A HISTORY OF COWLES MEDIA COMPANY

JAMES A. ALCOTT

A HISTORY OF COWLES MEDIA COMPANY

COWLES MEDIA COMPANY
Minneapolis, Minnesota
1998

© 1998 Cowles Media Company

All rights reserved. No part of this publication may be reproduced, stored in a retrieval system, or transmitted in any form or by any means without the prior written permission of the publisher.

Due to space limitations, most acknowledgements of permission to reprint previously published material are found following the index.

Library of Congress Cataloging-in-Publication Data

Alcott, James A.
    A history of Cowles Media Company / James A. Alcott.
        p.   cm.
    Includes bibliographical references.
    ISBN 0-86573-862-9. -- ISBN 0-86573-863-7 (pbk.)
    1. Cowles Media Company--History. 2. Newspaper publishing--Minnesota--Minneapolis--History--20th century. 3. Periodicals, Publishing of--United States--History--20th century. 4. Mass media--United States--History--20th century. I. Title.
Z473.C79A43 1998
070.5'09776'579--dc21   98-15417
                                                                       CIP

Printed in the United States of America.

Typefaces: Adobe Caslon and Meta
Type Composition: Page layouts were composed in QuarkXpress on a Power Macintosh 7600/132
Paper: Mead Signature Dull 80# text

TABLE OF CONTENTS

TIMELINE *iv*

ACKNOWLEDGMENTS *ix*

INTRODUCTION *xi*

CHAPTER 1   THE BASE *1*

CHAPTER 2   BRANCHING OUT *5*

CHAPTER 3   BUILDING *THE MINNEAPOLIS STAR* *9*

CHAPTER 4   THE FORMULA FOR SUCCESS *15*

CHAPTER 5   *THE MINNEAPOLIS JOURNAL* *23*

CHAPTER 6   *THE MINNEAPOLIS TRIBUNE* *29*

CHAPTER 7   A LEVEL OF SUCCESS *35*

CHAPTER 8   THE WAR YEARS *39*

CHAPTER 9   ONE OF THE BIGGEST AND BEST *45*

CHAPTER 10   THE FIFTIES *57*

CHAPTER 11   RADIO AND TELEVISION *65*

CHAPTER 12   DIVERSIFICATION *71*

CHAPTER 13   THE STRIKE *75*

CHAPTER 14   A GRADUAL TRANSITION *81*

CHAPTER 15   ADAPTABILITY AND RESPONSIVENESS TO CHANGE *87*

CHAPTER 16   A DECADE OF CHANGE *93*

CHAPTER 17   MERGER *103*

CHAPTER 18	SOMETHING OF A GAMBLE *109*
CHAPTER 19	BUFFALO *115*
CHAPTER 20	CONFIDENCE *121*
CHAPTER 21	CONTINUITY *125*
CHAPTER 22	NEW GROWTH STRATEGIES *135*
CHAPTER 23	THE FOURTH GENERATION *141*
CHAPTER 24	EPILOGUE — SUBSEQUENT EVENT *145*
	INDEX *251*
	PHOTOGRAPHY CREDITS *255*

APPENDIX A	John Cowles Sr. Memorandum on the Purchase of *The Minneapolis Star* *153*
APPENDIX B	John Cowles Sr. 1935 *TIME* Magazine Cover Story *157*
APPENDIX C	Data on Cowles Media Company (and predecessors) Stock *163*
APPENDIX D	Major Plant and Equipment Investments *167*
APPENDIX E	Newsprint *169*
APPENDIX F	"The Responsibilty of a Free Press in a World in Crisis," a Speech Given by John Cowles Sr. at That Time Being Awarded a Missouri Medal for Distinguished Services to Journalism by the School of Journalism of the University of Missouri *171*
APPENDIX G	Cowles Media Company (and predecessors) Corporate Airplanes *179*
APPENDIX H	John Cowles Sr. Memorandum on the Importance of the Electronic Media *183*
APPENDIX I	"The Newspaper Business is a Strange Animal," Speech by John Cowles Sr. to the Harvard Business School Club of the Twin Cities *187*
APPENDIX J	John Cowles Jr. Speech on the Rededication of the Guthrie Theater *195*
APPENDIX K	"How I Became Interested in Racial Justice," Article by Elizabeth Bates Cowles, Winter 1948 Issue of *Opportunity* Magazine, Published by the National Urban League *197*
APPENDIX L	John Cowles Jr. Speech Receiving the First Amendment Freedoms Award from the Society of Fellows of the Anti-Defamation League of B'nai B'rith *199*
APPENDIX M	Civic Responsibility of Cowles Media Company (and predecessors) *201*
APPENDIX N	John Cowles Sr. Remarks at his Retirement in 1973 *205*
APPENDIX O	Proposed Merger of the Minneapolis Star & Tribune Company and the Des Moines Register and Tribune Company *207*
APPENDIX P	Cowles Media Company News Release Regarding John Cowles Jr. Becoming Publisher of *The Minneapolis Star and Tribune* *211*
APPENDIX Q	The Heritage Center *215*
APPENDIX R	The 1985 Governance Changes *219*
APPENDIX S	Cowles Media Company (and predecessors) Board of Directors *221*
APPENDIX T	Cowles Media Company (and predecessors) Chronology *223*
APPENDIX U	The Family of Gardner Cowles *229*
APPENDIX V	The Family of John Cowles *231*
APPENDIX W	*Star Tribune* (and predecessor newspapers) Circulation 1935-1997 *233*
APPENDIX X	Cowles Media Company (and predecessor corporations) Financial Performance 1935-1997 *235*
APPENDIX Y	Glendalough *239*
APPENDIX Z	Selected Biographies *241*
APPENDIX AA	Excerpt from the Joint Proxy Statement for Special Meetings of the Stockholders of McClatchy Newspapers, Inc. and Cowles Media Company to be Held March 19, 1998 *245*

Purchase of *The Minneapolis Star*	Purchase of *The Minneapolis Journal*	Merger with *The Minneapolis Tribune*	Creation of the *Star Journal Tribune* Fund
1935	1939	1941	1945

1938	1940	1942	1949
John Cowles Sr. and family move to Minneapolis	Dedication of new plant addition	First dividend declared	New plant dedicated

1954	1959	1964	1968
Interest in WCCO-TV purchased	New plant addition	*The Rapid City Journal* acquired	John Cowles Jr. elected president; New building addition

1955	1962	1965	1973
Acquisition of KTVH-TV in Kansas	112-day strike	*The Great Falls Tribune* acquired; *Harper's* magazine and Harper & Row investments made	John Cowles Sr. retires as chairman

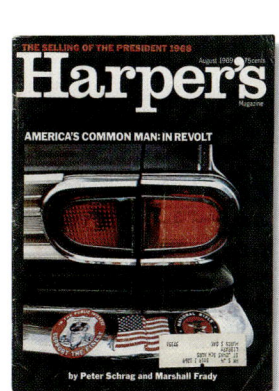

1976	1980	1982	1984
Sale of interest in WCCO-TV	27-day strike; Sale of *Harper's*; Creation of Cowles Family Voting Trust	*The Minneapolis Star* combined with *The Minneapolis Tribune*; Merger agreement rescinded; Closing of *Courier-Express*; Corporate name changed to Cowles Media Company	Sale of Buffalo cable television system; Bids made for Des Moines Register and Tribune Company; New production facility authorized

1979	1981	1983	1985
Acquisition of *Buffalo Courier-Express* and CableScope cable television system	Interest in Harper & Row sold; Plan made to merge with Des Moines Register and Tribune Company	John Cowles Jr. resigns as president; David Kruidenier elected president and CEO; Death of John Cowles Sr.	Washington Post Company acquires 17% interest in Cowles Media Company; *The Des Moines Register* and *Tribune* and 14% Cowles Media Company interest sold to Gannett; David C. Cox elected CEO

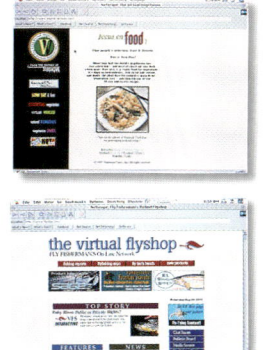

1986	1988	1993	1997
Acquisition of first consumer special interest magazine group	Purchase of Cowles Media Company stock from Gannett; Formal extension of voting trust to 2000; Acquisition of business magazine group	David Kruidenier retires from board; John Cowles III becomes chairman; Stock splits 6:1	Record revenue and earnings announced; Agreement in principle reached for sale of Cowles Media Company to McClatchy Newspapers Inc.

vii

1987	1990	1996	1998
Heritage Center production facility completed	Sale of Rapid City and Great Falls papers; Tender offer completed for Cowles Media Company stock	Voting Trust extended to 2010	Cowles Media Company acquired by McClatchy Newspapers Inc.

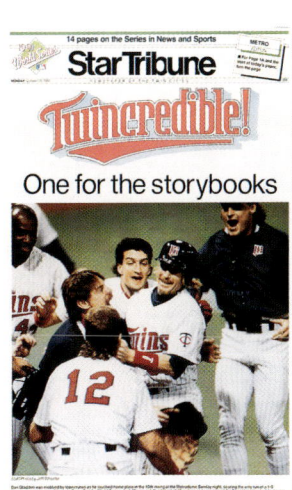
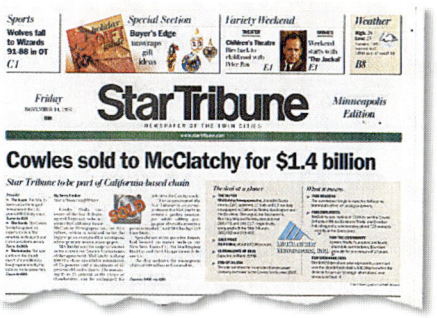

ACKNOWLEDGMENTS

Many people helped make this book possible. To them goes my appreciation and respect for their creativity and hard work.

Laura Anders and her associates at Anders Corporate Communications played several key roles — in researching and bringing together all the graphic materials which enliven and inform the pages, coordinating the work of the design team, working with Cowles Creative Publishing on production issues, and attending to the scores of details that go into getting the book from the writer to the reader.

James O'Shea Wade provided valuable editorial advice and counsel, helping keep the writing clear and focused for the reader.

Linda Henneman, Mary Legeros and the team at ThinkDesign Group provided both the basic framework for the physical book and the graphic concepts that made data intelligible on the page. Lars Hanson's photographic skills are evident throughout the book.

At Cowles Media Company, Frank Parisi, Jim Viera, Tony Lopesio, Jan Veith and Jean Karels provided vital information and help along the way. Helen Marn drew on her keen knowledge of the company to ensure accuracy and consistency and in general to keep things straight.

At the Star Tribune, Greg Anderson developed the schematic showing the growth in the plant and equipment installations; Tom Hardie provided data on newsprint prices; Lou Gelfand and Chris Mahai were generous with their perspectives on the interests of likely readers; Bob Jansen searched the resources of the library to bring appropriate material to the book; Dave Hage loaned key documents from his father's writings and made useful strategic editorial suggestions; Andrea Matthews and Robyn Kelly helped with the *Newsmakers* archives. Sue Mach steered me through the shoals of word processing.

Gail See's marketing advice helped ensure the right kind of distribution for the book. Martha Stevens was an invaluable source of information about Cowles Communications, Inc. and its predecessors. The Minnesota Historical Society, the State Historical Society of Iowa, the Minneapolis Public Library and the Wilson Library at the University of Minnesota all contributed their resources.

Inga Hoifeldt at the Cowles Library at Drake University and Pat Dawson, who catalogued the Cowles papers there, were generous with their time in helping me make use of those key files.

The support and help of these and many other people made putting the book together a pleasure.

James Alcott
Salem, New York
February 1998

A NOTE ABOUT THE AUTHOR

James Alcott joined Cowles Media Company in 1975 as president of Harper's *magazine. He was vice president of the Cowles Media Company from 1978-1996, responsible, at different times, for planning, administration, corporate communications and the contributions program. He was chairman of Cowles Media Foundation from 1993 to 1996.*

INTRODUCTION

THIS BOOK IS A HISTORY OF Cowles Media Company, and its predecessor, The Minneapolis Star and Tribune Company. It is not a history of *The Minneapolis Star Tribune* newspaper and its predecessors, nor is it a history of the John Cowles family. It necessarily includes some of both, but readers expecting extensive coverage of either the papers or the family may be disappointed. The objective of the book is to bring together in one place relevant information about the company, some of which may otherwise be lost in the future. Footnotes at the end of each chapter identify sources for much of the information. Most of the underlying documents (except for interview notes) are archived with the Cowles Media Company papers. Interested readers may contact the Star Tribune library for further information on the archives.

The book relies heavily on written records, such as the monthly employee newsletters, annual reports to stockholders, speeches, and the extensive files of John Cowles which are housed at Drake University. It also borrows from other published sources including three papers prepared by students at the University of Minnesota School of Journalism, contemporary newspaper and magazine coverage, monographs from Herbert Strentz at Drake University and William Friedricks at Simpson College, histories by the late George Hage, and two privately published books by members of the Murphy family.

Interviews with a number of people provided needed background and context as well as anecdotes and specific information. Those people include Joyce Swan, the late William A. Cordingley Jr., Willis Brown, Philip VonBlon, Kenneth Dayton, Bruce Dayton, Howard Mithun, Otto Silha, Norton L. Armour, John B. Dennison, Donald Dwight, John Cowles Jr., Morley Ballantine, Richard Ballantine, Elizabeth Ballantine, John Cowles III, James Rosse, Luther Hill Jr., David Kruidenier, Lois Harrison, David M. Winton, Frank Hatch, Barbara Flanagan, Richard Cooney, Kingsley Murphy Jr., David Cox, Randy M. Lebedoff, John R. Finnegan, and William R. Busch Jr. They were generous with their time and recollections; without their help the book would have suffered.

For those wanting more detail, several speeches and statements are included as appendices, together with short descriptions of issues and topics mentioned briefly in the text.

My attempt has been to let the record speak for itself to the extent possible. In many instances, however, it was necessary to tie the facts together with some interpretation. The Cowles family has been the subject of almost endless curiosity and speculation, much of it reported over the years as fact. John Cowles Sr. commented to Professor J. E. Gerald in 1961 that he was "constantly surprised to find persons working for him who are under the impression that he has declared such and such a policy when, in fact, he has done no such thing. For years employees thought there was a rule against printing pictures of employees or members of their families in the newspaper." Cowles' position was simply that he disliked having himself or members of his family played up unless there was some compelling reason for it — in contrast to some other publishers who encouraged such publicity. I have tried to avoid speculating about personal motivations and personalities, and to rely instead on observations of those closer to the individuals and events. The intent has been to capture the available information about Cowles Media Company and leave more detailed biographies to others.

THE BASE

1

COWLES MEDIA COMPANY had its beginnings in 1935 when the Cowles family purchased the Minneapolis Star Company. Its real roots, however, go back to the beginning of this century and are to be found in Iowa. The history of the Des Moines Register and Tribune Company has been well documented, but because it provided the model and the base for the subsequent success in Minneapolis, some coverage of its history is appropriate.

Gardner Cowles Sr. in 1903 joined his associate Harvey Ingham in acquiring *The Des Moines Register and Leader* and building it through acquisition and brilliant business tactics into the dominant newspaper not only in Des Moines, but in the entire state of Iowa by 1927. It was a time of newspaper consolidation throughout the country, but Cowles and Ingham built a position probably unique in the newspaper business. The so-called "Cowles formula" has been widely, if not consistently, described by others. Three key elements are strong local news coverage, an outstanding circulation system and strong promotion. *Time* magazine reported in 1935: "The news is rushed to the Register and Tribune's quarter million subscribers by the most elaborate and thoroughgoing carrier system in the U. S. Old 'G.C.' with his head full of route numbers and train schedules built an organization of 4,820 carriers who swarm over Iowa. Fifty-six circulation managers, 90 supervisors — all crack men — keep the machine running."[1] They treated the whole state as if it were a city. The population of Iowa in 1935 was 2.5 million, Des Moines itself was well under 200,000.

Gardner Cowles in 1884 joined his banker-father-in-law in a business that ran mail wagons from railroad stations to towns without train service in Iowa, Kansas and the Dakotas. They contracted with the government to serve more than 30 such routes. This experience, together with a strong interest in railroading, gave him an unusual understanding of the logistics of circulation.[2] The business was based in Algona, where Cowles had settled in 1882 as school superintendent.

THE DES MOINES REGISTER,
MAY 21, 1927

Editor Harvey Ingham laid out the basic philosophy this way: "A strong and fearless newspaper will have readers and a newspaper that has readers will have advertisements. That is the only newspaper formula worth working to…After making all allowances the only newspaper popularity that counts in the long run is bottomed on public respect."

Their philosophy was summarized in a statement of "three commandments" that guided the papers as well:

"1. We believe in presenting ALL of the news impartially in the news columns.

"2. We believe in expressing our own opinions as persuasively and forcefully as possible, but in confining those expressions to the editorial columns on the editorial pages.

"3. We believe in giving our readers also the opinions of other competent writers, representing ALL SIDES of important controversial issues, so our readers can form their judgments wisely."[3]

Many years later, Gardner Cowles said, "Without good newspapers, I doubt whether any people under modern conditions can preserve free institutions…The good newspaper must be honest. It must be fair. It must be truly efficient in every respect in the job of delivering to a free people with the maximum speed the information by which they alone can manage their common affairs themselves as a self-governing group."[4] *The Des Moines Register* had 254 state correspondents reporting on local news so that a single day's edition of *The Des Moines Register* and *The Des Moines Tribune* could be replated as many as 20 times to assure that the news was of special interest to all communities in the state.

HARVEY INGHAM AND GARDNER COWLES, 1937

Other sources suggest that there was more to the editorial formula. One writer suggested that while yellow journalism was repugnant to Cowles and Ingham, "Sex and crime, swathed in a sound moral lesson, or muffled by columns of serious matter, insulted the dignity of neither readers nor publishers."[5] The "formula" was further enhanced by careful attention to typography and to the skillful use of photographs. *The Des Moines Register* was the first Des Moines paper to have a Sunday rotogravure section containing many photographs, as well as advertising with a strong graphic content. It was said that photographs were its stock in trade. The emphasis on graphics and human-interest stories was balanced by strong economic and political coverage. The success of the Cowles newspapers in Des Moines provided both the critical knowledge of how to publish and market a successful newspaper and the substantial financial resources to permit replicating the Iowa experience elsewhere.

A second and key part of the history lies in the story of *The Minneapolis Daily*

IOWA RAILROAD MAP, 1884

DES MOINES SKYLINE, EARLY 20TH CENTURY

Star. In 1918, the Working People's Nonpartisan Political League began serious consideration of the possibility of launching a metropolitan daily newspaper sponsored by organized farmers and organized labor.[6] The League, a populist organization with activities in 13 Midwestern and Western states, was headquartered in St. Paul. They had established papers in North Dakota, and the president of the organization, Arthur G. Townley, considered himself "a newspaper man" and believed that for the movement to succeed, it needed its own newspaper, saying "…Minnesota is not going to be free until you have a press…."[7] A separate company, Northwest Publishing Company, was organized in 1919 and one million shares of stock were sold to members of the League and local labor unions, and especially to farmers who were enjoying the strong wartime and post-war demand for their products. The company built its own building and on August 19, 1920, printed the first issue of *The Minnesota Daily Star*.

A year later *The Minnesota Daily Star* claimed circulation in excess of 42,000 and apparently reached a peak of approximately 67,000 in early 1924. It was still losing $500 a day, in part because it failed to sell enough advertising; its political orientation made it difficult to attract advertisers.

THE DES MOINES REGISTER AND TRIBUNE BUILDING, 1940

John Thompson took charge of advertising and was able to reduce the losses somewhat, thanks to some success among department stores and the streetcar company. He had earlier been assistant to the business manager of *The New York Times*, and in 1916 he came west to manage the League's publications, over 100 daily and weekly newspapers, and serve as an advisor to its president. In August 1923, the owners obtained a $50,000 loan from A. B. Frizell, an advertising executive in St. Paul, but in February of 1924, the company went into receivership with 6,860 stockholders.

John Thompson was temporarily placed in charge, and in May he, Frizell and Thomas VanLear bought the company for $150,000. VanLear was a former Socialist mayor of Minneapolis, and he did not remain with the new company long. On July 1, 1924, the first issue of *The Minneapolis Daily Star* was published, with the new name to describe its focus on the Twin Cities rather than the entire state. By that time circulation had fallen to about 55,000. By the summer of 1926, circulation reached 68,000 and by 1934 was just over 75,000. Thompson felt that this concentration on local coverage by a paper with greater city circulation was a major factor in bringing in more advertising. People close to the paper stated that its new political independence also made it more attractive to advertisers and readers alike.

The consolidation of the newspaper business moved rapidly across the country. Most midsized markets experienced consolidation in the thirties as the Depression reduced both advertising and circulation. Ownership had been consolidated in Des Moines in 1927, in St. Paul in 1933, for example, and in Omaha and Kansas City during the same period. Minneapolis was ripe for the same consolidation, but no one would have predicted that *The Minneapolis Daily Star* would be the key in bringing it about.

1 "The Press," *Time* (July 1, 1935), p. 31.
2 "Saga of the Cowles Family Began in Des Moines in 1903," *Editor & Publisher,* February 6, 1943, p. 5.
3 Ibid., p. 5.
4 *Harvey Ingham and Gardner Cowles Sr., Things Don't Just Happen* (Ames: Iowa State University Press, 1977), p. 63.
5 "Don't Make 'Em Mad," *New Republic*, p. 20.
6 Harold L. Nelson, "A History of *The Minneapolis Daily Star*" (unpublished Master's thesis, University of Minnesota, July 1950), p. 51.
7 Ibid., p. 52.

2

JOHN COWLES GRADUATED from Harvard University in 1920 at age 21 and returned to Des Moines and *The Des Moines Register* as a "plain reporter." There he undoubtedly honed his legendary "intelligent inquisitiveness," through his ability to ask the questions that gave him the information he needed to run the newspaper or understand the issue at hand. As a college student he had worked summers at the paper, including one soliciting farm subscriptions. Although he was trained as an editor and reporter, he worked mostly on the business side. He was the fifth of six children — three girls and three boys; only he and his younger brother Mike (Gardner Jr.) were active in the business.

In 1923 he was named vice president, general manager and associate publisher. His father, Gardner, was publisher and president and Harvey Ingham was editor. W. W. Wymack was the chief editorial writer. In 1924 the Register and Tribune Company purchased *The News*, the Scripps Howard 27,000-circulation afternoon competitor, for $150,000. John Cowles participated with his father in those negotiations. On the day of the merger it was important to deliver *The Des Moines Tribune* to the homes of all former *News* subscribers. Because there were not enough circulation staff members to conduct a house-to-house canvass, John Cowles recalled that "some of the rest of us pitched in."[1]

In June of 1923 he married Elizabeth Bates, whom he had met while she was a student at Smith College and he at Harvard. She was born in Oswego, New York, and instead of completing her degree at Smith, she joined a friend and her parents on a trip to China. Their first child, Elizabeth Morley, was born in 1925, followed by Sarah Richardson in 1926, John Jr. in 1929, and Russell II in 1936. In addition to rearing her family, she was active in the civic life of Des Moines, founding the first birth control clinic in Iowa in 1935.

Bad business conditions in 1926 resulted in the

MINNEAPOLIS DAILY STAR,
MAY 26, 1927

merger of the two leading Des Moines department stores, a blow to newspaper retail advertising. The publisher of the *The Capital* suggested that his morning paper merge with the *The Des Moines Register,* but instead John Cowles purchased it for $750,000, acting for his father who was in the Far East. "Father was very restless at being away at such a time," John Cowles said. "He was very happy with the deal, though. He would have paid more than that."[2] Even so, there was concern whether having a monopoly on daily newspapers in Des Moines was a good idea, and Gardner Cowles wrote that it might be "four or five years before we will know if it was the right thing to do."

It is significant that only six years out of Harvard John Cowles had both the business acumen and the confidence of his father to make such a transaction. His brother Mike (Gardner Cowles Jr.) had joined the business in 1925 after his graduation from Harvard and concentrated his efforts on the news side of the business. John Cowles launched The Register and Tribune Syndicate in 1922 to sell news stories, serialized fiction and nonfiction, cartoons and photographs to other newspapers worldwide.[3] Referred to by some as the "syndicate in the sticks," it proved a very successful business venture. According to Mike Cowles, the syndicate was "a highly profitable move and later one of the key factors that carried the papers through the Depression." At its peak it offered 60 to 75 features, sold to more than 1,000 newspapers. It was sold to Hearst's King Features Syndicate in 1986 for $4.3 million.[4]

The Des Moines Register and *The Des Moines Tribune* did well during the twenties, more than doubling in circulation.

According to Mike Cowles, by 1935 he and John had decided that the time had come to branch out from Des Moines, a move in which his father heartily concurred, recognizing that the Register and Tribune Company was too small an operation for both his ambitious sons. John Cowles said: "My father realized that The Register and The Tribune was too small for Mike and me both. He was still more or less active and he had a good organization in Des Moines."[5]

Mike Cowles reported that they conducted "an elaborate search, looking for an evening paper with strong

PORTRAIT OF JOHN AND ELIZABETH COWLES, PAINTED BY OSKAR KOKOSCHKA

JOHN, RUSSELL, GARDNER SR. AND GARDNER (MIKE) COWLES JR., 1910

MINNEAPOLIS SKYLINE, 1928

reader loyalty and a high percentage of home-delivered circulation that served a relatively literate and educated market."[6] John Cowles said of the search: "We considered a number of cities, all of them bigger than Des Moines. We knew the Middle West, or thought we did. Minnesota had the same general policies as Iowa and it was convenient to Des Moines. It was the capital of a provincial empire, there was nothing to the west or northwest for miles and miles, and it was the center of a rich area — one of the provincial capitals of America, a retail buying and commercial center as well as a political center. Also, the Minneapolis people are more punctual in paying their bills, according to credit company surveys. They are thrifty, solid, substantial people."[7] (See Appendix A.)

Omaha was another market considered, but they decided that it was not a good bargain. They were looking for a newspaper property that would afford opportunities comparable to those the family had capitalized on in Iowa. The death in 1934 of A. B. Frizell, majority owner of *The Minneapolis Daily Star*, led to that opportunity.

Minneapolis had a 1930 population of 400,000 with a strong Scandinavian heritage; it had been settled by Protestant New Englanders who were attracted to the timber and the flour milling business, the mainstays of the economy through World War I. The falls on the Mississippi River provided the source of power that made Minneapolis "Mill City." Its twin, St. Paul, was older and smaller, with a large Roman Catholic population, predominantly of southern German, Austrian and Irish origins. The two cities were rivals from the outset, and were much more separate than their proximity would suggest. Minneapolis experienced serious labor strife in 1934-35. It was one of the strongest open-shop cities in the country with a well-organized employers' association. There had not been a successful strike in Minneapolis in the twentieth century, but the new National Recovery Act guaranteed the right to bargain collectively, providing critical support to unions. In 1934 two strikes in the trucking industry resulted in widespread violence and eventually the end to the long open-shop tradition. Several of the union leaders were members of the Communist League of America; their local was expelled from the American Federation of Labor in 1935, which set up its own drivers union. In 1935 there were strikes by iron workers and garment workers. The Twin Cities local of the Newspaper Guild was the second one established in the country. It was into this community that the new Cowles enterprise was about to enter.[8]

1 George Mills, *Harvey Ingham and Gardner Cowles Sr., Things Don't Just Happen* (Ames: Iowa State University Press, 1977), p. 90.

2 Ibid., p. 77.

3 William B. Friedricks, "The Newspaper that Captured a State: A History of The Des Moines Register, 1849-1985," *THE ANNALS OF IOWA* 54 (Fall 1995) (The State Historical Society of Iowa, 1995), p. 328.

4 Herbert Strentz, *Starting Points* (Des Moines, Drake University: Photocopied Publication, 1994), p. 2.

5 Mills, *Things Don't Just Happen*, p. 94.

6 Gardner Cowles Jr., *Mike Looks Back* (New York: Gardner Cowles Jr., 1985), p. 24.

7 "The Minneapolis Cowles - Papers," *P.M.*, May 21, 1944, p. 14.

8 Charles Rumford Walker, *American City* (New York: Farrar & Rinehart, 1937).

BUILDING *THE MINNEAPOLIS STAR*

3

THE PURCHASE OF *The Minneapolis Star* in June of 1935 rated a cover story in *Time* magazine, with John Cowles on the cover of the July 1 issue. (See Appendix B.) The story began: "When the Cowles family of Des Moines bought the Minneapolis *Star*, they acquired the third and weakest newspaper in that community last fortnight. To them that was no cause for discouragement."

The story then went on to chronicle the growth of the Des Moines newspapers as well as some history of the family, and to note that, "At 36…John Cowles is in effect the boss of the Des Moines *Register & Tribune*." Mike Cowles pointed out that while the $1 million price was reasonable, he and John underestimated the time required to make the paper profitable. He acknowledged that doing so "required three long years of aggressive promotion in the face of heavy losses" and said at one point his father said that the paper should be built up so that it could be sold.[1]

The contract of purchase for the Minneapolis Daily Star Company was made on June 12, 1935; the effective date of purchase was June 18, 1935. The officers of the company all resigned on June 14, and on June 15 John Cowles was elected president, Gardner Cowles Jr., vice president, Davis Merwin, vice president and treasurer, and John Thompson, secretary. The name of the corporation was changed to the Minneapolis Star Company on August 28, 1935. According to Basil Walters, while Gardner Cowles supported his sons in this new enterprise, he didn't want the boys to go into Minneapolis. "He summoned some of us and said: 'This is the boys' venture. You are to have nothing to do with it. Your interests are here in Des Moines. Some of you risked your money by buying stock in the Register and Tribune. We are not going to risk that money. The boys have some money and they can risk their own'."[2] Stock ownership records, however, indicate that John Cowles was initially the sole stockholder of record, and that later in 1935 he and Gardner Cowles Jr. (Mike) purchased

TIME
JULY 1, 1935

additional shares, a pattern that continued into 1937. In May 1936, the Register and Tribune Company held all the preferred stock, and other executives were listed as shareholders — John Thompson and Davis Merwin both had significant holdings, and 12 others (including Walters) had nominal amounts. (See Appendix C.)

There were two other, long-established daily newspapers in Minneapolis in 1935. *The Minneapolis Tribune,* founded in 1867, had been owned and run by W. J. Murphy and members of his family since 1891. The publisher was F. E. Murphy, W. J.'s brother. It was published morning and evening with a combined daily circulation of 140,500 in 1935 and a Sunday circulation of 201,800. Of those totals, 85,900 and 108,400 were city circulation. It carried 7 million lines of daily advertising in 1935 and 3.1 million on Sunday. It had a strong emphasis on the agricultural economy of the Northwest.

The Minneapolis Journal, which began in 1878, had been owned and run by the Jones family since 1908. Carl Jones was the publisher. It was also an evening paper, with a daily circulation of 114,700 and Sunday circulation of 159,200 in 1935. Of that, 65,700 and 76,400 were the city circulations. It carried 7.4 million lines of daily advertising and 1.9 million on Sunday, and was generally regarded as the "silk stocking" paper and the "mouthpiece of the bourbons," with great strength in the affluent 13th ward of Minneapolis.

The daily circulation of *The Minneapolis Star* was,

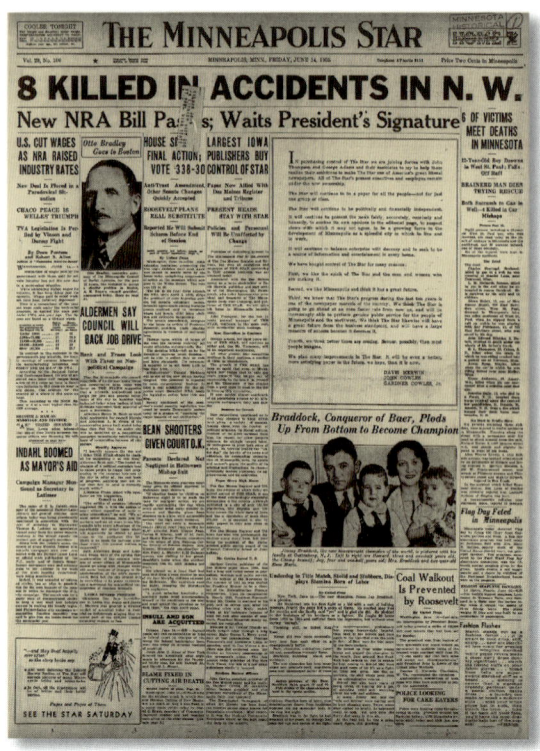

THE MINNEAPOLIS STAR

MINNEAPOLIS, MINN., FRIDAY, JUNE 14, 1935

Price Two Cents in Minneapolis

8 KILLED IN ACCIDENTS IN N. W.

New NRA Bill Passes; Waits President's Signature

U.S. CUT WAGES AS NRA RAISED INDUSTRY RATES

New Deal Is Placed in a Paradoxical Situation

CHACO PEACE IS WELLES' TRIUMPH

TVA Legislation Is Periled by Vinson and Dorsey Fight

Otto Bradley Goes to Boston

ALDERMEN SAY COUNCIL WILL BACK JOB DRIVE

Bank and Trust Look With Favor on Non-political Campaign

INDAHL BOOMED AS MAYOR'S AID

Campaign Manager Mentioned as Secretary to Latimer

FINAL ACTION; VOTE 338-30

Anti-Trust Amendment, Other Senate Changes Quickly Accepted

ROOSEVELT PLANS REAL SUBSTITUTE

Reported He Will Submit Scheme Before End of Session

BEAN SHOOTERS GIVEN COURT O.K.

Parents Declared Not Negligent in Halloween Mishap Suit

INSULL AND SON ARE ACQUITTED

BLAME FIXED IN CUTTING AIR DEATH

LARGEST IOWA PUBLISHERS BUY CONTROL OF STAR

Paper Now Allied With Des Moines Register and Tribune

PRESENT HEADS STAY WITH STAR

Policies and Personnel Will Be Unaffected by Change

DAVIS MERWIN
JOHN COWLES
GARDNER COWLES, Jr.

Braddock, Conqueror of Baer, Plods Up From Bottom to Become Champion

Coal Walkout Is Prevented by Roosevelt

POLICE LOOKING FOR CAKE EATERS

6 OF VICTIMS MEET DEATHS IN MINNESOTA

BRAINERD MAN DIES TRYING RESCUE

Flag Day Feted in Minneapolis

Fashion Flashes

SEE THE STAR SATURDAY

THE MINNEAPOLIS STAR,
JUNE 14, 1935

as represented by the sellers, about 79,000 at the time of purchase, causing Gardner Cowles Sr. to comment approvingly: "I have never known of a deal of equivalent size so clear in every particular as your representations in connection with the sale of the Minneapolis Star...."[3] (It was not uncommon for sellers to seriously misrepresent circulation, as happened when Cowles entered the business in 1903.) The paper had a large blue-collar readership and was regarded as "the labor paper." However, 57,100 of its circulation was in the city retail zone, the highest percentage of any of the papers. It was a distant third in advertising with 5.5 million lines, very little of which came from the major retailers. It had no Sunday edition. The business community was not friendly either to the paper or to the idea that two young men from a small place in Iowa had "invaded" their city. *Newsweek* said that advertisers had reluctantly "fed it enough money to keep it alive, largely as a buffer against possible rate

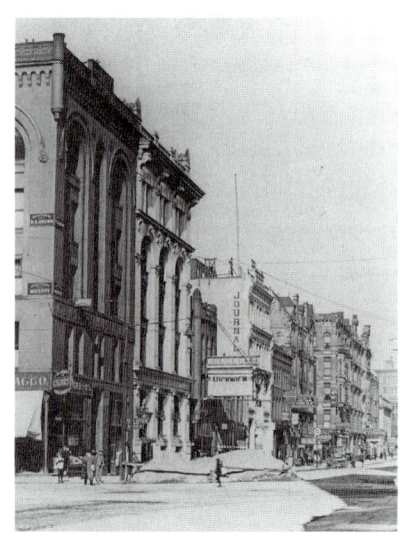

MINNEAPOLIS' "NEWSPAPER ROW" AT THE TURN OF THE CENTURY

increases" by the other two papers.[4]

Nonetheless, a civic luncheon was given to welcome the Cowles family to Minneapolis and John Cowles said: "We saw here, looking from the outside, a great future, a great era of development just beginning. You have every reason to be proud of the three newspapers you have at the present time. We merely want to join them in going forward."[5] The purchase was announced first on the front page of *The Minneapolis Star* of June 14, with the following statement signed by the new owners:

> "In purchasing control of The Star we are joining forces with John Thompson and George Adams and their associates to try to help them realize their ambitions to make The Star one of America's great liberal newspapers. All of The Star's present executives and employees remain under the new ownership.
>
> "The Star will continue to be a paper of all the people — not for just one group or class.
>
> "The Star will continue to be politically and financially independent.
>
> "It will continue to present the news fairly, accurately, concisely and honestly, to confine its own opinions to the editorial page, to respect the views with which it may not agree, to be a growing force in the development of Minneapolis as a splendid city in which to live and work.
>
> "It will continue to balance enterprise with decency and to seek to be a source of information and entertainment in every home."

On its face the statement seems innocuous enough today, but each line was carefully crafted to signal significant changes, some of which would be regarded as radical by conservative members of the community. In this and the subsequent acquisitions the Cowles brothers were careful to avoid major personnel changes — at least initially — and to foster a sense of continuity and local control. The old *Minneapolis Star* had not been a "paper of all the people," and its competitors tended to have clear constituencies. Like many papers across the country, editorial positions tended to influence news coverage and to dismiss other points of view. News

MINNEAPOLIS SKYLINE, 1935

coverage was often tailored to please advertisers and the business community. The three papers in Minneapolis had not been characterized by great enterprise, they carried liquor advertising, and did not regard themselves as educational forces in the Cowles manner. They were conservative in makeup, writing and news coverage. *The Minneapolis Star* had been a "liberal" paper from its early populist roots; the other two almost always supported the Republican Party.

Davis Merwin, a Harvard friend of John Cowles, with whom he had discussed his plans, was hired as publisher of the new *Star*. He became a stockholder and officer of the company. His family — together with that of his cousin and good friend, Adlai Stevenson — owned the Bloomington, Illinois, *Pantagraph*, which Merwin was running successfully after graduating from college. Other people and tactics were imported from Des Moines. The two immediate challenges were to transform the newspaper itself, by applying what other writers have characterized as repeating "the news formula" used successfully in Des Moines, and developing the

THE MINNEAPOLIS STAR BUILDING, 1928

circulation system that was at the heart of *The Des Moines Register* and *Tribune* organization.

Basil Walters, managing editor of *The Register*, replaced George Adams in September of 1935 as editor of *The Minneapolis Star*, a position he held until April when he returned to Des Moines. During that time he apparently made many of the changes that were expected to enliven the paper and make it more attractive to readers. Shortly after Walters became editor, Cedric Adams, a former *Star* reporter, was hired as a columnist. His first column, entitled "In This Corner" began: "Not since 1927 have I had my stomach up against a desk at The Star. It's the same desk. The stomach has grown and so has The Star. It's nice to be back among the old faces. And the new ones all look bright and happy."[6] The column — and Adams — went on to become enormously popular.

During the same time William A. Cordingley Sr., circulation manager in Des Moines, visited Minneapolis frequently to build the distribution organization. He had worked closely with Gardner Cowles, first as a grain clerk in Algona, Iowa, then in building the newspaper circulation operations in Iowa. During the first three years, Cowles apparently tried various circulation experts

THE GREAT DEPRESSION, 1933

before settling on Cordingley, whom he named circulation manager in 1906. He was said to have an optimism and enthusiasm that translated into a great ability to motivate circulation field men. Most of the earlier managers apparently were more inclined to rely on promotional gimmicks than on the solid, methodical approach that finally produced results. One example of the success was the fact that between 1928 and 1941 — the Depression years — circulation of the two dailies increased from 226,318 to 313,103. Others in the circulation operation would form part of the force that later shaped the circulation success of *LOOK* magazine.

In Minneapolis the two-pronged approach began to pay off quickly. Net paid circulation grew to 88,190 in October, to 94,196 in November, and reached 100,000 in December. For the six months ended March 31, 1936, *The Minneapolis Star* had the largest daily home delivered circulation in Minneapolis — 56,286. The total city circulation was 68,753 and total circulation, 102,158. In the first three months of 1936 classified advertising linage increased 63 percent, giving it a lead over both *The Minneapolis Tribune* and *The Minneapolis Journal* daily.

Willis (Bill) Brown had been hired by Mike Cowles to work in Des Moines on the strength of national recognition for his work at the Peoria, Illinois, *Transcript*, but the needs in Minneapolis took precedence and Brown went to *The Minneapolis Star*, as classified advertising manager, where he remained in a number of executive positions until his retirement in 1968. (He arrived in Minneapolis on the day after Christmas in 1935, without ever stopping in Des Moines.) Like a number of key people during that time, he was a graduate of the University of Missouri School of Journalism.

In spite of these circulation successes, profitability was not only elusive, losses were growing. In an interview with J. E. Gerald in 1961, John Cowles said that the paper lost $224,000 in the first year of operations and $325,000 the second. Beyond that, there was considerable antagonism toward the paper and its Iowa owners throughout the community. Davis Merwin resigned in October of 1937 "following my doctor's orders to sever this connection with The Star."[7]

Apparently Merwin had a problem winning the friends the paper needed within the business and advertising community, preferring instead to spend his time with those with whom he was socially comfortable.

His task was complicated by the fact that Minneapolis was insular and self-protective, resenting the Cowles absentee ownership when the other two papers were still run by the local families that had owned them for decades. Nelson Dayton, then head of the leading department store, was one of those with strong feelings about local ownership. John Cowles then made the decision — or, according to another source, was ordered by his father — to move to Minneapolis. He had retained his home in Des Moines, "commuting" to Minneapolis by overnight train.

MINNEAPOLIS STAR COMPANY
FIRST CERTIFICATE OF SALE OF STOCK
TO JOHN COWLES SR., 1935

1 Gardner Cowles Jr., *Mike Looks Back* (New York: 1985), p. 24.
2 Mills, *Things Don't Just Happen*, p. 94.
3 "Cowles Boys Make Amazing 6-Year Record in Minneapolis," *Editor & Publisher*, February 13, 1943, p. 7.
4 "The Fourth Estate: Iowa Publishers Hitch Evening Star to Their Wagon," *Newsweek*, June 29, 1935, p. 22.
5 "Minneapolis Welcomes Star Publishers With Civic Luncheon," *Editor & Publisher*, July 20, 1935, p. 8.
6 "In This Corner," *The Minneapolis Star*, October 4, 1935, p. 17.

THE FORMULA FOR SUCCESS

4

WHEN JOHN COWLES moved to Minneapolis with his family in September of 1938, it was with a flourish. He bought a house that was handsome, but without pretense, a square Georgian brick house that communicated both stability and great style. It was located on Park Avenue at 24th Street, approximately two miles from his office. *The Minneapolis Star* ran a two-column photograph of the house on page one of the local news section with a caption saying that the Cowles family, including their four children, had moved to Minneapolis to stay. Morley was 12, Sarah (Sally), 11, John Jr., 8, and Russell, 1. The girls were placed in Northrop Academy, and John in Blake School, each a bastion of the Minneapolis establishment.

According to an account in *Editor & Publisher*, "Working quietly and with a kindly manner so characteristic of the Cowles tradition, John started a one-man campaign to win over Minneapolis. Largely by his own effort he completely changed the picture in favor of the *Minneapolis Star*. He accomplished his mission by constant application, day in and day out. Such a personal program, combined with an excellent product, brought results in the form of advertising patronage and with it a public confidence in the management of the paper."[1]

That account is undoubtedly true, but it glosses over the hard work, time and perseverance required to bring about those results. According to Basil Walters, "John went out and hit the pavement soliciting advertising which came very slowly." Employees from the time recall that the Cowles "did a great amount of entertaining," and that he rented a summer house on Lake Minnetonka (called the Pink Palace) which helped with "the Woodhill crowd." (Woodhill was the country club for the Minneapolis establishment "at the lake.") Cowles believed it important for both himself and Mrs. Cowles to be accepted by the leading citizens of the community, and to be recognized as peers. Such acceptance was key not only to increasing advertising, but also to publishing a truly independent newspaper and being a

MINNEAPOLIS STAR JOURNAL,
NOVEMBER 24, 1939 CLASSIFIED ADS

HOME OF JOHN COWLES SR., MINNEAPOLIS

force in the community. One of his close associates was Stanley Hawks, a socially prominent person who was able to help provide entree to many of those skeptical about the outsider from Des Moines. Originally in circulation, Hawkes served in a number of assignments in the community. Bill Brown recalls an early dinner party at the house on Park Avenue: "They invited a dozen couples to dinner and dancing. And they had two or three other outsiders there. One whom I liked very much was the owner of the black newspaper."

At the newspaper itself, John Cowles was undoubtedly aided by the presence of John Thompson, one of the owners of *The Minneapolis Star* who remained with the paper in a number of executive capacities until his retirement in 1949. He was named publisher after Davis Merwin left, having previously been general manager. A Kentuckian, he was described as an avid sports fan whose greatest love was baseball. He was also a fan of Westerns, which he liked to review for the paper. He was apparently very popular in the organization; May of 1938 was proclaimed "John Thompson Month" in recognition of his 15th year with the paper. Each department in the paper set a special goal to achieve to honor Thompson. (This was a technique that had been used successfully in Des Moines to honor Gardner Cowles.) In 1936 John Cowles organized a surprise 60th birthday party for Thompson at the Minneapolis Athletic Club, which was described at length in the employee newsletter. One former employee recalls, "Thompson was the nice guy, the front man. He was tough, but he was a good guy."

For years Thompson reportedly was able to call every employee by his or her first name on his daily journeys through the plant. Another colleague said, "…what a great guy, what a friendly guy he was and smart — his little touches with people were something to behold. He was great with employees — quiet and he knew the answer to everything, as far as I was concerned. He taught people a lot of those things you don't get in the regular day's life. He would teach you as you went along. There were a couple of incidents where people had used the words 'Negro' and 'nigger.' That person would be brought in to

JOHN THOMPSON, 1947

John Thompson, actually by John Thompson. He didn't ask anybody else to do it. He'd go up to 'em and say, 'Joe, I'd like to talk to you in the office.' And he had the know-how to treat the situation and make them understand. But he did it in a soft, sincere way that was very effective. He was a great man to know." In July 1949, the Pressmen's union voted him the first honorary membership it ever offered.

The summer before he came to Minneapolis, John Cowles named Nelson Poynter as business manager, a new position. Poynter had been editor and publisher of the Columbus, Ohio, *Citizen,* but had to leave *The Minneapolis Star* after a year to return to his family's newspaper in St. Petersburg, Florida. Cowles also brought Basil Walters back to Minneapolis as editor; he had been managing editor at *The Des Moines Register* and *Tribune,* which he joined in 1928. He had served as editor of *The Minneapolis Star* from September 1935 to April 1936, when he returned to Des Moines and was replaced by John Thompson. That August, George Grim was hired from the King Features Syndicate in New York to do promotion. He had been promotion manager at the Worcester *Telegram* and, most importantly, had produced more than 1,100 newspaper radio programs.

Walters recalled that "when we first moved out there on Dupont Avenue, our next-door neighbors would not have anything to do with us. They thought of the Star, anybody working on it, as Commies," referring to the paper's early Socialist associations. (His neighborhood was solid *Journal* territory — its household penetration was roughly two-thirds.) This attitude apparently had little impact on Walters, who is generally credited with creating the changes in the newspaper that made it an overwhelming success in spite of the traditional antipathy toward it by many people.

The late George Hage, a professor of journalism at the University of Minnesota and student of Minnesota newspapers, hypothesized that "Cowles' formula for success in Minneapolis was to eliminate the competition by seducing readers with sensation and pursuing aggressive promotion and circulation policies, then to use his monopoly position to publish a responsible newspaper." His is a controversial assessment, but he admires the results. "To implement the first part of his formula, John Cowles imported Basil L. ("Stuffy") Walters from Des Moines and installed him as editor. His nickname better described his opinion of the (competing) Journal and the Tribune; stuffy, he was not. Typical of his news philosophy was his adjuration to reporters and editors: 'Tell your story. Don't write it.' Type, in all its dazzling variety of sizes and styles, was to be used to GET ATTENTION. Under Walters, the Star redefined the meaning of news. One issue carried an eight-column banner heading at the top of page one proclaiming, 'Mrs. Robin Has Twins,' with four accompanying bird photographs to confirm this thrilling natal event. Readers flocked to the Star. Between 1935 and 1939, the Star's circulation jumped from 75,770 to 150,056."[2] *The Minneapolis Star* emphasized sports, sending its own men to cover Big Ten games and furnished air transportation in order to speed up coverage and pictures.

In his master's thesis Peter Posel characterized "the formula" in this way:

> "John Cowles brought more than just himself and key staff members from Des Moines. He also adopted the formula which had made the Register and the Tribune such a success: bright writing, unusual makeup, pictures, features, small shorts of well-deplored sin, saturation of circulation and promotional razzmatazz that would let no Minnesotan forget the Star.
>
> "All were altered and refined to fit the new audience and the new competition. The foremost innovator was Basil Walters, who quickly realized that if the Star was to move from third to first in the race for circulation and advertising, it would be

necessary to adopt ideas not generally followed by newspapers.

"A necessary contributor to the success and failure of the three Minneapolis newspapers was an intangible factor called the news. How it was emphasized and commented upon often made the difference between selling and not selling a newspaper.

"There was some indication of sensationalism in the way the Star headlined and wrote the news. The same is true when the type of news it displayed is considered. By 1935, the least conservative of the three, the Star, became by far the most popularized. In fact, it often bordered on the sensational, as owner Cowles admitted:

'Naturally there are differences of opinion among our readers, and occasionally among our own editors, as to what is sensational and what isn't. But sensational news often has to be reported if our readers are not to be misled about the facts of life in the community and world they live in. We try not to over-emphasize sensational stories solely because they are sensational…

'Managing Editor Walters said, that when in doubt, he would throw out what was regarded as a five percent news interest story and replace it with a ninety percent reader interest picture. Among the stories most often consigned to the waste basket by Walters were what he referred to as 'the political speculation stuff'."[3]

Walters was interested in the more modern English newspapers, and had been familiar with the work of George Gallup while in Des Moines. (In the late 1920s Mike Cowles had employed Gallup, then a graduate student in journalism at the University of Iowa, to conduct readership surveys for *The Des Moines Register* and *Tribune*. The studies showed that the highest readership was tied to stories accompanied by related pictures or graphics.)[4] Walters said: "Quite frankly, I combined the English technique with the recommendations of Gallup. We encouraged reporters to write as they talked, and encouraged headline writers to try experiments both in type faces and editorial technique. But, with it all, we tried to put across all the news of the nation, the world and the city, in a very understandable fashion, and stressed accuracy. You can see the necessity for the latter, because, naturally in developing anything new, in order to get the effect, it would be very easy to slide into carelessness."[5]

Walters had three basic rules for writing: One was the six-line lead, another the elimination of jargon and a third the reduction of even the most complicated news to man-on-the-street terms.[6] These were all evident in his belief that war reports should be handled in a "letter to a friend" style. The situations in each country were reported in bold stroke fashion with emphasis on interesting detail and background, instead of on half-mile gains here and there around some town with a name that Walters thought would frighten off readers.

Whenever a personality began to attract attention, *The Minneapolis Star* carried interesting details about him right along with the news story. Does he drink, smoke, take cold baths before breakfast? This was Walters' way to sell what he called the "heavyweight news."[7] Whether the Walters approach qualified as "seducing readers with sensation" or simply as enlightened contemporary writing and editing, it found a place in the households of Minneapolis. Another historian said: "The staid, conservative makeup policies of *The Minneapolis Tribune* and *The Minneapolis Journal* simply were not adequate to meet the challenge of the interloper from Iowa. It took about two years before the challenge of the new makeup and news techniques penetrated *Journal* thinking. It was not until about 1938 that the *Journal* began enlivening its own makeup, but it did become more attractive. In addition, it began promoting its own good deeds and services more frequently. It was all to no avail, however. *The Star* apparently had too great a lead."[8]

Three policies instituted by John Cowles had major impact. The first was a decision not to accept liquor advertising, a longstanding policy in Des Moines. *The Minneapolis Journal* announced that it would reverse its policy and begin accepting liquor advertising, revenue that would help in its competition with *The Minneapolis Star*. The next day *The Minneapolis Star* announced that it would cease carrying liquor advertising. The ad began to position *The Minneapolis Star* as the family newspaper in Minneapolis. The page one story was headlined, "Minneapolis' Family Newspaper" and went on to say, "The Star, henceforth, will publish no advertising for any alcoholic beverage, whether liquor, wine or beer. The Star is being cordially welcomed in an increasing number of Minneapolis homes each evening, and is edited to appeal to all members of the family, young and old."[9]

Cowles said, "We let every minister in the state know that the Journal was taking liquor ads while we were dropping them. I'll bet 200 preachers preached against the good old Journal. I'm sure it added several thousand to the Star's circulation."[10] The potential loss in advertising revenue was significant, but the move was an important one in the overall strategy. Liquor advertising was accepted again in 1972, a move helpful in attracting national advertising. Critical reaction was "surprisingly small," in part a reflection of how much values and mores had changed.[11]

A second policy, also adapted from Des Moines, was the practice of printing news that other papers did not print, because, in most cases, the other papers did not want to upset their advertisers. *The Minneapolis Star*, for example, printed names of people arrested for traffic and other violations which most people would have preferred to remain secret. A prominent banker was arrested for taking more than the limit during duck hunting season, and the story wound up on page one. When salaries were released by the Internal Revenue Service, they were published — both those of national celebrities and of local business figures, including Nelson Dayton, head of the department store that was the market's leading retail advertiser.[12] Said John Cowles: "Printing the news greatly stimulated our circulation. It took many years for the business community to get used to the idea that news would be printed regardless of whose interests might be harmed."[13] He noted further: "This tactic persuaded the community that a serious competitor was in town. Several men who really had important business influence in town held aloof from the Star, however."[14] Similarly, he and the editors decided to cover labor's side of the news as well as the management side. His journalists were at first uncertain of John Cowles' true intention and were reluctant to cover labor views, but they came through nicely when he convinced them he meant what he said.[15]

Executives and family members were not spared from the practice. According to Bill Brown, one morning John Cowles was arrested for speeding, causing great concern in the news room. It took some time for anyone to muster the courage to ask Cowles how to handle the matter. His response was simple: "I told you whoever it is, he gets his name in the paper." His name was at the top of the list.

The third policy said that there would be only one advertising rate card. It was common for advertising salesmen to go in with a contract to be signed by a retailer, who would then talk with the business manager or other executive to negotiate a more favorable rate.

Minneapolis' Family Newspaper

The Star, henceforth, will publish no advertising for any alcoholic beverage, whether liquor, wine, or beer.

The Star is being cordially welcomed in an increasing number of Minneapolis homes each evening, and is edited to appeal to all members of the family, young and old.

THE MINNEAPOLIS STAR, JULY 15, 1935

Under John Cowles, the rate quoted by the salesman was the only rate. According to Joyce Swan, he meant business when he said, "This is our rate card. We don't have any other."[16]

John Cowles recalled that obtaining advertising was a problem. Donaldson's (the second largest department store) was the first of the big advertisers to come through with a sizable contract, enticed in part by an agreement that guaranteed them a page-three position indefinitely. Since Dayton's had that position at *The Minneapolis Journal,* Donaldson's saw the opportunity — especially with the strengthening *Minneapolis Star* circulation picture — to improve its advertising effectiveness. Swan credits Cowles as being, "the best salesman *The Star* ever had, finally persuading Powers Department Store to start 'upstairs' advertising. John had been cooling his heels for some time in Nelson Dayton's waiting room and at Donaldson's. He and the head of Powers became well acquainted and they finally signed the contract." The term "upstairs" advertising refers to the fact that department stores had "bargain basements" as well as regular merchandise. *The Minneapolis Star* had been relegated almost totally to running basement advertising by Dayton's, with only nominal advertising from the other major stores early in 1938. *The Minneapolis Journal* carried over half of the linage from the six leading retail advertisers, *The Minneapolis Tribune* around forty percent.

The other newspapers competed in many ways, not all of them honorable. There was an early attempt to identify the Cowles family as Jewish, saying that Morley Cowles' real name was Morgan, and that Morley was a nickname to conceal that fact. The story had it that she was a niece or grand niece of "the Jewish international banker, J. Pierpont Morgan."[17] This particular rumor was apparently quashed by letting people know that John Cowles' grandfather had been a prominent Methodist minister in Iowa.

At the business level, *The Minneapolis Tribune* hired more than 200 extra circulation "peddlers" who went door to door trying to sell their paper and displace *The Minneapolis Star. The Minneapolis Journal* attempted a number of promotional tactics, most dramatic the installation of a "Telesign" atop the Foshay Tower. The sign displayed "Sky Flashes" from *The Minneapolis Journal* newsroom, beamed in six-foot high letters from 9 to 11 p.m.[18]

Posel has described well the promotional activities that kept the name of *The Minneapolis Star* before the public. House advertisements were the backbone of the campaign — publicity about the newspaper and its promotions. *The Minneapolis Star* began sponsoring an annual Golden Gloves amateur boxing tournament in 1937 and deployed placards on streetcars. One of *The Minneapolis Star*'s key promotional tactics was a daily

A CHRISTMAS AD FOR THE DAYTON COMPANY, *MINNEAPOLIS STAR JOURNAL*, DECEMBER 21, 1939

FOSHAY TOWER TELESIGN, 1939

radio program at 1:15 p.m. on WCCO that featured the top stories. The show was directed by George Grim who described it as "aiming to make our news broadcasts more showmanly…By dramatizing the news bulletins we are giving the same treatment on the air that our editorial department does in striking layouts, action pictures, flash headlines."[19]

Many people say that Cedric Adams' column "In This Corner" and his evening radio program on WCCO were the most important contributors to widespread public acceptance. At one time it was estimated that perhaps half of *The Minneapolis Star*'s reader families turned first to his folksy column, which was described as a clearing house for charity, animals and the trite but all-inclusive what-not. He once suggested that people should water their pine trees and shrubs. The next day the water department reported an increase of eight million gallons over the same day the week before.[20]

He traveled to both coasts, filing reports along the way, and went to Canada to cover a visit of the King and Queen of England. Unfortunately, he filed his story of meeting the King and Queen before the fact. They were indisposed at the last minute and had not met with the press, but Adams' story was already on the front page.

A full explanation of the embarrassing event resulted in sympathy for Adams' plight and actually appeared to help *The Minneapolis Star*'s circulation and credibility.[21]

The Minneapolis Star had overtaken *The Minneapolis Journal* in daily circulation in 1936 and in 1938 at 150,100 daily, it was 15,000 ahead of *The Minneapolis Journal* and 2,000 more than the daily *Minneapolis Tribune*. In the Minneapolis retail zone, of special interest to many advertisers, *The Minneapolis Star* had grown from 57,100 in 1935 to 85,900 in 1938 — 15,000 ahead of *The Minneapolis Journal* and only 1,500 below the daily *Minneapolis Tribune*.

Advertising, however, was a somewhat different story. At 5.5 million lines in 1935, it was 2 million below the daily *Minneapolis Journal*. Linage grew to six million in 1936, then fell to 5.3 million in 1937, recovering to 5.9 million in 1938. *The Minneapolis Journal*, meanwhile, had held in the 7.5 million range. Both it and *The Minneapolis Tribune* showed decreases in 1938 while *The Minneapolis Star* added 600,000 lines. It was in classified advertising that *The Minneapolis Star* had substantial

CEDRIC ADAMS, 1941

MINNEAPOLIS DAILY NEWSPAPER CIRCULATION 1935-1941
(TOTAL DAILY CIRCULATION)

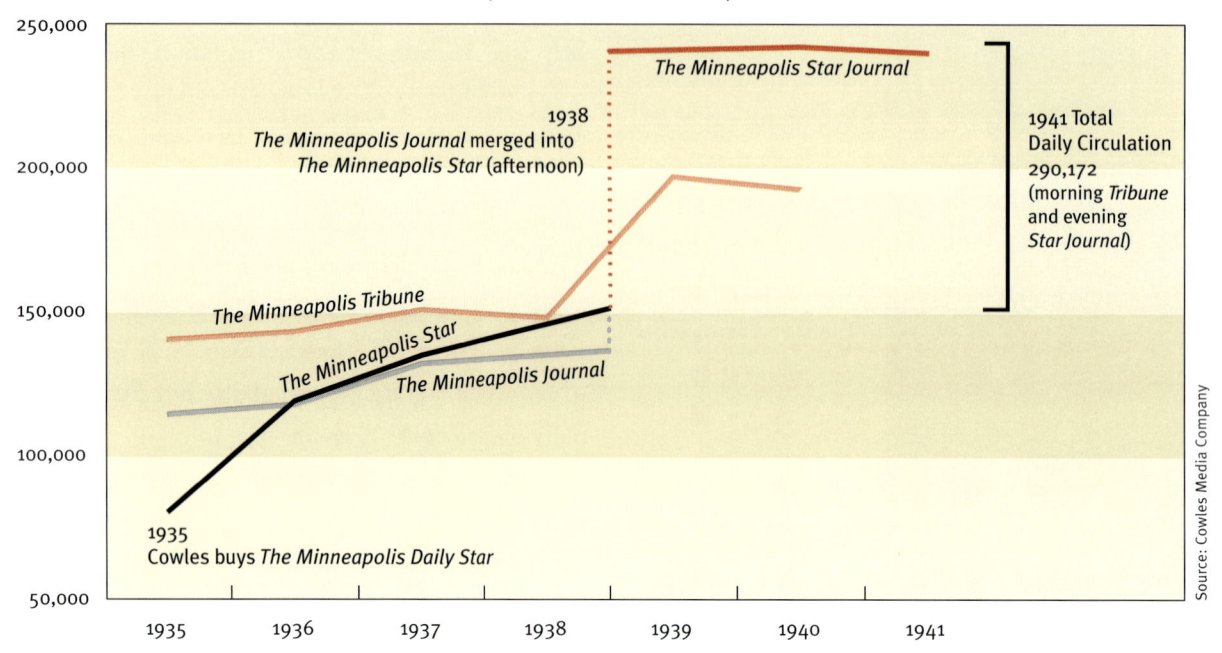

- The Minneapolis Star Journal
- 1938: The Minneapolis Journal merged into The Minneapolis Star (afternoon)
- The Minneapolis Tribune
- The Minneapolis Star
- The Minneapolis Journal
- 1935: Cowles buys The Minneapolis Daily Star
- 1941 Total Daily Circulation 290,172 (morning Tribune and evening Star Journal)

Source: Cowles Media Company

---

gains, passing *The Minneapolis Journal* in 1935.

By December 1938 John Cowles was optimistic. "The outlook appears relatively so bright from all angles that I have concluded to go ahead and expand the Star's mechanical facilities so that we will be in shape safely to handle a lot more circulation and substantially larger papers. Although no public announcement has been made, privately we are going ahead and build at least a large new press room and install additional presses."[22] Shortly thereafter he brought a key executive from Des Moines, Joyce A. Swan, a University of Missouri journalism graduate who had joined *The Des Moines Register* and *Tribune* in 1928, and served as promotion manager, personal assistant to John and Mike Cowles, and assistant business manager. (One chapter of Swan's memoirs is entitled "What Can a Man Do with a Name Like Joyce?" He was named for a prominent Methodist bishop in Illinois.)

1 "Cowles Boys Make Amazing 6-Year Record in Minneapolis," *Editor & Publisher,* February 13, 1943, p. 7.
2 George Hage, "Print and Broadcast Media," *Minnesota in a Century of Change* (St. Paul: Minnesota Historical Society, 1989), p. 305.
3 Peter Paul Posel, *The End of Newspaper Competition in Minneapolis 1935-41* (unpublished Master's thesis, University of Minnesota, June 1964), p. 44, 63 and 64.
4 Friedricks, "The Newspaper That Captured a State," p. 328.
5 John E. Allen, *The Modern Newspaper* (New York: Harper and Brothers, 1940), p. 81.
6 Mitchell V. Charnley, *Reporting* (New York: Holt, Rinehart and Winston, Inc.; Second Edition, 1966), p. 111-112.
7 Posel, "The End of Newspaper Competition," p. 4.
8 Ted Curtis Smythe, *A History of The Minneapolis Journal, 1878-1939* (unpublished Master's thesis, University of Minnesota, 1967), p. 327.
9 "Minneapolis' Family Newspaper," *The Minneapolis Star,* July 15, 1935, p.1.
10 "Forever Curious," *The Minneapolis Star,* June 17, 1974, p. 1B.
11 "Stockholders Hear Reports on Operations and Financial Details at May 16 Meeting," *Newsmakers,* June 1973, p. 6.
12 J.E. Gerald, author interview, 1961.
13 Mills, *Things Don't Just Happen,* p. 96.
14 Gerald interview, op. cit.
15 Ibid.
16 Joyce A. Swan, author interview, April 1996.
17 Ibid.
18 Smythe, op. cit., p.337.
19 Posel, op. cit., p. 89.
20 Ibid., p. 25.

THE MINNEAPOLIS JOURNAL

5

JOHN COWLES BELIEVED that a morning, evening and Sunday combination would be the strongest and soundest newspaper publishing operation. He wanted a morning and Sunday newspaper in Minneapolis and privately thought when he bought *The Minneapolis Star* that within a few years he would be able to take over *The Minneapolis Tribune*. He believed that the combination of the evening *Minneapolis Star* and the morning and Sunday *Minneapolis Tribune* would become overwhelmingly the leading newspapers in Minneapolis, even though *The Minneapolis Journal* continued to publish indefinitely.[1]

Discussions about acquiring both *The Minneapolis Tribune* and *The Minneapolis Journal* began very shortly after Cowles acquired *The Minneapolis Star*. In a letter to his father in December 1935, John Cowles said that F. E. Murphy "is clearly extremely anxious to sell the Tribune or consolidate it with the Star," and referred to the fact that Murphy's health was not good and that the Tribune organization was not strong. He goes on to say, "I kept suggesting a consolidation between the Tribune and the Journal," but that F. E. would only be receptive to a consolidation with himself as publisher if the other members of the Jones family could eliminate (the publisher) Carl.[2] Discussions were apparently ongoing: Three years later Gardner Cowles wrote John that he was "not very happy at the thought of a partnership deal with the Murphys" and that, "There seems to be some decided advantage in having the Journal and the Tribune consolidated if Ronald can bring it about; (it) would add materially to the value of the Star." (George W. Ronald was business manager of *The Minneapolis Journal* and brother-in-law of publisher Carl Jones.) He went on to discuss the difficulties connected with such a merger, saying that "the Cowles family are the only likely purchasers of the Tribune, unless Ronald can persuade the Jones family to try it, and I don't believe he can persuade them."[3]

The same day, John wrote to his father and brother to say that, "Jaffray called me and said that F. E.

THE MINNEAPOLIS SUNDAY TRIBUNE, MARCH 8, 1936

(Murphy) definitely wanted to make a merger with The Star." (C. T. Jaffray was president of the First National Bank.) "Jaffray said that F. E. told him that Ronald had spent all last evening with him trying to discuss a merger of the Tribune and the Journal. I told Jaffray that I would be simply delighted if the Journal and the Tribune consolidated because that could be worth a lot of money to The Star. Jaffray said there was going to be no consolidation."[4]

The daily city retail zone circulation of *The Minneapolis Journal* declined throughout the 1930s while *The Minneapolis Star* began to grow in 1933. *The Minneapolis Star* passed *The Minneapolis Journal* in 1935, and by 1938 *The Minneapolis Star* led, 81,326 to 63,192. It also had a growing lead in total daily circulation over both competitors. Cowles believed that *The Minneapolis Star* had "an incomparably superior circulation sales organization to that of either The Minneapolis Journal or The Minneapolis Tribune. This fact was at least as important as the improvement in news and feature content in explaining why the The Minneapolis Star made such a rapid and continuing circulation growth."[5] Its circulation gains were beginning to be converted into advertising linage by 1939. In a letter to Davis Merwin, John Cowles indicated that, "things are going pretty well. I am hopeful that Dayton's will materially increase its Star linage next year; but regardless of Dayton's, I think the chances are good we will be first in retail in 1939 anyway."[6]

Carl W. Jones, publisher of *The Minneapolis Journal*, joined that paper in 1919 at the urging of his father, leaving a promising advertising career in Chicago at Lord & Thomas and later Erwin Wasey. When Herschel V. Jones became ill in 1926, Carl was asked to take over. Two other brothers also worked at *The Minneapolis Journal*, Moses in circulation and Jefferson in editorial. George B. Bickelhaupt was business manager during both regimes; in 1936 he was succeeded by George Ronald.

When Herschel Jones died in 1928, he left controlling interest in *The Minneapolis Journal* to his widow, with the three sons working for the paper receiving identical shares, and the balance placed in trust for a fourth son and three daughters. During the Depression little money was spent on new promotions, new purchases of equipment were eliminated, and pay cuts instituted. In spite of these steps, the paper apparently lost money. During the profitable years of the twenties, very little money was put back into the paper, so that there were no reserves to help in a financial crisis. The 1890 building was outdated, inefficient and expensive to maintain, and inadequate for the needs of a modern metropolitan newspaper. The land occupied by the building was leased and there was no way to improve the facility.[7]

Apparently it was Mrs. Jones' concern about the paper

THE MINNEAPOLIS JOURNAL,
JULY 22, 1934

that led to bringing in George Ronald as business manager, replacing George Bickelhaupt who had evidently been resisting any overtures to sell the paper. According to Smythe, Mrs. Jones in 1939 determined that she would sell the paper. The bad financial situation also meant that there was very little in the way of profits to pay out to the owners, other than the three employed at *The Minneapolis Journal* at salaries of at least $12,000 to $18,000, considered excellent at the time. The brothers working at the paper wanted to keep it running and make a fight against Cowles, but their mother wanted to sell. One source has it that Mrs. Jones had returned to live in New York and wanted nothing more to do with the paper.[8]

John Cowles himself noted, in a letter to the author of a history of *The Minneapolis Journal*, that a shift in retail advertising was beginning to take shape. "A few months before the Journal was offered to us both Donaldson's and Powers, which were then the second and third largest retail advertisers, after months of tests as to relative sales results, began increasingly to concentrate their advertising copy in the Star and reduce it in the Journal. This was undoubtedly an important factor in the minds of the Journal's owners in influencing them to sell the paper. They could see the developing trend."[9]

Not reported in these earlier histories is the fact that Nelson Dayton, head of the largest retail advertiser in Minneapolis, told Carl Jones, as a courtesy, that Dayton's planned to begin advertising in *The Minneapolis Star*.

A DAYTON COMPANY AD, *THE MINNEAPOLIS JOURNAL*, DECEMBER 18, 1939

Until that time Dayton's had not used *The Minneapolis Star* at all, believing that merchants had a responsibility to support local businesses, he had continued to consider the Cowles as interlopers who were not a part of the community. The Dayton and Jones families were related by marriage, and Carl Jones never spoke to Nelson Dayton again after hearing the news. He must have concluded that it was time to sell *The Minneapolis Journal*, sensing that loss of even part of the Dayton's advertising would be followed by others as *The Minneapolis Star*'s circulation position continued to improve. Department stores used the evening newspapers extensively, and bought only minimal space in the morning paper. So the potential loss of even a portion of Dayton's advertising could be critical.[10]

According to John Cowles, in the summer of 1939 he was asked by a third party whether he "might be interested in buying the Minneapolis Journal. This came as a complete surprise to me," he wrote, "as I had made no overtures to the Journal's owners." He met with Carl Jones and George Ronald in the office of their attorney to discuss the sale. They offered to sell *The Minneapolis Journal*'s name, goodwill, circulation structure, press association membership, etc., but said they wished to keep *The Minneapolis Journal*'s building and equipment. John Cowles says they did not give him any information regarding *The Minneapolis Journal*'s financial position. His assumption was that it had been operating at a deficit for a number of years, and that the owners figured they could net more by making a sale sooner rather than later. According to Moses Jones, Cowles offered $2,250,000 for *The Minneapolis Journal*, which was accepted. According to Smythe it was a fair price, considering the inability of *The Minneapolis Journal*'s management to contest the evening field with *The Minneapolis Star*.

(Waring Jones recalls being with his father, Carl Jones, in South Dakota where they learned from an English reporter that *The Minneapolis Journal* was being sold. He also reports that his mother disputed a number of things said in the thesis (by T. C. Smythe) about the paper and its sale.)[11]

Cowles had three reasons for wanting *The Minneapolis Journal*: for its Associated Press membership, to gain a Sunday edition (which he was considering starting for *The Minneapolis Star*), and the prestige of *The Minneapolis Journal* and its position with major retail advertisers. It also must have presented a powerful opportunity to make *The Minneapolis Star* investment profitable.[12]

News of the sale of *The Minneapolis Journal* came first in a radio broadcast at six p.m. on July 31, 1939. There had been no leaks or rumors. Joyce Swan recalls that he and his family were on a fishing vacation in northern Minnesota where he got a call to come to Minneapolis. At 5 p.m. John Cowles announced the purchase and discussed the steps necessary to print the next day's edition as *The Minneapolis Star Journal*. Employees worked all night, going to *The Minneapolis Journal* plant to bring forms of type, ads, and news material back to *The Minneapolis Star* and getting them into production.[13] Bill Brown remembers being told late in the day to remain in the office until the five o'clock meeting, then going to *The Minneapolis Journal* and moving everything that had to do with advertising back to *The Minneapolis Star*.[14]

The 500 *Journal* employees learned of the sale from a notice posted on the bulletin board. The same information, in a statement from Carl Jones, appeared in the August 1 edition:

> "The Minneapolis Journal was enjoying at the present time an all time peak in daily circulation and its advertising patronage has suffered only the natural shrinkage of the recession.
>
> "However, there have been too many newspapers in Minneapolis to support a healthy constructive growth of any one of them. The changing times

MINNEAPOLIS STAR JOURNAL
MERGER NOTICE, AUGUST 1, 1939

THE STAR JOURNAL FROLIC, 1939

have brought revolutionary methods in mechanical equipment, news and picture gathering, handling of personnel and taxes, which required ever increasing resources.

"Because the majority of the stockholders of The Journal were not engaged in operating The Journal, it seemed wise to the respective managements that one ownership could more effectively meet the exigencies referred to. Mr. John Cowles and his associates, desiring to further the usefulness of the Minneapolis press, made a fair offer for purchase which was accepted by The Journal."[15]

John Cowles, in announcing the merger, said, "The Star Journal will have only one aim — to serve its reader with a clean, fair, reliable, constructive newspaper which will deserve the support of the community." An editorial on the same day reiterated the policy of no liquor advertising.[16]

The monthly employee communication made no announcement of the merger, other than to change its name from *Starmakers* to *Star Journal Makers*. Every attempt was made to avoid discriminating between "Star" and "Journal" employees. A "Star Journal Fall Frolic" was attended by 900 people at the Nicollet Hotel. "John Cowles welcomed new members of The Star Journal staff and declared that henceforth they would not be called 'newcomers' but would be part of the one organization. 'I am sure all of us — and all of our readers — are glad The Star Journal's future is ahead of us,' he said." He "spoke of the aims and possibilities of The Star Journal, declared the splendid spirit of our organization, the editorial content and the mechanical facilities to work will send it a long way."[17]

Public reaction to the sale was mixed. *The Minneapolis Journal*'s 135,300 subscribers received copies of the new paper—*The Minneapolis Star Journal*—with a request that they continue reading the new paper. Circulation in 1939 was 241,200, up from *The Minneapolis Star*'s 1938 total of 150,100. One former *Journal* reporter said that the new paper "looks like the Journal but feels like the Star," something he found unsatisfactory. To some people, losing *The Minneapolis Journal* was like losing a member of the family or a good friend.[18]

Joyce Swan characterized the general reaction as not bitter, but shocked. "I think the people simply couldn't understand why their favorite paper had suddenly become a part of The Star. But that gradually subsided as they began to understand that The Star Journal was helpful to the community, even though they didn't like some of the news stories (that sometimes stepped on the toes of prominent people)."[19] Most of the employees of *The Minneapolis Journal* were promptly offered jobs by *The Minneapolis Star* at the same compensation, or in some cases at higher salaries, in part because of the requirements of the new Sunday edition.

John Cowles reported that starting early in the morning of August 1, 1939, different *Star* executives began to contact *Journal* employees to ask them if they did not want to join the combined *Minneapolis Star Journal*. *The Minneapolis Star* needed to add the bulk of

> ## The Tribune Meets the Situation
>
> Beginning next Monday there will be two Minneapolis Tribunes.
>
> The Morning Tribune will be published each morning and Sunday.
>
> The Times-Tribune will be the evening paper.
>
> They will be wholly distinct newspapers, each complete in itself, each with its own editorial page, news staff, features and pictures and the full service of the Associated Press and auxiliary news services.
>
> F. E. Murphy, publisher, made the announcement and added the simple comment: "We will give Minneapolis and the northwest the best morning and evening newspapers the enlarged Tribune organization is capable of producing."
>
> The multitude of details involved in the building of what is practically a new newspaper are already well in hand and just two weeks from the day the Journal closed its doors and dismissed its employes the Times-Tribune will be on the streets, in Minneapolis homes and on its way to delivery throughout the northwest.
>
> The present Tribune news and editorial staffs will be augmented by many of the pick of the Journal's writers, reporters and executives.
>
> George H. Adams, for nineteen years managing editor of the Journal, will be managing editor of The Times-Tribune.
>
> Dowsley Clark, assistant managing editor of The Tribune for 10 years, will be managing editor of The Morning Tribune.
>
> Thomas J. Dillon, for 19 years The Tribune's managing editor, will be editor of both papers and Charles B. Cheney, chief editorial writer of the Journal, will contribute to the editorial page.
>
> Among others of the Journal's news staff coming to The Times-Tribune will be Leif Gilstad, widely known political writer, Dow Congdon, news editor, Merle Potter, one of the country's outstanding motion picture reviewers and commentators, Clifford Falls, for many years Journal telegraph editor, and Arnold Aslakson and Jay Edgerton, top-ranking reporters and news writers. Others are being engaged and The Tribune's present staffs of reporters, women's page writers and photographers will be further enlarged.
>
> The Tribune's office this week has swarmed with representatives of producers of newspaper features. The best of available features, comic strips and informative articles, many wholly new to Minneapolis, will appear in the Morning Tribune and Times-Tribune starting Monday.
>
> New headline type, now being rushed from the east, will give The Times-Tribune a new and modern dress.

**THE MINNEAPOLIS TRIBUNE
AUGUST 10, 1939**

The Minneapolis Journal production employees to publish the greatly enlarged daily and the Sunday editions. Intra-union jurisdictional problems were difficult, and eventually settled by the union chapels. He estimated that probably 95 percent of employees not of retirement age and who also wanted to work, found positions on *The Minneapolis Star Journal* or *The Minneapolis Times-Tribune*.[20] George Ronald and Moses Jones were among the executives who made the move. Ronald was elected an officer and director in 1940, but left within a year.

The Minneapolis Tribune created a completely new afternoon edition to replace its 24-hour service, and renamed it *The Times-Tribune*. Circulation of the morning and evening *Minneapolis Tribune* newspapers increased from 148,100 to 197,100 in 1939. Under a story headlined, "The Tribune Meets the Situation," the new addition was announced with the note that the new paper would appear "…just two weeks from the day the Journal closed is doors and dismissed its employees."[21] Two dozen former *Minneapolis Journal* writers were hired by this new daily, and the paper included its best features and comics in the afternoon edition, some taken from the morning paper.

1   John Cowles Sr., Letter to Professor J.E. Gerald, June 1, 1963.
2   John Cowles Sr., Letter to Gardner Cowles Sr., December 21, 1935.
3   Gardner Cowles Sr., Letter to John Cowles Sr., December 1, 1938.
4   John Cowles Sr., Letter to Gardner Cowles Sr. and Gardner Cowles Jr., December 1, 1938.
5   John Cowles Sr., Letter to Ted C. Smythe, October 3, 1937.
6   John Cowles Sr., Letter to Davis Merwin, December 22, 1938.
7   Smythe, *A History of* The Minneapolis Journal, p. 398.
8   Ibid., p. 392.
9   John Cowles Sr., Letter to Ted C. Smythe, October 3, 1967.
10 Kenneth N. Dayton, author interview, May 2, 1996.
11 Waring Jones, author interview, May 10, 1996.
12 Smythe, op. cit., p. 401.
13 Joyce Swan, author interview, April 1996.
14 Willis Brown, author interview, February 1996.
15 "Star and Journal in Consolidation, Statement by Carl W. Jones," *The Minneapolis Star Journal,* August 1, 1939, p. 1.
16 Ibid., p. 1.
17 "Star Journal Fall Frolic," *Star Journal Makers,* October, 1939, p. 2-3.
18 Smythe, op. cit., p. 403.
19 Swan, op. cit.
20 John Cowles Sr., Letter to Ted Smythe, October 3, 1967.
21 "The Tribune Meets the Situation," *The Minneapolis Tribune,* August 10, 1939, p. 1.

THE MINNEAPOLIS TRIBUNE

6

WITH THE ACQUISITION of *The Minneapolis Journal*, *The Minneapolis Star* had a daily circulation now significantly larger than *The Minneapolis Tribune*, and it was all in the evening, the preferred time by advertisers. Advertising linage passed *The Minneapolis Tribune* in 1939. While the Sunday paper was still smaller than *The Minneapolis Tribune*, it grew from 160,200 in 1939 to 197,500 in 1940 — closer to *The Minneapolis Tribune*'s 214,200, which had actually declined a little.[1]

The Minneapolis Tribune was a venerable paper, founded in 1867. Like many newspapers of the time, it passed through a number of ownerships over the years. In 1891, it was owned by the Minneapolis Rapid Transit Company, in turn owned by Thomas Lowry, a prominent Minneapolis businessman. The paper was losing money, and he was looking for someone to return it to profitability. In a discussion with Senator Pierce of North Dakota, he learned that a young lawyer in North Dakota had taken over a newspaper in Grand Forks and made a success of it quickly. The man was W. J. Murphy, then 32, who had acquired the *Plaindealer* in a financial deal which was contingent on his collecting the paper's debts, which he did. He also owned electric power companies in the area.

Murphy had already sold the *Plaindealer* and was on a train to New York when he received a telegram in Chicago. He returned to Minneapolis to talk with Lowry, who made him executive editor of *The Minneapolis Tribune*. He acquired total ownership of the paper in a short time, subject to his ability to pay off a $1 million debt to the transit company. He sold the Grand Forks Gas and Light Company in 1908 to pay off the debt to Lowry and achieved clear ownership of *The Minneapolis Tribune*.[2]

Murphy was from a large family in New Richmond, Wisconsin, and he employed a number of relatives in the paper from time to time, including his brother Frederick (F. E.). He succeeded through hard work, skillful management, and tough labor policies. W. J.'s grandson, Kingsley H. Murphy Jr., relates a story told

MINNEAPOLIS TRIBUNE, NOVEMBER 12, 1940

him by his father who worked in the press room as a 13-year old one summer. He observed to W. J. one morning at breakfast that the heat in the press room was stifling and that putting in fans there might improve productivity. His father erupted at the idea and called his son a "little socialist" and told him that if he wanted his advice, he would ask for it.[3]

The Minneapolis Tribune prospered through the early years of the century, but W. J. Murphy's personal life did not. In 1916 a daughter, Josephine, was killed in an automobile accident. Murphy began drinking heavily from time to time, and essentially walked out on his family. He became determined to build a paper mill at Manistique, Michigan. (Many newspaper companies built their own newsprint mills to control supply and prices.) The mill turned out to be much more costly than estimated, and by 1917 conditions had become so bad that the secured lenders, Minnesota Loan and Trust of Minneapolis, removed Murphy from active management. He died in the flu epidemic of 1918. His will was complicated, with distributions of Minnesota Tribune Company stock going to his immediate family, the University of Minnesota for a School of Journalism,[4] and to his brothers and sisters. The lawyer appointed by the bank as president of the Tribune company was ousted by the family members who brought Frederick E. Murphy back to run the paper.

F. E. Murphy had been running the Femco farms in western Minnesota. Agriculture was his

W. J. MURPHY, ABOUT 1910

EARLY OFFICES OF *THE MINNEAPOLIS TRIBUNE* WERE IN THE MINNEAPOLIS CITY HALL, CIRCA 1870

lifelong passion, although he had worked at the newspaper for many years under W. J., his brother. F. E. Murphy was apparently able to restore *The Minneapolis Tribune* to financial health, although much of his attention was devoted to resolving ownership issues created by W. J. Murphy's will. He first acquired the stock that W. J. gave to the University of Minnesota; part of the financing was a $350,000 loan from a group of 14 businessmen which included Charles Blandin (who then owned the St. Paul newspapers), Reuell Harmon of Webb Publishing, George Dayton of the department store family, and James Ford Bell of General Mills. In 1924 these and the other Murphy family shares in the Minnesota Tribune Company were placed in the Mutual Holding Company. That company then held 5,400 of the 9,800 shares outstanding, the rest owned largely by the W. J. Murphy family — his widow and two sons.[5] *The Minneapolis Tribune* was highly profitable during the 1920s, able to pay annual dividends of $75 per share.

Leo Owens, one of W. J.'s nephews, returned from World War I expecting to reclaim his job at *The Minneapolis Tribune*, but was told that his job had been filled. He later took a job in New York and in 1927 went to St. Paul to see Charles Blandin about newsprint supplies. Blandin was then owner of *The St. Paul Pioneer Press* and *Dispatch,* as well as his paper mill in Grand Rapids, Minnesota. Blandin suggested that Owens buy the paper. He had no money and proposed to the Ridder family in New York that they purchase the papers jointly, with Owens holding a 20 percent interest which was later increased to 25 percent.

In 1934 Owens found that he could buy radio station WRHM in Minneapolis for $140,000. The Ridders did not want to invest the full amount, so he persuaded his uncle F. E. Murphy to have the Minnesota Tribune Company buy a half interest. The call letters were then changed to WTCN, standing for Twin City Newspapers. At about the same time he proposed to F. E. that he purchase *The Minneapolis Star,* saying that it could be bought for $900,000. F. E. declined (even though Kingsley H. Murphy, W. J.'s son, agreed to the proposal) with the comment that, "We can buy the paper cheaper next year."[6]

In 1938 the Ridder family asked for Owens' resignation; he went on to publish other newspapers and retained his stock in the company. B. H. (Ben) Ridder succeeded him as publisher. He quickly set up a program to encourage St. Paul women to shop in St. Paul (not Minneapolis) stores. The Women's Institute of St. Paul held programs and promotions until 1971, initially twelve a year, later reduced to ten as costs escalated. Each drew 12,000 women to the St. Paul Auditorium to hear people ranging from Eleanor Roosevelt to Liberace.

The Depression years were difficult for the Tribune organization, dividends were cut to $5 per share (from $75 in the later twenties), and the company had to borrow $1.5 million. The economic problems were apparently exacerbated by F. E.'s devotion to agricultural diversification and the Femco farms, into which he poured much of the newspaper's profit instead of putting it back into the newspaper. Concerned about the Midwestern over-reliance on wheat, he emphasized the value of "the cow, the sow and the little red hen." Over time he was looked to as a spokesman for Minnesota agriculture and became an influence on national agricultural policy.

F. E. Murphy died in February of 1940, with his will providing for continued control of the Minnesota Tribune Company in the Mutual Holding Company. Control of the holding company was placed in the hands of three trustees — Charles Blandin, George Bickelhaupt, who had come to *The Minneapolis Tribune* from *The Minneapolis Journal,* and Northwestern National Bank and Trust Company. As W. J.'s son and a large stockholder, Kingsley H. Murphy wanted to become publisher, but F. E. had been very much opposed to that possibility and had set up the holding company specifically for the purpose of keeping him out of management.

In 1939 F.E. had brought his nephew W. J. McNally back to *The Minneapolis Tribune* in part to help launch an evening paper to compete with *The Minneapolis Star Journal.* The paper had begun losing money in 1938, the result of depressed advertising revenues and the new competition. An additional factor,

RADIO'S REACH MADE IT AN IMPORTANT INVESTMENT FOR THE COWLES

reported by McNally but not reported elsewhere, was a commitment to pay one-third of *The Minneapolis Tribune*'s profits to *The Minneapolis Star Journal* each year until a total of $450,000 was reached. This was an agreement made with F.E. and Kingsley Murphy, presumably on the theory that *The Minneapolis Tribune* would benefit from the demise of *The Minneapolis Journal*, being better able to compete for circulation and advertising.[7]

THE MINNEAPOLIS STAR JOURNAL COMPANY STOCK CERTIFICATE, 1940

The Minneapolis Tribune's efforts to increase circulation and to create a separate evening paper were very costly and were not producing the desired results. Advertisers wanted evening circulation, but the new *Minneapolis Times-Tribune* was not able to provide it. The physical plant of both the newspaper and the pulp and paper mill were "hopelessly obsolete," since nothing had been spent on them for years.

There is no record of discussions with John Cowles after the death of F. E. Murphy, and it does not appear that McNally was apprised of earlier discussions. Shortly after the acquisition of *The Minneapolis Journal*, Mike wrote to John that he was opposed to a joint ownership with the Murphys. "The only real argument seems to be that we are going to have to spend a large amount of money for the Sunday Star Journal. The net of all this is that this is not a propitious time to attempt to work out anything with Murphy. Possibly next March or next June something could be worked out."[8] The same day his father wrote to John that, "It is probably too soon to consider any further clean up of the Minneapolis daily newspaper field. Sometime in the future it will be a real question. It probably will do no harm to let Murphy outline a proposition; be slow about making any positive commitment."[9]

William J. McNally succeeded his late uncle as president of the Minnesota Tribune Company in April 1940. He concluded that *The Minneapolis Tribune* could be saved only by a sale or merger. There were no likely buyers, so he decided to get in touch with John Cowles to discuss a merger. Cowles was heavily involved in Wendell Willkie's presidential campaign and almost continuously absent from Minneapolis. They finally encountered each other by chance in November, at a party given by the James Ford Bells honoring Claire Booth Luce, and agreed to have a lunch the following Monday — November 18, 1940. McNally proposed that the two properties be merged, with each predecessor company owning 49.5 percent of the stock in the new company and an outside individual holding the remaining one percent. McNally had determined that a consolidated operation "could easily turn in a minimum profit in excess of two and a half million dollars a year before taxes."[10]

John Cowles was interested, but concerned about tax consequences of a transaction and his strong feeling that he needed to be in control of a consolidated property. They met again on November 27 with attorneys, who had concluded that a down-stream merger could be accomplished without incurring any tax liability, and agreed to study the matter further. In January, however, Cowles went to London with Willkie, was difficult to reach afterwards, then left for a winter vacation in Arizona. *The Minneapolis Tribune* losses in January and February were "appalling" and McNally was becoming concerned that Cowles might not be serious about a merger. In March he obtained reluctant permission from his board to launch a 13-papers-a-week plan in the hope that doing so would force *The Minneapolis Star Journal* to follow with a morning edition, at great cost.

Cowles returned to Minneapolis in March, and the two met on March 19, 1941. On April 2 they met again and agreed to form a new company in which the Minnesota Tribune Company would own one third — 50,000 shares. The combined corporation assumed a $2.9 million loan from the Des Moines Register and Tribune Company, with an additional debt of $1,450,000 owed to the Minnesota Tribune Company. Cowles also asked for the Tribune Company's half interest in WTCN; McNally refused and offered the Glendalough game farm instead. Further discussions were held in New York during the annual meeting of the American Newspaper Publishers Association. Mike Cowles attended some of those meetings, and McNally observed that he was not nearly as keen about the proposed deal as his brother. Kingsley Murphy was then advised of the pending merger, to which he subsequently agreed, and the contract was signed in Minneapolis on April 29, 1941. Thus began a long and often uneasy relationship between the Cowles family and the Murphys.

The merger took the owners of the Minnesota Tribune Company out of a rapidly deteriorating situation. It also provided John Cowles with the opportunity to begin making significant profits in Minneapolis after several years of continuing investment. Both parties benefitted, but this did not make them allies. The completed agreement provided that the sellers deposit in escrow 25,000 shares (half of their interest) in the Minneapolis Star Journal and Tribune Company for a period of three years to ensure fulfillment of all obligations. The agreement also provided that the seller could not sell any stock in the combined company without first offering it to the president of the company at the same price offered by another prospective purchaser.[11] Kingsley Murphy subsequently agreed to give John Cowles a similar right of first refusal on any of his own stock in the Minnesota Tribune Company. The agreement, however, permitted transfers among stockholders of the holding company.[12]

The company remained completely separate from the Des Moines company, and in 1940 and 1941 the stock then held by the Register and Tribune Company was distributed to its shareholders. John and Mike Cowles had roughly equal holdings in the Star Journal and Tribune Company, and were major stockholders in the Register and Tribune Company.

1 Posel, *"The End of Newspaper Competition,"* p. 106.
2 C. J. Mulrooney, *Recollections* (St. Paul: MTC Properties, Inc., 1978), p. 10.
3 Kingsley Murphy Jr., author interview, 1996.
4 At the time, the Murphy gift for a journalism school was second in size only to one from Joseph Pulitzer to Columbia University.
5 Mulrooney, *Recollections,* p. 61.
6 Ibid., p. 69.
7 W.J. McNally, *Tale of an Assignment* (St. Paul: MTC Properties, Inc., 1956), p. 4.
8 Gardner Cowles Jr., Letter to John Cowles Sr., October 23, 1939.
9 Gardner Cowles Sr., Letter to John Cowles Sr., October 23, 1939.
10 McNally, op. cit., p. 14.

A LEVEL OF SUCCESS

7

WHILE THE "REALIGNMENT" of the Minneapolis newspapers, as it was termed, tended to dominate much of the activity of the 1939-41 period, *The Minneapolis Star* itself had been moving toward some financial success by itself. At the 1939 annual shareholders meeting, John Cowles complimented personnel on the improvement of *The Minneapolis Star* and said that it was showing a profit — not a great profit — but a profit as contrasted to previous years during which losses were incurred. He noted that advertising had increased greatly in volume, indicating *The Minneapolis Star*'s acceptance by advertisers and the favorable state of mind of the Minneapolis business community. He indicated that it would be advisable to raise advertising rates in the near future.

The purchase of *The Minneapolis Journal* followed shortly after that meeting, and construction of a new plant had begun. At the 1940 annual meeting Cowles again complimented personnel on the continued improvement, but noted that the paper had not yet reached the level of success it deserved, was not receiving the percentage of available advertising that its circulation position had really earned, nor was circulation commensurate with the paper's coverage of world and local news. He acknowledged that the property was showing a profit, but not at the level that should be paid on the company's great investment.[1] He urged each stockholder to exert his influence to the fullest to see that *The Minneapolis Star Journal* reached its potential and asked them to sign a pledge to that effect. (The stockholders present were nearly all management employees.)

A new building was dedicated in July of 1940 with the entrance on Portland (then Sixth) Avenue. A fifty-foot sign was erected on the roof of the building with daily circulation announced in green neon numerals six feet high — leaving no doubt in the mind of the public that *The Minneapolis Star Journal* had become the leading circulation newspaper. The new plant was said to be the last word in newspaper building construction, the finest

MINNEAPOLIS STAR JOURNAL,
APRIL 30, 1941

THE MINNEAPOLIS STAR BUILDING, 1920

THE MINNEAPOLIS STAR BUILDING, 1960

plant between Chicago and the Pacific coast. More than 16,000 visitors attended the open house.

With four stories and a basement, the building was both a renovation of the original building and new space. Along with new stereotyping equipment, a Goss eight-unit high-speed color press and three additional black and white units made a total of 22 black and white units. Outstanding features were described as including a new, faster passenger elevator, new lavatory facilities with the latest in modern equipment, and a complete ventilation system for the mechanical departments. In January 1941, a new Sunday magazine section was introduced, printed on the new color press. (See Appendix D.)

Other activities took the time and attention of John Cowles. He was involved with his brother, Mike, in the launch of *LOOK* magazine, in which the two invested $500,000. Mike initially thought it could be a Sunday newspaper supplement, but John and his father convinced him that was not the proper tack to take. They learned that Henry Luce and Roy Larsen of Time Inc. were also planning a picture magazine, *LIFE*. John and Larsen were Harvard classmates; the four met to discuss their respective plans and agreed that the two magazines were different enough that they would not be competitive. Luce even made a small investment in *LOOK*, later repurchased when the magazines turned out to be highly competitive. (John Cowles had been unsuccessful earlier in bringing Larsen to The Register and Tribune Company.)

The magazine got off to a strong start in 1937, but by the summer of 1938 circulation was in trouble, in part because the U.S. economy had turned down sharply. Because of the losses, John favored killing the new magazine. Mike, however, turned renewed attention to the magazine, building both the editorial product and the circulation capability, and it began to turn the corner. John served as chairman of the new Look Corporation.[2]

The brothers met Wendell Willkie in April 1940 at the annual meeting of the American Society of Newspaper Editors in Washington. John Cowles was an avowed internationalist at a time when isolationism and

GARDNER COWLES JR. (MIKE), LEFT, AND JOHN COWLES SR., RIGHT, AT *LOOK* MAGAZINE, ABOUT 1940

opposition to becoming involved in the war in Europe were running high, and he opposed the nomination of Senator Robert Taft of Ohio, an isolationist. John and Mike decided to help Willkie secure the Republican nomination for President. John Cowles arranged for him to be the main speaker at a Republican dinner in St. Paul, and Mike arranged for a similar opportunity to meet delegates in Des Moines. In both instances, Willkie was a huge success, and the brothers supported him strongly throughout the campaign.

Beginning in May *The Minneapolis Star Journal* began extensive coverage of Willkie, and the editorial page strongly endorsed his candidacy. John wrote Willkie's acceptance speech for the convention and was a strong influence on the selection of the vice-presidential candidate, Senator Charles McNary of Oregon. Willkie asked Cowles to become chairman of the Republican Party, but he was not interested in the assignment. Cowles was concerned about his role in the campaign because he strongly believed that any newspaper could be seriously injured if its head involved himself in partisan politics. He went on to say, "I worked for Willkie's nomination only because I thought it was an extremely critical time for the country and it might be fatal if an isolationist who would not build up the country's military capabilities were elected."[3] John Cowles was not active in partisan politics in Minnesota, and was not part of a group of leading businessmen who met in Room 452 of The Minneapolis Club to agree on candidates (usually Republican) for important state offices.

After defeating Willkie in November, President

JOHN COWLES SR., LEFT, WENDELL WILLKIE, CENTER, AND GARDNER COWLES JR. (MIKE), ABOUT 1941

Roosevelt asked him to go to England to work on the idea of Lend-Lease in January of 1941, accompanied by John Cowles. Upon his return, Cowles gave a firsthand report to employees of the paper and later addressed the Minnesota Legislature in joint session.

Meanwhile, discussions with the Murphys continued, and, on April 30, 1941, the merger was announced in the paper:

"A complete re-alignment of the companies publishing the Minneapolis newspapers has been effected, to the end that all three Minneapolis dailies The Star Journal, The Morning Tribune and The Times-Tribune, may remain in the field, preserve their separate editorial individualities and have more assurance of permanency of life than they have had in the past.

"It is an open secret that for many years the Minneapolis newspapers, as a whole, have been operated at a loss. It has long been apparent that casualties were inevitable unless some readjustment was made. This readjustment has been made in order to ensure the continued existence of the three dailies.

"Under the new setup, the present owners of The Star Journal will also have a financial interest in The Morning Tribune and The Times-Tribune, and present Tribune stockholders will similarly have a financial interest in The Star Journal."[4]

With the Tribune merger completed, the business began to concentrate fully on consolidating its position in the market and to effect the efficiencies inherent in the new organization. William J. McNally joined the operation as vice president of the new Minneapolis Star Journal and Tribune Company; he also wrote a column for the morning paper. He and Kingsley Murphy were named directors. *The Minneapolis Times-Tribune* was renamed *The Minneapolis Daily Times* and George Bickelhaupt named publisher. Thomas J. Dillon carried over as editor-in-chief.

After the merger, the Newspaper Guild sued for severance pay, alleging it was due its members under their contact, even though they kept working after the change in ownership. This was the first overt or public union problem under the Cowles ownership. A state judge awarded the Newspaper Guild $160,000. John Cowles felt that the verdict was unfair since many Guild members continued to perform the same work as before for a newspaper of the same name. In spite of this inequity, he felt it unwise to appeal the decision, given the strong presence of organized labor in Minneapolis and the labor unrest a few years earlier.

The Guild apparently saw their action in a national context in which they "wanted to make it as tough and expensive as we could to close up papers." The local executive of the Guild said: "The Cowles don't like to come out in public against the Guild. They have a monopoly here, they have boosted circulation and advertising rates. They are in a defensive position as to labor. They are trying to do nothing outwardly hostile."[5] The conflict left some bitterness on both sides.

Cowles was very much aware of the importance of public relations, especially in an essentially monopoly situation. He said: "We probably emphasize our public relations program more than some newspapers. We try to take the leadership as a newspaper and as individuals in all civic matters related to our community. We work just as hard outside our columns to be good citizens and

THE MINNEAPOLIS TIMES-TRIBUNE,
AUGUST 14, 1939

we encourage all our key executives to be active in community affairs." These activities included such things as an annual pheasant dinner for disabled veterans, drives to get personal supplies for servicemen, and assisting with Sister Elizabeth Kenny's passport extension so that she could remain in Minneapolis and open her clinic — the Elizabeth Kenny Polio Institute.[6] He was not involved in local organizations himself, both because of the press of business and because he had played that role extensively in Des Moines. His executives, however, participated in a range of civic activities.

Summing up the 1935-41 period, John Cowles said that the greatest obstacle to be overcome in attaining control of the field was reader habit. "Our formula was simply this — give them a superior product, deliver it better and promote it effectively. By giving our readers a good editorial product and breaking down their habits of reading other Minneapolis newspapers, we were able to offer our advertiser a productive advertising medium. They too, however, had to learn to change their habits in favor of our paper, but they eventually wanted to buy space from us."[7]

On December 12, 1942 the company declared its first dividend: $1.00 per share.

1 Minneapolis Star Journal Company, Minutes of the Annual Meeting of Stockholders, July 11, 1940.
2 Gardner Cowles Jr., *Mike Looks Back*, p. 62.
3 John Cowles Sr., Letter to J. E. Gerald, August 8, 1963.
4 "An Announcement," *The Minneapolis Star Journal,* April 30, 1941, p.1.
5 *P.M.,* May 21, 1944, p. 14.
6 "Cowles Boys Make Amazing 6-Year Record in Minneapolis," *Editor & Publisher,* February 13, 1943, p. 7.
7 Ibid., p. 7.

THE WAR YEARS

8

THE WAR YEARS WERE marked by considerable personnel turnover, newsprint rationing, high tax rates and the general constraints faced by all businesses.

In December of 1941, 143 men from the organization were in the armed services, and a large display was installed in the lobby listing each one. By July of 1943 the number had grown to 175, and by August of 1944, to 212. In all, 247 *Minneapolis Star Journal* and *Tribune* employees were in the military service; over half returned to their former employment. The company established a death benefit for the families of men who were killed — eight in total. Total employment increased slightly during the war — from 1,055 in 1942 to 1,113 in 1945, with a jump to 1,345 in 1946. The mechanical departments — almost totally male and union — added only six from 486 in 1942, but jumped to 623 in 1946.

A shortage of newsprint forced hard decisions on the newspaper. In July of 1943, papers were ordered to use five percent less than in the similar period in 1941; in September the order was raised to ten percent. And in January 1944, consumption was cut to 74.5 percent of 1941 consumption. All forms of advertising were rationed; national and classified advertisers were reduced by not less than 30 percent, and local display advertisers were able to use only 80 percent of their 1943 linage.

Newspapers had, in effect, the option of reducing circulation, news coverage, or advertising. John Cowles believed that it was in the best interest of the public and the paper to reduce advertising, in spite of the loss of revenue. Circulation of *The Sunday Minneapolis Tribune* grew from about 350,000 in 1941 to 465,000 by 1946. During the same period, the morning *Minneapolis Tribune* grew from a little over 50,000 to 130,000, and the evening *Minneapolis Star Journal* from just under 250,000 to 270,000. The relatively slow growth of the evening paper was a preview of the future of its circulation.

According to Joyce Swan: "…John wisely made the decision, 'Let's ration advertising.' Which meant about a one-third cut in advertising, and let the circulation grow because after the war that increased circulation is going to

MINNEAPOLIS MORNING TRIBUNE, DECEMBER 8, 1941

be very helpful to the advertisers. Now the advertisers, of course, didn't understand that until after the war, when they realized that they had much better circulation."[1]

In January of 1943 John Cowles went to Washington to become assistant to Edward W. Stettinius Jr., head of the Lend-Lease Administration, a subject to which he was introduced during his work with Wendell Willkie.

In June of 1943, John Cowles went to North Africa as part of his Lend-Lease assignment, and narrowly missed being named public relations officer on General Eisenhower's staff. The general needed help with the press, and Milton Eisenhower had recommended that he draft either C. D. Jackson or Cowles, whichever arrived in Africa first. Jackson, who was then with the Office of War Information on leave from Time Inc., arrived first because Cowles was delayed by bad weather.[2] John Cowles completed his work for Stettinius and returned to Minneapolis in August.

Mike Cowles had gone to Washington in 1942 to head the domestic division of the Office of War Information (OWI), succeeding Archibald McLeish. He told President Roosevelt that he would rather enlist in the Air Force, but he was persuaded by the President to go to Washington with the OWI. Even that move concerned his father, since neither son was then on the scene in Des Moines. Mike's rationale was that it made more sense for him to be based in Washington, where he could be reached by telephone at any time, than being overseas with the military.

Even with their wartime assignments, John and Mike were never far from their business interests. Late in 1943 Mike tried to persuade John that they should consider entering the Indianapolis newspaper market, one of the few that had not yet "solidified." He favored buying *The Indianapolis Times* from Roy Howard, then buying the *Star* which had a Sunday edition. The competition was *The Indianapolis News*. The success of *The Sunday Des Moines Register* led him to believe that the Sunday paper could be the key in Indianapolis, if it were teamed with morning and evening dailies. John's concern was that the *News* had incomparably better retail advertising than the others and that great effort would be required. He said, "Indianapolis would be attractive if you or I had a twin brother who would live there, but it frankly doesn't appeal to me at all. I would think that with one-fifth the investment and effort, we might make far greater profits and have more influence through establishing a new magazine, for example."[3] There is no indication that the matter was pursued.

John Cowles was invited to join the board of the First National Bank of Minneapolis in 1944, a solid sign that he had become accepted by the business establishment. Mike was a director of the Iowa Des Moines National Bank, part of the Northwestern Bank Corporation, owner of the other large bank in Minneapolis. John had more friends on the Northwestern Bank board, but concluded that the First National directorship would be better.[4] Less than a year later he joined the board of General Mills, confirming his status in the community. Although he was concerned about the arguments against a newspaper publisher

THE WAR MEMORIAL IN THE LOBBY OF
THE MINNEAPOLIS STAR AND TRIBUNE BUILDING

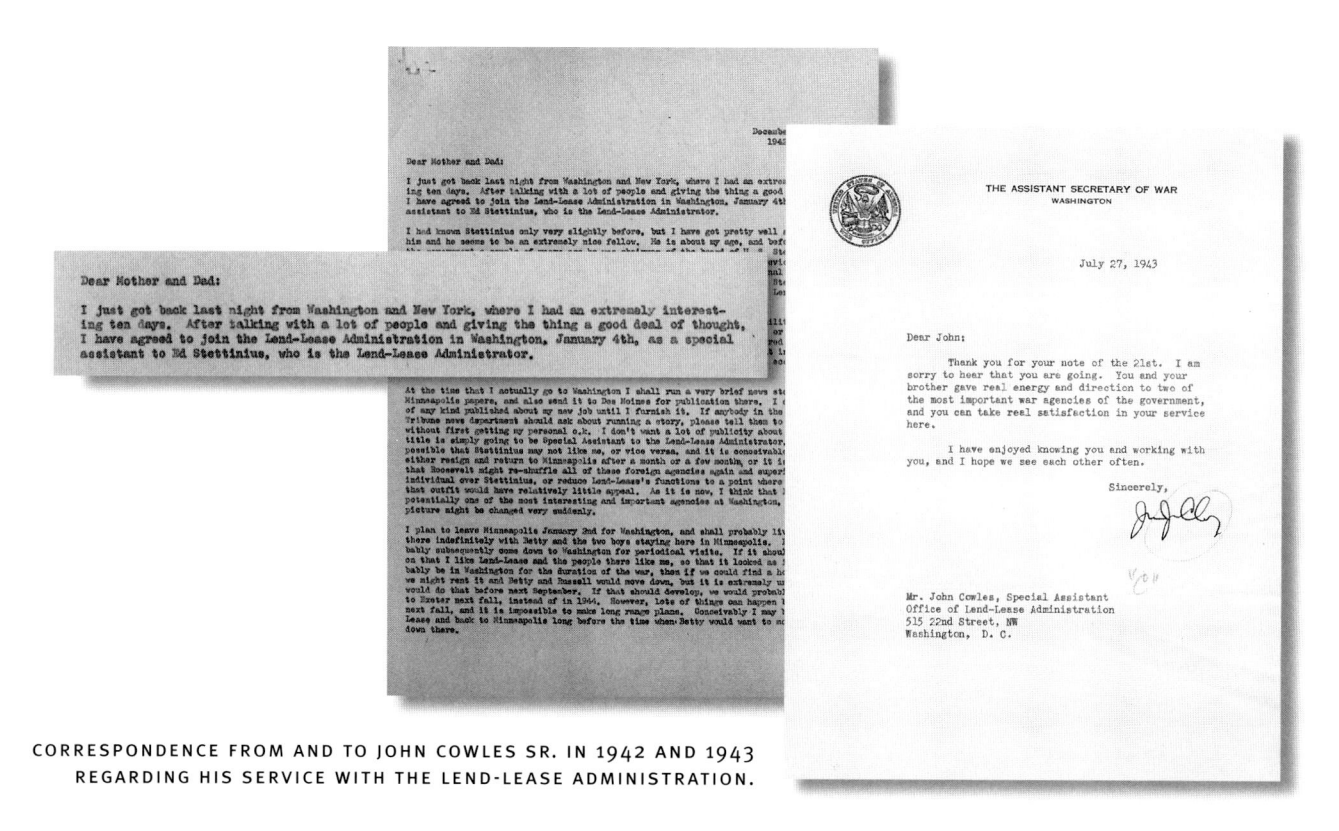

CORRESPONDENCE FROM AND TO JOHN COWLES SR. IN 1942 AND 1943 REGARDING HIS SERVICE WITH THE LEND-LEASE ADMINISTRATION.

having outside business affiliations, he apparently felt that his visible presence in the business community was more important. In 1945 he joined the board of General Electric, an indication that he had a national reputation in the business world as well.

In April 1944, George Bickelhaupt retired as publisher of *The Minneapolis Times*, which had been acquired with *The Minneapolis Tribune* and continued as a second afternoon paper. Bickelhaupt had joined the organization in the Tribune merger, and was apparently not aggressive in building the paper, which had yet to make money. One reason for continuing to publish *The Minneapolis Times* was to capture advertising that might otherwise be lost. (Wartime newsprint allocations were based on past usage, so that *The Minneapolis Times* would "use" its surplus newsprint to capture advertising that *The Minneapolis Star* could not take.) Another reason for continuing to publish was the desire to have competitive newspapers, to help avoid a monopoly in the community. Cowles attempted to sell *The Minneapolis Times* to Gannett, Jack Knight, and many other publishers, but there were no takers. He also offered the paper to Nelson Dayton and to James Ford Bell, then the chairman of General Mills.[5]

Joyce Swan replaced Bickelhaupt as publisher. In a letter to his father, Cowles commented: "We are going to have to turn down so much advertising here at the Star Journal that it is certain that the Times will have a big increase in advertising. Swan is full of ambition and drive, and I think we'll instill some enterprise into the Times organization and eliminate some of the dead wood that is still there from the old days."[6]

The Minneapolis Times became marginally profitable under Swan's leadership, but publication was finally suspended in 1948 when it became clear that the market could no longer support two afternoon newspapers, especially at a time of increasing production costs. It was merged with *The Minneapolis Star* and *Tribune* on

May 17; most of its features and more than half of its employees moved to those papers.

In May 1944, Basil "Stuffy" Walters resigned as executive editor of the newspapers and as an officer of the company to join the Knight newspapers. Early in the year he told John Cowles that he had an extremely attractive offer from another publisher and was considering leaving. John mentioned the possibility of buying an Indianapolis newspaper and said that if he wanted to have the top job in a newspaper, perhaps the Indianapolis possibility might work out, but suggested that he might be happier staying permanently as executive editor in Minneapolis. In a letter to Mike, John said that he "had every expectation of living in Minneapolis the rest of my life and that, of course, I would always be the top man here."

In fact, Cowles' interests and Walters' had begun to diverge. He told Professor Gerald: "He (Walters) had an extraordinary talent in human interest news selection and for news display, and played a major role in building the Star. Stuffy and I simply didn't share the same philosophy on international affairs. Gideon Seymour had a much broader knowledge of the world than Stuffy, and philosophically Gid's views and mine were quite similar."[7]

Seymour had trained in Des Moines under editor Harvey Ingham and W. W. Waymack, the editorial page editor who later succeeded Ingham. (Each was an early mentor of John Cowles, who had also been influenced by the two when he was a reporter there in the twenties.) Seymour had worked for the Associated Press in several countries and been an assistant managing editor of *LOOK*. He joined the Minneapolis papers in 1940 to run the editorial page, reporting directly to Cowles. In an article in May 1944, *P.M.* reported that, "Seymour is the man who sees the most of John Cowles when Cowles is in his Minneapolis office."[8]

A third departure occurred in July of 1944: William J. McNally resigned in an exchange of highly cordial letters, because of the "pressures of other numerous other duties, particularly those as President of the Minnesota Tribune Company."[9] (He had split his time between the two companies, serving as an officer of the Star Journal Tribune Company — and columnist in *The Minneapolis Tribune* — and managing the affairs of his family's Tribune Company.) He was finding conflicts between his role as a senior executive at the newspaper and as head of the Tribune Company.

In December 1943, John Cowles had reached an

GIDEON SEYMOUR, CIRCA 1945

THE S.J.T. MAKERS, FEBRUARY 1942

agreement to purchase 480 shares of Minnesota Tribune Company stock from Kingsley Murphy, who had not offered them first to other Tribune Company shareholders, a source of concern and resentment by those shareholders. More important, however, was the fact that ownership of Tribune shares gave Cowles an ownership interest in radio station WTCN, owned jointly with the Ridders, who also owned the St. Paul newspapers. Cowles' new ownership of a small interest in WTCN would leave the Tribune Company and Murphy with fewer shares than the Ridders. Neither Murphy nor Cowles had recognized the situation, because they were focusing on the fact that the Tribune Company shares were convertible into 2,400 shares of Star Journal and Tribune Company stock. It then fell to McNally to repurchase the Minnesota Broadcasting Company (WTCN) shares from Cowles to restore the critical 50:50 ownership balance with the Ridders.

Then, early in 1944, Kingsley Murphy wanted to buy KSO, the second Cowles radio station in Des Moines, which the Federal Communications Commission had ordered the Register and Tribune Company to divest. John Cowles insisted that the purchase be accomplished with 6,000 shares of Star Journal and Tribune Company stock. Murphy proposed trading his existing stockholding in WTCN to the Minnesota Tribune Company for those shares. The WTCN shares

MINNEAPOLIS MORNING TRIBUNE, MAY 8, 1945

were then paying higher dividends, but the Star Journal and Tribune stock was judged to have greater potential. Rather than see Murphy's WTCN shares be sold to others, the Tribune Company reluctantly agreed to the trade. The transaction also completed separation of the common ownership interests of Kingsley Murphy and the Minnesota Tribune Company, except for the Star Journal and Tribune Company.

McNally, representing MTC's 15 percent ownership in the Star Journal and Tribune Company, had been privy to financial information as an officer and director of the company, almost on a daily basis. Early in 1944 that access was cut off, and he concluded that tensions over stock ownership issues would make his further employment untenable and that his best course of action was to resign and to find a pretext to do so. On July 3, Seymour (who was, with McNally, one of two vice presidents of the company) suggested that McNally turn his office over to him for use as a second office, and that he would find another office for McNally elsewhere in the building. The next day, he went to John Cowles and resigned. Cowles apparently tried to dissuade McNally, who chose not to tell him the real reasons for his resigning.

1. Joyce Swan, author interview, April 2, 1996.
2. J.E. Gerald, author interview, May 21, 1963.
3. John Cowles Sr., Letter to Gardner Cowles Jr., December 27, 1943.
4. John Cowles Sr., Letter to Gardner Cowles Sr., January 24, 1944.
5. J.E.Gerald, author interview, October 16, 1961, and John Cowles Sr., Letter to J.E. Gerald, June 1, 1963.
6. John Cowles Sr., Letter to Gardner Cowles Sr., March 29, 1945.
7. Ibid.
8. *P.M.* was a tabloid published in New York.
9. William J. McNally, Letter to John Cowles Sr., August 4, 1944.

ONE OF THE BIGGEST AND BEST

9

DURING THE WAR YEARS the newspaper business — like most others — had been essentially on hold, coping with shortages, restrictions and loss of experienced employees. As World War II drew to a close, there was a tremendous optimism about what the future would hold. These sentiments are best expressed in excerpts from a letter John Cowles wrote to all Star Journal and Tribune company employees then in the military service:

> "The Star Journal and Tribune can start carrying out some of those plans that all of us have had in our minds for after the war. If we don't succeed in making the Star Journal and Tribune one of the biggest and best newspaper institutions in the country, it will be our own fault. We will have the opportunity to do many of the things the war prevented our doing earlier, after our Minneapolis newspaper realignment.
>
> "Our first circulation goal will be for 500,000 Sunday subscribers and much larger circulation figures for the daily papers than they have now. We'll need a larger mail room and various expansions in the mechanical equipment in order to handle the bigger circulations. We're making plans now for a sizeable addition to the SJT plant. We are going to try to improve our papers editorially, universally recognized by competent professional journalists as the equal of those anywhere. The years immediately ahead should be the most prosperous peace time era the nation has ever had, with high level employment and with active, expanding business."[1]

In less than four years —14 years after the purchase of *The Minneapolis Star* — those goals had been met and more. Sunday circulation had topped 600,000 by September 1949, up from 350,000 in 1941. *The Minneapolis Star* had grown from 240,000 to just over 300,000, a level it was to sustain well into the 1960s. *The Minneapolis Tribune* increased from 64,000 in 1941 to 180,000 in 1949, a growth that continued, if at a slower rate.

The newspapers had been profitable enough during the war to pay off most of the debt incurred to acquire them. Dividends were modest, but began to increase in

MINNEAPOLIS MORNING TRIBUNE, AUGUST 15, 1945

POSTWAR NEWSPAPER CIRCULATION
(CALENDAR YEARS)

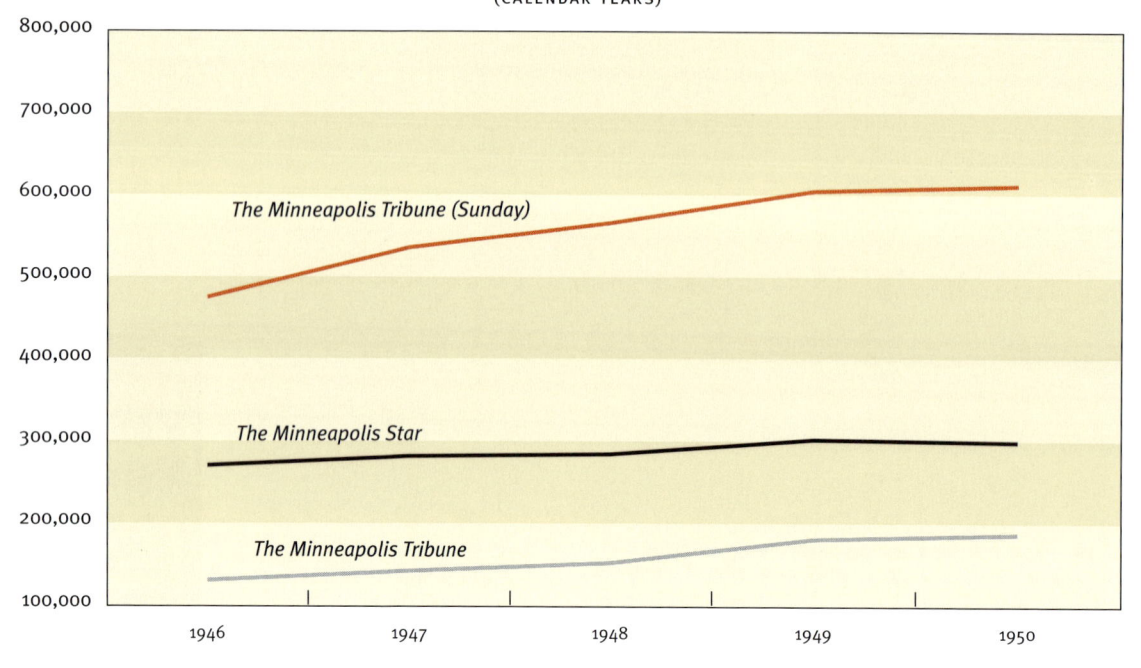

1945 from $1.00 to $1.50.[2] *Editor & Publisher* estimated (correctly) in 1949 that revenues were at the $20 million level. Approximately half of advertising revenue came from the retail display category, with the rest evenly split between classified and national accounts. That year the papers ran 14,210,000 lines of classified advertising, 21,734,000 of retail, and 4,304,000 of national advertising.[3]

An executive team had been assembled and an organizational structure adopted that guided the papers through the next two decades. The name of the company was changed to Minneapolis Star and Tribune Company in 1947, and the name *Journal* was dropped from the evening paper the following year when the evening *Minneapolis Times* was closed.

PLANT

The opening of a new plant in May of 1949 symbolized the success of the immediate postwar years. The new building doubled plant capacity to 260,000 square feet in an Art Moderne building at Fifth and Portland, the site of the original 1920 *Minneapolis Star* building.

That building had been doubled in size before the war with a new press room to accommodate the capacity needs of *The Minneapolis Journal* and its Sunday edition. Fourteen new Goss Headliner press units were added in 1949 to the 34 black and white units already in place, all

THE MINNEAPOLIS STAR AND TRIBUNE BUILDING, ABOUT 1949

now visible through large glass windows from a corridor off the main lobby.

A five-story entrance facade of Indiana limestone and black granite displayed six large stone medallions portraying the six principal industries of the Upper Midwest region: lumber, fishing, farming, mining, dairying and milling. These were the work of sculptor Ivan Doseff of the University of Minnesota. The rest of the block-long building was faced with buff and black brick. The Fifth Street side and much of the Portland Avenue side were four stories. Architects for the building were Larson & McLaren, and general contractors were C. F. Haglin & Sons, both Minneapolis firms.

The composing room housed 42 typesetting machines, four of which were new in 1949. At 23,000 square feet the mailing room (as it was called then) had twice the floor space of the pressroom, making it one of the largest in the country. Twelve overhead conveyors carried papers from the pressroom to the counting, bundling and tying operations that in turn delivered bundles of papers directly to the truck dock for distribution. Much of the capacity was required for the large Sunday circulation, which was distributed to Rapid City, South Dakota, and beyond into Montana, over 500 miles west. (See Appendix D.)

CIRCULATION AND PROMOTION

In today's business lexicon, circulation would be described as the organization's core competency or driving force. Just as in Iowa, the Minneapolis newspapers placed great emphasis on building solid circulation, preferably home-delivered, which required continuing investment in equipment. The building of a sophisticated distribution system was coupled with aggressive promotion of the papers, the function that knit together the many elements of the business — circulation, advertising, editorial and news coverage, and public service. Promotion was, in effect, the marketing arm of circulation, providing comprehensive advertising and other support services.

THE MINNEAPOLIS STAR AND TRIBUNE GOSS PRESSES, 1949

Nearly 8,000 "carrier boys" in Minneapolis and beyond in 1949 were the largest such group in the country. Carrier service extended to 1,082 towns and cities outside the Twin Cities metropolitan area; 606 were in Minnesota, 1,996 in North Dakota, 197 in South Dakota, 81 in Wisconsin and one in Montana. Twenty carriers were selected each year to receive a $250 college scholarship and were eligible to participate in a range of sporting events, airplane trips around the state, and a "Parade of Champions" dinner for the top 1,500 carriers — featuring sports celebrities like Leo Durocher and Jack Dempsey. In 1947 the papers provided 1,700 carriers with their first helicopter rides, covering 120 cities and towns throughout the region. In connection with the dedication of the new plant in 1949, one 15-year-old carrier was sent on a seven-day, around-the-world trip on Pan American Airways to deliver the official May 22 dedication edition to officials in 13 countries.

The carrier force eventually grew to over 10,000.[4] An elaborate system of district managers was key to the smooth functioning of this sales force, as was a sophisticated trucking system involving vehicles of the company and of independent contractors. Trucks and cars delivering the newspapers were estimated to travel almost nine million miles a year.

A contest in the late forties resulted in the name "Upper Midwest" to describe the market area of the papers — Minnesota and the Dakotas — where half the families received *The Minneapolis Sunday Tribune*. That theme was used for more than two decades by the papers and was adopted by others as well. John Cowles felt it important that the papers "get our roots down deep in the whole region," and the emphasis on the Upper Midwest was part of that effort. Of total circulation revenue, 47 percent came from the metropolitan area, 40 percent from regional circulation handled by the papers' own distribution system, and the balance from contractors in rural areas.

CARRIER BOY, CIRCA 1941

Important as the regional market was, half of the Sunday circulation growth, three-fourths of the morning growth, and nearly all of the evening growth came from the Twin Cities metropolitan area, excluding St. Paul and its suburbs.

ADVERTISING

During the war John Cowles had made the strategic decision to use scarce newsprint to build circulation, rather than advertising, figuring that a large and solid circulation base would have a long-term payoff when the war was over. In part because of the strong growth in circulation, the newsprint shortage was sometimes acute, resulting in actual curtailment of advertising. In a letter to his father John Cowles commented: "The Star Journal and Tribune's newsprint situation is much more acute than that of The Register and Tribune. We are declining far more national advertising than Des Moines is and are cutting our local display customers more heavily. We also have eliminated the bulk of our classified from the country editions, all in order to have sufficient newsprint so that we can accommodate additional circulation."[5] (The Des Moines papers had achieved strong circulation coverage many years before, and were not growing at the rate of the Minneapolis papers.)

In December 1945, he described the newsprint situation as "extremely acute," with only a five or six-day supply on hand. He speculated that it might even be necessary to eliminate all or a large part of advertising from the papers between Christmas and New Year's, but that did not happen. A ten-year newsprint contract with the Blandin Paper Company had been turned over to the Minnesota and Ontario Paper Company, which was unable to fulfill the Blandin contract. The contract was acquired as part of the purchase of *The Minneapolis Journal* in 1939, but by 1945 Blandin itself had effectively gone out of the newsprint business.

Minneapolis retailers enjoyed a strong market after the war; Dayton's, Donaldson's and Powers all expanded their downtown stores, investing millions in additional retail space. Donaldson's, for example, had about $7 million in revenue in 1942 and almost $13 million by 1945. Dayton's was by then at the $30 million level. In 1939 Donaldson's had been given preferred positions in *The Minneapolis Star*, in part to secure long-term advertising commitments that had not been forthcoming until that time. Ten years later, Donald Dayton, president of The Dayton Company, wrote to John Cowles pointing out that Dayton's should

THE MINNEAPOLIS STAR, PARADE OF CHAMPIONS COVERAGE, MAY 24, 1949

now receive better positioning. "We feel that we are entitled to top notch consideration in your papers for several reasons. Dayton's spent $94,000 more on your two papers than your second largest advertiser. We are the only major advertiser who has not recently left your papers to use television and other media. We believe that the prestige of our store is such that our advertising, as much as almost any other single item in your paper, tends to produce readership." Then he went on to request specific positioning.[6] The earlier commitment to Donaldson's was kept, and other means found to satisfy Dayton's.

National advertising was very important to newspapers, and the Minneapolis papers had a strong position with those advertisers, in part because they could reach the entire "Upper Midwest" on Sundays, the only medium other than radio to do so. *The Minneapolis Star* and *Tribune* received a quarter of their advertising revenue from national

THE DAYTON COMPANY AD
THE MINNEAPOLIS STAR, DECEMBER 7, 1948

accounts, a higher proportion than most newspapers. In 1963 Swan told stockholders that national advertising was the newspapers' most profitable linage.[7] To help increase national market share, 1949 milline rates (cost of advertising per line per million of circulation) were kept sightly lower than in 1941 and were about half that charged by the average metropolitan daily newspaper and 20 percent lower on Sunday. Retail advertising rates were also below 1941 rates for both the Sunday and morning papers, slightly higher for *The Minneapolis Star* which was the preferred advertising medium.

The Minneapolis Star and *Tribune* typically had one of the highest promotion linage figures of any newspaper as well as one of the largest national advertising promotion programs, both in trade publications and national consumer publications such as the weekly news magazines, *The New York Times* and *The New York Herald Tribune*. The papers used local radio extensively, with as much as 210 minutes of air time per week, including both public service community calendar programs and its own columnists like Cedric Adams who became one of the most popular personalities in the Upper Midwest. It was said that airlines pilots in the fifties could tell when his evening radio show ended by observing the number of houses below turning off their lights. His columns were excerpted and published as advertising in *The New Yorker* for several years and eventually compiled in a book.

CEDRIC ADAMS COLUMN
THE NEW YORKER, 1949

JOHN COWLES AND GLOBE, 1959

The Minneapolis Star had a World Affairs program that involved more than 675,000 students in the Upper Midwest in the study of current events through the newspaper. It sponsored an annual dinner for hospitalized veterans who were served game contributed by Minnesota sportsmen. Other public activities included support for women's organizations, summer community sings, the Golden Gloves boxing tournaments, an annual social conservation competition, high school journalism clinics for thousands of students, and the annual Spelling Bee.

John Cowles was always sensitive to the perception that the newspapers were a monopoly, pointing out that there were scores of other media in the Upper Midwest — other daily and weekly newspapers, radio, billboards and direct mail. In a talk in 1949 he asserted, "Minneapolis papers supplement the local papers." He went on to say that bigger papers actually increased advertising volume for smaller papers by pioneering new national advertising campaigns, and pointed out that regional dailies had circulation increases comparable to the Minneapolis papers.[8] John Cowles Jr. said that his father had great concern about the possibility of antitrust allegations, even into the sixties. In his 1959 annual meeting speech, attended largely by employees, he said, "I know many of you hear critical comments about the single ownership of newspapers in Minneapolis" and went on to discuss the nationwide trend to single ownership and the recent demise of *The Globe-Democrat* in St. Louis.[9]

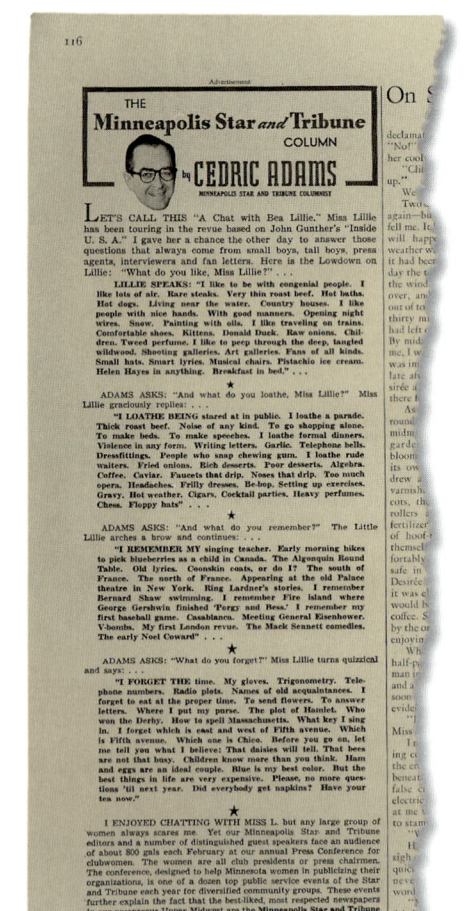

MANAGEMENT STYLE

Concern for and interest in employees characterized the organization almost from the beginning, when care was taken to retain as many employees of *The Minneapolis Star*, and later *The Minneapolis Journal* and *The Minneapolis Tribune* as possible. One report said: "Another component of the Cowles formula for publishing success was company paternalism. A 'family atmosphere' was engendered in top men by frequent policy meetings and considerable free rein. Cynical big-city newsmen were unwelcome; wholesome young Midwesterners were hired from smaller papers or direct from college and paid partly in experience and prestige."[10] He did not rely exclusively on Midwesterners, however. After World War II a number of young "Easterners" were attracted by the growing reputation of the newspapers and an opportunity to develop their careers. Among them were Francis W. "Frank" Hatch, recruited by Cowles at a Harvard dinner in Boston, and Arthur Ballantine, who later married Morley Cowles. Both men started out in the newsroom, covering local politics, the courts and state government. Hatch returned to Boston in 1950, and in 1952 Arthur and Morley Ballantine moved to Durango, Colorado, to publish *The Durango Herald* together.

There was the monthly *Newsmakers* for employees, which covered a wide range of personal as well as company news. There were picnics, the Girls Club, the Golferoo, bowling leagues, the Twenty Year Club, and a credit union. Employee stock ownership began almost immediately, and at the time of the 1945 annual meeting there were 95 employee stockholders. Selected employees were offered an opportunity to buy stock and

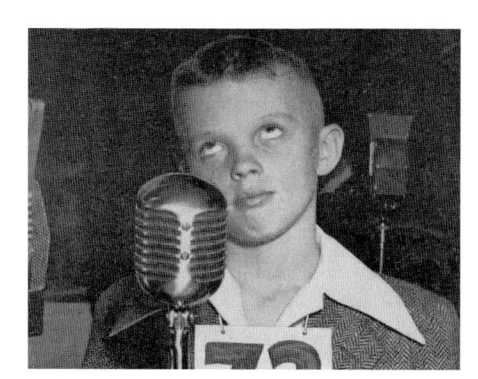

SPELLING BEE, 1965

MINNEAPOLIS STAR TRUCK, ABOUT 1936

JOHN COWLES SR. REGULARLY WROTE TO EMPLOYEES ABOUT THE COMPANY'S FINANCIAL PROGRESS IN *NEWSMAKERS*, INCLUDING THIS REPORT IN 1956 UNDER THE STANDARD HEADING OF "HOW ARE WE DOING?"

borrow the purchase price from the company, to be repaid in part with dividends received. While most employees held fewer than 100 shares, several were able to retire as wealthy men, with more than 1,000 shares.

In 1944 "hospital service benefits" and $1,000 in life insurance were made available to employees at no cost. In 1949 a pension plan, paid by the company, was begun. It covered all employees working at least 30 hours a week; credit was given for service since 1942. Male employees were able to retire at age 65, women at 60, with a minimum pension of $40 per month. About 50 employees became eligible immediately. John Cowles compared the plan to one introduced by Ford Motor Company later that year, and concluded that it would pay significantly more than Ford's.

Working conditions were always a concern, and the 1949 renovation included a first aid and medical center, a cafeteria and a rooftop sun deck. A member of the University of Minnesota medical faculty was available six hours a week and a registered nurse on duty 40 hours a week. The cafeteria, seating 234 people, was open 24 hours a day. One report said that "three cooks, one baker and 23 additional personnel are kept busy 24 hours daily preparing wholesome food." John Cowles believed that personnel issues were important: "Many large newspapers are backward in the field of employee relations and the establishment of personnel departments than are other types of business of comparable size."[11] The progressive nature of Cowles personnel policies was underlined by the creation, in 1973, of a program to help employees with alcohol problems. In 1976 the company made a psychiatrist available to employees in the plant four afternoons a week.

Published stories on John Cowles and the company frequently commented on the "conference style" of management, a practice developed in Des Moines. *Time* reported in 1935 that "'G. C.' had the wisdom to hire the best men available, pay them well, and above all, get them to work together. Register & Tribune conferences are serious business. Every Monday there is a conference of all departments, at which any man can — and is expected to — speak his mind on any subject, criticize anyone from old 'G. C.' down. Fridays at lunch the 'planning committee' meets to plot promotion stunts and civic campaigns."[12] *Fortune* reported that "John Cowles is a stickler for conferences and intercommunication between departments, and, as a result, 'Everybody in the organization knows just where we're going and why'."[13]

He used his annual reports to stockholders — which were reprinted in the employee newsletter under the title "How Are We Doing?" — as a way to let employees know just that. The reports were comprehensive, with statistics on circulation, advertising, costs and productivity. They also included his critique of the past year's performance, dealing with shortcomings and mistakes as well as recognizing achievement in all departments. Cowles believed that better decisions resulted when all executives were aware of the decision-making process and that it was important for them to have a perspective beyond their own functional areas. While he was clearly the dominant person in the process, it afforded great learning opportunities for others. He told Professor Gerald that he exercised control largely through his contacts with department heads and assistant department heads, all of whom he knew, and through other employees. It was perhaps an early example of "management by walking around."

A small executive committee, made up of officers of the company, was augmented with others in the next level of management at other meetings. Attendance at these meetings was prized for the opportunities it provided to learn and participate. The pattern continued under John Cowles Jr. In 1969, for example, the executive committee met every other Monday for two hours, with board of directors meeting alternating. In addition there were meetings with editors and with department heads.

One key to making the management style work was a system of promotion from within and the underlying continuous training, mentoring and evaluation that went with it. Cowles had no system of formal performance evaluation. Many of the early executives were either recruited from *The Des Moines Register* and *Tribune* or had strong Des Moines roots — Joyce Swan, Gideon Seymour, Stuffy Walters, Lyle Anderson, William A. Cordingley Jr., and Jack McCambridge. Many others in the next generation of management began their business

CORPORATE REPORT, AUGUST 1979

careers in Minneapolis, including Otto Silha, Robert Weed, Robert Witte, Richard Cooney and Howard Mithun. In 1966 Swan reported that there were 207 supervisors, compared with 134 in 1949. All but a handful were promoted from within the organization, possible he said because of the abilities of those staff members and the fact that "they got themselves ready for promotion." As in Des Moines, there were separate staffs for each paper's newsrooms and editorial departments, all reporting to an executive editor who reported to John Cowles. Rivalry between the newsrooms was genuine.

In 1979 *Corporate Report* magazine carried a long profile on John Cowles Jr., after ten years of running the company. He had made it a company goal to reduce earnings dependence on the Minneapolis newspapers and to achieve modest revenue growth of two percent above inflation. He said he liked to give people "a lot of rope," an approach referred to as "functional distance." Responding to the needs of a larger and more complex organization, the company was just instituting a form of management by objectives. He suggested that he had been "too gentle with the organization that I inherited" and that instead of trying to raise the sights of people working for him, he should have hired more from the outside. The article noted that he gave complete authority for the news and editorial pages to the editors of the two papers, "an act thought to be an abdication of responsibility by some Twin Cities businessmen."[14] He responded to the writer of the article with a letter that noted several minor errors and the following observation: "Of course, there are a few other things I wish you'd mentioned, including my work for The Associated

Press, Pulitzer Prize Board, etc., as well as my army service. Most of all, I am sorry you made no reference to the absolutely central role that Otto Silha has played for so many years in the life of the Minneapolis newspapers and this company. Nevertheless, I have received many favorable comments (on the article), and I thank you for a job well done."[15]

The separation of the news and editorial staffs continued well after John Cowles left active management, and was carried even further by his son. There were many similarities in their management styles, as well as notable differences. Leo Bogart, a leading figure in the newspaper industry through the Newspaper Advertising Bureau, had this to say: "John Cowles Jr. was in the third generation of his family to own and run newspapers in Minneapolis. In the mid-1970s his venerable father was still an imposing presence at management meetings within the paper. John Jr. was somewhat withdrawn and shy, but he was urbane, highly intelligent, literate and charming. Exhibiting an impulse not uncommon in those born to great wealth, he was eager to show what he could do on his own and took steps to expand his company into a communications empire, with Silha his confederate in this enterprise."[16]

Like his father, John Cowles Jr. valued meetings with his associates and others in the organization, and the ensuing discussion. His approach was to put great emphasis on creating structure within which the organization would operate and to rely more heavily on written articulation of policy. He created a formal system of what was called "Management By Objective," job descriptions for executives, employees and the board of directors, and structured compensation programs. He was influenced by the "human potential" movement of the 1960s and '70s, attending programs like that for executives at the Menninger Foundation and sending other executives to them. He created a mission statement for the company that was subject to periodic revision, but always centered on the special role of the newspaper in society.

In a 1977 interview he listed integrity as a most important quality in a manager, followed by sociability, defined as getting along easily with and enjoying all kinds of people. At the executive level he said that technical expertise was not as important as an ability to manage people, and that attitude is more important than education. Communication was another important quality — "When people under a manager don't know what's going on, maybe he hasn't taken the time to explain things." The last characteristic listed was curiosity: "Any executive has to be curious not only as to how the world is today, but how it's going to be five or ten years from now…and try to anticipate these changes."[17]

MISSION STATEMENT

The first objective of the Minneapolis Star and Tribune Company

To help people manage both their private lives and the public affairs of democracy:

· by gathering, organizing and marketing information, entertainments and ideas of high quality and keen interest.

· in newspapers and other socially responsible enterprises recognized for the excellence of their personnel and performance.

STAR AND TRIBUNE COMPANY ANNUAL REPORT, 1980

"JOHN COWLES SETS SJT GOALS IN LETTER TO SERVICEMEN"

The S.J.T. Makers
September 1945

After returning from his visit to the Pacific theater, John Cowles sent the following letter to all SJT-Makers in service. It is of great interest to all Makers as it tells of plans for the future.

To All SJT-Makers in the Service:

The end of July I left San Francisco at the invitation of the navy and war departments for a tour of our army, navy and air bases and installations in the Pacific. By good luck I was on Okinawa, only a few hundred miles from Japan, where Herb Paul has done such a fine job as our correspondent, when the first Japanese surrender proposal was received.

As a result of this trip, I am sure I have a much better understanding of what those of you fellows who are out in the Pacific have been going through, and a deeper appreciation of what you have done for the rest of us who have been here at home.

Now that the world is actually at peace again, the Star Journal and Tribune can start carrying out some of those plans that all of us have had in our minds for "after the war." Our future looks potentially brighter to me than ever before. If we don't succeed in making the Star Journal and Tribune one of the biggest and best newspaper institutions in the country, it will be our own fault. Before long we will have the opportunity to do many of the things that the sudden Jap strike at Pearl Harbor, which plunged the nation into war only a few short months after our Minneapolis newspaper realignment, prevented our doing earlier.

Every department — as soon as newsprint rationing ends and abundant paper again becomes available, which we hope will be early 1946 — will have fine opportunities for improvement and expansion.

Our first circulation goal will be for 500,000 Sunday subscribers. Half a million is a nice round number! Of course, we won't rest on our oars after getting 500,000. I sincerely believe that the more circulation a paper gets, the easier it is to get still more. Of course, I also expect to push the daily papers to much larger circulation figures than they have now.

We'll need a larger mailroom and various expansions in mechanical equipment in order to handle the bigger circulations. We're working on plans now for a sizeable addition to the SJT plant and hope to start actual construction of it early in 1946.

We are going to try to improve the papers editorially all along the line, making them more complete, better written, more informative, more readable and attractive and better illustrated, and more serviceable to this great upper Mississippi Valley region than ever before. We're lucky to be situated just where we are. There's no reason, except the limitations our brains, why we can't make our papers universally recognized by competent professional journalists as the equal of those anywhere.

If the United States follows wise governmental, economic and political policies, the years immediately ahead should be the most prosperous peace time era the nation has ever had, with high level employment and with active, expanding business. There should be widespread opportunities for individuals who have initiative and brains, for people who are willing to work and to assume responsibility, to get ahead.

If our advertising departments are on their toes, and sell aggressively and intelligently, we ought to carry a larger volume of advertising, morning, evening and Sunday, than we ever have before.

We've been experimenting with airline delivery of the papers to a few towns. We are thinking about various other possible developments, all of which would increase the variety and scope of our operations. We have made an application for a permit to construct an entirely new Twin Cities broadcasting station, 1,000 watt power on 580 kilocycles. We're also planning to apply before long for both A.M. and F.M. (frequently modulation) and a television station here in the Twin Cities.

We're hoping all of you fellows who were members of the SJT family before you went into the service will want to rejoin us as soon as you are back in civilian clothes again. Like you, we hope that you will get your honorable discharges soon!

It would be helpful to us if you let J.T., your individual department head, or me know whether or not you are definitely planning to rejoin the organization, and also approximately the date, insofar as you can guess it, when you think this may be. Some of you may have developed new interests and decided that you want to follow a different postwar profession or occupation. Others may have concluded that the California climate or the New York skyscrapers appeal to you more than life in Minnesota. Some of you may have learned new skills and may feel that while newspaper work is still what you want to do, you would prefer a different type of job from that you held with us before you went to war. If you would let us know what your current thinking is, we'd appreciate it, as it will help us in this transition period in our planning here. Every member of the Star Journal and Tribune family joins me in expressing renewed gratitude to you for the service you have performed for the country during the war. We hope we'll be seeing each of you back here at the SJT plant soon again. In the meantime, good luck!

Sincerely,
John Cowles

1. "John Cowles Sets SJT Goals in Letter to Servicemen," *Star Journal Tribune Makers,* September 1945, p. 1.
2. Star Journal Tribune Company, U.S. Tax Returns, 1945.
3. "Stockholders' Charts Tell Story of S and T Progress," *Star and Tribune Makers,* July 1949, p. 4-5.
4. "Star & Tribune Growth is Stirring 14-Year Saga," *Editor & Publisher,* June 4, 1949, p. 3.
5. John Cowles Sr., Letter to Gardner Cowles Sr., March 29, 1945.
6. Donald Dayton, Letter to John Cowles Sr., December 9, 1949.
7. "Swan Comments on Advertising, News Production, Distribution Equipment," *Newsmakers,* June 1963, p. 5.
8. "Minneapolis Newspapers Dedicate New Building," *Editor & Publisher,* June 4, 1949, p. 2.
9. "Report to Stockholders," *Newsmakers,* June 1959, p. C.
10. "Don't Make 'Em Mad," *New Republic,* December 1, 1947, p. 20.
11. "Star & Tribune Growth is Stirring 14-Year Saga," op.cit., p 4.
12. "The Press," *Time,* July 1, 1935, p. 32.
13. "The Prudent Publishers," *Fortune,* August 1950, p. 88.
14. "Inside John Cowles," *Corporate Report,* August 1979, p. 44.
15. John Cowles Jr., Letter to Wayne Christensen, August 15, 1979.
16. Leo Bogart, *Perceiving the Problem* (New York: Publisher, 1996), p. 59.
17. "Integrity is Important," *Newsmakers,* March 1977, p. 6.

THE FIFTIES

10

THE 1950S WERE A TIME of building and expansion, for the economy generally and for newspapers. Gross domestic product grew 44 percent, although there were recessions in the fall of 1953 and again in the fall of 1957. Revenue at the Star and Tribune Company increased from $22.5 million to $36.9 million, with net earnings growing from $1.4 million to $3.0 million. Total advertising linage was up by one third to 57.6 million lines.

Two problems occupied management's attention. Payroll costs rose from $7.9 million in 1952 to $13 million in 1960 and the cost of job benefits rose from 15 to 17 percent of payroll.

The price of newsprint continued to increase significantly, as it had immediately after World War II. Price per ton increased from $59 in 1945 to $107 in 1950 and $159 in 1965. Newsprint accounted for a quarter or more of total newspaper costs, and was (and is today) a significant factor in earnings. But equally important was the sheer availability of newsprint, which was sometimes rationed or available only at a significant premium on the spot market. (See Appendix E.)

Newsprint shortages plagued the industry throughout the fifties, although the decade was generally a profitable one. The acquisition of *The Minneapolis Tribune* included a contract with the Manistique Paper Company, subsequently assumed by the Minnesota and Ontario Paper Company which had purchased Manistique's newsprint operations. In 1949 the company began purchasing stock in M&O in part to obtain a stronger bargaining position for both price and supply. It was also a logical place to invest earnings to reduce taxation. Many newspaper companies had gone into the newsprint business, building or acquiring mills directly or in joint ventures.

In 1956 the company signed ten-year newsprint supply contracts with four mills. The largest of these was with the M&O, later acquired by Boise-Cascade, which remained the principal supplier into the nineties. In 1955 earnings had been hurt by the fact that 7,000

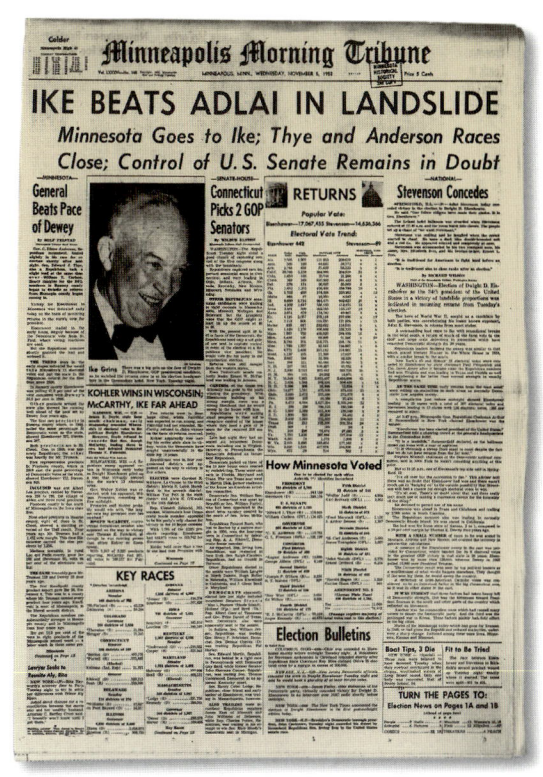

MINNEAPOLIS MORNING TRIBUNE, NOVEMBER 5, 1952

MINNEAPOLIS STAR AND TRIBUNE COMPANY
(FISCAL 1950-1960)

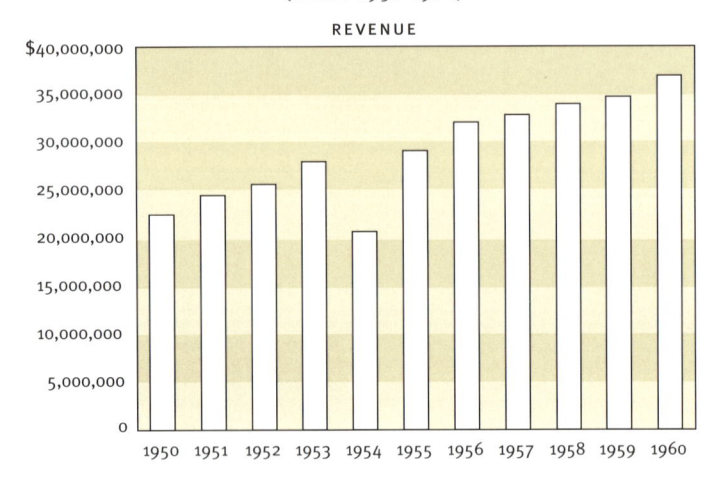

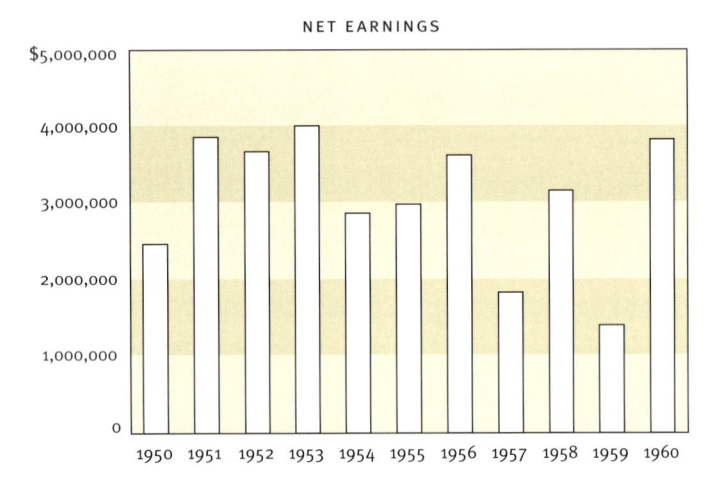

REVENUE

Year	Revenue
1950	~22,500,000
1951	~24,500,000
1952	~25,500,000
1953	~28,000,000
1954	~21,000,000
1955	~29,000,000
1956	~32,000,000
1957	~33,000,000
1958	~34,000,000
1959	~35,000,000
1960	~37,000,000

NET EARNINGS

Year	Net Earnings
1950	~2,500,000
1951	~3,900,000
1952	~3,700,000
1953	~4,000,000
1954	~2,800,000
1955	~3,000,000
1956	~3,700,000
1957	~1,800,000
1958	~3,200,000
1959	~1,400,000
1960	~3,900,000

tons of newsprint — almost ten percent of total usage — had to be acquired at a premium of up to $100 per ton to assure an adequate supply. Newsprint cost $131 per ton at the beginning of 1956.

The decade was a time of recognition of John Cowles' accomplishments. In 1950 he was asked by Henry Ford to become one of the first outside trustees of the Ford Foundation. He received nine honorary doctorates, including one from Harvard in 1956. The newspapers were awarded a University of Missouri Medal for Distinguished Service to Journalism May 4, 1951. (See Appendix F.) That event resulted in the company's purchase of its first airplane, a DC-3. With him on the trip to Missouri were Joyce Swan, Gideon Seymour and Otto Silha, respectively the business manager, executive editor and promotion director. Their overnight train was stopped in Iowa by flood waters. Swan was dispatched to find other means of transportation, and somehow located a farmer with an airplane, a Fairchild, who flew Cowles and Seymour on to Columbia in time for the award ceremonies. Swan and Silha followed in a Piper Cub. Joseph Pulitzer, owner of *The St. Louis Post-Dispatch*, offered to fly the Cowles party back to Minneapolis in that company's DC-3. At its meeting on May 8 the Board authorized purchase of an airplane "to conserve the time and health of executives in their travel and improve facilities for rapid gathering of news and pictures."[1] The idea of having an airplane was not new. In 1928 John Cowles had purchased one in Des Moines where it was used extensively for both news and promotional activity.[2] The airplane was the first of three; the last was sold in 1976. (See Appendix G.)

In his Missouri acceptance speech Cowles talked about one-newspaper towns, arguing that the result of consolidation, in almost every instance, was a newspaper superior to the ones that preceded it. One reason was the ability to resist the constant pressure to over sensa-

JOHN COWLES SR. RECEIVED MANY HONORARY DEGREES, INCLUDING THIS LL.D. FROM HARVARD UNIVERSITY, AWARDED IN 1956

ASSURING SUFFICIENT NEWSPRINT SUPPLIES AT MANAGEABLE PRICES WAS A CONTINUAL ISSUE FOR THE COMPANY

THE STAR TRIBUNE COMPANY OWNED THREE AIRPLANES, BEGINNING WITH THIS DC-3, FROM 1951 THROUGH 1976

tionalize the news and the pressures of immediacy that made for shoddy reporting. He then went on to say that television would almost certainly fall short of its potential to educate because competition among stations would push programs down to the lowest common denominators of interest, and their competition for audiences would tend to vulgarize their programs.[3]

John Cowles was one of the early backers of Dwight Eisenhower for President in 1952. At the beginning of a round-the-world trip for the Ford Foundation, he stopped in Paris to persuade the general to accept the Republican nomination. As in 1940, when he supported Wendell Willkie for the Republican nomination, the other leading candidate was Senator Robert Taft, a conservative from Ohio who did not share Cowles' internationalist views. By 1952, Cowles was able to write to Eisenhower: "I feel certain that the Republican Convention will nominate you if the situation in Europe should develop in a such a way that you would feel that you could get relieved of your NATO job and come home, say, in May and make a number of speeches setting forth your views on domestic problems." Then in May: "The campaign for your nomination seems to be rolling along. I think it would be wiser for you to resign your Army commission immediately after you make your report to President Truman. I hope you will stress your belief that government spending can be substantially reduced through more competent management."[4]

Cowles devoted considerable time to the 1952 campaign and to the early days of the Administration. *The Minneapolis Star* and *The Minneapolis Tribune* strongly endorsed the candidacy. A writer in *Harper's* described John Cowles as "a Republican the way that de Gaulle is a Frenchman — by birth, instinct, tradition, and resolve."[5] He supported Eisenhower again in 1956, although he was critical of Secretary of State John Foster Dulles' foreign policy, which he faulted as "moralistic" and inflexible. He had been a strong supporter of Dean Acheson, Secretary of State under President Truman and a winter-time neighbor in Antigua where he had bought a house. There was often speculation that Cowles wanted to be Secretary of State because of his great interest in international affairs. His daughter Morley believes that he had no interest in the job and that he thought that no one from west of the Mississippi could aspire to anything but Interior or Agriculture.[6]

The long-time working relationship between John and Mike Cowles was altered in 1951 when Mike Cowles began to sell his stock in the company. After World War II Mike had become heavily involved in

JOHN COWLES SR. AND PRESIDENT DWIGHT D. EISENHOWER AT THE COMPANY'S
GLENDALOUGH RETREAT IN WEST-CENTRAL MINNESOTA, IN 1952

LOOK magazine which he had built into one of the major consumer publications along with *Life, The Saturday Evening Post* and *Collier's*. In 1945 he had moved to New York to run the magazine and begin building a company that owned a number of other publications and broadcast properties. His wife, Lois Thornberg Cowles, did not want to leave Des Moines, and they were divorced in 1946. He then married Fleur Fenton, an advertising woman who began to work at *LOOK* and to (in her view at least) upgrade both the content and graphics of the magazine. She apparently wanted to change the magazine more than Cowles and his associates felt appropriate, and he suggested that she start her own magazine. *Flair* was launched in 1950, an aesthetic success but a financial disaster. By the end of 1950 — after eleven issues — before-tax losses totaled almost $2.5 million and the magazine was closed.[7] In 1949 Mike had launched *Quick*, a weekly pocket-size news magazine designed for newsstand sale. It was an immediate circulation success, but did not make a profit and was closed in April 1953. While *LOOK* itself was successful, with a circulation over three million and advertising revenue of $21 million in 1952, it was in a highly competitive field with ongoing circulation battles.

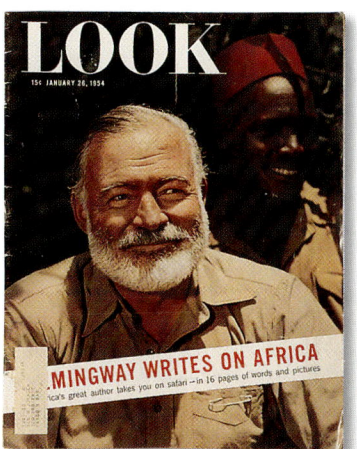

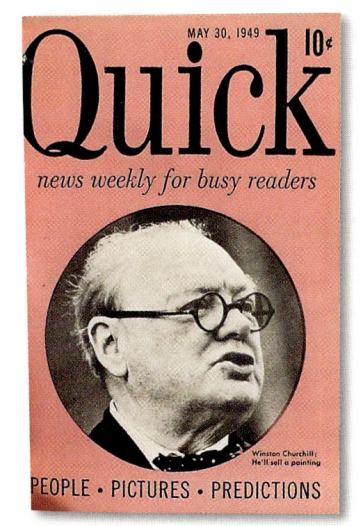

Mike and John initially held equal interests in both the Minneapolis Star and Tribune Company and in Cowles Magazines, Inc., the parent company of *LOOK*, so the financial well-being of each was important to John Cowles. At the urging of his wife, Elizabeth Bates Cowles, John sold his holdings in Cowles Magazines and Mike sold his stock in the Minneapolis Star and Tribune Company. She was concerned that problems with the magazines would require more and more investment on John's part. In her

COWLES MAGAZINES, INC., LATER COWLES COMMUNICATIONS, INC., HEADED BY GARDNER COWLES JR. (MIKE), PLAYED A PROMINENT ROLE IN THE NATIONAL MAGAZINE SCENE WITH SUCH TITLES AS *LOOK, QUICK,* AND *FLAIR*

view the purchase of *The Minneapolis Star* had been a significant gamble that had paid off handsomely, and there was no reason to jeopardize that success. Beyond that, she did not approve of Mike's marriage to Fleur. In 1953 Mike resigned as a director and chairman of the board of the company; John severed his ties with Cowles Magazines, Inc. The Des Moines Register and Tribune Company became their principal common ground, with each of them sharing responsibility for it until the late sixties.[8] John Cowles never had a formal compensation arrangement with the company until 1953 when the board established one. He was to receive two percent of earnings, calculated before depreciation and taxes. The arrangement continued until the early 1970s, when he ceased to be active in the business.

At the 1956 annual meeting of stockholders Cowles talked about his concern that *The Minneapolis Star* was not growing and later discussed the fact that changes in the paper had not resulted in expected circulation increases. *The Minneapolis Tribune*, on the other hand, continued to grow in circulation, but it was still not making money. Advertisers greatly preferred the evening paper, and Sunday advertising was growing rapidly for at least two reasons: 1) the development of preprinted advertising inserts (including coupons) and 2) the fact that Dayton's began Sunday advertising in March of 1954. (G. Nelson Dayton, who died in 1950, had a long-standing policy against Sunday advertising; the store was not open, and display windows were covered as well.)

There were other differences between *The Minneapolis Star* and *The Minneapolis Tribune*, beyond their financial performance. *The Minneapolis Tribune* had become much more the "newspaper of record" with stronger emphasis on national and international news. According to Carl Rowan (later Deputy Assistant Secretary of State), "Circumstances and John Cowles made *The Minneapolis Tribune* the 'prestige' newspaper. They were content to have *The Minneapolis Star* be the money-maker."[9][10] According to the *Harper's* account: "A subscriber to the Minneapolis Tribune can get the New York Times drama review of last night's opener on Broadway delivered to his doorstep at virtually the same time it's delivered to a Times subscriber."

Despite the fact that Minneapolis was considered "a union town," the newspaper had avoided the strikes and other labor disputes that were beginning to occur across the country. John Cowles had correctly predicted in 1945 that the country was in for a lot of labor strife after the war, largely on issues of manning and jurisdiction. Cowles was considered a generous employer with good wages and good working conditions. People generally liked to work for the papers, and there was something of the conventional lifetime job mentality among

MINNEAPOLIS MORNING TRIBUNE, MAY 15, 1948

employees. They were proud of the product, and the craft union members enjoyed working in a good plant with good equipment. The unions, however, took strong positions on staffing and jurisdictional issues which often tended to cause friction between management and employees and to separate the two, reinforcing the traditional class lines.

There were two factions in the labor movement in general — the progressives ("progs") and the conservatives. For many years the printers had been the dominant newspaper union, followed by the International Typographical Union. The Stereotypers went on strike for a short time in 1949, the company's first strike. It was not supported by other unions, and management employees were able to do the work necessary to publish the paper. By the fifties, the Teamsters were becoming a powerful force in newspapers, and there was a seven-day drivers' strike in Minneapolis in 1953. Change was coming to the industry with the availability of new technologies such as photocomposition. Additional change was driven by the need for greater productivity in places like the mailroom where advertising inserts were handled manually, an activity not present when jobs and jurisdictions were established years before.

Within the plant changes in the postwar labor force were being felt. An increasing number of production employees — including the mailroom — were better educated, probably more than management generally recognized. They were also more ambitious than most veteran workers who remembered the Depression and the serious labor strife in Minneapolis then. It was difficult for production employees to aspire to management ranks, a situation that caused some resentment toward the company. Beyond that, the more radical elements tended to dominate negotiations, and their focus was very much on the traditional concerns of wage rates and jurisdiction.

Booze was an ever-present problem in the plant. Many employees frequented nearby bars — including the Press Row Bar and Cafe directly across Portland Avenue from the plant — when there were long lulls in the production process. The Press Row was described as a "a home away from home" — before, during and after work.[11] (Problems of drinking were not confined to the plant; there are numerous stories of managers who were overly fond of alcohol, including one who unexpectedly appeared as a participant in a rodeo during a large newspaper industry meeting in Dallas.)

By the end of the fifties, growth of the newspapers — especially the Sunday edition and inserts — required another plant expansion, largely of the mailroom. In addition to the growth of inserts, classified advertising had increased so much that *The Minneapolis Tribune* ranked fifth among newspapers in North America in classified linage, *The Minneapolis Star* was fourth, and *The Minneapolis Sunday Tribune* was eighth. Sunday circulation had reached a new one-day record at 680,000.

One response to increasing labor costs was to invest in new plant and equipment to get improved productivity. Ten new Goss press units were installed in 1957, and in 1959 construction was begun on a 200,000 square foot addition — two additional floors along the north end of the Portland Avenue side of the building, resulting in its current exterior configuration. It was the last major reconstruction of the building until 1995 when the four-level space

PRESS ROW BAR AND CAFE, CIRCA 1948

STAR TRIBUNE BUILDING, 1997

occupied by the old pressroom was rebuilt to provide offices and conference and meeting facilities. Mechanical systems were extensively replaced at the same time. (See Appendix D.)

As the size of the organization grew and became more complex — and as his own outside interests grew — in 1952 John Cowles designated Joyce Swan as his second in command for all non-editorial functions, paralleling the responsibilities of Gideon Seymour, executive editor, for news and editorial operations. Cowles kept the titles of publisher and editor, and continued to play the dominant role in management. And in 1958 he resigned "quietly" from the board of General Mills, where he had served since 1945, expressing his desire to cut back on his business responsibilities to have more time to travel. The customary exchange of felicitous letters followed. One story has it, however, that he and James Ford Bell (General Mills' chairman) differed sharply on political issues and that Bell wanted him off the board. (Ironically, he left the General Electric board in 1949, because the Department of Justice expressed concern that both companies made and sold small household appliances.)

Earlier Bell had floated the idea of starting a competing newspaper in Minneapolis because he was so opposed to the editorial views of the newspapers. (In 1947 he had turned down the opportunity to buy *The Minneapolis Times*.) The story has it that some time in the mid-fifties he summoned Donald Dayton, who succeeded his father as president of Dayton's in 1954, to discuss the idea. The Dayton brothers demurred and the attempt foundered.[12] Bell went on to invest in several suburban weekly newspapers.[13]

1 Joyce Swan, author interview, April 1996.
2 Friedricks, *The Newspaper That Captured a State*, p. 328.
3 John Cowles Sr., "The Responsibility of a Free Press In a World In Crisis," (speech presented at the awarding of the University of Missouri Medal for Distinguished Service to Journalism, St. Louis, Missouri, May 4, 1951).
4 John Cowles Sr., Letters to Dwight D. Eisenhower, February 14 and May 7, 1952.
5 William Barry Furlong, "The Midwest's Nice Monopolists: John and Mike Cowles," *Harper's*, June 1963, p. 66.
6 Morley Cowles Ballantine, author interview, June 7, 1996.
7 Amy Fine Collins, "A *Flair* For Living," *Vanity Fair*, October, 1996, p. 220.
8 John Cowles Jr., author interview, November 12, 1996.
9 "The Midwest's Nice Monopolists: John and Mike Cowles," *Harper's*, June 1963, p. 73.
10 According to Carl Rowan, he was hired very soon after John Cowles Sr. challenged Seymour: "Gid, you'll never convince me that in all these United States you can't find a Negro man or woman capable of being a reporter on my papers." (See *Capital Karnea*, Autumn 1996, p. 19.)
11 "The Press Row — 10 cent beer and bouncer named Big Rube," *Newsmakers*, January 1977, p. 66.
12 Bruce Dayton, author interview, June 6, 1996, and Letter from Paul Parker to James Alcott, October 18, 1996.
13 David Duff, author interview, March 13, 1997.

RADIO AND TELEVISION

11

DIVERSIFICATION THROUGH the acquisition of newspapers in other markets was a common strategy in the newspaper industry throughout much of the last half of the twentieth century. Much of the earlier growth of newspaper companies was like that of the Minneapolis Star and Tribune Company and the Des Moines Register and Tribune Company — consolidating multiple newspapers in a single market.

After it became clear that the Cowles venture in Minneapolis was successful, discussion began about the possibility of moving into other markets. In 1943 Mike Cowles had raised the possibility of buying *The Times* in Indianapolis from Roy Howard, as the base for consolidation there, followed by purchase of *The Star*, which had the only Sunday paper at the time. He was "increasingly impressed by what a large share of our profit in Des Moines arises from the Sunday Register."[1] The idea was apparently not pursued in depth, in large measure because of John Cowles' view that success would require the presence of a member of the family on the scene (as it had in Minneapolis), and that neither he nor Mike were available.

The second, and apparently stronger, interest was in Phoenix in 1946 — *The Arizona Republic* and *The Phoenix Gazette*. There John Cowles met with one of the principal owners, the publisher Wes Knorpp, and was given financial information. The asking price was $5 million. He and Lyle Anderson, the company treasurer, worked through the financing and tax implications of a purchase. Their financial analysis suggested that Cowles could pay little more than $4 million because of his concern about possible tax liabilities and understated expenses, competition from *The Shopping News* that had been recently purchased by members of the Roosevelt family, the presence of minority shareholders, and the need for a new plant estimated to cost more than $1 million. Knorpp and Charles Stauffer, the other principal owner, were pushing for a quick decision, saying that Roy Howard was also actively interested. Again, John expressed his reluctance to "spend any time,

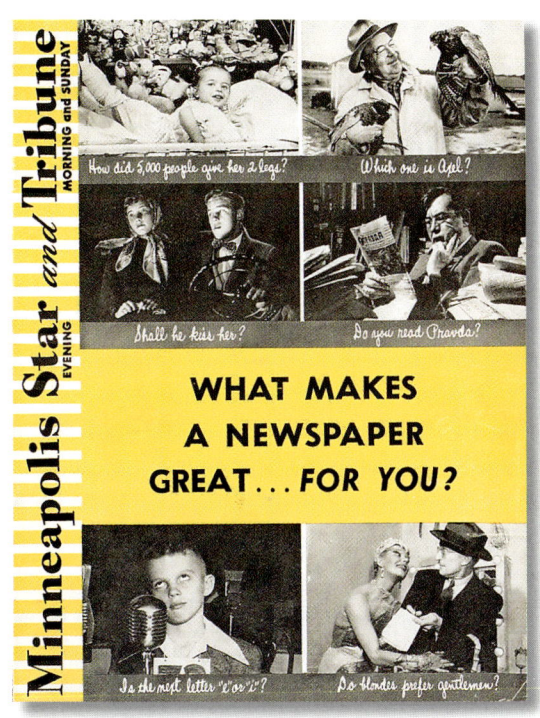

MINNEAPOLIS STAR AND TRIBUNE, ADVERTISING SUPPLEMENT, 1955

and certainly not any substantial amount which I think would be required, cultivating Phoenix advertisers and clipping nickels and dimes off Phoenix's operating expenses."[2]

John Cowles' conclusions are instructive: "Phoenix will probably continue to grow substantially and the Phoenix paper would prove a good buy at $4.5 million. However, I have absolutely no desire to assume the additional work and responsibility for running it. If you (Mike Cowles) are 100 percent sold on our pushing this thing, I will acquiesce, but am completely unenthusiastic. The more I think about some of these other papers, the more I am inclined to think that spending the same amount of energy on Minneapolis would produce more dollars, net, with no risk. We haven't begun to develop Minneapolis as intensively as we can. If Phoenix is worth what they are asking for it, just figure out in your own mind what SJT stock is worth."[3]

The Phoenix papers were sold in 1944 to Central Newspapers (the Pulliam family), owners of *The Indianapolis News* and *Star* for $2.9 million; the cost of improving the plant brought their investment to roughly $4 million. In the course of considering the Phoenix situation, Joyce Swan examined the Wichita market and concluded that there was a possibility of acquiring *The Wichita Eagle*, then *The Beacon* there. This was apparently not pursued.[4]

By 1949 Mike Cowles was established in New York as president and editor of Cowles Magazines, Inc., while continuing as president and treasurer of the Des Moines Register and Tribune Company. An extensive story in *Advertising Age* reported that "the Cowles brothers plan to acquire or start no other newspapers." By this time, the Minneapolis papers were larger than the ones in Iowa with a value estimated by *Advertising Age* to be $20 million, compared to $15 million for Des Moines.

Discussing the two newspaper markets and radio stations in Des Moines and Yankton, S.D., the story went on to speculate: "A strong nucleus, you might say, for a nationwide newspaper chain. But John and Mike Cowles believe that newspaper publishing must always be an owner-manager, personal responsibility business. It should never become too big or too widespread for the owners to be actively identified with each part of it. 'The hired manager plan won't work,' said Mike."[5] The article also quoted Mike as saying that "we plan definitely to have television stations in Des Moines, Minneapolis and Boston."

The Register and Tribune Company entered the radio business in 1922 and in 1931 established the Iowa Broadcasting Company as a subsidiary with three stations. KSO was moved from Clarinda to Des Moines in 1932 and KWCR in Cedar Rapids moved to Des

"There are many indications that in the next decade newspapers as we now know them will become relatively less important and broadcasting progressively more important as a means for the dissemination of news, information, pictures, advertising, entertainment, and all other forms of public service."

Confidential Memorandum
From John Cowles Sr., September 1, 1944

Moines in 1935 where its call letters were changed to KRNT.[6] The success of the radio business itself and its ability to reinforce the newspaper franchise caused John Cowles to be deeply interested in broadcasting. From 1943 until 1954 he devoted considerable time and energy to obtaining radio and television licenses in Minneapolis. The effort was only partly successful and involved repeated negotiations with the Federal Communications Commission, which was formulating rules for market entry throughout the period. In 1943 he wrote Stanley Hawks, one of his key executives: "The things that I have read about FM and television in the last couple of weeks tend to intensify my conviction that we simply must get into it, and that we cannot afford not to have the best station here in the Twin Cities as an insurance policy against a shift from newspapers, if nothing else."[7] Almost immediately he began to pursue the possibility in the Twin Cities with inquiries about siting radio or television towers on the First National Bank Building in St. Paul. On January 26, 1944, the Board of Directors authorized the president to enter the broadcasting field in the Twin Cities at the earliest date he determined advantageous. He reported that he had taken the necessary steps for the company to join the American Network. At the same meeting, Gardner Cowles Jr. was elected chairman as well as a vice president.

At about the same time John Cowles began discussion with Kingsley Murphy, who was owner of almost 20,000 shares (approximately 13 percent) of the company, about Murphy's acquisition of radio station KSO in Des Moines. (The new so-called duopoly rule of the Federal Communications Commission required the Register and Tribune Company to sell one of its two radio stations in Des Moines, so KSO was the one put up for sale.) John Cowles insisted that Murphy pay for KSO with stock in the Minneapolis Star Journal and Tribune Company, leading to a complex transaction.

Murphy was also a shareholder — with the Minnesota Tribune Company and the Ridder family of St. Paul — of Minnesota Broadcasting Corporation, owner of radio station WTCN. He sold his Minnesota Broadcasting stock to the Minnesota Tribune Company for approximately 6,000 shares of Minneapolis Star Journal and Tribune Company stock, which he then paid to Cowles for KSO in the summer of 1944.

The two brothers then bought radio stations WCOP in Boston and WHOM in Jersey City in June of 1944, the latter after losing out in an effort to purchase WPEN in Philadelphia, with plans to buy others. They approached various existing Twin Cities radio stations with no success. In August they decided to apply for a license for frequency 580 in Minneapolis, recognizing the fact that ownership of half of WTCN by the Minnesota Tribune Company could be a problem. Their representative in Washington wrote to Mike: "We'll have to proceed as rapidly as possible on the 580 application. The site is an excellent one for AM/FM and television. My only concern is the relationship between minority stockholders of the company and WTCN. It may be necessary to divorce the Star Broadcasting Company as a subsidiary of the company. A visit by John or yourself with the Chairman of the FCC might prove fruitful."[8]

On September 1, 1944, John and Mike Cowles announced that they had formed Northwest Broadcasting Company, owned separately from the newspaper company by the two of them. They judged it not feasible for the Minneapolis Star Journal and Tribune Company to enter the radio broadcasting field directly, because one of its stockholders (Minnesota Tribune Company) had a competing radio interest in the Twin Cities. The duopoly policy of the FCC prevented granting a new broadcasting license to any corporation, any of whose officers or substantial stockholders had a direct or indirect interest of any kind in another radio station in that same community.

The cross-ownership issues were becoming increasingly complex. On September 3, John wrote to his father: "Our Minneapolis radio station situation is further complicated by the fact that Kingsley Murphy is a big stockholder and director of the Star and Tribune, and also the licensee of KSO which competes with KRNT in Des Moines. The FCC says it cannot see why it should grant the Star Journal Company a radio license here when Kingsley would share ownership when we are vigorous competitors in Des Moines. If Kingsley would re-sell us his Star stock, that barrier would be eliminated."[9]

John Cowles requested permission to appear before the Minnesota Tribune Company board on September 15, 1944. He began his presentation with an analysis of the "postwar radio field": FM, television, and facsimile, and the desirability of their being allied with newspapers. He predicted that in the next decade newspapers as then constituted would become relatively less important, and broadcasting progressively more important as a means for the dissemination of news, information, pictures, advertising, entertainment and all other forms of public service. He reviewed the many options that might permit the Star Journal and Tribune Company to acquire a broadcast license, and urged the board to sell its stock in the company and get out of the newspaper business.[10] The Minnesota Tribune Company Board declined to sell. As John Cowles told his father: "The more I suggest their selling their Star Journal and Tribune stock, the more anxious they are to hold onto it. And the more I suggest they sell their WTCN radio stock, the more anxious they are to hold on to that. I would guess that nothing will happen for a long time."[11] He was right. (His memorandum on the subject is included as Appendix H; it details some of the complex ownership issues.) Shortly thereafter the Northwest Broadcasting Company filed a license application and entered into negotiations with ABC to replace its CBS affiliations in Des Moines and Yankton with ABC and to make its proposed new station in the Twin Cities an ABC affiliate as well, taking that affiliation from WTCN. In September 1945, the Northwest Broadcasting application for the Twin Cities license was withdrawn for antitrust reasons.

The trade press in 1948 reported that Cowles Broadcasting Company (the Des Moines-based company) had earmarked $1 million for television construction in Boston, Minneapolis and Des Moines and that applications for the first two had already been filed. The Minneapolis application was granted on March 11, subject to the condition that within 90 days the Minnesota Tribune Company divest itself of its ownership in either

CROSS-OWNERSHIP CONCERNS COMPLICATED THE COWLES' EFFORTS TO EXPAND THEIR OWNERSHIP OF BROADCASTING PROPERTIES, INCLUDING WTCN-TV IN MINNEAPOLIS.

the Star and Tribune Company or the Minnesota Broadcasting Corporation. Again, the shareholders of the Minnesota Tribune Company declined to sell either. Discussions with the FCC continued until September 9, 1949, when the commission formally canceled the construction permit.

In 1948 Stanley Hubbard, owner of station KSTP in the Twin Cities, discussed with Stanley Hawks the possibility of the company buying 48 or 49 percent of KSTP, an idea he had raised with John Cowles earlier.[12] Hubbard believed that he would need additional capital to expand his programming when television became more competitive in the Twin Cities market. He indicated that one alternative to a Cowles investment would be a public offering for part of his company. The discussions later went so far as Hubbard furnishing audited financial statements, which the brothers discussed with the management of their Des Moines broadcast operations, but in the end they did not invest. Hubbard apparently also had discussions with the Ridder family during this period, which also did not come to fruition. Had these discussions led to a transaction, the Ridders would have sold their half interest in WTCN, a possibility that interested John Cowles greatly.

Minnesota Broadcasting Company had received a construction permit for a television facility in 1948 and was on the air by 1950 as WTCN-TV.[13] CBS had owned radio station WCCO since 1932, and it was the dominant station in the market. In November of 1950 John Cowles was authorized by his board to negotiate the purchase, if possible, of substantial holdings in the Minnesota Broadcasting Company, but the purchase was not pursued. Instead, preliminary discussions began with Frank Stanton and William Paley of Columbia Broadcasting System about a new television station in Minneapolis which would be jointly owned with Cowles interests. In August 1952, however, CBS and Minnesota Broadcasting merged their respective local radio and television interests, with CBS holding a 47 percent stake in the new corporation, called Midwest Radio-Television, Inc. The call letters were switched to WCCO-TV.

In November 1953, the FCC again changed its rules on ownership of television stations, causing CBS to decide to sell its interest in Midwest Radio-Television. John Cowles immediately approached William McNally, president of MR-T, about acquiring the CBS ownership interest. McNally concluded that Midwest Radio-Television itself did not have the resources to buy CBS out and that a sale of that interest was inevitable. He believed that a purchase by Cowles would be preferable to other possibilities, since it would eliminate a potential competitor and add the clout of the region's largest newspaper. The Ridders were initially opposed to the idea of Cowles ownership, but eventually agreed with McNally's position.

The deal struck with CBS called for a purchase price of $3,950,000 for its interest in MR-T, of which $950,000 would be considered payment for an agreement to compensate CBS for agreeing not to compete in the market for a period of ten years. The non-compete agreement, which would be deductible to the Star

THE KANSAS CBS AFFILIATE WAS PURCHASED BY COWLES IN 1955

and Tribune for tax purposes, would have been taxable as ordinary income to CBS however, and CBS balked. Cowles eventually agreed to the CBS price with the understanding that the company would be given preference in acquiring another CBS television station later. That opportunity came the next spring with the acquisition of CBS-affiliate KTVH in Kansas, acquired for $1 million. For more than a decade, all diversification efforts had centered on a broadcast interest in the Twin Cities; newspaper acquisitions had not been pursued.

1 Gardner Cowles Jr., Letter to John Cowles Sr., December 21, 1943.
2 John Cowles Sr., Letter to Gardner Cowles Jr., July 10, 1946.
3 John Cowles Sr., Letters to Gardner Cowles Jr., July 10, 1946 and July 15, 1946.
4 Joyce Swan, Memorandum to John Cowles Sr., July 12, 1946.
5 "Cowles Brothers Build a $50,000,000 Empire," *Advertising Age*, August 1949, p. 7.
6 Friedricks, *The Newspaper That Captured a State*, p. 327.
7 John Cowles Sr., Letter to Stanly Hawks, December 30, 1943.
8 Tam Craven, Letter to Gardner Cowles Jr., August 9, 1944.
9 John Cowles Sr., Letter to Gardner Cowles Sr., September 3, 1944.
10 John Cowles Sr., Memorandum, September 1, 1944.
11 John Cowles Sr., Letter to Gardner Cowles Sr., September 15, 1944.
12 Stanley Hawks, Memorandum, November 6, 1948.
13 Minnesota Broadcasting was jointly owned by the St. Paul newspapers (the Ridder family) and the Minnesota Tribune Company (members of the Murphy family, excluding Kingsley Murphy).

DIVERSIFICATION

12

INTEREST IN NEWSPAPER acquisitions began to surface again in the middle fifties. The television issue had been resolved, and profits continued to exceed amounts needed for reinvestment in Minneapolis. In 1956 the Orlando newspaper was considered, and John Cowles visited with the owners on two occasions. The papers were acquired by the (Chicago) Tribune Company. In 1957, John Cowles corresponded with a banker in Baltimore about the possibility of acquiring *The Florida Times-Union* in Jacksonville, then owned by the Atlantic Coast Line Railroad interest. He said: "I want to make crystal clear my serious interest in the *Times Union*…and would pay what I think a reasonable person would regard as a liberal price. We are in a position to pay all cash."[1] It was later sold to Morris Communications. The same year Otto Silha visited Austin, Texas, to check out the possibility of acquiring *The American-Statesman*, subsequently sold to Cox Newspapers. In 1959 Lyle Anderson and Joyce Swan met with owners of newspapers in Rockford, Illinois, and made an offer of $6 million. It was subsequently bought by Gannett.

According to Joyce Swan, there were many reasons for not acquiring these papers, but the general finding was that the asking prices could not be justified — especially when compared to prices paid for the Minneapolis newspapers. A second reason was that Cowles was primarily interested in the Minneapolis market and did not like the idea of "chains," of owning newspapers simply as financial entities. A third reason for going slow on acquisitions was the fact that Cowles wanted his own people in management positions, and his best people were needed in Minneapolis. Dale Larsen, who had been in circulation and promotion departments in Minneapolis since 1942, went to the Wichita television station in 1956. Later acquisitions in California, South Dakota and Montana were headed by managers with long histories with the company.

In 1961 executives investigated the San Bernardino, California, morning, evening and Sunday newspapers.

MINNEAPOLIS MORNING TRIBUNE, OCTOBER 29, 1962

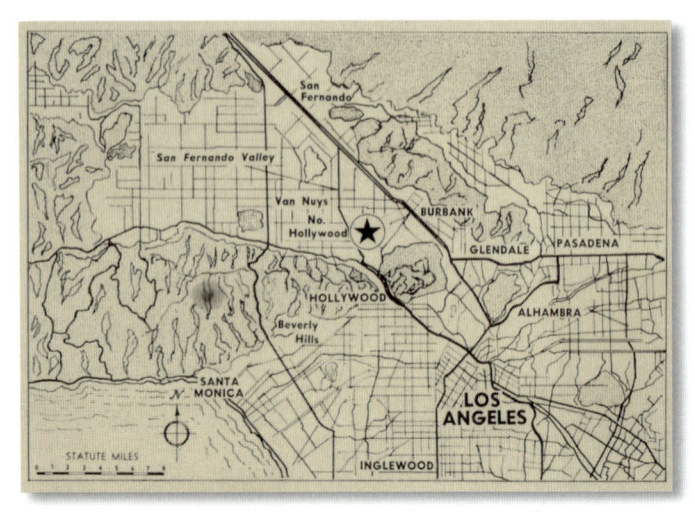

THE SAN FERNANDO VALLEY, ABOUT 1960, SERVED BY *THE VALLEY TIMES*

John Cowles visited with the principal owner, who, while he said the papers were "not for sale," furnished financial data and encouraged an offer, which was not forthcoming. He later asked to meet again in April at the ANPA convention, and Cowles noted that he thought it unlikely the owners would reduce their price to a figure that he would regard as attractive. It was purchased by Times-Mirror Company. He urged Swan and other executives to continue looking for other possible newspaper purchases in other markets.

The next major acquisition opportunity came in November 1958, with a lead from Philip Graham, publisher of *The Washington Post*. The Anaconda Copper Company owned six newspapers in Montana — in all the major cities except Great Falls — and had decided to sell them. John Cowles immediately made contact with Anaconda and arranged for Joyce Swan and others to visit the Montana locations. The papers were of interest in part because Montana was a logical extension of the Upper Midwest, still a strong marketing concept for the Minneapolis papers. Negotiations proceeded, Cowles traveled to New York for further discussions and invited the chairman of Anaconda, C. E. Weed, to be his guest at the 1959 Gridiron Dinner in Washington in February. He went to New York afterward, expecting to meet with the Anaconda board to conclude the transaction. That meeting did not take place, negotiations became stalled, and in May 1959, the papers were sold to the Lee Syndicate, now Lee Enterprises. Discussions were then held with Lee to determine whether they would be willing to sell the paper in Billings or Missoula, but they were not.

One account of the sale to Lee is that a key Lee executive was a native Montanan; he promised to move back to Montana and help provide a sense of local ownership.[2] A second account, not necessarily contradictory, is that under Cowles ownership the papers would have been too independent and liberal for Anaconda, a major economic force in Montana noted for a strong anti-labor stance and highly conservative positions on most political and social issues.

Swan immediately began looking at other newspaper markets in the West with trips to Denver, Salt Lake City, Seattle, Portland and Sacramento.[3] In Portland, for example, he looked at both newspapers, then locally owned. He concluded that *The Journal* was beyond hope and that *The Oregonian* was either too big or not available. Si Newhouse later told him that he "woke up one night thinking about Portland, called the next morning to see if the Oregonian was for sale, was told it might be, and offered $5 million without seeing any numbers."[4]

During the course of these investigations, a suburban Los Angeles newspaper became available. *The San Fernando Valley Times* served a rapidly growing group of communities near Los Angeles and was judged to have significant potential under Cowles ownership, making use of the circulation, promotion and editorial techniques that had been so successful in Minneapolis. It was also of interest because it appeared to be growing when afternoon newspapers in general were declining in circulation. John Cowles told stockholders in 1960: "By

THE GREAT FALLS TRIBUNE AND THE RAPID CITY JOURNAL

operating *The Valley Times*, we hope that we may learn why the Los Angeles metropolitan afternoon papers are not doing well in their competition with suburban newspapers, and consequently know how to improve the editing of The Minneapolis Star so as to reduce the likelihood of any such adverse trend developing here." He pointed out that in the New York market suburban papers like *Newsday* were becoming highly profitable, and that *The Valley Times* might become a valuable asset and a good diversification move.

The newspaper was acquired in 1960, and Robert Weed — then business manager in Minneapolis — went to California to run the new operation under the direction of Joyce Swan (who had engineered the acquisition) and other executives. Swan also acquired several acres of prime land to be used for a new plant for the paper, which would give it added visibility in the marketplace. Difficulties became apparent almost immediately; the investment required was greater than expected and operating losses accumulated. Early on, John Cowles wrote a memo comparing the experience there with the first year with *The Minneapolis Star*, noting that in comparable dollars the purchase price was about the same as that paid for *The Minneapolis Star*, yet operating losses were twice those experienced in Minneapolis.[5]

He recorded his view again in a handwritten letter to Swan from his home in Antigua: "My thinking about The Valley Times has pretty much crystallized. We made a mistake in buying it and I favor selling it as rapidly as we reasonably can. I am 100% opposed to pouring a lot of additional S&T cash into it in the vague hope that in a couple of years it might become modestly profitable."[6] Two years later he wrote: "The more I analyze regarding The Valley Times Today, the more I am inclined to believe we ought promptly to try to dispose of the property, even at a substantially lower figure than we have previously talked about. There is no disgrace in making an error in business judgement."[7]

In addition to the business problems of the paper, politics were a troubling factor. In 1962 Richard Nixon was running for governor, opposed by the John Birch Society, a potent force in Republican politics in Southern California. John Cowles wrote the publisher: "I don't see how we could support avowed members of the John Birch Society when its head has stated that former President Eisenhower is a conscious agent of the Communist conspiracy. Although I realize that Nixon has his faults … it is my present view that The Valley Times Today either ought to support Nixon or be neutral on the governorship."[8]

By 1963 steps were taken to sell the paper, and a number of potential buyers were contacted, including Gene Autry, a movie star known because of his early participation in some *Minneapolis Star* and *Tribune* promotion activities and his involvement in major league baseball. (Swan had been instrumental in building a baseball stadium in Minneapolis and convincing the American League to approve the move of the Washington Senators to the Twin Cities.) The eventual buyer in 1963 was Lamont Copeland Jr. who, in spite of his (duPont) family fortune, proved unable to meet his contractual obligations. Most of the purchase price of $2,650,000 was eventually recovered, and the land acquired as a plant site had appreciated in value so that its sale produced a profit. The total write-off from the investment was just under $500,000.

In 1962, consideration was again given to the newspapers in Wichita, but the Minneapolis newspaper strike put acquisition activity on hold until 1964. Early that year conversations and negotiations began with the owners of newspapers in Great Falls, Montana, and Albuquerque, New Mexico, about their possible acquisition. In September, negotiations began for the acquisition of *The Tucson Daily Star*, a morning and Sunday paper. An offer was not accepted and two months later the paper was sold to the Pulitzer Publishing Company. At about the same time, Swan determined that the owners of *The Rapid City Journal* in South Dakota were interested in selling. The evening and Sunday paper had a circulation of approximately 31,000. It was acquired in December for $3.5 million, plus modest noncompete agreements for two principal owners, members of the Morrell and Lighter families.

Negotiations to acquire the Great Falls Tribune Company in Montana from the Warden family were concluded in April 1965. The morning paper had a circulation of 36,000 and Sunday, 42,000. The purchase price was approximately $3.5 million, plus the customary noncompete agreements. The Wardens took pride in their status as the independent newspaper in the state and told Cowles that they were "proud of it before and will be after you take it over," that Cowles was not too liberal for them.[9] In the case of both Rapid City and Great Falls, John Cowles made sure that both Otto Silha and John Cowles Jr., visited both communities with the admonition: "Never buy a business in a town you wouldn't have lived in."[10]

Willis Brown, then assistant advertising director of the Minneapolis newspapers, was made publisher of *The Rapid City Journal*; Joyce Swan was president. Brown had come to Minneapolis in 1935 and spent his career in advertising. William A. Cordingley Jr. was named publisher of *The Great Falls Tribune*, with Swan as president. A Des Moines native, Cordingley had joined the advertising department of *The Minneapolis Star* and *Tribune* in 1940 and had been director of national advertising since 1950. Speaking of John Cowles, Cordingley recalled: "I remember he asked me to the Minneapolis Club for lunch, and we talked for about three hours. Next thing I know, he offered me the job."[11]

A different kind of diversification move was also made in April with the creation of a jointly owned venture with Harper & Row for *Harper's Magazine*, then owned entirely by the publisher. The company purchased its half interest for $700,000 and made a loan of $375,000 to the newly formed Harper's Magazine, Inc. John Cowles Jr., was named president of the new company.

At the annual meeting of stockholders in 1965, following the acquisitions, John Cowles gave three reasons for the purchase of the Rapid City and Great Falls papers: 1) They were well-edited, well-managed papers with a bright future; 2) He wanted the company to grow and provide opportunities for advancements; and 3) While outside *The Minneapolis Star* and *Tribune*'s normal circulation area, they are an integral part of the great Upper Midwest. In his remarks Swan cautioned that both papers were paying interest on heavy bank borrowings (each had five-year bank loans of $1.5 million).

1 John Cowles Sr., Letter to Mercantile Safe Deposit and Trust Company, July 1959.
2 Joyce Swan, author interview, April 1, 1996.
3 Joyce Swan, Memoranda, August 31, 1959 and October 20, 1959.
4 Joyce Swan, author interview, April 1, 1996.
5 John Cowles Sr., Memorandum, November 19, 1960.
6 Cowles Cowles Sr., Letter to Joyce Swan, April 2, 1961.
7 John Cowles Sr., Memorandum, May 22, 1963.
8 John Cowles Sr., Letter to the Publisher of *The Valley Times,* June 11, 1962.
9 John Cowles Jr., author interview, December 6, 1996.
10 Ibid.
11 William A. Cordingly Jr., author interview, February 6, 1996.

THE STRIKE

13

THE 1960S WERE A period of economic growth for the country as a whole, a prosperity in which the company shared, in spite of a brief recession in 1960-61. Real gross domestic product grew an average of 3.8 percent annually during the decade. The company's revenue grew by half from $37 million in 1960 to $55 million in 1969. Net earnings more than doubled from $3.0 to $6.1 million, and total dividends went up 78 percent from $1.8 to $3.2 million. Price of the stock, set periodically by Board resolution, went from $40 in February of 1960 to $58 in June 1969, adjusted for stock splits.[1]

Advertising linage — the largest source of revenue and profit for a newspaper, grew as well. Sunday linage rose 54 percent during the sixties, reflecting in part the growth of preprinted advertising inserts, although it was still only a quarter of total linage. *The Minneapolis Star* continued to be the leader in advertising linage — and especially retail advertising — although its share of total linage dropped from 48 to 46 percent of the total. *Minneapolis Tribune* advertising continued to trail *The Minneapolis Star* with just under 30 percent of the total.

One important aspect of the bright earnings picture arose from federal tax rules concerning profits of closely held corporations. Earnings that were not reinvested in the business or distributed in the form of dividends (which were taxable at high personal income rates) could be subject to surcharges, a situation that led to aggressive acquisition and diversification programs in many publishing companies.[2] The company's investment in new plant and equipment was more or less continuous — almost $20 million during the sixties. Following a 1956 investment of more than $2 million in air conditioning and new presses, a $3 million investment in the mailroom and pressroom began in 1959 with ten new press units. Another $3 million investment in new and improved presses beginning in 1960 brought 12 new press units and raised the speed on all presses from 48,500 to 60,000 papers per hour. Additional investment in the mailroom was made to handle the growing volume of preprinted inserts.

But the event that shaped the sixties perhaps most

THE MINNEAPOLIS STAR, NOVEMBER 22, 1963

MINNEAPOLIS STAR AND TRIBUNE COMPANY
(FISCAL 1960-1970)

REVENUE

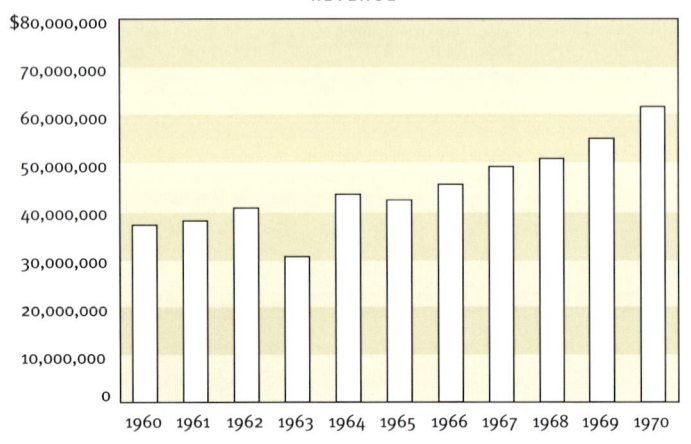

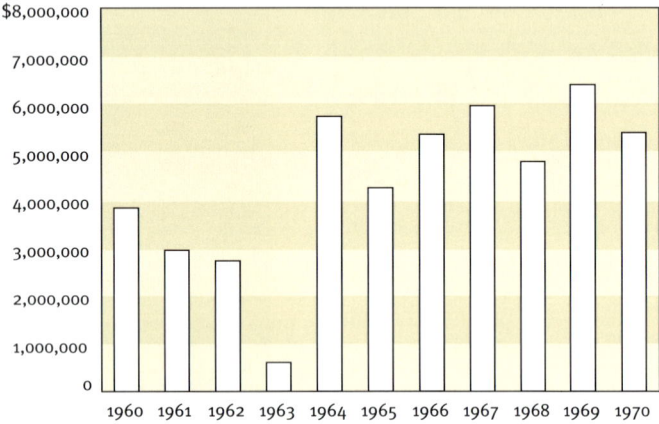

NET EARNINGS

profoundly was the labor disruption in 1962, the first serious labor stoppage in the company's 27-year history. The 116-day strike was the culmination of several forces that had been building since the late forties. Its impact on costs and on circulation were long lasting. As early as 1945 John Cowles had predicted in a letter to his father: "We are going to have a tremendous lot of labor trouble in this country in the next few years." A brief labor stoppage by the Stereotypers in the winter of 1949 came to a halt shortly after John Cowles ordered hot coffee served to the picket line.[3] Wages and benefits increased significantly during the fifties, but there was a brief strike by the Teamsters in 1953. When the threat of the strike became imminent, Cowles left for his home in Antigua, telling Joyce Swan not to contact him and to accept a strike if necessary to protect the business. He first learned of the strike in *The New York Times* four days after it had started.[4]

At the 1959 annual meeting John Cowles reminded stockholders (most of whom were employees) that negotiations in 1958 had been "extremely tense," but that a contract was agreed upon without a strike. He went on to describe strikes in other markets and the fact that *The Minneapolis Star* and *Tribune* wage scales ranked with those in the ten largest cities in the country. He concluded: "The Star and Tribune will continue to pay good wages for good work, and I hope our unions will not be unreasonable in their pay requests or in clinging to outworn restrictions which hamper productivity increases that are necessary to pay for wage increases." In 1960 the company increased its contribution to employee retirement plans from 1.0 to 1.5 percent of payroll, a decision based at least in part on a survey of employee attitudes about pay and benefits. The cost to the company was $250,000 annually. The total benefits package — referred to as job dividends — during the late fifties amounted to about 15 per cent of payroll, including holiday and vacation pay, health and life insurance, retirement plans, etc.

Beginning in 1957, Cowles' presentations at annual meetings included productivity measures, comparing output trends for four major production departments. (John Cowles Jr. had become

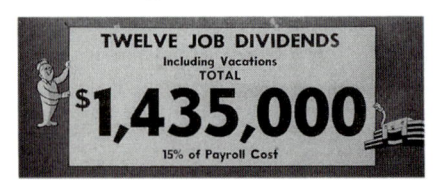

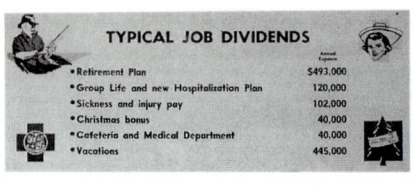

NEWSMAKERS, 1956
JOB DIVIDENDS REMINDER

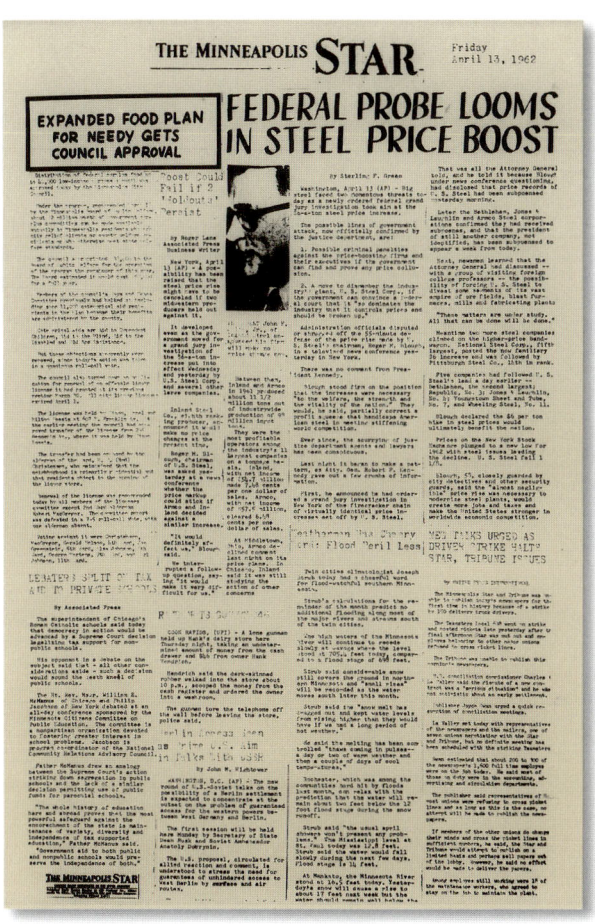

THE MINNEAPOLIS STAR (STRIKE EDITION), APRIL 13, 1962

interested in the productivity issue while working in the various "business" departments and saw the need to establish quantifiable measures of productivity.) These comparisons were paired with comments about the resulting declining profit margins — and in some years, actual profits. He pursued the same theme at annual speeches before the Twenty Year Club. In 1957 he commented that in general newspapers were slow to improve their production, machinery and methods, and that it had cost more each year for the past 10 or 12 years to produce each page of *The Minneapolis Star* and *The Minneapolis Tribune*. In 1961 he commented that productivity in some departments was declining, saying "that is bad for everyone."

The strike began on April 12, 1962, when Teamsters picketed, joined soon by Typographers and Mailers, then Stereotypers, Pressmen and the rest of the ten craft unions. The issues focused on wages, pensions and manning and work procedures — the number of men required to handle the volumes of inserts and the introduction of new labor-saving equipment. Some of the underlying motivations were complex. The strike was triggered by the Mailers, whose leverage came from the fact that they handled the profitable newspaper advertising supplements — inserts — that were growing in volume and importance. In general newspaper lore, the Printers had been considered the most highly skilled of the craft unions, and the Mailers the least skilled. That sentiment was exploited by some of the more radical members, including one mailer who had come from Des Moines, who was generally agreed to detest the Cowles organization and for whom the strike was a personal vendetta. He convinced the Teamsters to strike first, telling them (wrongly) that otherwise they could not get benefits during the strike.

Negotiations were handled first by Gale Freeman, a lawyer and former legislator who was the company's business manager. He reported to a committee of senior management including Otto Silha, Joyce Swan, Howard Mithun and John Cowles. As the seriousness of the situation deepened, Howard Mithun — general counsel — entered the negotiations, and at one point John Cowles met with representatives of the unions. Cowles proposed that the two sides submit their cases to binding arbitration, with the swing member of the panel to be selected by President Kennedy. Shortly after the strike started, he met with the Mailers Committee to offer a guarantee that no regular full-time employee would be laid off involuntarily if new equipment or methods were introduced. He then went to his home in Antigua where he was kept abreast of developments.

THE MINNEAPOLIS STAR, AUGUST 7, 1962

The union refused the offer. During the strike the newspapers continued to "publish" *The Internal Journal,* a mimeographed daily circulated within the organization. It maintained a record of local news that was read over educational television.[5]

Negotiations moved slowly until August, when the Typographers agreed to settle. They were followed by all the other unions — including the Mailers — except the Teamsters. A strike newspaper called *The Minneapolis Herald* had begun publication by Maurice McCaffrey, a St. Paul advertising man. Circulation reached 75,000 daily and a number of *Minneapolis Star* and *Tribune* people worked there, drawing wages as well as strike benefits, in violation of federal labor law. With only the Teamsters holding out, Mithun telephoned Jimmy Hoffa, national president of the Teamsters Union, and explained to him that some drivers were being paid off the books by *The Herald,* in violation of wage laws. The strike ended the next day.[6]

John Cowles was dismayed by the strike, believing that he had gone well beyond what other publishers would have offered and that his proposition was entirely just. He voiced his feelings later that year at a Press Club dinner: "When The Star and Tribune offered both the commitment that we would not lay off any of our existing employees because of the introduction of new equipment or new operating methods, and when we offered to go to binding arbitration, I had taken it for granted that our strike would be speedily settled. I was amazed that when we offered both this absolute job protection to existing employees and also offered to go to binding arbitration on any differences, the unions would not promptly agree, that we could resume publication. The only reason that The Star and Tribune was able to weather the four-month strike as successfully as we did was because the company had been conservatively managed for many years. Newspapers simply must be financially strong in order to be independent of outside pressures for news or editorial slanting and to be able to survive advertising recessions or strikes."

At the 1963 stockholders meeting, he added: "Our strike demonstrates that we did not have the relationship based on confidence and understanding and recognition of the mutuality of interest between the employees and the management that I had assumed we had."

Following the strike, the company's retirement plan was split into two parts: The existing Plan "O" was designated for office workers, including Guild members, and a new Plan "A" was set up for other union employees, except for the Teamsters who opted to have their contributions made directly to the Central Teamsters Fund. Existing funding remained with Plan "O." As an example of the bitterness on both sides, the "annual" Christmas bonus, which had been paid since 1935, was

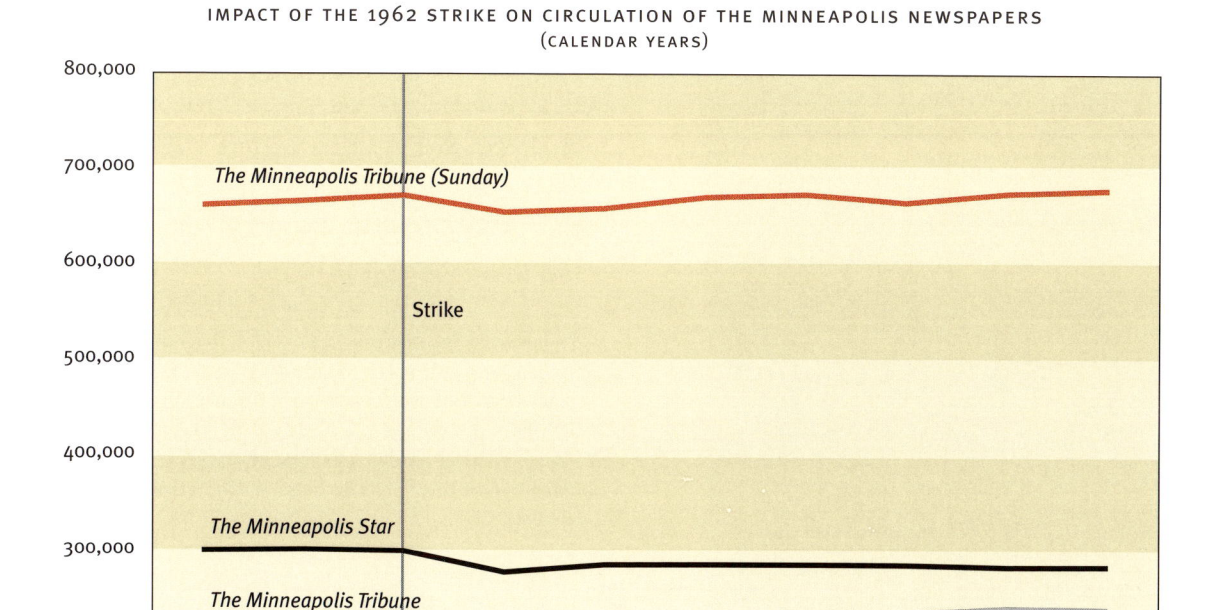

IMPACT OF THE 1962 STRIKE ON CIRCULATION OF THE MINNEAPOLIS NEWSPAPERS
(CALENDAR YEARS)

discontinued. In spite of the fact that the unions could have forced the payment they chose not to do so.[7]

The papers began publishing almost immediately on August 7, amid strenuous circulation promotion efforts. By March of 1964 *The Minneapolis Star* had a six-month circulation average of 286,881, down 12,000 from the pre-strike March 1962 level. *The Minneapolis Tribune* at 221,981 was off by 8,000. The Sunday paper at 658,764 was down 14,000. The Sunday and daily *Minneapolis Tribune* made up their losses by the following year, but *The Minneapolis Star* never again significantly exceeded its pre-strike circulation. Advertising, on the other hand, rebounded well. Total linage grew from 56.9 million in the year before the strike to 61.2 million the year after. Job dividends increased from 17 percent of payroll in 1961 to 19 percent in 1963.

For several years customers' reading habits had been changing, as had their lifestyles. Circulation of *The Minneapolis Star* peaked at 302,000 in 1960 and had recovered to only 278,000 by 1969, reflecting both the disruption of the strike and the impact of television as a source of news. Walter Cronkite began his tenure as anchor on the "CBS Evening News" in 1962. While *The Minneapolis Star* grew very little, *The Minneapolis Tribune* grew modestly during the sixties, from 225,000 to 240,000, and *The Minneapolis Sunday Tribune* grew from 662,000 to 678,000, a number not exceeded until 1992.

Management was sufficiently scarred by the strike that negotiations throughout the sixties and into the seventies were marked by a very strong reluctance to incur strikes and their attendant loss in advertising and circulation. Mailers union officials were able to see all their demands met repeatedly. John Cowles Jr. feels today that the company erred in not recognizing that the need was to change attitudes (not win the strike) and that he should have been more deeply involved in labor relations, pressing for those changes and for an overall labor strategy that overrode executive rivalries.[8]

The company was cited by the Harvard Business School Club of the Twin Cities as its Outstanding

THE MINNEAPOLIS STAR, JUNE 4, 1965

Company for 1963. In his response, John Cowles characterized the newspaper business as a "strange animal because it is a mixture of a business and a profession, and at times there appear to be conflicts between what might seem expedient if the decision were to be based solely on short-run business advantages rather than on professional standards and intellectual convictions." He went on to describe both the economic character of the business and his own publishing philosophy.[9] (See Appendix I for the full text.)

1965 marked the 30th anniversary of the acquisition of *The Minneapolis Star* by the Cowles. *The Minneapolis Star* itself had grown in circulation from 80,401 to 287,193, *The Minneapolis Tribune* had grown from 78,479 to 226,663 under Cowles ownership, and *The Minneapolis Sunday Tribune* rose from 190,868 to 670,436. Much of that circulation growth had occurred before 1950, leading

Joyce Swan to characterize the first of the three decades as the "circulation decade." Advertising ran between five and 10 million lines annually for each of three papers until 1945, when it began to grow dramatically. By 1965 *The Minneapolis Star* had grown to 30 million lines, *The Minneapolis Tribune* to almost 20 million, and the Sunday paper to over 15 million.

1 Minneapolis Star and Tribune Company, U.S. tax records, 1960 to 1969.
2 Personal income tax rates were as high as 90 percent during World War II and 70 percent as recently as 1973, when corporate rates were 48 percent.
3 Francis W. Hatch, author interview, June 1997.
4 Interview between John Cowles Sr. and Professor J.E. Gerald, October 16, 1961.
5 Bradley L. Morison, *Sunlight on Your Doorstep* (Minneapolis: Ross & Haines, Inc., 1966), p. 131.
6 Joyce Swan and Howard Mithun, author interviews, 1996.
7 John Dennison, author interview, February 27, 1997.
8 John Cowles Jr., author interview, December 6, 1996.
9 John Cowles Sr., "The Newspaper Business Is a Strange Animal" (speech to the Harvard Business School Club of the Twin Cities), September 24, 1963.

A GRADUAL TRANSITION

14

JOHN COWLES JR. BEGAN working for the company in 1947 as a summer intern in the St. Paul Bureau as a reporter for *The Minneapolis Tribune.* After his discharge from the U. S. Army in 1955 he worked in a variety of assignments in the business departments, before taking on management responsibilities in 1958. He was a 1951 graduate of Harvard, majoring in American history and literature. In 1952 he married Sage Fuller, who was pursuing a career in dance. They had three children — John III (Jay) born in 1953, Jane in 1955, and Fuller in 1961. (Sage had a daughter, Tessa Flores, from a previous marriage.) During the sixties and seventies they lived in a house designed for them by architect Edward Larrabee Barnes, overlooking Long Lake in a western Minneapolis suburb. In 1980 they moved into Minneapolis, first to a large house on Mount Curve Avenue in Kenwood, and eventually to a converted warehouse building located between downtown and the university.

John Cowles Jr. worked first for Lyle Anderson in finance on a number of special projects and task forces, which he enjoyed because they tapped his interest in mathematics. (Later, when he chose an editorial role instead of finance, Anderson told him that he would have been "a great treasurer.") Working next as assistant to the Business Manager, Otto Silha, he had assignments in retail advertising, circulation, promotion and production.

While working in production he became interested in productivity issues, a concept that had yet to enter the newspaper business in a serious way. He made a speech on the subject to the Northwest Production Association,

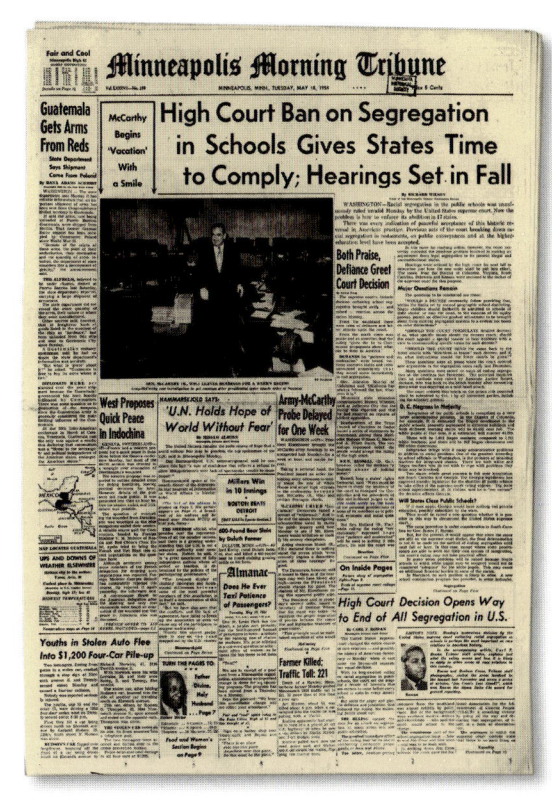

MINNEAPOLIS MORNING TRIBUNE, MAY 18, 1954

a group not accustomed to hearing that kind of analysis. When he came to the production department he was struck that pages arrived in the pressroom randomly, often resulting in delays and complications in the production process. As the papers had become larger with more pages per issue and more copies per pressrun, the problems began to strain the ability of pressmen to improvise. John instituted a system of page deadlines, designed to create a smooth, predictable flow of work to the pressroom. The change created consternation among some involved in the production process, accustomed to setting their own deadlines informally and independently, but apparently it cheered the newsrooms and the circulation force, both of which could plan their own work more effectively.

In 1959 his father wanted him to take an operational job, in either finance or news. He became assistant executive editor, feeling that the need was greater in news. Gideon Seymour, who had become executive editor of both papers in 1944, died in 1954, leaving a significant gap in the organization, where he had been one of the most powerful people and a confidant of John Cowles. Seymour had been replaced by William Steven who was hired in 1944 as managing editor of *The Minneapolis Tribune*, in part to complement Seymour's strong interest in national and international affairs. He had come from *The Tulsa Tribune* and was regarded as something of a wunderkind.

Cowles did not want to be seen as favoring *The Minneapolis Star* over *The Minneapolis Tribune*, and wanted the paper to have adequate resources. The typical news cycle generally meant that morning papers were better positioned to carry breaking stories and "hard news," about which he cared greatly. After World War II *The Minneapolis Tribune* under Seymour developed what *Harper's* called a staff of thoughtful specialists in science, labor, sociology, foreign affairs and education. While *The Minneapolis Star* had long been the money maker and leader in circulation, *The Minneapolis Tribune* was making its mark as the newspaper of record, dwelling more on national and international stories, developing its newsroom staff accordingly. *Newsweek* in 1958 said that of the two papers *The Minneapolis Tribune* was generally the newsier and, at the same time, the more serious. Steven had worked extensively with the promotion department to build circulation of *The Minneapolis Tribune*, and often went to some lengths to develop stories or features that would appeal to the Upper Midwest audience. He was a very different person from Seymour, and there was friction between the two almost from the outset.

According to John Cowles Jr., he and Steven got along well enough, but had significantly different ideas as to what was required for a quality newspaper. The two worked together much more closely than Steven had with his father. Cowles says that he "probably made his life miserable" with the constant interaction every day. Steven left in 1960, apparently frustrated by the relationship, a departure described as "not voluntary."[1] When Steven left, John Cowles Jr. became executive editor of both newspapers, with Bower Hawthorne serving as managing editor of *The Minneapolis Tribune* and David Silverman, managing editor of *The Minneapolis Star*.

1960 marked the 25th anniversary of the purchase of *The Minneapolis Star*, and John Cowles told stockholders that he had complete confidence in the executive organization of the company and that he was increasingly delegating operating responsibilities, although he expected to continue to participate in policy decisions. The following year he appointed Joyce Swan publisher and John Cowles Jr., editor of *The Minneapolis Star* and *The Minneapolis Tribune*, noting that, "Too often heads of companies tend to keep operating power too exclusively in their own hands when the organization would be better served by a gradual transition to younger men... Then, when the time of my retirement or death comes, there will not need to be any abrupt change in the management or uncertainty about the future policies of the institution."[2]

Lyle Anderson retired unexpectedly in 1960, at the age of sixty, to move to Arizona, where he had a winter home, in part because it had become clear that he would

JOHN COWLES SR. TURNING OVER THE REINS

"Next month will mark the 25th anniversary of the purchase of the old Minneapolis Star by the Cowles family, and the 25th anniversary of my presidency of this company. This quarter of a century has been a time of great development and great change, both for the world and this newspaper organization. Only an individual who was familiar with the operations of the Minneapolis newspapers 35 years ago can realize the extent of the change and the degree of the improvement in the quality of the Minneapolis papers during this period.

"Although I have no present intention of retiring and expect to continue to participate in the making of top policy decisions, I am increasingly delegating all operating responsibilities to Joyce Swan, as executive vice president and general manager, and to our other vice presidents. Consequently, I do not expect to be as close to the details of our operations in the future as I have been in the past, as I have complete confidence in the judgment and effectiveness of the executive organization that we have built."
John Cowles Sr.
Newsmakers, June 1960

"Too often, I believe, heads of companies tend to keep operating power too exclusively in their own hands when the organization would be better served by a gradual transition of operating control to younger men.

"If the directors immediately following this meeting re-elect me president of the company, as I assume they will, my first action will be to appoint Joyce Swan publisher, and John Cowles Jr., editor, of the Star and Tribune. I have held both of those titles for many years, in addition to being president of the company.

"Joyce has been gradually taking over, at my suggestion and with my encouragement, more and more of the functions and responsibilities that are normally performed by the publisher of a newspaper, and I believe he thoroughly merits and should have the title of publisher.

"Similarly, John Cowles Jr., has been gradually assuming the functions and responsibilities of the editor, and I think should have that title.

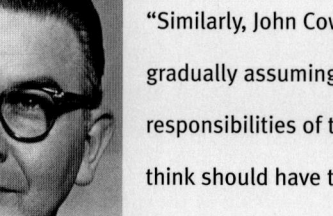

JOYCE A. SWAN, 1963

"As president and chief executive officer of the company, my interest in the institution's success will in no way lessen. Simply more of the operating decisions will be made directly by Joyce and John Jr., without their needing to refer them to me. I have been so closely associated with Joyce and John Jr., over so many years that I am sure that their and my journalistic and business philosophies are similar, and I am completely confident of their abilities to handle the enlarged responsibilities of their respective new positions. Then, when the time of my retirement or death comes, there will not need to be any abrupt changes in the management or uncertainty about the future policies of the institution."
John Cowles Sr.
Newsmakers, June 1961

GUTHRIE THEATER, 1974

not move higher in the organization. He joined *The Minneapolis Star* in 1938 as auditor, coming from the business department of the Des Moines Register and Tribune Company. He was made an officer in 1941 and a director in 1945. As treasurer, he had been an important person in the growth of the company, and an important adviser to John Cowles on tax strategy and in acquisitions.

In 1961 John Cowles announced the appointment of Philip VonBlon, then a marketing executive at International Milling Company. He wrote to Anderson: "Ever since you retired I have been increasingly convinced that we need to strengthen our top management on the business side. On several occasions you have expressed the view to me that we needed more business executives who had 'the money sense.' I believe and hope VonBlon has it. Those divisions at International Milling for which he has direct responsibility made more than $2.5 million last year ... substantially more than the comparable divisions at either General Mills or Pillsbury."[3] He was the first senior executive brought into the company from outside its ranks. He was also one of the leaders — along with John Cowles Jr. — in building the Guthrie Theater. In addition to the usual responsibilities of a chief financial officer, he was also responsible for managing the company's large investment portfolio.

The Guthrie Theater was a highly significant event in the civic life of Minneapolis. The noted Irish director, Tyrone Guthrie, announced in 1959 that he intended to establish a professional repertory theater in the United States, outside New York, and began a search for a city to be home to his project. John Cowles Jr. championed the idea, persuaded Guthrie to come to Minnesota, and led the campaign to raise the $2.3 million to launch the theater. His style in this regard contrasted with his father, who supported many civic endeavors, but not in a leadership role himself, using Stanley Hawks, Joyce Swan and others instead. John Cowles Jr. even had a working desk in the jade gallery of the Walker Art Center, where the embryonic theater was housed. It opened in 1963, less than three years after the idea was announced, and the reputation of Minneapolis for an exceptional quality of life was greatly enhanced. (See Appendix J.)

Many people had been skeptical about raising that much money. The Guthrie campaign was then followed by those of the other major cultural institutions, providing them a financial security unmatched in most cities and furthering the reputation of the Twin Cities nationally. The development of the theater and its continued success led to John Cowles Jr.'s being acknowledged as a member of the civic leadership in his own right. The next year he was named one of the ten outstanding young men of 1964 by the U. S. Junior Chamber of Commerce. Their citation said that he had "exerted a singularly persuasive influence upon his community… and demonstrated an editor's ability to contribute immeasurably to the economic and cultural development of a community and a state."[4]

1   Morison, *Sunlight on Your Doorstep*, p. 112.
2   "How Are We Doing?," *Newsmakers*, June 1961, p. 6.
3   Letter from John Cowles Sr. to Lyle Anderson, August 17, 1961.
4   "John Cowles Jr. Chosen as One of 10 Outstanding Young Men," *Newsmakers*, January 1965, p. 1

ADAPTABILITY AND
RESPONSIVENESS TO CHANGE

15

IN 1963, JOHN COWLES JR. outlined his philosophy for newspaper publishing and for *The Minneapolis Star* and *Tribune*. He stated his firm belief that newspapers should be able to remain the country's basic medium for advertising and news, but that papers did not have a "monopoly" position because of the many other avenues available to the public. He expressed concern that the principal disadvantage of the papers' leadership in the community was a "public resentment," based on a fear that they would try to use their strong position unfairly. He went on to emphasize that the company published two newspapers, with "their own distinctive personalities or separate characters," giving the newspaper reading public a choice between two daily versions of what is entertaining or interesting. He felt that greater public awareness of the separateness would reduce concern about a supposed monopoly and would create a greater likelihood that people would buy and read both papers. "Better understanding by the public of us and our newspapers will be necessary, I think, if we are to realize our full potential both as a business and as an institution of public service."[1] These themes directed much of his thought and action over the next two decades.

The same year an article in *Harper's* said that "unlike most monopoly publishers the Cowles don't see the papers as tools to make money so much as they see money as tools to make better newspapers." Bower Hawthorne said, "We'd rather send ten or twenty men overseas every year and have them come back here to handle the news from abroad more intelligently than maintain a large staff overseas that has no 'feel' for the people they're talking to."[2] The article also quoted John Cowles Jr. as saying: "Obviously a newspaper has to be financially strong to be independent." He persuaded his father to loosen the news hole to include op-ed pieces and letters to the editor. The paper was one of the first to have more than one editorial page, and its op-ed page preceded that of *The New York Times*.

In 1964 *Time* magazine named *The Minneapolis Tribune* as one of the ten best newspapers in the country and *Saturday Review* placed both papers in the top

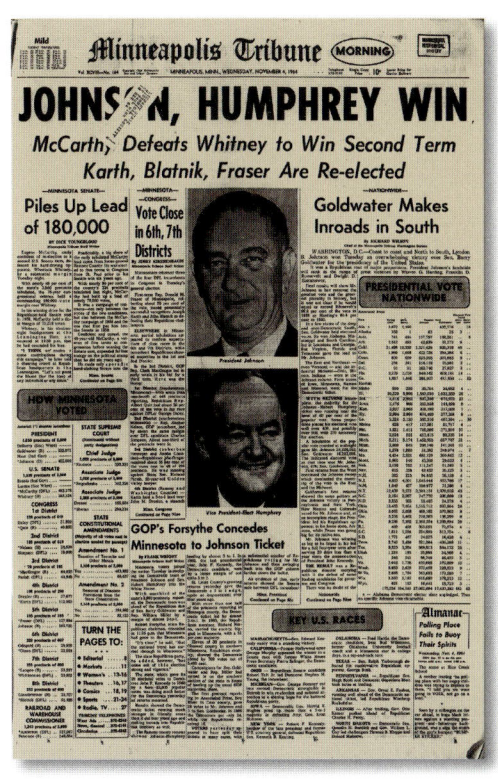

MINNEAPOLIS TRIBUNE,
NOVEMBER 4, 1964

JOHN COWLES JR., 1978

twenty. *Time* said: "Few newspapers work harder than *The Minneapolis Tribune* at expanding the boundaries of reader interest."³ *The Minneapolis Sunday Tribune* was repackaged with a new look which "brought favorable response from both readers and advertisers." John Cowles Jr., instituted *The Minneapolis Tribune*'s Science Reading Series which won the American Newspaper Publishers Association award as "Best Idea of the Year" in 1964.

Following the strike in 1962, there was renewed interest in diversification and acquisitions. Over the years the company had acquired real estate, both downtown adjacent to its plant and in the suburbs. In 1959 the company had acquired approximately 21 acres of land in the near western suburbs, at the intersection of two important highways. In 1963 an additional 30 acres were acquired and a joint venture to develop the land was formed with Baker Properties, a commercial real estate firm. The property was sold in 1974 after it had been fully developed. A large farm northwest of Minneapolis was also acquired in 1963, and held until the 1980s when surrounding suburban development made it necessary to develop a master plan for the property and begin a series of land sales that continue into the nineties. The downtown property — five contiguous square blocks — are used today principally for the newspaper operations and for employee parking.

While most of the diversification attention in the sixties was focused on newspapers, John Cowles Jr. was interested as well in other publishing opportunities. His father-in-law, Cass Canfield, was chairman of Harper & Brothers (later Harper & Row), the distinguished New York book publishing house. He discussed with Canfield the possibility of buying a periodical, and mentioned two or three magazines. Canfield countered with the suggestion that he consider buying stock in Harper & Row, and the company began acquiring stock in 1964.⁴ Earlier he had become acquainted with John Fischer, editor-in-chief of *Harper's Magazine*, which was owned by Harper & Brothers. At one point Fischer offered him a job there, a possibility he considered seriously, and which stimulated his interest in magazines.

As its book publishing business had grown, the ownership of the monthly magazine became somewhat peripheral, and Harper & Row became interested in selling it. In April 1965, the company became a joint owner of *Harper's*, with John Cowles Jr. as president. In describing the acquisition to shareholders he said that one of the practical benefits would be gaining operating experience in magazine publishing to supplement that in newspapering and broadcasting. (The company had no operational relationship with Cowles Magazines.) His father was skeptical of the acquisition, believing that it would not be profitable, and concerned that his son would be attracted

> "Few newspapers work harder than *The Minneapolis Tribune* at expanding the boundaries of reader interest."

HARPER & ROW, PUBLISHERS
New York
Hagerstown
San Francisco
London

1817

to New York. (In later years he urged Kingsley Murphy Jr., David Kruidenier and Luther Hill Jr., new outside directors, to consider selling the magazine.)[5]

The 1962 merger of Harper & Brothers with Row, Peterson was not working well, and in 1965 John Cowles Jr. was asked to join the board of directors. He had become acquainted with senior management during the negotiations setting up the new ownership structure for *Harper's* magazine, and they were impressed with him. Because he was well regarded by both the Harper and Peterson factions and regarded as impartial, he was able to assume a strong role on the board. It was on the Harper & Row board that he came to understand the important role of outside directors. He was instrumental in recruiting Winthrop Knowlton as president and in establishing the appropriate relationship between the board and management. John Cowles Jr. became chairman in 1968 and remained in that post until 1979. He left the board in 1981 when the company sold its stock in Harper & Row, which by then was 33 percent of the outstanding stock.

By 1969 the company had increased its ownership in the magazine from 50 to 100 percent, and taken a 16 percent interest in Harper & Row. The two then created Harper's Magazine Press as a joint enterprise. At the time John Cowles Jr. commented, "Our ownership of *Harper's* magazine, our participation in Harper's Magazine Press, and our investment in Harper & Row all may prove valuable to the Minneapolis Star and Tribune Company not only in future earnings but also in the cross-stimulation between the men and women publishing our newspapers, the magazine and books. We are seeking to expand the company's participation in the broadening business spectrum of communications, information and education."[6]

In 1966 he had talked about the future of communications, pointing out that the differences between what used to be "quote" separate and distinct media of communication were blurring and overlapping, that the clearly separated segments were becoming almost a continuum. He said, "(this) is why it is so important for our company to acquire practical operating experience in many different aspects of the communications business."[7]

The investment in *Harper's* did not pay off financially. Magazines that tapped into specific consumer interests — often around sports like skiing, tennis, or boating — were in the ascendancy, and there was less interest in the more general interest magazines, either intellectual or popular. It was during this time that the large circulation magazines like *Life, LOOK, Saturday Evening Post* and *Colliers* went under. In an attempt to create a larger audience, *Harper's* and *The Atlantic* formed a joint advertising sales venture, but neither the demographics nor the content were of strong interest to most media buyers. In 1967 Willie Morris was made editor-in-chief of *Harper's* magazine and began immediately to turn it into a "hot book" by paying higher fees and bringing in some of the most famous names in contemporary literature. Norman Mailer, William

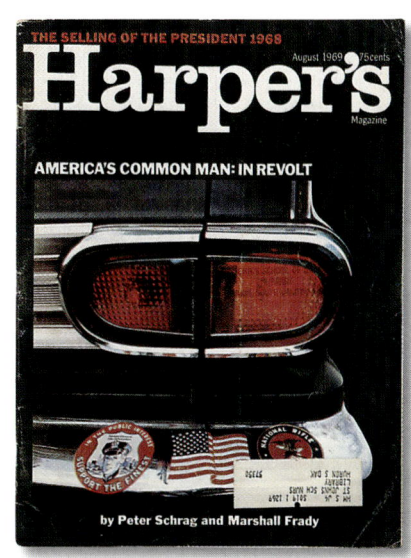

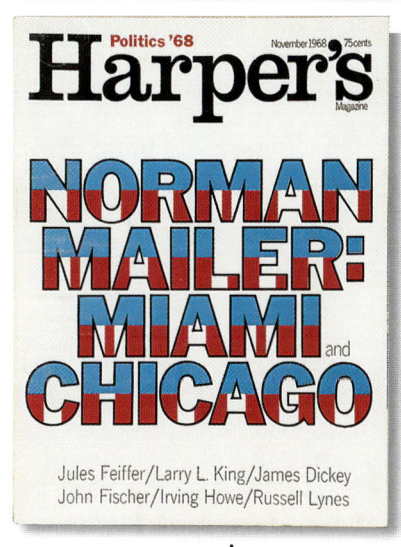

HARPER'S, NOVEMBER 1968, AUGUST 1969

Styron, Robert Penn Warren, George Plimpton, Truman Capote, Larry McMurtry and Philip Roth were among those who wrote for the magazine. The problem, however, was that while circulation rose, the losses continued. After three years, Cowles began insisting that the magazine be run on a more businesslike basis. In February 1971 — after a bitter and raucous meeting at The St. Regis Hotel in New York — Morris and most of his writers left the magazine, creating a great stir in the New York literary world, later fanned back to life occasionally by Morris in a new book.

BOWER HAWTHORNE, 1967

ROBERT W. SMITH, 1969

He was later succeeded by Lewis Lapham, who developed a distinctive, serious voice for the magazine, which won National Magazine and other prestigious awards. Renewal rates were high and rising, but circulation did not grow appreciably and the magazine — along with *The Atlantic* — was unable to attract advertisers in the numbers needed to turn a profit. In 1980, after talking with more than two dozen possible buyers, it was announced that *Harper's* would close. When the announcement was made, the magazine was acquired by a venture created by the then-new MacArthur Foundation and the Atlantic Richfield Foundation, and it became officially a nonprofit publication.

In 1967 the top news and editorial structure of the Minneapolis newspapers was reorganized. Bower Hawthorne had been executive editor for both newspapers since 1960, responsible for all news operations. He now became executive editor of *The Minneapolis Tribune*, with authority over both news and editorial content.

Robert W. Smith, previously editor of the editorial pages for both newspapers, was appointed executive editor of *The Minneapolis Star*. In announcing the changes, John Cowles Jr. emphasized that they were consistent with the objective of making each a separate, competitive and complete newspaper. He did not expect, he said, that the papers would differ sharply on major issues, but that they would frequently make different judgments about what was of interest and/or significance to the public and to that newspaper's readers.

The 1968 stockholders' meeting marked the formal changing of the guard. John Cowles Jr. succeeded his father as president and chief executive officer, and Otto A. Silha became publisher, succeeding Joyce Swan. John Cowles Sr. remained as chairman of the board; Swan was named vice-chairman and shortly afterwards became publisher of *The Rapid City Journal*. The new CEO took the occasion to talk about change — of reader styles and tastes, in the marketing of consumer products and services, of the technology of gathering and disseminating information. He said: "I believe that probably the most important characteristic that we shall have to reinforce within our Company is adaptability and responsiveness to change."

As president, John Cowles Jr. completed the separation of *The Minneapolis Star* and *The Minneapolis Tribune*, a process begun when he became editor, by making the editorial pages separate, each with its own editor. He could see that the tide was turning and that it was desirable for the two to compete by developing

"...WE ARE A THRIVING, GROWING COMPANY."

"We have prospered and grown because we have worked hard, have adapted our methods and our operations to changing conditions, and have been willing to take risks. And because our management under Father and Joyce (Swan) has been prudent as well as imaginative, our company is in healthy financial shape to tackle the new problems, the new opportunities and the new challenges in our society that will continue to confront us.

"Change is the hallmark of the world we live in today, and these characteristics of our newspaper and our company — namely, increasing productivity, adaptability to change, and willingness to experiment, to try something new, to take reasonable risks — will be needed more than ever in the years ahead.

"As your new president — only eight months in office — I do not want to mislead you with over-optimism. But I have worked directly with many of you during the past 15 years, and I know many more of you. Consequently, I am confident that we can keep this a thriving and growing company, with each of us taking increasing satisfaction and pleasure and pride both in our own jobs and in the contribution we know these newspapers and our company make, in a small way at least, to the welfare and happiness of all Americans."

John Cowles Jr.
Newsmakers
February 1969

OTTO SILHA, 1968

distinct personalities with separate, competitive staffs. The final step in the separation of the papers was Cowles' relinquishing the editor's title in 1969, and taking the new title of editorial chairman of the company. Hawthorne was named editor of *The Minneapolis Tribune* and Robert W. Smith, editor of *The Minneapolis Star;* each had been executive editor before. He explained that he was making the move because as president he was "no longer able to keep as well informed with news and editorial matters" as the editor should.[8]

The late sixties was a time of considerable social upheaval, when the issue of racial justice came to the fore. The company held "sensitivity" meetings in the summer of 1968 at which John Cowles Jr. outlined the company's policies. "The Star and the Tribune have editorially supported the concept of equal justice and equal opportunity for Negroes for many years; but within the past year it has become plain that the time has also come to act, not merely talk, within our own company."[9] He set the goal of doubling employment of black Americans by the end of the year — to 64 employees. (By that time there were 60 blacks and 17 other minorities.) He called for intensifying recruiting, adapting hiring standards, allowing department heads to exceed normal employment levels on a temporary basis. Other speakers at the meetings included Milton Williams, director of a North Side Minneapolis community center called The Way Unlimited. He spoke about black history and black power; he had earlier written a series of articles on African American history for *The Minneapolis Sunday Tribune.* Cowles himself was a founding member of the Minneapolis Urban Coalition, and the company was the first newspaper to participate in Project Equality. Progress on the hiring of minority employees was reported at subsequent annual stockholders' meetings. In 1970 the number had increased to 94 (of whom 73 were blacks) and by 1973 the number stood at 118. One of those was W. Harry Davis, who was hired as assistant to the publisher; minority employment was one of his assignments. A prominent leader in the black community, he had been president of the Urban Coalition and was chairman of the Minneapolis Board of Education.

The emphasis on racial justice was not new for the newspapers, but the times gave the issue a heightened sensibility. Elizabeth Bates Cowles had been a strong advocate for racial justice for years, and in 1948 published a landmark essay in the publication of the National Urban League. (See Appendix K.) She served as a board member of the Minneapolis Urban League for 15 years, was a vice-chairman of the United Negro College Fund, and received an award from the Minnesota-Dakota Conference

MINNEAPOLIS TRIBUNE JULY 3, 1964

ELIZABETH COWLES ARTICLE, OPPORTUNITY, WINTER, 1948

of the National Association for the Advancement of Colored People for her human rights activities in 1965. Morison quoted Cecil E. Newman, the editor of *The Minneapolis Spokesman* as saying, "You fellows on the Tribune keep beating me to the punch. I can't improve on many of your editorials championing the rights of Negroes, so I simply reprint them."[10]

In 1977 the Anti-Defamation League of B'nai B'rith presented its First Amendment Freedoms Award to John Cowles, John Cowles Jr., and the two newspapers for "outstanding dedication to the basic rights guaranteed a free people by the First Amendment to the Constitution of the United States." (See Appendix L.)

1 John Cowles Jr., "A Philosophy for Newspaper Publishing," (speech to *The Minneapolis Star and Tribune* Advertising Sales Conference), January 14, 1963.
2 "The Midwest's Nice Monopolists," *Harper's,* June, 1963, p. 73.
3 "The Press," *Time,* January 10, 1964, p. 59.
4 Cass Canfield, *Up & Down & Around* (New York: Harper's Magazine Press, 1971), p. 232.
5 Kingsley Murphy Jr., private interview, March 10, 1997, and Luther Hill, private interview, May 9, 1996.
6 "*Harper's* Magazine Enters Field of Book Publishing," *Newsmakers,* February, 1969, p. 5.
7 "Cowles States Views on Communications Future," *Newsmakers,* February, 1966, p. 6.
8 "Hawthorne and Smith Named VP's, Editors of *Tribune, Star*," *Newsmakers,* March, 1969, p. 1.
9 "Cowles Jr. Outlines Company's Minority Employment Policies," *Newsmakers,* July-August, 1968, p. 6.
10 Morison, *Sunlight on Your Doorstep,* p. 109.

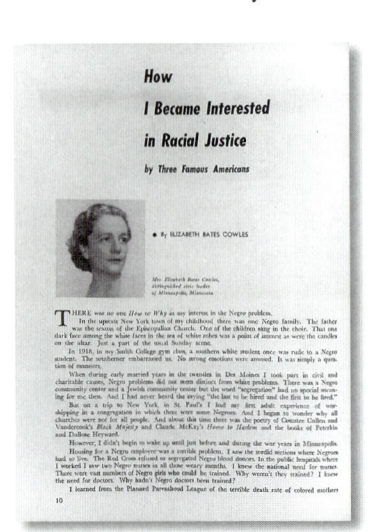

A DECADE OF CHANGE

16

THE DIVERSIFICATION ACTIVITY of the late sixties and seventies differed in focus from earlier efforts. The company acquired an additional television outlet, two groups of weekly suburban newspapers, and eventually a large daily newspaper and cable television system.

Several changes in executive responsibilities were linked to the company's emerging growth strategy. In February 1969, John Cowles Jr. relinquished his role as editor and became editorial director, a new position removed from direct operating responsibilities. The following February, Gale Freeman (then industrial relations director) was made vice president for operations; Philip VonBlon was made vice president for finance and environment with responsibility for investments, real estate, *Harper's,* and "matters of environmental concern"; and Robert Witte was shifted from vice president and business manager to what were described as "largely corporate duties." Cowles explained: "These changes will strengthen the team responsible for the publication of the two Minneapolis newspapers, and at the same time will strengthen the company's capabilities for growth throughout the wide spectrum of activities associated with publishing, communications and education."

Late in 1968 an agreement was reached for the sale of the Wichita television station to the Oklahoma Publishing Company for $4.4 million. The reasons cited for the sale were the satisfactory price, the need for substantial capital outlays for the newspapers both in Minneapolis and in Rapid City and Great Falls, and the fact that the company was interested in other segments of the communications business. There was also reluctance to engage in a business heavily regulated by the government. The Federal Communications Commission challenged the sale on antitrust grounds and the sale agreement was permitted to expire. At the same time, the commission was considering the renewal of licenses for WCCO television and radio (in which the company had a 47 percent ownership), amid concerns about new ground rules regarding overlapping media ownership in a market.

In 1971 the company acquired 15 weekly community

THE MINNEAPOLIS TRIBUNE, JULY 21, 1969

newspapers in the Denver metropolitan area, with a circulation of 150,000, and created Community Publications Company. They were joined two years later by a similar group of 12 papers in the Baltimore area with a circulation of approximately 80,000, Stromberg Publications. In New York, the company had acquired an opinion polling firm, then a promotion firm, and an interest in a country music magazine. *Harper's* launched *Harper's Weekly* and a biweekly book publishing newsletter. *Harper's Weekly* was actually a biweekly revival of a publication made famous by its reporting of the Civil War, including engravings by Winslow Homer. The contemporary version was notable in that it was to be written entirely by readers.

By 1975 the weekly newspapers accounted for six percent of revenue. The next year *The Great Falls Tribune* bought two small newspapers in Idaho, the company increased its ownership in Harper & Row to 39 percent, and acquired a UHF television in Louisville for $6.5 million. The company had also invested over $20 million in new technology and facilities to improve efficiency in existing operations, including an electronic news system for the Minneapolis papers and an automated newsprint warehouse adjacent to the downtown plant. The warehouse was clad in Cor-Ten steel, a new material that formed an oxidized surface giving it a rusted appearance, puzzling to some.

In 1974 the company joined with IBM and seven

THE STAR AND TRIBUNE NEWSPRINT WAREHOUSE, 1982

COMPUTER COMPOSITION, 1968

other newspaper organizations to develop a computerized full page composition system, which would permit the news and advertising copy, photographs and graphics to be transmitted directly to a film for conversion to printing plates. The project was indicative of the investments the company made almost continuously in new technology. While the project itself was not completely successful, it was the basis for the electronic news system and — indirectly — strategic changes in labor negotiations.

An unplanned diversification move was triggered by a lawsuit filed in 1975 by Sun Newspapers, Inc., publishers of a group of suburban weekly newspapers in the Twin Cities. Their principal owner, Carroll E. Crawford, had acquired a number of papers in 1967 from John Tilton and then purchased others until the group included 17 weeklies. (Tilton's financial partner in the venture had been James Ford Bell, who acquired some of the papers in the late 1950s.) The lawsuit alleged that the Minneapolis and the St. Paul newspapers had engaged in anti-competitive activities in violation of antitrust laws. The company had long been cautious about possible antitrust matters as a result of its leading place in the market. It had not developed substantial circulation in St. Paul, principally because that city remained quite separate from Minneapolis both socially and economically.

Discovery continued until January 1978 when a

settlement was reached. The Minneapolis Star and Tribune Company agreed to purchase all outstanding shares of Sun Newspapers. Crawford was the majority stockholder, but the deal was contingent on all shares being acquired, and he was unable to get agreement from holders of 14 percent. The largest of these was Scott Donaldson, the former owner-publisher of *The Bloomington Sun,* who eventually agreed to sell in September.

THE MINNEAPOLIS STAR AND TRIBUNE COMPANY PURCHASED THE SUN NEWSPAPERS INC. IN 1978

The agreement provided that the 17 newspapers be sold by Sun through an independent broker, after which the company would assume ownership of the real estate and the commercial printing and community directory businesses. In November, the papers were sold for just over $1 million to a group of investors headed by Elmer L. Andersen, owner of the Princeton (MN) weekly newspaper, and a former governor of Minnesota. The U. S. Department of Justice found no objection to the settlement and it was completed. The suit was dismissed with prejudice and on the merits. A few days later a local businessman sued to void the sale, on the basis that he was legally entitled to buy the papers. His suit was dismissed by a Hennepin County District Court judge who ruled that he had no contract. The suit was appealed and finally terminated in 1986. As a result of the settlement, the company found itself in the business of printing newspaper advertising inserts and community telephone directories, adding to the number and diversity of its operating units.

One of the notable events of the seventies was the 1976 sale of the company's interest in Midwest Radio-Television (WCCO). That year Ridder Publications, which included the St. Paul newspapers, merged with the Knight newspapers. Knight-Ridder announced that it would sell their broadcasting operations in markets where it also owned newspapers. (Since 1974 the U. S. Department of Justice had urged the FCC not to renew licenses for WCCO because of "the high degree of concentration in the dissemination of local news and advertising"; the two newspaper companies [Cowles and Ridder] together accounted for 73.5 percent of the ownership.) That meant the sale of the Ridders' 26.5 percent interest in Midwest Radio-Television, owner of WCCO radio and television. The radio station started life as WLAC in 1922 and was purchased by the Washburn Crosby Company. The call letters were changed to WCCO and the "Gold Medal Station" went on the air October 1, 1924. In 1929, the company, by then General Mills, sold a one-third interest to William S. Paley, who was starting the Columbia Broadcasting System. The same year WCCO was awarded one of 40 "clear channel" frequencies, and in 1932 CBS purchased the remaining two-thirds. The CBS radio station was merged with Minnesota Broadcasting Company (owned by the Murphy's Minnesota Tribune Company and the Ridders) to form Midwest Radio-Television in 1952.

Knight-Ridder sold its 26.5 percent interest to the Minnesota Tribune Company, owner of the other 26.5 percent. Cowles exchanged the company's 47 percent interest in Midwest

THE MINNEAPOLIS STAR AND TRIBUNE COMPANY
(FISCAL 1970–1980)

REVENUE

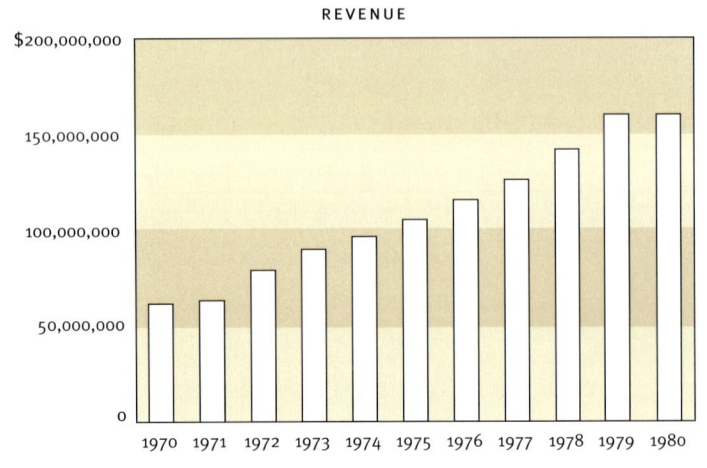

NET EARNINGS

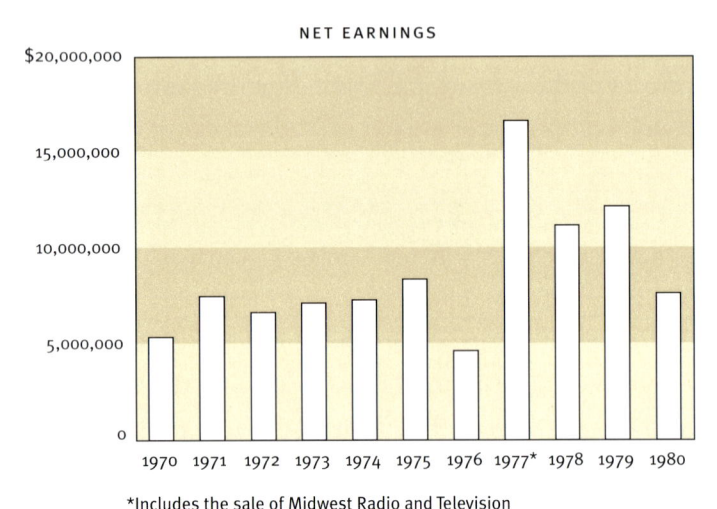

*Includes the sale of Midwest Radio and Television

Radio-Television for the stock in the company that the Minnesota Tribune Company had held since the merger in 1941, plus $1 million in cash. After 35 years the company had eliminated one large minority stockholder and ended the broadcast ownership position it had worked so hard to achieve during the forties. John Cowles Jr. reported that his father was delighted with the transaction, and he told stockholders that year: "The purchase of 47 percent of WCCO in 1954 has turned out to be one of Father's best investments."[1]

In 1977, the company's attention again turned to daily newspapers, this time large metropolitan newspapers. *The Oakland Tribune* was considered when it came on the market. After an initial review, the board voted not to make an offer. It was bought by Combined Communications. The same year, John Cowles Jr. and others made visits to *The Tacoma News Tribune*, whose owner was considering a sale. No offer was made. The paper was sold several years later to McClatchy Newspapers.

The economic climate of the 1970s was far different from the earlier postwar period. Over the decade real growth of the economy dropped one percentage point, from 3.8 to 2.8 percent average annual growth rate. 1970 was a recession year, and the recession of 1973-75 was the sharpest since the thirties. Perhaps worst of all was the rapid inflation, much of it traceable to the "energy crisis" of the early seventies. Cost escalations had begun in the late sixties in part because of inflationary pressures from the Vietnam war, but also in large measure due to labor settlements. In the mid-sixties there was some improvement in productivity as measured by payroll cost per page, but that was reversed by the 1969 settlements. Payroll costs increased 17.5 percent and job dividends 20.9 percent during the twelve months ended February 1970. Newsprint cost was up almost ten percent during the same period. John Cowles Jr. told stockholders in May 1970 that during the past four years the Minneapolis newspapers added more than $16 million in revenue, none of which had been converted to earnings.

At the annual meeting of stockholders in 1973 financial results were announced for the first time. In previous years these reports had included advertising and circulation figures, job dividends, payroll, employment, and productivity numbers — but financial information in dollar terms had been a closely guarded secret. Balance sheet information was added in 1976. Salaries of the top three officers were announced in 1977 and quarterly earnings reports begun. Cowles commented: "We have no plan to take the company 'public,' but we continue to believe that many of the disciplines and reporting requirements for publicly held companies are, on the whole, beneficial also for private companies like ours."[2] He also believed that the company should be as public in its disclosures as those businesses its papers reported on.

In spite of the economic climate, financial performance improved during the seventies with a great growth in classified advertising and advertising supplement inserts. From fiscal year 1972 (the 12 months ended in February) though fiscal year 1979 revenue more than doubled from $78.8 to $162.5 million and net earnings increased from $6.7 to $12.2 million. (The FY'72 figures included income from WCCO; a comparable increase would have been more than double.) From FY'72 to FY'75 the operating margin dropped from 5.6 percent to 5.0 percent, well below the industry average. Margins then began to improve steadily to 6.1 percent in FY'79, but still below the company's goal of 7.5 percent. Return on stockholder equity had reached 16.2 percent, higher than either Knight-Ridder or The New York Times Company.[3] The balance sheet in FY'75 showed total assets of $76.9 million and stockholders' equity of $58.7 million, with no long term debt. By FY'79 assets had grown to $114 million and stockholders' equity to $75.2 million.

By 1972, other management and board changes were

MINNEAPOLIS TRIBUNE
APRIL 30, 1975

developing. Robert W. Smith and Gale Freeman were appointed associate publishers of *The Minneapolis Star* and *Tribune* newspapers, as part of a continuing executive development program intended to provide greater flexibility and 'back-up' at the senior management level. The change also permitted Publisher Otto Silha to take on increasing corporate responsibilities. Bower Hawthorne was made vice president for public affairs, a new corporate post, and Charles Bailey, former chief of *The Minneapolis Tribune*'s Washington Bureau replaced him as editor of *The Minneapolis Tribune*.

The company had long been a leader in corporate responsibility, both through its giving programs and participation of its senior management in community organizations and projects. Together with The Dayton Company, the company began in the forties a practice of contributing to charity five percent of its pretax profits. John Cowles and Bruce Dayton worked closely on questions about appropriate levels of support for various organizations, and they led giving by business community. John Cowles Jr. used Hawthorne's appointment in 1972 to underscore the company's civic commitment. He said that the new post "reflects our belief that helping improve the social, economic and physical environment wherever a company does business is a major obligation of that company as well as a matter of long-range self-interest." (See Appendix M.)

David Kruidenier, president of the Des Moines

Register and Tribune Company was elected a director of the company in 1972. His mother, Florence, was an older sister of John and Mike Cowles. He was followed in 1973 by Kingsley H. Murphy Jr., whose father was a director from 1941 to 1953; his grandfather, W. J. Murphy, had acquired *The Minneapolis Tribune* in the 1890s. Kruidenier and Murphy were the first outside directors in 20 years, each representing significant minority stock ownership. In the case of Kruidenier, a grandson of Gardner Cowles and cousin of John Cowles Jr., that interest was the Register and Tribune Company's 11.3 percent stock ownership. Murphy himself held a 12.7 percent ownership interest, which dated from the time of the merger with the Tribune Company in 1941; an additional 14.7 percent was owned separately by the Minnesota Tribune Company controlled by his relatives. The next year Luther L. Hill Jr., a Des Moines lawyer and board member of the Register and Tribune Company, and Publisher Robert Smith became directors. Hill's father had been publisher of the Des Moines newspapers and actively involved in their broadcast operations.

John Cowles Sr. announced his retirement as chairman of the company in 1973, choosing the annual dinner of the Twenty Year Club on February 25 as the occasion for his announcement. He extended his gratitude to the 500 members of the Twenty Year Club as the backbone of the institution. He had then served as either president or chairman for 38 years, and noted the infirmities of old age. He quoted a line from Rudyard Kipling that he had learned from his father: "It ain't the individual nor the army as a whole, but the everlasting teamwork of every blooming soul." (See Appendix N.) He also paid tribute to Joyce Swan: "… none was more dedicated or effective than Joyce in helping build The Star and Tribune into the institution it has become."

John Cowles Jr. succeeded his father as chairman, and Otto Silha became president. Robert W. Smith was named publisher of the Minneapolis newspapers, Howard Mithun retired as general counsel, Joyce Swan retired as vice chairman and was succeeded in that office by David Kruidenier. Swan was succeeded as president of the Rapid City Journal Company by his son, James W. "Rusty" Swan, who had become publisher in 1971. A new generation of management had been established and outside directors now represented significant ownership. The board established a compensation committee to set executive compensation, and formally outlined the duties and responsibilities of the top officers and the board.

In 1975, Smith informed John Cowles Jr. confidentially that he would like to retire (early) as publisher sometime in 1976. Cowles hired an executive search firm to find a replacement and, in October of 1975, Donald R. Dwight was hired as associate publisher and vice president, the first senior manager to be hired from outside the company since Philip VonBlon in 1961. (VonBlon left the company in 1970.) A former Republican lieutenant-governor of Massachusetts, Dwight had been general manager of *The Holyoke* (MA) *Transcript-Telegram* and was an officer and director of Newspapers of New England, a company owned by his family.

In announcing Dwight's appointment, Smith said that the move "completes the restructuring of the publisher's office for the present." Dwight was to be responsible for the news and advertising department, while the other operations remained with Gale Freeman, the only other person in the newspapers who knew of Smith's plans. Two months later, in December 1975, Smith died of a heart attack at 59. Silha

DONALD DWIGHT, 1980

resumed the title of publisher until the next annual meeting, May of 1976, when Dwight was named publisher and Freeman, general manager. Dwight was also elected a director, along with John B. Davis Jr., president of Macalester College in St. Paul, and Lois Cowles Harrison, a daughter of Mike Cowles, and Winthrop Knowlton, president and CEO of Harper & Row.

When Dwight was hired, John Cowles Jr. gave him three major challenges: management structure, labor and cost structure, and *The Minneapolis Star*. A series of organizational changes had resulted in many executives being in positions and functional areas with which they were not familiar. Productivity had continued to decline in spite of continuing investment in new technology and equipment, and the cost of newsprint (25 percent of all expenses) had increased over two years by 40 percent, to $260 per ton. The energy crisis was creating significant economic dislocations. Circulation of all the papers had been dropping slowly, in part because of the need to reduce distant circulation, but was especially worrisome in the afternoon; like most evening papers, its circulation was dropping more significantly.

A program of "lateral movement" was instituted in the summer of 1973 to increase understanding of inter- and intra-departmental problems. Employees were moved on temporary assignment to other departments. Some shifts included the editor of *The Minneapolis Star* becoming vice president for advertising; the operations director

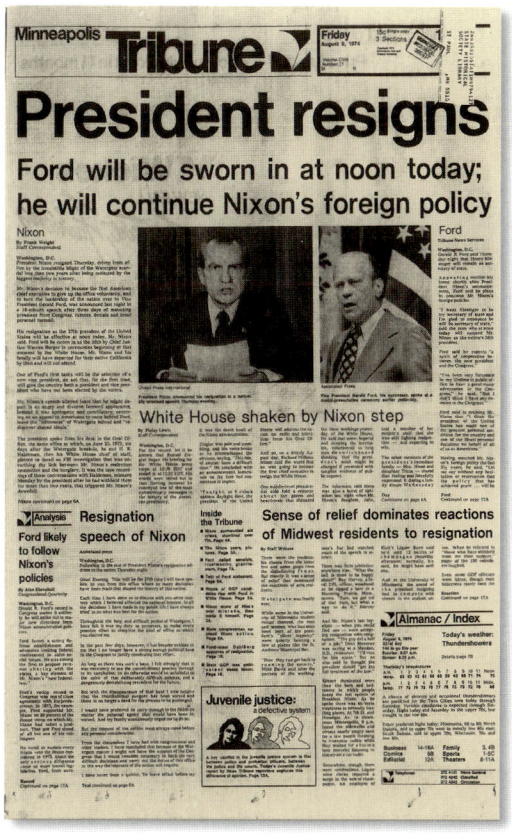

MINNEAPOLIS TRIBUNE
AUGUST 9, 1974

became executive editor; the executive editor became assistant to the publisher with responsibilities for press project planning and then to promotion; the marketing director became operations director. These changes resulted in numerous others in the next level of the organization. As Dwight characterized the situation in the 1976 annual report: "Unquestionably a certain amount of confusion was created. Top managers were learning new assignments under front line conditions. Yet the goal of breaking down ancient walls between departments is being achieved and vitality is also apparent."

One of the legacies of the 1962 strike was a strong reluctance to take another strike, significantly reducing management's leverage in negotiations. Between fiscal 1963 and 1972 there had been progress in holding — and reducing in the case of stereotyping and the mailroom — hours required to produce a page, one measure used to gauge productivity. Payroll cost per page, however, had increased over 50 percent in both the composing department and the pressroom, with a 25 percent increase in the mailroom.

In 1975 and 1976 many managers and nonunion employees in advertising and other departments began receiving training in production at the industry-sponsored SPPI (Southern Production Program, Inc.) facility in Oklahoma City. The training concentrated on composition, press and plate-making, so that they could help supervisory production personnel put out a paper in case of a strike. Newspapers had generally been unwilling or unable to publish during a strike, but in 1975, after violence in the pressroom, *The Washington Post* was able to continue publishing during a long strike, using management and supervisory personnel. The industry began to revise its thinking.

An innovative labor contract was negotiated with the typographical union, representing the Printers, in 1975. As the result of technological advances it had become possible to eliminate the "double keyboarding" of material going into the paper, a practice whereby all copy was entered first by a clerical person in advertising or by a reporter in the newsroom, then retyped into a Linotype machine by a printer. Under existing labor law, the company had the ability to eliminate workers whose jobs were no longer needed.

The International Typographers Union was well aware of what changing technology could mean for its members, and was interested in having a contract that would meet both their needs as well as those of the company. The result was a precedent-setting negotiation in which the company received full freedom to automate and assign work required by the new technology. The union received a guarantee of lifetime jobs for 361 full-time and 28 part-time printers, with the number of jobs to be reduced by attrition and buyouts to a minimum of 130, i.e. a "floor" for the future size of the union itself. The Printers also agreed to tie their compensation to that of other unions in the plant. The ten-year contract was the first in the local union's 103 year history to be longer than three years.

At the Star and Tribune Company, a practice had developed in contract negotiations — usually on a two- or three-year cycle — in which the last union to sign held out for more than the others; thus effectively undercutting the "plant pattern" at the expense of those unions that had created or followed the pattern. In 1976, this history of pattern and then pattern-breaking began to change when the Teamsters negotiated a wage package and also agreed that they would support a strike of another union only up to the level of the wage increase given to the Teamsters, but not beyond that level.

In late 1978, the 18-member Machinists union, the last to settle, suddenly struck, rejecting the pattern that had been established in what were described as lengthy, strenuous and sometimes bitter negotiations. No other unions endorsed the strike, and one criticized the machinists for giving no warnings to other unions of their strike plans. Few union workers were willing to cross the picket lines, even though they generally felt that the issues did not warrant a strike. One local union official characterized the position as "very dumb" and said that the unsettled issues were "not the kind you shut down the Minneapolis Star and Tribune Company over." There was violence one night — roughing up Gale Freeman, the general manager of the papers, and damaging trucks and other vehicles. For the first time in its history the company produced newspapers with its mechanical unions on strike and the Newspaper Guild honoring the picket lines. With the Teamsters willing to report to work, the strike collapsed after four days.[4]

The next round of contract negotiations was in 1980. That year the Mailers and the Guild went on strike on September 13 and did not return until October 10. The Teamsters "sat out" the strike with no commitment, and were not drawing strike benefits since they were technically not on strike, only honoring the picket line. They concluded that the company was not being unfair and told the Guild that they would cross the picket line if the Guild did not settle because they did not want to get into an all-out war if the company brought in drivers from other cities, which Dwight was ready to do. During the strike management and non-union employees alternated publishing the two daily papers, although in an abbreviated version. They were sold from the plant, about 6,000 daily and 25,000 on Sundays. If the Teamsters were to cross the picket line, the company would possibly have been willing and able to publish indefinitely and hire replacement workers, as *The Washington Post* had done.

The 1980 strike had four important results: (1) further consolidation of the plant pattern concept being applicable to each union covered by it, regardless of the sequence of settlements; (2) recognition that the company would no longer avoid strikes to keep labor peace, (3) confirmation of the company's ability to publish under strike conditions and (4) recognition of a willingness to distribute papers during a strike. The Mailers signed a three-year contract that produced vital productivity gains. Guild members accepted the same economic contract that was offered to them on the day they voted to strike, and the accepted terms were consistent with those already accepted by other unions.

The Guild had struck in part over issues of electronic work jurisdiction rights, and the ability of the company to "re-sell" previously published material from the newspaper to electronic media. The newspapers had joined the Associated Press and eleven other newspapers in an experimental electronic delivery of news to customers through CompuServe, and Guild members wanted extra compensation based on profits of such a venture; that demand was dropped.

1 Minneapolis Star and Tribune Company, *Annual Report,* Fiscal 1976.
2 Minneapolis Star and Tribune Company, *Annual Report,* Fiscal 1977.
3 "Annual Report Shows Earnings Up 19%," *Newsmakers,* June 1978, p. 1.
4 "18-Member Union Strikes Star and Tribune Co.," *The Minneapolis Star,* December 4, 1978, p. 1A.

MERGER

17

THE SEPARATION OF THE company and the newspapers was made dramatically clear in the spring of 1979 when the corporate headquarters was moved nine blocks to the IDS Center. The official announcement said: "The establishment of separate corporate headquarters will emphasize physically the operational independence of The Minneapolis Star and Tribune newspapers under Publisher Donald R. Dwight. At the same time, this move will aid those of us in corporate management to focus more intensely on emerging business opportunities separate from the Minneapolis newspapers." Some fifty people in the legal, public affairs, financial, and affiliate operations (the subsidiaries) departments were involved. As John Cowles Jr. described it: "One of our reasons for making the move is to get out of old habits," referring to the fact that many members of top management had once held similar jobs at the newspapers and still took a keen interest in operation of the papers. He went on to say that as the company moved from having one profit center to multiple profit centers (there were then seven outside the Twin Cities) the character of top management "has to change."[1] Moving corporate headquarters from the newspaper building was also intended to reinforce the fact that John Cowles Jr. did not interfere in news and editorial decisions, a fact which many people did not believe but which was a policy established first by Gardner Cowles Sr. in Des Moines.

In 1977, at the urging of Kenneth Dayton, then the CEO of Dayton Hudson Corporation, Cowles had assumed chairmanship of the Stadium Site Task Force of the Minneapolis Chamber of Commerce, a group charged with finding financing for a new domed football/baseball stadium in downtown Minneapolis. There was significant controversy about the stadium itself, and — in the newsrooms — about the appropriateness of the chairman of the newspaper company leading the effort. On March 1, 1979, a group of 45 employees placed an ad in *The Minneapolis Tribune* stating that their professional principles had not been undermined by Cowles' involvement, that he had not tried to influence *The Minneapolis Tribune*'s coverage, but that

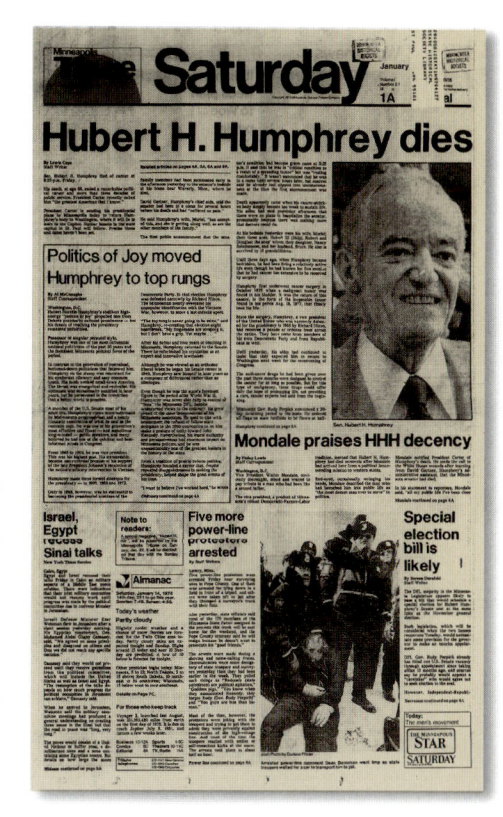

MINNEAPOLIS TRIBUNE, JANUARY 14, 1978

management should avoid a leadership role in sensitive political and economic issues. The task force raised almost $15 million to acquire the site and ensure that the facility would be in downtown Minneapolis. About one-third of the total was contributed by the Minneapolis Star and Tribune Company in cash and land. The site was turned over to the Metropolitan Sports Stadium Commission, the agency created by the legislature to build and operate the new stadium.

On September 21, 1979, John Cowles Jr. announced that he would become president of the company, retaining the CEO title, and that Otto Silha would be chairman. Cowles was to oversee the Minneapolis newspapers, all other operating units except those in Buffalo, and the corporate staff. Silha was given responsibility for the board of directors, new acquisitions, *Harper's* magazine, and the newly acquired newspaper and cable television system in Buffalo. The switch was puzzling to many, described by Cowles as "slightly unconventional." He believed that it was desirable to separate the governance function of the chairman from the management responsibility of the CEO. Most important, it permitted him to work directly with operating management, including Dwight, whom he had hired and who was considered his potential successor. Ten years older than Cowles, Silha would be moving toward retirement.

Cowles was concerned about strengthening his management team, particularly the need for sophisticated financial management and the ability to bring about change. In 1980, a search began for someone who would bring those skills and a business executive whose experience was outside the newspaper industry. He selected David C. Cox, whose background was in large consumer product companies, and gave him direct responsibility for the corporate staff and for all the operating units except those in Minneapolis and Buffalo. Cox was introduced to Cowles by Dwight, who had worked with him on the board of the Guthrie Theater. Both were named executive vice presidents, a strong indication that a new management team was in place.[2] Cox was 43, Dwight, 49, and Cowles, 51.

Cowles recognized that he needed more profitability, and Cox brought the business discipline to do that. There was a clear need for a meaningful budgeting system and the business processes to implement a financial plan.

MINNEAPOLIS SKYLINE, SHOWING
THE HUBERT H. HUMPHREY METRODOME, 1993

THE IDS TOWER,
MINNEAPOLIS, 1978

DAVID C. COX, 1980

Cox took responsibility for developing such a system for all operating units, not just those reporting to him. Past meetings with operating units had not focused adequately on financial performance; after a few such meetings Cox told operating management "don't come in for another meeting unless you talk about profit." Prior to setting the annual budget itself, Cox instituted budget objectives — operating managers' best estimates of their performance, based on specified assumptions about their market, cost structure, marketing tactics, etc. When the first budget objectives were presented in the fall of 1981 it was clear that they were not adequate, and that alternatives had to be developed. That, in turn, set the stage for significant changes throughout the organization. The discipline Cowles had sought was beginning to take hold.

In 1977, *The Kansas City Star* was sold to Capital Cities Communications. The sale raised the awareness of other independent, privately held newspaper companies around the country, because that newspaper was owned by its employees and thought unlikely to come on the market. That same year differences within the Knowland family led to the sale of their *Oakland Tribune*. Some family members involved in management had complained that the paper was being run more for civic pride than for profit. Three generations of Knowlands had been U. S. Senators, and had used the newspaper as their power base. Barry Bingham Jr., publisher of the Louisville newspapers, was quoted as saying that the idea of family-owned newspapers in the future was not probable.[3] There were over two dozen major newspaper mergers and acquisitions during the seventies. The informal family relationships that had traditionally governed the ownership of the newspapers in Minneapolis and Des Moines had always been assumed adequate to assure family control. John and Mike Cowles had discussed the possibility of a voting trust or other arrangement to assure control, but had never pursued the matter. Ownership in the Des Moines company was becoming more dispersed among the descendents of the six children of Gardner Cowles Sr., few of whom lived in Iowa or had any ties to the newspapers.

The Des Moines management and several principal stockholders engaged as a consultant A. James Casner, a professor of law at Harvard, to advise them on setting up a mechanism to help assure continued family control of the Des Moines Register and Tribune Company. In 1978 a Voting Trust Agreement was completed and signed by over 60 stockholders, most of them members of the Cowles family, and by the Des Moines Register and Tribune Company itself. Voting rights for their shares were to be exercised by the five trustees — David Kruidenier, John Cowles Jr., Luther L. Hill Jr., Morley Cowles Ballantine, and Michael Gartner. The first three were also directors of the then Minneapolis Star and Tribune Company; Ballantine was the daughter of John Cowles and Gartner was president of the Register and Tribune Company, which was a party to the agreement.

At the end of 1978 a suit was filed in U. S. District court by members of the family of Harry T. Watts, a former employee of the company; they held 1.49 percent of the Register and Tribune Company's stock. The suit sought to bar establishment of the trust and asked remedies also on several other points. (It would be settled in 1984.)

In 1980, a separate, much simpler voting trust was established in Minneapolis, where family ownership was concentrated among John Cowles and his four children.

The company was not party to that agreement. The trustees were John Cowles Jr., Luther L. Hill Jr., David Kruidenier, Morley Cowles Ballantine, and Lois Cowles Harrison, a daughter of Gardner Cowles Jr. All but Harrison were also trustees of the Des Moines Register and Tribune Company Trust. Cowles, Hill and Kruidenier were directors of both companies, Harrison was on the board in Minneapolis and Ballantine in Des Moines. By 1982 approximately 39 percent of the company's voting stock was held by the John Cowles family voting trust; in Des Moines 51 percent of that company's voting stock was held in the Des Moines Register and Tribune Company voting trust.

In spite of having overlapping ownership and some directors in common, the Des Moines and Minneapolis companies had operated independently over the years. In 1978, as the Des Moines management was eager to grow the business, they approached the Minneapolis company with two possible joint investment opportunities. The first was *The Everett (Washington) Herald*, the second a group of radio stations based in Denver. The two companies agreed to pursue the acquisition of *The Herald* together, on a 50-50 basis, at a price not to exceed $25 million. The bid was not accepted and the paper was acquired by The Washington Post Company. The radio acquisition was not of interest in Minneapolis, and the Register and Tribune Company then bought it for $27.7 million. In 1980 the boards of the two companies met concurrently

THE DES MOINES REGISTER, SEPTEMBER 10, 1981

for two days at a resort in Illinois.

By 1981, earnings in both companies were down sharply, largely because of the recession that was especially severe in the Midwest. Both had taken on significant debt to finance acquisitions — approximately $40 million in Des Moines and $30 million in Minneapolis. In Des Moines, interest expense was $4.4 million and operating earnings only $4.1 million. On August 7, 1981, the Minneapolis Star and Tribune Company loaned the Register and Tribune Company $2.3 million at the prime rate plus 1/4 percent, then almost 19 percent. In connection with the loan, a merger of the two companies was also discussed and continuing discussions authorized.

The Des Moines Tribune carried the story on August 11, 1981, following a meeting of the Register and Tribune board, saying that the merger idea was triggered by a suggestion of Michael Gartner, president of that company, that it sell a portion of the stock it held in the Minneapolis company to help reduce debt. According to the story, one attraction of merging the two companies was that the combined company could more easily develop a public market for its stock, helping provide greater liquidity for shareholders and permitting acquisitions using stock instead of cash. The story went on to quote "board sources" as saying that the plan gave Minneapolis executives too much power in the merged company, and that Gartner would be given a "top executive position" in the merged company while maintaining control of

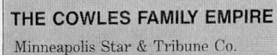

BUSINESS WEEK ARTICLE
DECEMBER 7, 1981

the Des Moines newspapers. A preliminary merger agreement had been approved by the board in Minneapolis, but the Des Moines board deferred action. On August 13, John Cowles Jr. and David Kruidenier announced a suspension for two or three weeks, saying that participants at both companies needed a "breather."[4] Annual revenue for the Minneapolis company was then about $237 million and total assets about $130 million; in Des Moines revenue was then $89 million and total assets $81 million.

On September 9, an agreement in principle for a merger was announced, subject to a definitive agreement on terms and approval by shareholders and relevant regulatory bodies, expected early in 1982. Cowles was to be chairman and CEO; Kruidenier, president; and Silha, vice-chairman. Headquarters were to be in Minneapolis with Dwight and Cox joined as executive vice presidents by Gartner and Gary Gerlach (then executive vice president and general counsel in Des Moines). The announcement said that the combined company did not plan to offer stock to the public initially, but that a secondary public market was anticipated. (See Appendix O.) Kruidenier was quoted as saying that the new company would provide a strong financial basis that would mean "continued strong, quality, independent journalism in Iowa." He also said that the Cowles family would maintain control.[5] Each company hired investment bankers to determine the values to be used in the transaction.

An article in *Business Week* characterized the proposed merger more bluntly with the headline "Cowles consolidates to survive."[6] In February, the Des Moines merger committee voted unanimously to end the merger talks, reportedly because of disagreements over values to be assigned to the properties to be combined and, hence, the exchange ratio for their stock. Cowles said he was greatly disappointed because "the two companies have a great deal of common ownership and share very similar objectives."[7] Shortly thereafter Katherine Graham, chairman of The Washington Post Company, visited Kruidenier in Des Moines. According to Gartner, "She said the Washington Post would be interested in buying the Des Moines Register and Tribune Company, but he told her the company wasn't for sale."[8]

In August 1982, the Register and Tribune Company announced that its shares would be sold on the open market for the first time. It also announced the closing of the afternoon *Des Moines Tribune* in September and the sale of two radio stations in Denver for $9 million. The company sustained a loss of $816,000 for 1982, which it attributed to costs of closing the afternoon *Des Moines Tribune* and the poor Iowa economy.

1 "Inside John Cowles Jr.," *Corporate Report,* April 1979, p. 42.
2 An article in *Minnesota Monthly* (July 1991) suggested that Cowles had thought about retiring early, hence his emphasis on building the organization.
3 Benjamin M. Compaine, *Who Owns the Media* (White Plains, N.Y.: Knowledge Industry Publications, Inc., 1979), p. 33.
4 Minneapolis Star & Tribune Company, news release, August 13, 1981.
5 "Minneapolis, R&T Papers Plan Merger," *The Des Moines Register,* September 10, 1981, p. 1.
6 "Cowles Consolidates to Survive," *Business Week,* December 7, 1981, p. 100.
7 "Des Moines Papers Call Off Merger Proposal," *The Minneapolis Tribune,* February 7, 1981.
8 "Washington Post Co. Rebuffed Over Offer to Buy Des Moines Register & Tribune Co.," *The Wall Street Journal,* March 1, 1982, p. 15.

SOMETHING OF A GAMBLE

18

BY 1981, IT WAS CLEAR to Dwight that fundamental changes would be required to achieve needed levels of profitability. He said: "A look at other newspaper companies around the country is instructive. They operate in the same economy and the same competitive environment as we do, yet their profit margins are appreciably healthier. Something's out of kilter here." He characterized the newspapers as overweight, slow moving, uncompetitive and paternalistic, and concluded that there was no choice but to change. He pointed out that "we manufacture, sell and distribute 15 percent fewer newspapers than we did 10 years ago and distribute in a smaller geographic area." Yet, total employment had increased from 2,473 to 2,864, with all but 100 of the increase in part-time people.

He then went on to describe a "Plan for the 80s." In it he said: "The consequence could be a change in a fundamental news and marketing strategy of the newspapers: the end of total differentiation." This marked a distinct change from the concept of two totally separate, competitive newspapers. He proposed combining the business sections and speculated that food and entertainment sections could follow, eventually leaving only the basic news sections separate and differentiated as they had always been. He reviewed the economic structure of the business: "Fixed costs are just that...newsprint cost is going to be increasing each year...further reductions in programmed costs (travel, promotion, research, etc.) do not make good business sense. That leaves labor costs, 48.8 percent of our expenses. And that's what we are going to fix, starting today."[1]

A Voluntary Incentive Retirement Plan resulted in the early retirement of 124 senior employees in March 1982. They included Otto Silha, chairman of the company, Gale Freeman, general manager, and Richard Cooney, director of operations of the Minneapolis newspapers and a number of other senior newspaper executives. Several of the retirees became consultants to the newspapers.

Not mentioned in the plan was *The Minneapolis Star*. Concern about its stagnant circulation began in the fifties. In his annual report in 1956 John Cowles dis-

MINNEAPOLIS TRIBUNE, JANUARY 21, 1981

cussed the situation publicly for the first time. He talked about changes, including news color pictures five days a week and opening up the first four pages for more news content; he described them as real improvement and as progressive, but went on to say: "Most of us now agree that we made too many changes on The Star too swiftly and jolted established reading habits too much all at one time. I hope we'll remember that lesson in the future. The circulation effort based on the new Star did not meet with anything like the success we had hoped."[2] Circulation in 1956 was around 300,000; by 1978 it had dropped to 238,000 with most of the losses in Minneapolis itself and the 107 counties outside the metropolitan area.

NEWSMAKERS, NOVEMBER 1981

There were modest gains in the rapidly growing suburbs. Compared to other evening newspapers, however, *The Minneapolis Star* was not doing badly. It retained its national circulation ranking — it was 17th largest in 1956 and still in 1976. *The Minneapolis Tribune* was seeing some circulation loss as the result of cost-related reduction in its circulation area, but in 1978 its circulation topped *The Minneapolis Star* for the first time. More critical than the circulation numbers themselves was the fact that household penetration in the core of the metropolitan area had dropped below 50 percent, causing dissatisfaction among advertisers. Still, as late as 1979 *The Minneapolis Star* still carried almost 100 pages more advertising linage than *The*

MINNEAPOLIS DAILY NEWSPAPER CIRCULATION 1970-1982
(TOTAL DAILY CIRCULATION)

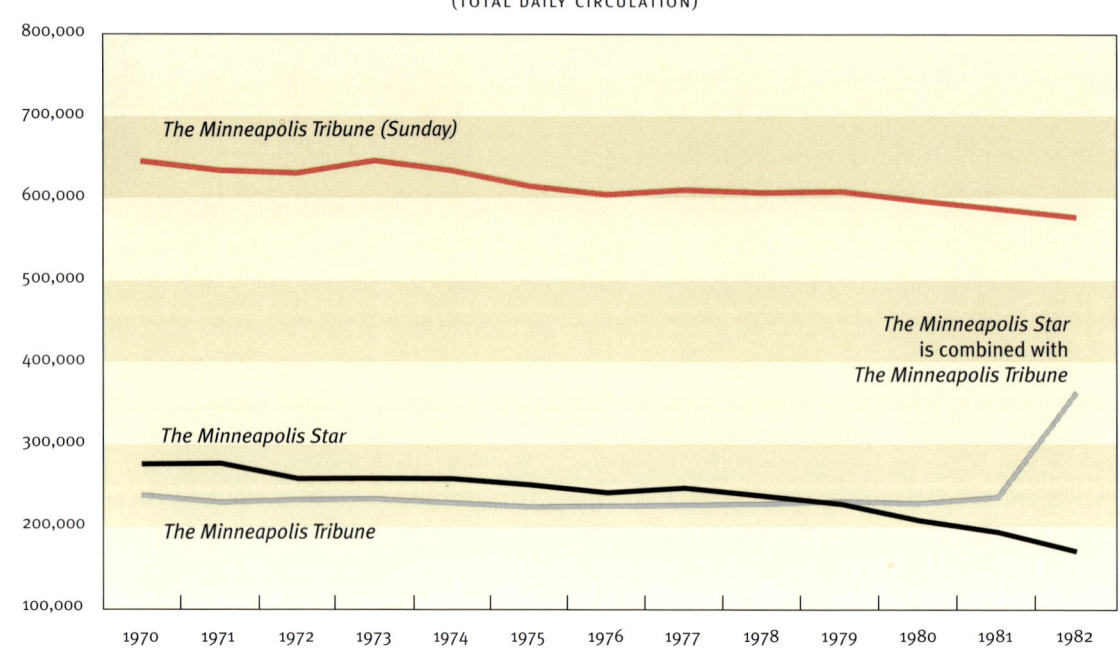

Minneapolis Tribune, with most of the difference accounted for by retail display.

In March of 1978, Stephen D. Isaacs was named editor of *The Minneapolis Star.* He had been at *The Washington Post* since 1961 in a number of positions, including city editor, editor of the Sunday picture magazine, and director of their news syndicate, and was described by *Time* as a "wunderkind."[3] Isaacs, Dwight and Cowles were under no illusions about the difficulty of the challenge. The new editor conceded that there was probably only a 50-50 chance at reversing the long-term circulation decline; Dwight characterized the task as trying to find the base readership. Isaacs' approach was to involve the newsroom in developing a strategy for the paper, participatory management — a new approach in the newspaper business. Isaacs set up eight committees to look at everything from design and writing to allocations of space, manpower and money. The editorial budget was increased by $1.4 million and ten new reporters were added by 1979.

By May of 1979 Dwight was able to tell stockholders that *The Minneapolis Star* had become an entirely different newspaper — "a daily magazine that seeks to explain the world around us in terms of the impact of that world on people." (He characterized it earlier as "a warmed-over daily news report that was neither timely nor very interesting.")[4] He acknowledged that the changes were "something of a gamble, but a gamble taken with an understanding of the shifts in interests of readers."[5] Changes at *The Minneapolis Star* were accompanied by continued major investments in technology. During 1978 an "ATEX" electronic news writing and editing system had been put in place. A new Goss offset press and new Ferag stacking equipment in the mail room were installed to replace outdated equipment and improve quality and efficiency. There was a long-term study on press and mailroom needs, testing

ATEX SYSTEM, 1978

of a computer-based classified advertising order entry system, and development of a computer-based central business system that would eventually take the carriers out of the billing and collection process. *The Minneapolis Star* expanded its zoned editions within the metropolitan area from four to eight and increased its supporting news staff from 13 to 22, to provide local community news each Thursday. These and other changes were costly, and they did not stem the circulation decline. The average for the six months ending September 30, 1980, dropped below 200,000 for the first time since the merger with *The Minneapolis Journal* some forty years earlier; a year later the six-month average was at 174,000 and it had slipped another 5,000 by March 1982.

On April 5, 1982, *The Minneapolis Star* was combined with *The Minneapolis Tribune* into a single all-day paper distributed primarily in the morning, Monday through Friday. It marked the end of *The Minneapolis Star* as an evening newspaper after 62 years. Ironically, by the time it was closed it had become the 12th largest evening newspaper in the country, having been number 20 only three years before — evidence of the irresistible national trend.

Planning for closing *The Minneapolis Star* had begun several months before, and growing rumors about its demise were consistently denied, then not commented on, up until the announcement was made. The rationale for the secrecy was obvious: there were too many unanswerable questions, advertisers would move out of the paper, employee morale would suffer, unions would be concerned, the community would be confused. Nonetheless, many employees felt they had been betrayed and attacked Dwight personally. It was hard to see that it could have been done much differently, although Dwight later reflected that the approach was not the most effective, that at least the process should have been shortened. It would have been better, he believes, to have acknowledged the need to think seriously about *The Minneapolis Star*'s future and taken the hits in public rather than in secret.[6]

Dwight made the announcement to the combined news staff on March 24, 1982, telling them that 55 news and support employees would be laid off, and that an additional 35 would lose their jobs in other areas.

Layoffs were based on seniority. He pointed out that the combined paper would have 20 percent more news space and 50 percent more news staff than either paper had before. Those laid off would be offered separation pay and benefits substantially more generous than required by trade union agreements.[7]

Among those leaving was Steve Isaacs. In a long commentary piece he detailed changes in the local and national environments that were killing afternoon newspapers — television viewership (from half to two-thirds of all households watching in the evening), a news cycle that favored morning papers, the growing number of working women (at 68 percent, almost 20 percent higher in Minnesota than nationally) and the fact that nationally people were spending only 14 minutes a day with newspapers. He concluded, "In the end, what we created was a kind of newspaper that no one had ever seen the likes of before. All along, the question was whether we could summon the creativity and the talent and the resources to pull it all off…That we didn't succeed is obvious, as of today. But anybody who ever set foot inside the doors of 425 Portland Avenue knows how very hard we all tried to fight off the inevitable."[8]

Two afternoon press runs of the combined paper were reduced to one in May, and by October the afternoon edition was scrubbed altogether. The

THE MINNEAPOLIS STAR FINAL EDITION, APRIL 2, 1982

THE MINNEAPOLIS STAR, MARCH 25, 1982

papers announced in October that an additional 75 jobs would be eliminated, in part because there had not been the attrition expected in the spring. The layoffs included 28 in news and editorial, leading Charles Bailey, editor of the combined daily, to resign, an event that was prominently covered in the national press. He wrote to Dwight: "I feel so strongly that it is wrong to reduce the news and editorial staff through layoffs that I have concluded it is the only course I can properly follow." Bailey had intended to resign as editor later in the year and return to the Washington Bureau, but said that "with news people being laid off in Minneapolis it would be unthinkable for me to rejoin the bureau as I had planned."[9] A St. Paul business writer reported that "Cowles denied that there was any plan to replace Dwight, who increasingly has been a target of employee animosity arising from a 1980 strike by the Newspaper Guild and from the Star-Tribune merger."[10]

On November 1, however, Cowles announced that he would become publisher of *The Minneapolis Star and Tribune*, that he had asked Dwight to relinquish that position as part of a reorganization. He said he was assuming the publisher's role "to help strengthen the sense of teamwork and common purpose … because the Minneapolis Star and Tribune is by far our biggest operating unit it is important that I spend more time with it." (See Appendix P.)

1 "A Plan for the 80's," *Newsmakers,* November 1981, Extra section.
2 "How Are We Doing?," *Newsmakers,* June 1956, p. 3.
3 Press: "Democracy in Minneapolis," *Time,* April 23, 1979, p. 49.
4 Ibid., p. 49.
5 "Minneapolis Newspapers Division/1979," *Newsmakers,* May 1979, p. 6.
6 D.R. Dwight, author interview, January 24, 1997.
7 "Star, Tribune to Combine," *The Minneapolis Star,* March 24, 1982, p. 1A.
8 "Editor Says The Star Tried Hard, But Life is Killing Evening Papers," *The Minneapolis Star,* March 25, 1982, p. 1A.
9 "Editor Resigns, Cites Newsroom Layoffs," *The Star Tribune,* October 7, 1982, p. 1A.
10 "Star-Tribune Cuts 75 Jobs, Editor Quits," *The Pioneer Press-Dispatch,* October 7, 1982, p. 1A.

BUFFALO

19

THROUGHOUT THE LATE seventies, revenues, earnings and profit margins were all increasing with some consistency. Significant capital investment had been made in the two television stations, at *The Great Falls Tribune,* and at the Minneapolis newspapers. The separation of the corporate headquarters had been decided, and the time seemed ripe for acquisition activity.

In his report to shareholders in 1978, Cowles discussed the company objectives. The first really described the mission of the company — "To help people manage both their private lives and the public affairs of democracy: — by gathering, organizing and marketing information, entertainments and ideas of high utility and keen interest — in newspapers and other socially responsible enterprises recognized for the excellence of their performance." He focused, however, on two other objectives — a modest diversification of sources of earnings and a modest growth in earnings per share, measured in constant dollars. He then went on to say: "We may be somewhat more aggressive in pursuing acquisitions in the future because I think we are once again beginning to demonstrate a competence to manage fairly well. In our kinds of acquisitions, however, you seem to pay either a *very* high price for reasonably assured earnings or a reasonable price for quite uncertain earnings."

Operating earnings had increased in each of the five preceding years, and the stock was split, two-for-one —

BUFFALO SKYLINE, 1982

"to maintain similarity and comparability with publicly held publishing companies, although we have no plan to take the company 'public'."[1] Earnings were up again in fiscal 1979, and investment in plant had doubled to $13.5 million, with a forecast of $20 million for the next year. By mid-1979, however, the Minneapolis newspapers — hit by rising costs of gasoline, ink and newsprint — instituted a 3.5 percent cut in all operating budgets.

The two newspapers in Buffalo, New York, had long been owned by local families. The dominant *Evening News* was purchased in 1977 by Blue Chip Stamps, owned by investor Warren Buffett. The three members of the Conners family running the *Buffalo Courier-*

Express — the morning and Sunday paper — were concerned by the prospect of aggressive competition and wanted to sell. Silha commissioned an internal analysis in late 1978 that concluded "the situation certainly deserves further exploration." The company was well aware that evening newspapers were a dying breed, and it seemed clear that the Conners "had apparently not utilized aggressive management techniques." The morning paper had a circulation of about 125,000, compared with 220,000 for the evening paper. Its Sunday paper circulation was over 150,000 in a market of 1.3 million and almost 500,000 households. (The Twin Cities population was then just over 2 million with 700,000 households, and *The Minneapolis Sunday Tribune* had a circulation of approximately 600,000.) In addition, the paper owned the cable television system in the City of Buffalo with over 30,000 subscribers and a 25 percent penetration. The reported asking price was $15-16 million, and at going prices the cable system alone was worth that much.

A further study, concluded in April 1979, recommended that evaluation continue and that an offer be formulated. The cable system was determined to have nearly 40,000 subscribers. The author of the report believed that the paper "can be turned around and moved from a negative to a modestly profitable profit picture in two or three years."[2] The report made these observations:

> "The market is capable of supporting a modestly profitable morning and Sunday newspaper, but not two profitable Sunday newspapers.
>
> "Substantial capital investment in new press equipment should not be required in the next five years, but mailroom inserting equipment is in immediate need of upgrading.
>
> "A joint publishing venture with *The Buffalo Evening News* should be viewed as a longer-term contingency plan.
>
> "Top level management is passive to competition and unsophisticated in the use of current management tools. This factor is of primary importance in assessing reasons for the current financial dilemma and in evaluating the potential for improvement of the newspapers.
>
> "Circulation figures have stabilized and Sunday circulation losses have been moderate in view of the launch of a Sunday edition by *The News,* priced under the *Sunday Courier-Express.*
>
> "Display linage figures show momentum favoring the weekday and *Sunday Courier-Express* and classified markets are underdeveloped.
>
> "Opportunities exist to reduce newsprint and labor expense by significant amounts."

Arthur D. Little, Inc. was commissioned to make a study of the market, and eventually concluded that prospects were good. The studies probably underestimated the strength of *The News,* which had (without a Sunday edition) 75 percent more revenue than the *Courier-Express* and the highest household penetration of any major market daily.

Negotiations were authorized by the board of directors on April 30, 1979, a letter of intent was signed on May 10, and the purchase of the *Courier-Express* and its cable television system was announced June 23, 1979. The acquisition was completed on August 24, and James B. Shaffer was named acting publisher. Shaffer had been with the company since 1970 in planning and financial capacities, before becoming general manager in 1977 of the weekly newspaper group in the Baltimore area. A search began for a new president and publisher. In September the board authorized borrowings of $30 million to finance the acquisition, the first significant debt since the realignment with *The Minneapolis Tribune* in 1941. In November the Baltimore-area weekly newspapers were sold at a profit of $1 million.[3]

Roger P. Parkinson became publisher and president in February 1980, reporting to Silha who had senior management responsibility for Buffalo operations. Parkinson came from The Washington Post Company where he had worked at *Newsweek* magazine, then at *The Post* newspaper as assistant to the general manager and as vice-president-administration. He brought in a new management team, including Shaffer, and in December 1980 selected as executive editor of the paper, Joel Kramer, who had been an assistant managing editor for news at *Newsday,* the successful Long Island newspaper owned by Times-Mirror Company. One of their top priorities was to improve the news and editorial quality of the paper.

Shortly after Buffett acquired *The Evening News* in 1977 he decided to launch a Sunday edition, in direct competition with the *Courier-Express* for which the Sunday paper provided its profit. Two weeks before the planned launch, the *Courier-Express* (then owned by the Connors family) sued *The Evening News* for violating the Sherman (antitrust) Act by using the weekday strength of the daily *News* (its ad revenue was four times that of the *Courier-Express*) to subsidize a money-losing paper on Sunday. In November of 1977, the court issued an injunction against *The News,* pending a trial, permitting it to publish on Sundays, but with very limited marketing. An appeals court reversed the lower court early in 1979, two months before the company bought the *Courier-Express,* and *The News* was free to compete vigorously on Sundays. By 1982 its circulation reached 200,000, compared to 265,000 for the *Courier-Express.*

The company did not pursue the litigation for two reasons: It was not at all clear that the suit was winnable and management believed there was some advantage in not alienating Buffett unduly. Establishing a joint operating agreement[4] with *The News* was always considered to be a possibility, even though Buffett and his associate, Charles Munger, indicated no interest in the subject when it was discussed with a special master appointed by the court to pursue ways of ending the lawsuit. Buffett and Munger had made it clear that if the suit were continued they would intensify the competition with the *Courier-Express.*

In the annual report to stockholders in May 1982, Silha and Cowles said that "the *Courier-Express* was able to increase advertising market share moderately and to maintain circulation penetration despite substantial price increases. This meant the *Courier-Express* performed within budget and reduced its operating loss from the previous year." CableScope, the cable television system, was described as "one of our most rapidly growing and profitable operations."[5] Three months before, in connection with his early retirement, Silha had relinquished his operating responsibility for CableScope to Cox and for the *Courier-Express* to Cowles.

The 1982 annual report also announced that the company's net earnings had dropped to less that $1 million, from $7 million the year before — largely the result of operating revenue shortfalls and costs of the early retirement program in Minneapolis. *The Evening News* was losing money too, but less than the *Courier-Express.* There were reports that the *News* would not continue beyond 1982 unless its losses diminished, although Buffett insists that he would have continued publishing *The Buffalo News* "forever," regardless of what the *Courier-Express* did — unless there was a very prolonged strike that crippled the operation.[6]

The board met in Buffalo on August 3, 1982. At a reception for prominent Buffalonians, Cowles and Silha both spoke briefly, expressing enthusiasm for the enterprise, and leaving listeners with the impression that the company intended to remain in Buffalo in spite of its losses. Roger Parkinson recalls that Cowles was much more measured in his remarks than Silha. Cowles also indicated to the board members that Dwight would likely be his successor.[7]

By mid-August planning had begun to sell or close the *Courier-Express.* Early in 1982 Cox commissioned an internal present value analysis of the *Courier-Express,* which concluded that its cash flow would never make it a profitable investment. Parkinson had come to a similar conclusion regarding the probable value of a joint operating agreement with *The News.* Cowles said that a financial review of the newspaper's performance in early August following the board meeting once again triggered a consideration of whether the *Courier-Express* could be viable.[8] The board held a special meeting on September 1 in Minneapolis. The principal agenda item was the *Courier-Express* and resolutions were passed to suspend publication and to enter into a letter of intent with News America. There was also discussion of selling the television station in Louisville and the weekly newspapers in Denver.

On September 7, Cowles and Silha announced that the paper would cease publication on September 19 unless a buyer could be found. They estimated that annual pretax losses had averaged about $8.6 million. They said: "We hoped to increase our share of market, both advertising and circulation, as we improved the management and editorial quality of the paper. Unfortunately, our hopes were overrun by our losses."[9] They discounted the possibility of a sale.

On September 13, a conditional sale of the paper to News America Publishing was announced, subject to a substantial reduction in annual payroll and related costs being negotiated between News America and the

BUFFALO COURIER-EXPRESS FINAL EDITION, SEPTEMBER 19, 1982

Courier-Express unions by September 16. The sale would save jobs of approximately 700 of the 1,100 employees. News America, owned by Rupert Murdoch, would not pay cash for the paper but would assume liabilities. The sale was blocked by members of the Buffalo Newspaper Guild, representing 156 news and editorial employees. The closedown resulted in after-tax charges of $8.1 million; net cash outflow caused by the closedown itself was estimated to be approximately $4 million. Cowles and Silha said they had considered a joint operating agreement with *The Evening News,* but concluded that the time required made that option unfeasible. *The News* bought some production equipment from the paper and the antitrust litigation was dismissed. Severance arrangements followed non-union personnel policy and union contract provisions, and the company provided extensive outplacement services to assist employees in seeking new jobs.

At the same time, the decision was made to take steps to sell the cable system, which by then had almost 60,000 subscribers. The system would require significant ongoing investment to keep up with new technology. The company had no expertise in the field, it was becoming increasingly clear that the industry was undergoing significant consolidation, and household penetration had essentially peaked. The franchise under which the system operated expired in February 1986, and extending the franchise was necessary to obtain full

THE BUFFALO NEWS, DECEMBER 26, 1983

value. The Buffalo Common Council was petitioned in June 1983 to extend the franchise until 1991, to add new services to the system, and to transfer ownership to Tele-Communications, Inc., the largest cable system operator in the country. Negotiations continued through 1983; the Common Council unanimously approved the extension and sale in December, with final approval in January 1984. The purchase price was $41.5 million; the after-tax gain on the sale was $15.6 million which yielded net after-tax cash proceeds of $29.7 million.

Shortly thereafter, the company's Louisville television station was sold to Blade Communications for a gain of $1 million, and cash proceeds of $8.7 million.

1 Minneapolis Star and Tribune Company, *Annual Report,* Fiscal 1978.
2 Internal Memorandum, April 16, 1979.
3 Cowles Media Company, *Letter to Shareholders,* September 2, 1982.
4 The Newspaper Preservation Act permits two newspapers in a market to combine all their business operations and continue to publish two newspapers if it can be determined that one of them is failing financially. Such combinations permit greatly reduced operating expenses and provide for the two papers to share profits without violating antitrust laws.
5 Cowles Media Company, *Annual Report,* Fiscal 1982.
6 Warren Buffet, Letter to Hugh J. Klein, January 21, 1997.
7 Interviews with directors present at the Cowles Media Company Board of Directors' Meeting, August 3, 1982.
8 "Cowles Media Closing Buffalo Courier-Express," *The Minneapolis Star and Tribune,* September 8, 1982, p. 5C.
9 Cowles Media Company, news release, September 7, 1982.

CONFIDENCE

20

THE ANNOUNCEMENT THAT John Cowles Jr. was taking over as publisher was widely reported in the national press. *Editor & Publisher* led with "Donald R. Dwight was fired on Monday."[1] *The New York Times* said "… staff cuts, consolidations and management shake-ups have not solved The Minneapolis Star-Tribune's continuing fight against declining profits."[2] The story in *The Wall Street Journal* said that Cowles was moving his offices back to the newspaper building, "remedying 'a mistake' he said he made in moving to a downtown building several blocks away. Cowles dismissed as 'a canard' industry reports that the newspaper and the company itself were for sale."[3] *Advertising Age* referred to the move as "a dramatic indication that Cowles Media has reluctantly come to realize that the lifeblood of its corporate well-being centers on the revitalization of the embattled Star Tribune flagship… a sign the parent company is backing away from an ill-conceived acquisition binge."[4] *Ad Age* went on to recount specific problems which they said included an inability to attract talent to three top positions, low employee morale, and advertiser resentment over "surprise hikes of 40% and 50%" in retail advertising rates.

Cowles outlined his plans and aspirations in employee meetings, soon after he returned as publisher in November 1982. He told them, "It feels good to be back at the Star and Tribune in my new role as publisher." He summed it all up: "Excellence and teamwork — if we practice a commitment to those two ideas, I think the future of this newspaper and company can be very rewarding to everyone who helps make it happen." He spoke specifically about profit performance and pointed out that good earnings are fundamental to great newspapering, saying "we must bring our earnings up to industry standards."[5]

Cowles made two key appointments in conjunction with his own move. David C. Cox was named chief operating officer, responsible for all corporate staff functions and operating units other than *The Minneapolis Star and Tribune*. Roger Parkinson, who had been publisher in Buffalo, was named deputy publisher of the

MINNEAPOLIS STAR AND TRIBUNE, NOVEMBER 7, 1984

Minneapolis paper. Cowles hoped to select a new editor within the next few months.

Directors of the company were restive. They had been greatly surprised by the decisions to close the *Courier-Express* and to ask Dwight to leave, and felt that they should have had some warning and/or been consulted. Most directors had thought the Buffalo acquisition a good one that would make the company more than a large newspaper with a few small subsidiaries. They were troubled by what they saw as a lack of communication and were concerned about Cowles' abilities as an operator and manager. Outside directors began talking among themselves, frustrated that too many important issues were given inadequate time on board agendas and that too much time was taken with unimportant details instead of strategic discussion. They met with Cowles in late November and told him they wanted a plan they could count on, a rationale for decisions they could understand, and talked about the need for a strong manager to replace Dwight.

ROGER PARKINSON, 1983

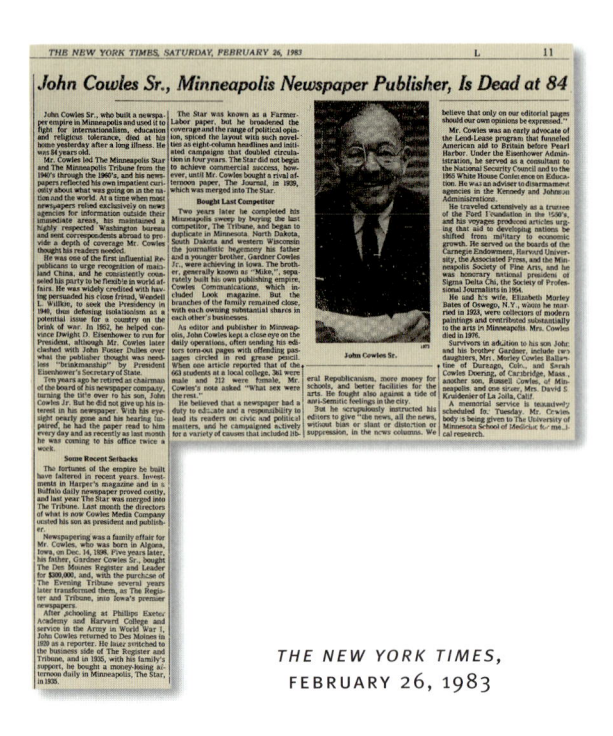

DAVID C. COX, 1985

By the time of the January 1983 board meeting, the die was cast. Cowles had not regained the confidence of the board. Recollections of the meeting vary among the participants, but there is agreement that the board asked for Cowles' resignation and that he countered with the suggestion that the company be sold instead. The outside directors were unanimous about the resignation, and only Kingsley Murphy voted to sell. Kruidenier was elected president and CEO, while remaining as chairman and CEO of the Register and Tribune Company. Cowles was to remain on the board.

After several years of deteriorating health, John Cowles Sr. died on February 25, 1983, at 84. *The New York Times* said that he "built a newspaper empire in Minneapolis and used it to fight for internationalism, education and religious tolerance."[6] Among the many tributes in his own newspaper was a note Bruce Dayton had written at the time of Cowles' retirement in 1973 in which he referred to "the great leadership you have given to the community over the years. You have been a magnificent citizen. You have been out in front of every worthwhile effort that has made Minneapolis the most attractive and interesting city in the country. You built a newspaper that ranked as one of the best in the nation and which was instrumental in pressing the community to move forward as boldly as it has. You coupled your

THE NEW YORK TIMES, FEBRUARY 26, 1983

leadership with exemplary generosity."[7] *The Des Moines Register* quoted from a 1950 article in *Fortune*: "There is a temptation to regard John Cowles in the full dress of an empire builder, or Lord of the Press, rather than in the shirt sleeves of the working newspaperman he is."[8]

In the newspaper coverage, the characteristic most frequently commented on was his curiosity, perhaps best captured in his own paper by Leonard Inskip: "It happened in the late 1970s. Some Indians were holding a powwow in the inner-city park at Franklin and Park Avenues. A frail old white man, bundled against the cold and hanging onto the arm of his black companion, crossed Park and moved toward the crowd for a closer look. John Cowles, his life near an end, had always taken a closer look — be it in the presence of presidents, generals, business tycoons, scholars or artists. His was the constant curiosity that good journalists have. He mixed it with good business judgement and built a good newspaper, this one."[9]

At the 1982 annual meeting stockholders voted to change the name of the company to Cowles Media Company (CMC) to reflect its more diversified operations; to issue a convertible preferred stock to shareholders who were entitled to sell shares back to the company under employee shareholder contracts; and to elect two new directors — Morley Cowles Ballantine (daughter of John Cowles Sr.) and David Cox. The fiscal year end was changed from the last Saturday in February to the Saturday closest to March 31, in part to make easier

MINNEAPOLIS STAR AND TRIBUNE, FEBRUARY 26, 1983

comparisons with the performance of publicly owned companies. In July the company announced the $12 million sale of the Wichita television station. The same month it also divested itself of its ownership in Harper & Row.

In 1975 the company had sued the State of Minnesota to revoke a use tax on newsprint and ink used by publishers spending more than $100,000 per year on those items — a tax clearly aimed at the Twin Cities newspapers. In March of 1983, the U. S. Supreme Court in an 8-1 decision ruled that the tax was unconstitutional, and that the company was entitled to a refund of $10.9 million for taxes paid since 1974, plus accumulated interest. It was a landmark First Amendment case, joined by other newspapers around the country.

As the new CEO, Kruidenier had many challenges — filling several key management positions at *The Minneapolis Star and Tribune* newspaper, restoring employee morale and confidence in the company, restoring profitability, and dealing with the need for a new production facility in Minneapolis. Ten days after assuming the job, Kruidenier took the opportunity to

IN 1982, THE COMPANY'S NAME CHANGED TO COWLES MEDIA COMPANY IN RECOGNITION OF THE COMPANY'S DIVERSIFYING MEDIA BUSINESSES.

talk about his intentions at the annual meeting of the Twenty Year Club on February 6, 1983. He reminded members that he had begun his career working for the company in 1948 under the tutelage of his uncle, John Cowles Sr. He worked in circulation, traffic, news, production and retail advertising before returning to Des Moines in 1952. He discussed the need for adequate earnings to have a quality newspaper and said that he wanted to see *The Minneapolis Star and Tribune* recognized as one of the great regional newspapers in America. He intended to be in Minneapolis on Wednesday and Thursday of each week. He reported that the board had reaffirmed its position that the company was not for sale, and that there was no current interest in merging with the Register and Tribune Company.

The board had named Parkinson publisher of *The Star and Tribune* in January, and Joel Kramer was named executive editor in March, a job he had held briefly in Buffalo. Cox remained chief operating officer, working closely with both Kruidenier and Parkinson. By

DAVID KRUIDENIER, 1983

the following March, *Editor & Publisher* carried a story, "A Star is Reborn," saying that a major investment and change of direction is being made to revitalize the 117-year old *Minneapolis Star and Tribune*. The *Washington Journalism Review* heralded "A Comeback in Cowles Country."

For the fiscal year that ended March 31, 1984, the financial turnaround was impressive. Earnings from continuing operations were $10.4 million, and the sale of the Louisville television station and the Buffalo cable system brought another $16.9 million. Debt was down and the balance sheet greatly strengthened. Kruidenier was quoted in a local business weekly as crediting John Cowles Jr. with making "all the hard decisions necessary to get this company going again before I got here. All I had to do was come in and put a management team together."[10]

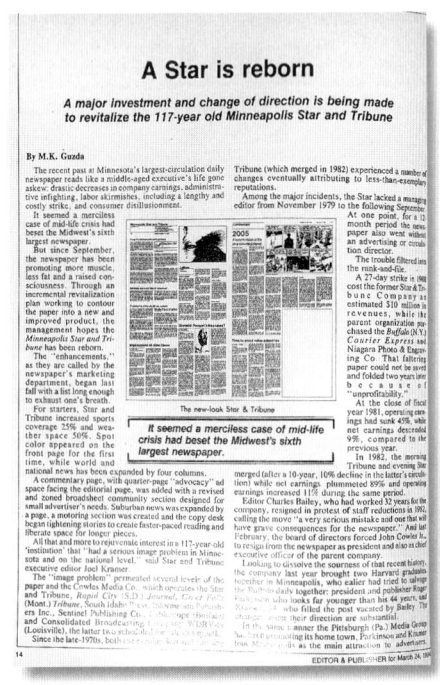

EDITOR & PUBLISHER,
MARCH 24, 1984

1 "Cowles Replaces Dwight as Minneapolis Publisher," *Editor & Publisher,* November 6, 1982, p. 14.

2 "Cowles Takes Charge at Troubled Minneapolis Paper," *The New York Times,* November 8, 1982, p. A14.

3 "Head of Cowles Media Takes Charge of Paper," *The Wall Street Journal,* November 3, 1982, p. ?.

4 "Cowles Taking Control," *Advertising Age,* November 8, 1982, p. 1.

5 John Cowles Jr. (remarks made at employee meetings), November 10, 1982.

6 John Cowles Sr., "Minneapolis Newspaper Publisher Is Dead at 84," *The New York Times,* February 26, 1982, p. 13.

7 "Memories of a Newspaperman," *The Minneapolis Star and Tribune,* February 26, 1983, p. 8A.

8 "John Cowles is Dead at 84: Former R and T Chairman," *The Des Moines Register and Tribune,* February 26, 1983, p. 1A.

9 "Memories of a Newspaperman," *The Minneapolis Star and Tribune,* February 26, 1983, p. 8A.

10 "Rebound at Cowles Media," *CityBusiness,* September 12, 1984, p. 1.

CONTINUITY

21

BY 1980 IT HAD BECOME clear that *The Minneapolis Star and Tribune*'s production equipment and facilities were fast becoming inadequate. Most of the presses and related equipment had been installed between 1947 and 1958. In 1976, the letter press units had been converted to a DiLitho (lithography) process, which permitted the presses to print from aluminum offset plates instead of the 40-pound lead stereotype places used for decades. Metal type had been replaced by "cold type" using film to produce images. The presses themselves, however, still required ever-increasing maintenance because of their age. One new offset press was installed in 1978, and automated mailroom equipment the next year. In 1990 a new building was built primarily to handle the expanding needs of the circulation operations that were being changed by computer systems that enabled direct customer billing instead of collection by carriers.

These and other changes were necessary to keep up, but they did not deal with the larger issue — producing papers in the future would require much more space and modern technology. Capacity was no longer sufficient to meet circulation demands without overtime, deadlines were frequently missed, and the risk of significant breakdown of the old equipment was high and increasing. Planning for a new production facility began in 1983 with a special task force that included active employees and some who had left under the special early retirement program in 1982. Two key questions were where to locate the new facility and what press technology to choose. The overriding issue was the optimum investment needed to meet the newspaper's long-term needs.

Initial analysis focused on expanding the existing downtown plant onto land owned in the adjacent blocks. That option was not feasible because technology called for a plant with a linear production process on one level — with rail cars of newsprint coming in at one end and finished newspapers loaded onto delivery trucks at the other end. A 20-acre site at the edge of downtown Minneapolis was selected and construction began

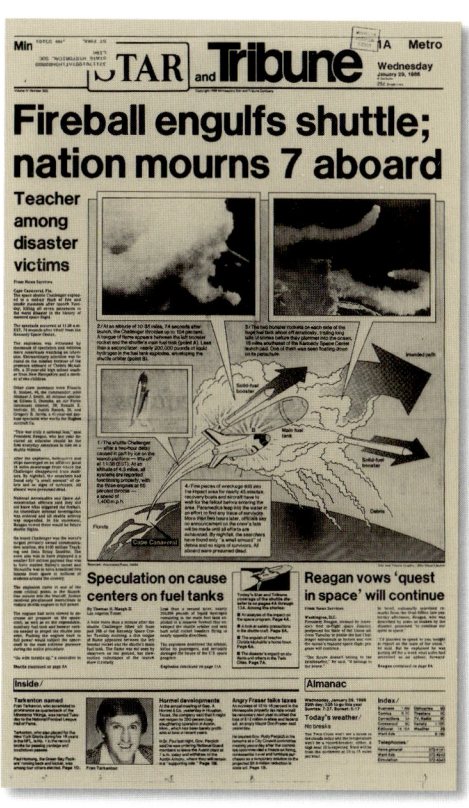

MINNEAPOLIS STAR AND TRIBUNE, JANUARY 29, 1986

October 24, 1985. Flexography was considered as an alternative to conventional offset presses because potentially it offered the advantage of using water-based ink. It was not a proven technology, however, and during the planning process did not develop as expected, so the decision was made to install offset presses. The facility was first planned for three phases, over five to nine years; they were combined into a single project for completion in 1988. It was called the Heritage Center, the name taken from the historic neighborhood where it was located.

The 425,000 square foot plant began operation in March 1987 with two of the five presses. At a cost of $110 million, the facility was a landmark investment expected to last a generation or more. Three-quarters of the total was spent on equipment and supporting systems, and most existing production equipment was sold or scrapped. (See Appendix Q.) The start-up was scheduled to last until the summer of 1988, with production split between the old and the new plants. Three more presses came on line later in 1987; all daily production moved by the beginning of 1988, with Sunday production moving the following summer.

Parkinson was responsible for both the production project and for a new marketing strategy. In addition, he was heavily involved in developing the labor strategy needed to realize the productivity levels attainable in the new facility. He established three objectives for labor negotiations: wage increases consistent with comparable newspapers (market pricing), manning levels appropriate to the tasks required (publisher's manning), and flexibility in work scheduling. With the upcoming move to the new plant it was also highly desirable to have contracts with terms longer than two or three years.

For the new Heritage Center investment to pay off, significant improvements in productivity — inherent in

HERITAGE PLANT, 1997

HERITAGE PLANT, 1988

the new equipment and systems — would be required. That in turn would require extensive negotiations with the unions to get an overall reduction of 26-28 percent in manning levels. The five new Goss press lines were the heart of the new plant, and negotiations began with the Pressmen. The newspaper's business manager, Bruce Gensmer, advised the union that the company would have to move to Heritage on its own terms, and hoped it could have the union's consent in achieving maximum efficiency and elimination of restrictive work rules. Management said it was willing to share savings realized, and provide lifetime job guarantees to current employees if they would agree to the management's manning guidelines. These guarantees would be comparable to those provided the Typographers in 1975 for their jurisdictional concessions.

Gensmer and others took union personnel to visit pressrooms in Albuquerque, Gainesville, Los Angeles and Baltimore, to see how those facilities operated and that the proposed manning was feasible and fair. Massive training programs equipped the Pressmen to operate the new state-of-the-art presses and they were encouraged to participate on decisions about working conditions. The resulting five-year contract included wage increases and a new health insurance program. The most important aspect of the settlement was agreement to pay the Pressmen approximately half of the projected estimated savings resulting from management's reduction in crew sizes. That contract was later extended to 1997 with provisions to "buy out" most remaining restrictive work rules, practices that the Pressmen agreed were no longer relevant. Contracts similar in length and concept were negotiated with the other production unions, using the Pressmen as the model.

The transition to Heritage was made with no labor disruption — no strikes or lockouts, no lost time and, in fact, a better labor environment than before the move. By the end of 1988 press production records were being set routinely, reflecting the willingness of all employees there to make the new integrated production systems work well. Between 1982 and 1988, 17 contracts were settled without any work interruptions, many for periods of five years and longer.

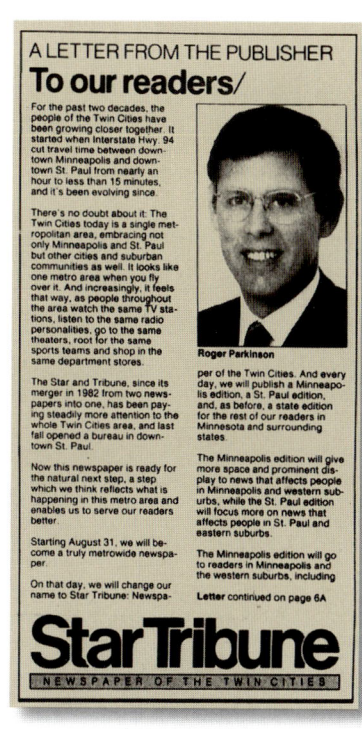

STAR TRIBUNE
JULY 1, 1987

Midway through the Heritage start-up process, Parkinson announced that the *Star Tribune* would become a Twin Cities-wide newspaper, aggressively marketed throughout the entire market. Adding an edition to serve the eastern part of the market (principally parts of St. Paul and its suburbs) placed added, but planned, demands on the production process. An extensive market analysis resulted in what was described internally as the Metro Strategy. It was based on the premise that the Twin Cities market was really one, and that the traditional Minneapolis – St. Paul distinctions were no longer valid. The shopping, employment and entertainment habits of people had blurred those lines. The two cities — and St. Paul especially — had prided themselves on their separateness. Settled earlier, many St. Paulites considered Minneapolis something of an upstart. The Ridders, who owned the St. Paul newspapers, actively promoted St. Paul merchants to their market and refused to accept advertising from Minneapolis retailers until 1950. Sears was primarily a Minneapolis operation, Montgomery Ward in St. Paul. Dayton's did not have a store in St. Paul until 1959 when it purchased Schuneman's; Dayton's had stores in Sioux Falls and Rochester in 1954 and had opened their first large suburban store — Southdale — in 1956.

Major advertisers had stores throughout the metropolitan area, and the major suburban shopping centers (where most retail sales occurred) drew from a wide geography. Building on the so-called umbrella model developed by James Rosse,[1] an economist and newspaper expert at Stanford University, it became obvious that the newspaper should cover the entire area comprehensively. "Minneapolis" was removed from the flag in August 1986, and the *Star Tribune* adopted a tag line "Newspaper of the Twin Cities." A St. Paul edition joined the Minneapolis and state editions, and a significant circulation marketing effort began in selected neighborhoods of St. Paul and suburban Dakota County.

The success of the Minnesota Twins in 1987 — winning the American League Championship, then the World Series — placed further strains on the system. Demands for more and larger papers were enormous, resulting in more than $100,000 in extra production costs. On the day after the series, presses ran from 7 a.m. to 7 p.m. to accommodate the demand for additional single copies — 176,000 copies. The play-offs and the series also produced one of the most successful newspaper promotions ever seen — the Homer Hanky.

Two million of the 14-inch square handkerchiefs were sold, each emblazoned with the *Star Tribune* logo and "Twins 1987 Championship Drive."

In addition to its importance within the newspaper, the decision to invest over $100 million in a new production facility had a significant impact on members of the Cowles family, and specifically the five trustees of the voting trust. For management to recommend and the Board to approve such a large investment meant that it would need to be favorably viewed by the major stockholders. Kruidenier was concerned that the voting trust expired in 1990, and that management needed a longer time frame for planning the investments. He and Cowles began to discuss "some agreement to provide for a more stable environment and to heal the family breach."[2]

At a special meeting of the voting trustees in August 1984 there was discussion of the company's large investment requirements and the need to assure management that the company would continue in its present ownership status. Cowles was reported to favor the investment and to state his belief that the family would continue to own the company at least for the duration of the voting trust, which expired in 1990. He had retired from the board earlier that month with the comment that he expected to remain "a very interested shareholder." The facilities plan was substantially completed by the end of October and presented to the Board on November 7, 1984, and approved in February 1985.

STAR TRIBUNE,
OCTOBER 28, 1991

The principal topic of discussion at the August 1984 meeting of the voting trustees, however, was the possibility of reviving the merger between Cowles Media Company (CMC) and the Des Moines Register and Tribune Company.[3] Cowles noted various concerns including the capital needs of both companies, the fact that Kruidenier at 63 was CEO of both companies, the vulnerability of the Des Moines Register and Tribune Company (R&T) to takeover, and the fact that the investment world was puzzled by the fact that the two companies were not already merged, given the extent of common ownership. He saw a merger as a means to an end, not an end in itself.[4] There were further discussions about a merger, including one with director Kingsley Murphy on September 27 which prompted him to call the Skadden Arps law firm in New York and Morgan Stanley and Company.[5]

Concerns about a possible appeal by other R&T stockholders of the Watts lawsuit settlement agreement (which had been reached in March 1984) put the merger discussions on hold in October. The R&T management wanted board approval to develop a strategy to remain independent, and the subject was to be discussed by outside directors on November 5. Instead the board received a surprise $112 million ($100 per share) offer from Dow Jones, two R&T officers — Gartner and Gerlach — and two other Des Moines private investors. At the CMC board meeting two days later, there was concern about what would happen to the CMC stock owned by the R&T, then 14 percent of the total outstanding.

On November 11, Murphy wrote Kruidenier to tell him that "it is not in my family's interest to continue to hold an investment in the company," and that he had retained Morgan Stanley and Skadden Arps to advise him on how to realize most fully the value of his family's investment in the company. Morgan Stanley had advised him that the current value of Cowles Media was significantly more than $100 per share; the last known trade took place in October at about $40.

The information reached the press, and Kruidenier issued a statement that Murphy spoke only for himself, that the position of the board was that Cowles Media is not for sale.[6] Press reports also said that Gannett had hired Otto Silha as a consultant to advise it and *USA Today* on marketing, noting that he was a former chairman of Cowles Media.[7] (Silha left the Cowles Media board in August.) On November 20 Al Neuharth (CEO of Gannett) sent

HOMER HANKY

THE DES MOINES REGISTER, DECEMBER 11, 1984

Kruidenier what he characterized as "a letter from a friend … hand-delivered to you by our mutual friend Otto Silha." In it he included a preliminary valuation of the R&T Company, including its Cowles Media stock, at between $134 and $140 million, between $120 and $125 per share. His estimate for Cowles Media was $360-375 million. He hoped that the companies would be "able to retain their present private structure or modify it with a merger internally," pointing out that if that were not possible, Gannett would be a desirable successor owner. He stressed that his letter was not a bid or purchase offer. A copy also went to Cowles.[8] (In his autobiography Neuharth says that Silha assured him that he had a close relationship with Kruidenier and the family. Neuharth negotiated a deal to pay Silha a consultant's fee, if Gannett acquired the R&T, based on a percentage of the price. Kruidenier refused to see him when he attempted to deliver the letter, so Silha left it on the secretary's desk. The fee ultimately turned out to be $1,080,000.)[9]

Other offers for the R&T ensued, and in December First Boston Corporation was hired to be its investment banker with responsibility for managing a process to sell the company. Elizabeth Ballantine, a niece of Cowles

---

Minneapolis, MN – January 10, 1985 — The following statement was issued today by David Kruidenier, Chairman of the Board and Chief Executive Officer of Cowles Media Company, and John Cowles Jr., a major shareholder and former Chief Executive Officer of Cowles Media Company:

"Many members of the Cowles family feel that, in light of the potential sale of The Des Moines Register and Tribune Company, it is important to make clear that they agree with the Board of Directors of the Cowles Media Company that the company is not for sale.

"Cowles Media is a strong, well-managed company. We have the highest regard for David Cox, President and Chief Operating Officer, and Roger Parkinson, Publisher and President of The Minneapolis Star and Tribune. The Twin Cities is an outstanding market, and we see excellent growth prospects for The Minneapolis Star and Tribune and the other operating units of Cowles Media Company. With the knowledge that management of Cowles Media is considering strategic plans which include a major investment in plant and facilities in Minneapolis, we believe that confirming at this time long-term commitment to the continuity of independent ownership and professional management is very important to the orderly implementation of those strategic plans.

"To ensure continuity of ownership, we have agreed to take the steps necessary to extend the Voting Trust for an additional 10 years, through the year 2000, and additional members of the Cowles family, from the third and fourth generations, have agreed to join the Voting Trust, which will increase the percentage of voting shares held by the Trust to more than 50 percent. We will both continue as Trustees of the Voting Trust.

"We both, together with other members of the family, are confident that these steps provide the stable framework on which the company can grow and prosper, meet the financial goals necessary for that growth, and maintain the standards of excellence long associated with the Cowles name."

and Kruidenier, told *The Des Moines Register* that "David hoped to persuade John (to oppose a sale), but he was not successful. It probably wouldn't have made any difference anyway. The view that the paper should be sold was just too widespread in the third generation."[10] Kruidenier said that the Voting Trust decided unanimously to "let the board deal with the question of bidding."[11] She went on to agree with her uncle, David Kruidenier that her generation was less attached to the newspaper. She noted that she was once turned down for a reporting job at the Minneapolis newspapers, although she was a reporter at *The Des Moines Register* for several years.

At the same time Kruidenier announced that Cowles Media was not for sale. Speculation about a possible sale was rampant, causing concern among management and employees. Cox met with Cowles in mid-December to express those concerns and to say that revitalizing the company would be possible only if Cowles confirmed his long-term ownership commitment. Kruidenier and Cowles discussed management's concerns and the options for creating a more stable situation.

On January 7, 1985, Cowles wrote Kruidenier to outline his recommendations. They included changing the Voting Trust to have the trustees reflect the ownership of the John Cowles family and extending the term of the Trust, and the appointment of Cox as CEO with Kruidenier remaining as chairman of the board. (See Appendix R.)

On January 10, Cowles and Kruidenier issued a statement, which they discussed with reporters. In it they confirmed the family's "long-term commitment to the continuity of independent ownership and professional management…To ensure continuity of ownership, we have agreed to take the steps necessary to extend the Voting Trust for an additional 10 years, through the year 2000, and additional members of the Cowles family, from the third and fourth generations,[12] have agreed to join the Voting Trust, which will increase the percentage of voting shares held by the Trust to more than 50 percent."[13] (The Trust previously held 44.6 percent of the voting stock.) When asked about the 14.3 percent of the Minneapolis company owned by the R&T, Cowles said he hoped that it would not be sold to a new owner, but distributed to R&T shareholders.[12] The announcement was reported widely in the press nationally, and most accounts indicated that the Trust had been extended to the year 2000.

With the prospect of ownership uncertainties being resolved, Cox focused on strategic planning for the company, and talked with John Cowles III (Jay) about returning to the company with responsibility for developing such a plan, with emphasis on acquisition opportunities in the communications industry. Jay Cowles had worked on a capital planning project two years earlier, during the summer of his Harvard Business School program.

On January 16, Kingsley Murphy filed suit to have the extension of the Voting Trust declared null and void, to prohibit implementation of the amendments to the Trust and the repurchase the block of Cowles Media stock owned by the R&T, and to grant damages in excess of $40 million, the alleged loss of value of the Murphy stock resulting from the changes in the Voting Trust. The defendants were initially the five Voting Trustees, and the suit was later amended to include Cowles Media and its directors. Murphy contended that the changes in the Voting Trust were part of a plan to derail the sale of his stock. He had told Cowles on January 4 that he was going to receive a firm offer for his stock on January 7; that offer was made at about $45 million with a potential increase to $60 million. After the announcement by the Voting Trustees and press conference, the offer was withdrawn.[15]

COWLES MEDIA COMPANY BOARD OF DIRECTORS, 1991

The press gained access to the court documents at the end of January, and the widespread coverage tended to focus on the fact that Kruidenier would be replaced as CEO by Cox, and on the November 20 letter from Neuharth to Kruidenier, noting that it included an offer of employment and an opportunity to repurchase parts of the R&T on a favorable financial basis. One story noted that the concept of extending the Trust was only a verbal commitment since under Delaware law the life of the Trust could not be extended before 1988.[16]

On January 31, Gannett agreed to pay $165 million for *The Des Moines Register,* well above Neuharth's preliminary evaluation of $140 million (which included approximately 14 percent of Cowles Media stock and several other broadcast and newspaper operations) and the $112 million Dow Jones group bid. Other bidders were reported to be Hearst at $130 million and The Washington Post Company at $115 million.[17] The decision on disposing of the Register and Tribune Company's Cowles Media stock was deferred. On March 14 The Washington Post Company agreed to purchase the stock owned by Kingsley Murphy and his family; terms were not disclosed, and the buyer characterized the purchase as an investment. Speculation focused on whether the Post would also be successful in acquiring the 14.3 percent stock interest owned by the R&T. Disposition of that stock was scheduled for an R&T board meeting on March 25. Gannett again proved to be the high bidder, acquiring an interest in Cowles Media for $130 per share, a total cost of approximately $56 million.

Between June 1985 and June 1986, both companies increased their stock holdings significantly. The Washington Post Company acquired an additional 29,332 shares and Gannett, 19,899, at prices as high as $200 per share. At the time of the 1986 Cowles Media stockholders meeting, the Post owned approximately 20 percent of the voting stock and Gannett about 15 percent. Each sought to reach 20 percent in order to consolidate a proportionate share of CMC earnings with its own for accounting purposes.

At the 1985 annual meeting, David Cox was named chief executive officer, replacing David Kruidenier who remained chairman of the board. For the first time, the CEO was not a member of the Cowles family. Lois Cowles Harrison and Kingsley Murphy did not stand for reelection. They were replaced by Anthony L. Andersen, CEO of the H. B. Fuller Company, and William A. Hodder, CEO of Donaldson Company, Inc., both clearly independent outside directors. Their appointments reflected John Cowles Jr.'s January suggestion that two business executives be recruited, "on the younger side if possible, experienced in the management of larger business organizations." Operating earnings from continuing operations had rebounded from the loss in fiscal 1983 (related to the *Courier-Express*) to $10 million in 1984 and $15.7 million in 1985. Long-term debt was down to $5.5 million from a high of $32.4 five years earlier. Dividends had increased from $1.08 per common share in 1982 and 1983 to $1.52.

1. James Rosse became a director of Cowles Media Company in 1990; while completing his doctorate at the University of Minnesota in the 1950s, he worked in *The Star Tribune* mailroom.
2. In the Court of Chancery of the State of Delaware in and for New Castle County, Kingsley H. Murphy Jr., Georgia M. Johnson, Kingsley H. Murphy III, Cecily M. Murphy, Barrett B. Murphy, Katherine B. Johnson, Evan R. Johnson, and Gerald H. Friedell as Trustee for Georgia M. Johnson, Kingsley H. Murphy III, Cecily M. Murphy and Barrett B. Murphy, Plaintiffs, v. David Kruidenier, Morley Cowles Ballantine, Lois Cowles Harrison, Luther L. Hill Jr., John Cowles Jr., David C. Cox, Roger P. Parkinson, Winthrop Knowlton, John B. Davis Jr., and Cowles Media Company, a Delaware corporation, Defendents. Civil Action No. 7916. January 21, 1985.
3. Ibid.
4. John Cowles Jr., handwritten notes, August 28, September 4 and October 18, 1984.
5. Kingsley H. Murphy Jr., author interview, March 10, 1997.
6. Cowles Media Company, news release, November 13, 1984.
7. "Cowles Media Co. Chairman Says Firm Is Not For Sale," *The Washington Post,* November 15, 1984, p. B1.
8. Al Neuharth Letter to David Kruidenier with copy to John Cowles Jr., November 29, 1984.
9. Al Neuharth, *Confessions of an S.O.B.* (New York: Doubleday, 1989), p. 201.
10. Referring to the family of Gardner Cowles Sr.
11. "R and T Put On the Block by Directors," *The Des Moines Register,* December 11, 1984, p. 1.
12. Referring to the descendents of Gardner Cowles Sr.
13. John Cowles Jr., and David C. Kruidenier, Announcement, January 10, 1985.
14. "Family Members Move to Strengthen Their Control of Cowles Media Co.," *The Star Tribune,* January 11, 1985, p. 1A.
15. Op. Cit., Complaint in the Court of Chancery of the State of Delaware, January 16, 1985 and amended January 21, 1985.
16. "Documents Detail Cowles Feud," *The Washington Post,* January 30, 1985, p. F4.
17. Neuharth, *Confessions of an S.O.B.,* p. 202.

NEW GROWTH STRATEGIES

22

BY THE END OF 1985 the strategic planning was well underway and its overall direction presented to the board. It had four parts: building on the Twin Cities base by pursuing the "metro strategy," acquisition of medium-size newspapers like those in Rapid City and Great Falls, adding new business areas such as special interest consumer and business magazines to take advantage of trends in market segmentation, and realizing the full value of the company's real estate assets. The plan had three major financial objectives: growth and profitability levels equal or above those of the industry; better utilization of cash and debt capacity; and diversification of the earnings base to be less dependent on the *Star Tribune*'s operations.

With Heritage Center and the metro strategy underway, Cowles Media Company attention was directed to other areas. The major investments required for the newspaper had been made, and it was generating cash well beyond its foreseeable needs. For its long-term growth the company needed to invest in ventures that had higher growth potential than the newspaper offered. A long-term dividend policy was established to provide predictable growth and return and to be competitive with other companies in the publishing category, paying out roughly one third of earnings.

In December 1986 the company entered the consumer magazine business with the acquisition of Historical Times, Inc., from its founder, Robert Fowler, who felt that the values he saw in Cowles would ensure that his magazines had a good home. A Pennsylvania publisher of several history magazines, *Fly Fisherman* and a continuity book series, the purchase became the model for an ongoing series of similar acquisitions. The next acquisition was Empire Press, a Virginia-based publisher of history magazines, followed later by publications in the equestrian, health, collectibles, and other niche markets appealing to enthusiasts. Unlike *Harper's*, these magazines all met two criteria developed in the strategic planning process: they took advantage of the segmentation of the market into highly specialized areas, and circulation provided well over half the revenue. The

STAR TRIBUNE, OCTOBER 20, 1987

MINNEAPOLIS DAILY NEWSPAPER CIRCULATION 1983-1993
(TOTAL DAILY CIRCULATION)

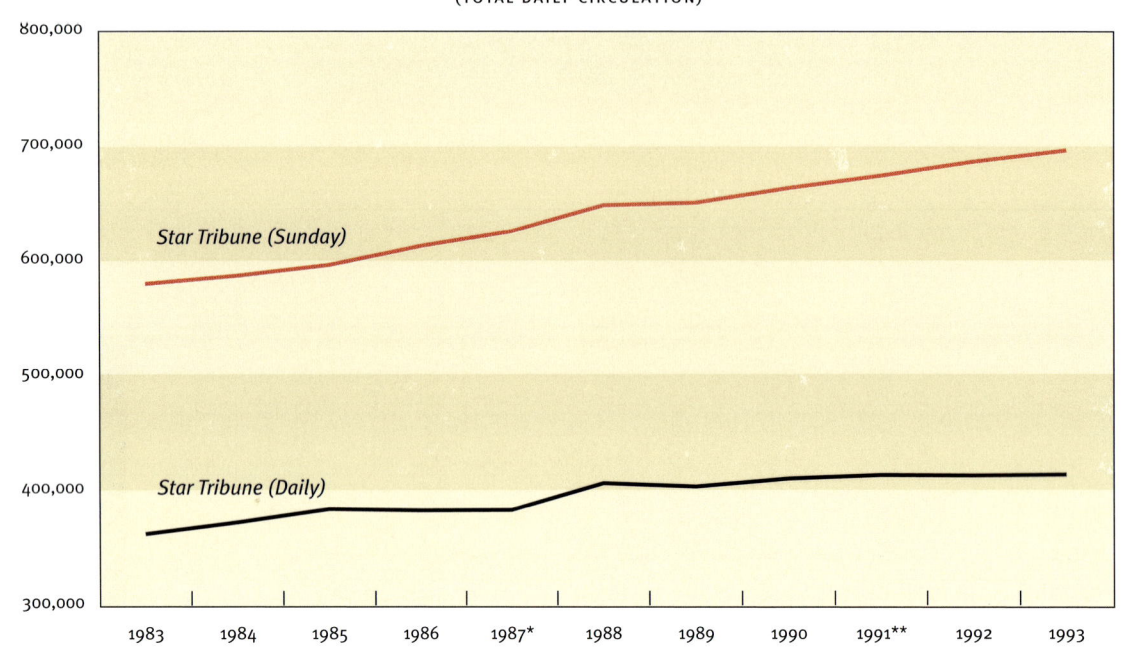

Star Tribune (Sunday)

Star Tribune (Daily)

consumer magazine business was called Cowles Magazines, later renamed Cowles Enthusiast Media, to better reflect its scope and emphasis.

Two years later came the acquisition of Hanson Publishing Company in Connecticut, whose magazines and allied trade shows were dominant in the magazine and catalog businesses. They became the base for adding other business-to-business publications in media and marketing, largely through acquisition. It was renamed Cowles Business Media.

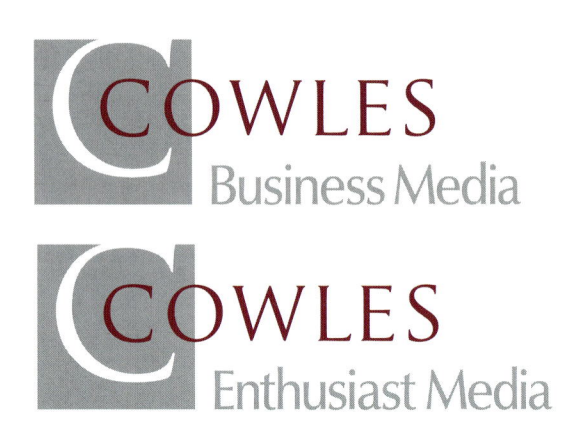

In 1987, the company had an opportunity to acquire *The Scottsdale Progress,* a six-day paper in the Phoenix market. While it did not fit the model of Rapid City and Great Falls, it served a distinct niche in its rapidly growing market with a respected, well-written publication, and it was purchased that year. The company made a bid for *The Sheboygan* (Wisconsin) *Press,* but it was sold at a higher price to Thomson. Late in 1987 the morning and afternoon papers in Enid (Oklahoma) came onto the market, and were seriously considered. The analysis of the papers concluded that achieving the financial return required by the price was impossible without compromising standards and creating serious community relations problems, neither of which Cowles Media was willing to do.

During the discussions about the Enid papers, Gannett approached management about selling its investment in Cowles Media, either to the company or to another buyer. After an analysis of alternative investment possibilities, management concluded that purchasing the stock from Gannett would be attractive, providing a higher long-term return than purchasing additional mid-market newspapers. The purchase was concluded early in 1988 at a price of $128 million, financed through a revolving credit arrangement and senior notes; in combination they afforded a highly flexible repayment schedule. At the same time the company redeemed the preferred stock issued in 1982.

At the annual stockholders meeting in 1988 John Cowles, speaking as managing trustee, announced that Voting Trust participants had agreed formally to extend the Trust for an additional ten years, to the year 2000, fulfilling the ownership-continuity commitment made to management in 1985.

The price paid to Gannett in 1988 was approximately $200 per share, well above the trading range in the limited market for Cowles Media stock. In the fall of 1989 the price was around $125, and there was little activity. The limited market did not provide the immediate liquidity that some stockholders desired, and there was concern about liquidity generally. In November of 1989 the company offered to purchase from its stockholders up to 250,000 shares (roughly ten percent of the outstanding) at $200 per share, a total cost of $50 million. The tender offer was fully subscribed, and 180 stockholders participated.

At the same time the company announced its intention to sell the Great Falls Tribune Company and the Rapid City Journal Company, using its investment bankers, Goldman, Sachs & Co. Together the two papers had revenue of approximately $21 million, just under

SCOTTSDALE PROGRESS, OCTOBER 14, 1990

seven percent of the CMC total. The 1985 strategy had contemplated acquiring additional mid-size market newspapers, but the acquisition prices being paid by other bidders precluded an adequate return on such investments. With only two papers, it was difficult to achieve any substantial economies of scale or management. Cordingley, who had been publisher in Great Falls since 1965 retired in 1984. Rusty Swan, who succeeded his father as publisher in Rapid City in 1971, retired in 1985 following completion of a new production facility there.

The decision to sell was difficult because both papers were highly profitable and well respected in their markets and in the industry, but it no longer made sense to own only two papers of this size with no apparent opportunity to build on that base. The sales were completed in 1990 and resulted in a pretax gain of $47 million, with net cash proceeds of $84 million. The Great Falls paper was sold to Gannett, and Rapid City to Lee Enterprises, which had bought the other major papers in Montana in 1959.

The suburban newspapers in Denver were sold to local buyers in 1991. The Scottsdale paper was sold in 1993 to Cox Newspapers, owners of three other suburban papers in the Phoenix market. The *Star Tribune* remained the company's only newspaper investment.

Shortly after completing the tender offer in 1990 the company established an employee stock plan, making stock available to substantially all employees on the basis of the company's profitability. Operating much like a profit sharing plan, the plan was unusual in that the eligibility and profitability criteria were recommended to the board by a committee of 20 employees from throughout the company. In the first two years of plan operation the company made contributions totaling $2.1 million to the plan, representing over 10,000 shares. It was a complement to a long-term incentive plan developed in 1987 which awarded restricted stock to executives using criteria tied directly to long-term profitability. In 1988 the company had adopted a charter — a statement of values — that included both the need to create superior long-term value and to reward employee performance and results. The stock plan was one way of reinforcing those values.

Two parts of the growth strategy adopted in 1985 had proved to be highly successful by 1993. The company was well established in magazines and related publications, and the "metro strategy" had firmly established the *Star Tribune* as a newspaper serving the entire Twin Cities market. Targeted circulation promotion had produced the desired coverage in the eastern (St. Paul) part of the market, and advertisers responded accordingly. In 1992 that eastern circulation grew approximately 12 percent. In August 1992 the largest retail and entertainment center in the country opened in suburban Bloomington — the 4.2 million square foot Mall of America — and the advertising of its major retailers went principally to the *Star Tribune*, encouraging other retailers to do the same.

In 1990, *Star Tribune* reporters Lou Kilzer and Chris Ison won the Pulitzer Prize for investigative reporting, confirming the growing quality and reputation of the paper — one of Parkinson's major objectives and the

PULITZER PRIZE, 1990

COWLES MEDIA COMPANY CHARTER

· We are a trusted source of information and ideas that help people pursue their interests and enrich their lives.

· We are a family of independent companies responsible for their own success and corporate citizenship.

· The skill and dedication of our people working individually and together are essential to our success.

· We produce high-quality products and act with integrity while achieving competitive financial returns to create superior long-term value.

· Customer satisfaction is a fundamental responsibility for each of us.

· We aim high, accepting the risks and rewarding performance and results.

· We believe in an open and fair environment, one that values diversity of backgrounds and ideas, and encourages personal growth.

first Pulitzer for the paper since the fifties.

The key elements in the corporate strategy were to build the *Star Tribune* as a great metropolitan newspaper and to invest available cash flow in highly focused consumer magazines and business-to-business communications. The financial strategy was to create superior long-term stockholder value measured by cash-on-cash return on invested capital. The business was defined in terms of traditional products, although senior management was almost continuously involved in discussions about how to achieve strong growth in a rapidly changing

NEW GROWTH STRATEGIES

JOEL KRAMER, 1995

media landscape. The *Star Tribune* began a review of its strategy in 1992, led by Joel Kramer, who took a leave from his responsibilities as executive editor.[1] The traditional mission of the organization — at least since 1935 — had been to produce a great regional newspaper, the highest quality newspaper the area could support. The strategy required strong emphasis on editorial quality, growing circulation, and selling mass advertising — most recently demonstrated in the metro strategy. In the course of the review, the *Star Tribune* redefined its mission: To enrich the shared life of the community by being the area's leading provider of information and communications that people value.

In some respects the traditional "Cowles formula" had been superseded in response to changing market forces and opportunities. In other respects, there was a strong parallel to John Cowles Sr.'s concern about and interest in the new "wartime electronics discoveries and uses" in 1944 and in his keen attention to such things as extensive sports coverage and the use of photography to appeal to readers for whom these were important. Implicit in the new mission was moving from a single product to multiple products, from serving only a mass market to serving both mass and niche audiences. The strategy had two components — the first was to build stronger relationships with readers and advertisers and the second to become much more flexible in meeting customers' needs — within and outside the newspaper.

The *Star Tribune* then implemented an organizational restructuring around its customers — readers and advertisers — instead of the traditional organization around functions and products. The new organization and the elimination of many traditional titles, especially in the newsroom, was controversial and became the object of criticism in both the local and national press. It also led to serious consideration of similar moves by many other newspapers. As part of the restructuring, there was a thoroughgoing remake of the newspaper itself, redefining traditional sections and the way in which stories were prepared and presented.

New sections were introduced and new products launched, separate from the newspaper itself. An on-line service was started in the fall of 1995, since joined by a World Wide Web site and related digital services.

The involvement of scores of employees in building Heritage Center had triggered a number of organizational changes that effectively pushed decision-making responsibility down in the organization. That in turn resulted in significant changes — first in circulation, and later in

COWLES MEDIA COMPANY'S OPERATING UNITS DEVELOPED A WIDE RANGE OF ELECTRONIC PUBLISHING SITES INCLUDING THE STAR TRIBUNE ONLINE (TOP), THE VIRTUAL VEGETARIAN (LEFT), THE VIRTUAL FLYSHOP (RIGHT) AND MEDIA CENTRAL (BOTTOM)

both advertising and in news, as well as the support functions — all involving the creation of teams to address problems and eventually to meet customer needs more effectively. In 1993 the paper instituted an annual cash awards program to reinforce the high level of employee involvement.

The company had participated in 1983 in an experimental videotext system with a group of newspapers led by the Times-Mirror Company, and in 1985 launched a public access downtown directory and information service using touch-screen terminals in the Minneapolis sky-way system. The system was not a financial success and closed the following year. The interest in "electronic publishing" ventures remained. Cowles Business Media began to move toward "electronic publishing" in 1992, under the leadership of Hershel Sarbin, its president. Business press customers were increasingly receptive to new channels of communication, and it was becoming clear that the company must go beyond its traditional print orientation, to become media neutral or media versatile. In 1993 CBM began on-line services, which have continued to build. The same forces were present in consumer markets, as well, and a number of non-print products and services were introduced by Cowles Enthusiast Media, some of which succeeded, while some did not.

By 1995 Cowles Media had redefined itself as "a leading information providing company, …using communication technologies rather than developing them." Each of its operating units had similarly defined itself more in terms of function than product: The Star Tribune as a leading Twin Cities information source through its core product, the *Star Tribune* newspaper, and other print and digital products and services; Cowles Enthusiast Media, the consumer magazine group, as a diversified publisher of media for special-interest consumer communities; and Cowles Business Media as publisher of magazines, newsletters, research, conferences and on-line products about and for the publishing, media and marketing industries. All recognized the importance of serving markets as defined by customers and technology, not by the content providers.

LEFT TO RIGHT, THE TITLES PRODUCED IN 1997 BY STAR TRIBUNE, COWLES ENTHUSIAST MEDIA, COWLES BUSINESS MEDIA AND COWLES CREATIVE PUBLISHING

[1] In June 1992, Joel Kramer succeeded Roger Parkinson as publisher and president of the *Star Tribune*.

THE FOURTH GENERATION

23

AT THE ANNUAL MEETING in July 1990 Luther Hill retired from the board; John Cowles III (known as Jay) was elected to the board together with K. Prescott Low, whose family owned the newspaper in Quincy, Massachusetts, and James N. Rosse, provost of Stanford University. Terry Saario, then president of the Northwest Area Foundation, had joined the board in 1987.

In August 1990, John Cowles flew to Denver to visit his son Jay, who was working as director of operations at the Sentinel weekly newspaper group there, still owned by the company. He came to tell Jay that he wanted to sell the company, and that David Kruidenier and at least one other Voting Trustee also favored a sale. John said that he had tired of family leadership responsibilities, which had included managing his father's estate and resolving a very large number of trusts.

Jay talked with his cousin Richard Ballantine, who was a director of Cowles Media Company (CMC), and later with Richard's sister Elizabeth. They were opposed to the idea of the sale and asked, in effect, "Can't we do something?" Jay had already decided to leave his management role at the company and was more than willing to help take on the leadership role from his father's generation. He took the lead in putting together the case to his father and Kruidenier that the next generation deserved a chance. Jay, sometimes with one of the Ballantines, met with many of their cousins to gain their support. While the board itself was not involved, the three talked with two individual outside directors, each the CEO of a family-controlled company. They encouraged the younger generation's interest and were eloquent in urging John Cowles to reconsider his position. He agreed to do so.

On December 3, 1990, John Cowles, as managing trustee of the Voting Trust, announced that two new trustees had been elected — Elizabeth Ballantine and Jay Cowles. He, Morley Ballantine and David Kruidenier resigned their seats. Sarah Doering and Russell Cowles II, both siblings of John, continued as trustees. Elizabeth, a lawyer, was a staff writer at *The Des Moines Register* from 1976 to

STAR TRIBUNE,
JANUARY 17, 1991

JOHN COWLES III
(JAY), 1991

1982. She noted that, "Successions are never simple and easy" and pointed out that unlike many families, "I really think we share a much more common point of view." The new trustees said that their succession boded no change in the company's values or in the independence of the *Star Tribune*. Jay Cowles said: "The change was the result of strong expressions of commitment and interest on the part of the fourth generation[1] members of the family to continue independent ownership and journalistic excellence at the *Star Tribune* and Cowles Media."[2] Jay maintains that the common point of view about values and the integrity of the newspaper had its origins in the family gatherings at Glendalough when he and his siblings and cousins were growing up. Their parents and grandparents were vitally interested in the world of public affairs, and the children were encouraged to become interested and informed as well. The dinner table at the camp at Glendalough had a strong influence on members of his generation.[3]

Jay Cowles was elected vice-chairman of the board in January 1991, to understudy his uncle, David Kruidenier. Elizabeth Ballantine became managing trustee of the Voting Trust. In February, Elizabeth Bullitt (the daughter of Sarah Cowles Doering and Jay's cousin), and Gardner (Pat) Cowles III (a second cousin) were elected Voting Trustees, joining Jay, Elizabeth Ballantine, and Russell Cowles II, their uncle. In 1993 David Kruidenier retired from the Board of Directors, Jay Cowles was elected chairman, and Elizabeth Bullitt and Elizabeth Ballantine were elected directors. Richard Ballantine, who was elected to the board in 1988, retired from the board in 1993. In 1994, Herbert P. Wilkins Sr., was elected a director.

The transfer of responsibility to the next generation was complete, a process set in motion by John Cowles Jr. in 1985. The separation of the governance and management functions was confirmed with a Cowles as chairman of the board and a professional manager as president and CEO, the only management member of the board. Three members of the family of John Cowles Sr., who were also Voting Trustees, were among the nine directors of the company, and the five other directors had no connection with either the family or the company.

The final step in the realignment of ownership occurred in 1996 when the Voting Trust was reconfigured with a new expiration date in 2010. The Trust then held 56.4 percent of all voting shares in CMC, down slightly from the 60 percent held a year earlier. Gardner Cowles III was replaced as a trustee by Joe Scofield, the son-in-law of David Kruidenier. In announcing the changes Elizabeth Ballantine said, "Our decision to extend the Voting Trust underscores our intention to continue Cowles family involvement and independent ownership of CMC and our satisfaction with the company's performance, steady growth and strategic direction."[4]

Over a period of ten years, the three financial objectives of the strategy developed in 1985 had been achieved. Profitability as measured by after-tax cash return on invested capital was in the top quartile in the industry. For the five years ended March 29, 1997 operating revenue had increased from $335 to $517 million, much of it from the two magazine companies; operating earnings increased from $36 to $54 million; earnings per share from $1.09 to $2.13; dividends from $0.52 to

COWLES MEDIA COMPANY
(FISCAL 1985-1997)

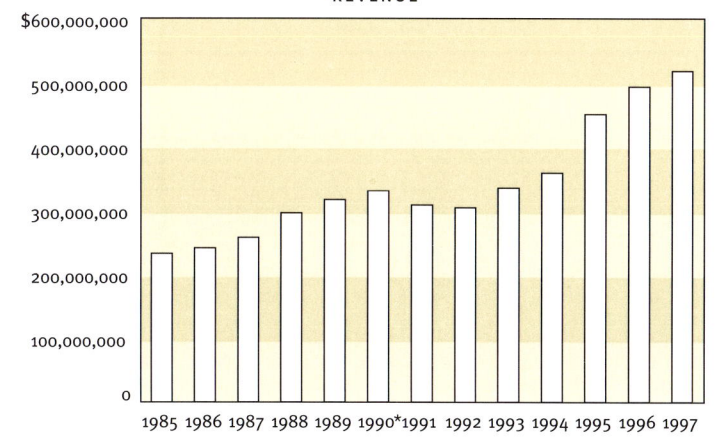

REVENUE

NET EARNINGS

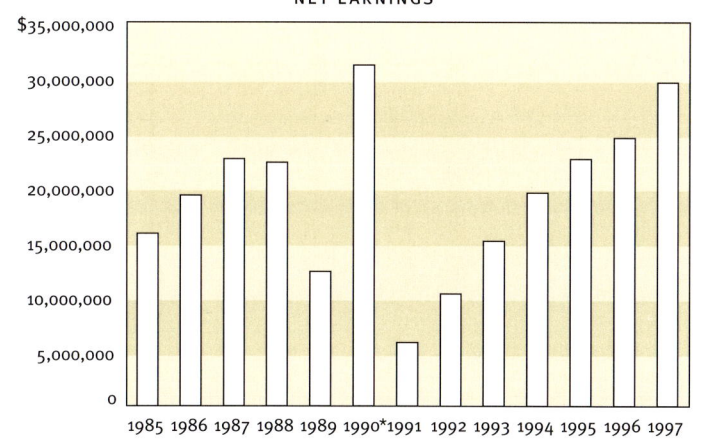

*Includes the sale of *The Great Falls Tribune* and *The Rapid City Journal*.

1. Referring to the family of Gardner Cowles Sr.
2. "Two Replace Parents on Cowles Media Family Trust," *Star Tribune*, December 4, 1990, p. 4D.
3. John Cowles III, author interview, March 5, 1997.
4. Cowles Media Company, news release, October 31, 1996.

$0.64. The company had a sophisticated capital structure designed to create long-term value, including flexibly-structured long-term debt and unused borrowing capacity. Revenue from non-newspaper operations, while still significantly less than the *Star Tribune*, increased more rapidly than the newspaper revenue. All the operations were moving to position themselves for a world in which digital technology was becoming increasingly important.

EPILOGUE — SUBSEQUENT EVENT

24

THE COWLES FAMILY VOTING Trust had held semi-annual meetings for several years, usually in late January or early February, then again in late July or early August, at the time of the annual meeting of stockholders. Meetings were attended by family members whose stock had been placed in the Trust, and often their spouses. Various topics were discussed at the meetings, but the ever present topic — whether on the agenda or not — was stockholder liquidity. At the summer meeting in 1996 members of the Voting Trust agreed to extending the Trust until the year 2010. (The expiration of the existing trust, created in 1980, was May 20, 2000.)[1]

The Trust then held 56.4 percent of total voting shares, down from 60 percent, reflecting largely the withdrawal of shares by descendents of Gardner Cowles, Jr. The extension of the Trust was announced October 31, 1996, following a meeting of the five voting trustees the day before.[2] The announcement said: "Our decision to extend the Voting Trust underscores our intention to continue Cowles family involvement and independent ownership of CMC and our satisfaction with the company's performance, steady growth and strategic direction."[3] The extension also served to reaffirm the solidity of the family around its traditional values and — in effect — to signal to potential acquirers that the company was "not for sale."

The question of shareholder liquidity had been a key strategic issue for many years, and significant time had been devoted to analyzing various alternatives that would both create a broader public market for Cowles stock, more nearly reflecting its underlying value, and still allow the family to retain control. Several media companies — Times Mirror, New York Times, Pulitzer, Washington Post, McClatchy — had achieved those dual objectives. A secondary offering — the sale of existing shares by current shareholders (largely members of the Cowles family) — would achieve both objectives. The other option was an outright sale of the company.

By 1996 the market for newspaper stocks and the consistent financial success of the company provided a

*STAR TRIBUNE,
APRIL 20, 1997*

STAR TRIBUNE,
SEPTEMBER 4, 1997

highly favorable environment for exercising either option. Approximately 25 family members participated in the Voting Trust; few of them lived in the Twin Cities and fewer still were involved in the media business. The fundamental issue for the trustees was how long the family would want to retain its large equity position in the company. For many of them, the financial aspects of holding the stock were becoming more important than maintaining the family's role in the *Star Tribune* in the Twin Cities. It was important to the leadership of the Voting Trust to be able to consider all options carefully and completely at a time when there were no distractions of other pressing issues and the external environment was strong.

A secondary initial public offering (or IPO) had been generally assumed to be the preferred option to assure the best future for the *Star Tribune*. The winter 1997 meeting of members of the Voting Trust was the logical time to consider whether a secondary offering was appropriate, given the bullish state of the market and the continuing profitability of the company. The fiscal year that would end in March would again see record earnings; non-newspaper operations now accounted for one-third of the company revenues and their profitability was reaching industry norms.[4]

The recent sales of Affiliated Publications and of the Providence Journal Company, and of some smaller newspaper groups, suggested that the quoted price of Cowles Media stock — around $25 — could be less than one-third of its potential market value.[5] An offering of at least $50 million of stock would be required for a successful secondary offering — from a quarter to a third of the Cowles family's non-voting shares. A secondary offering of their stock might bring the sellers no more than $40 per share, while a sale of the total company could bring as much as $80 per share. A secondary offering, then, would be a very high price to pay for liquidity in a broader public market, even if the company continued its strong earnings growth. From a purely financial point of view the secondary offering would not offer the most potential, especially when the proceeds would be all cash — fully taxable with none of the opportunities for tax deferral available in other transactions. The subsequent purchase of the papers in Kansas City and Fort Worth by Knight-Ridder confirmed the probable high value the market would place on Cowles Media.

If the company were to be sold, it was important to the Voting Trustee leadership that a buyer would share the journalistic and civic values the Cowles family had built and maintained in the Twin Cities over 60 years. The strong family cohesion around those values — and the Voting Trustees control — presented an opportunity to continue the influence, independence and success of the *Star Tribune*.

The two leaders of the Voting Trust — Elizabeth Ballantine and Jay Cowles — developed information about alternatives and met with family members with a series of questions. What level of risk were they willing to assume as stockholders? What were their own investment needs and objectives for their stock? Was a broader public market feasible? Did members of the family want to be more involved in the company and the Twin Cities? There was not agreement on all points, but there was a consensus that a sale of the company was probably the best resolution for both the family and the *Star Tribune*. There was no compelling vision in the family to maintain their control position over the long-term. Members of the fourth generation were involved in the governance of the company, but not in its operation and direction, and they lacked the experience and training to play a significant management role. They were concerned about management succession; there was no clear candidate to succeed David Cox as CEO, a decision that would need to be made within the next few years. The family's principal interest in the company was almost entirely in the newspaper, and it did not engage and motivate the family as it once had.

By the time of their summer meeting the Voting Trustees had established a process to ensure appropriate influence regarding any transaction. Directors and a very few senior officers were informed of the family's inclinations. At the time of the annual meeting of stockholders in late July, members of the Voting Trust requested that the Board explore strategic alternatives available to the company and expressed their interest in a transaction that would include both tax deferral and liquidity. Goldman, Sachs & Co., the company's longtime investment bankers,[6] made a presentation to the board and senior management on July 29, 1997, the day after the stockholders' meeting. They were formally engaged two weeks later as financial advisor to the company. Joel Kramer, publisher of the newspaper, later told employees that he was informed about the decision two weeks before the public announcement.

On September 4, 1997, Cowles Media Company announced that it was exploring possible "strategic alternatives" with other U. S. media firms, at the request of the Cowles Family Voting Trust. Jay Cowles, speaking for the Voting Trust, said: "We decided to pursue strategic alternatives because we believe future success in the media industry may come to more broadly-based organizations." The announcement was made, at least in part, because of speculation in the industry and the company's need for an orderly process that would minimize disruption within the organization. Goldman Sachs obtained confidentiality agreements from potential bidders and reviewed non-binding proposals with the Board on October 20. Candidate bidders made presentations to senior management and board members during the week of November 3, and definitive proposals followed. McClatchy initially proposed either an all-cash transaction, or one in which 25 percent of the consideration would be paid in McClatchy stock. That proposal was modified to provide for a minimum of 15 and a maximum of 25 percent in stock. (Detailed information about the bidding process is included as Appendix AA.)

National press coverage of the announcement was relatively muted, especially when compared with coverage of the sale of the Des Moines Register and Tribune Company in 1984 and the acquisitions of Cowles Media stock by Gannett and the Washington Post Company. Voting Trustees were unavailable to the press,

Cowles ponders sale or merger
Star Tribune's owner reviewing strategic options

By Terry Fiedler and Susan Feyder
Star Tribune Staff Writers

Cowles Media Co., owner of the Star Tribune, said Thursday it is pursuing "strategic alternatives" that could result in the merger or sale of the company that has been under family control since 1935.

The move comes at a time when media companies are commanding high premiums, and analysts estimated that the Minneapolis-based publisher could fetch $1 billion or more. The Washington Post Co. is regarded by some analysts as the leading candidate to make the purchase because it already owns 28 percent of Cowles stock.

The decision was prompted by members of the Cowles family who control 56.6 percent of the company's voting stock. The family has spent the past few years discussing various ways of cashing out of their holdings, at one time considering a public stock sale. Momentum for a possible sale to another media company seemed to build after a July board meeting.

STAR TRIBUNE, SEPTEMBER 5, 1997

and Cowles Media communications were directed almost exclusively to employees. *The Washington Post, The Wall Street Journal* and *The New York Times* carried brief stories; *The Journal* and *The Times* ran somewhat longer stories in October, commenting that prices for newspaper properties were probably at their all-time high and the pending transaction was creating anxiety in the organization.

News reports speculated that a sale of the company would bring between $850 million and $1.2 billion. The *Star Tribune* calculated that at $1 billion ($73 per share) a sale would bring $340 million to members of the Voting Trust. The quoted bid price of the stock in its limited over-the-counter market rose to $40 on September 5 and to $50 by September 25, up from $26 before the announcement.

The only family member who spoke at length with reporters was Charles Edwards, a great grandson of Gardner Cowles. A nephew of David Kruidenier, he was publisher of *The Des Moines Register* from 1984 to 1996. "For the last number of years the family has looked at strategic options to give shareholders more liquidity — a way to let the larger, older shareholders cash out," he said.[7] He went on to speculate that current changes in federal inheritance and capital gains taxes may make it easier to pass along inheritances from a successful family enterprise. He indicated that the decision was made by the Voting Trust, that he and other family members outside the trust had not been consulted, and that he was surprised by the decision. Lois Cowles Harrison, a former director and member of the Voting Trust, also indicated that she had not known of the possibility of sale before reading about it in *The New York Times*.[8] David Kruidenier responded, "Was I surprised? No."[9]

The Washington Post Company was widely thought to be the most likely buyer, given its existing 28 percent ownership.[10] Anthony Ridder, CEO of Knight-Ridder, said that his company would face "prohibitive antitrust problems" because it already owned the St. Paul Pioneer Press.[11] Other media companies mentioned frequently as likely buyers included Times Mirror, The New York Times Company, The Tribune Company, The Hearst Corporation and Advance Publications (owned by the Newhouse family). Gannett was generally considered unlikely because of its ownership of a Twin Cities television station. As time went on, speculation grew about more elaborate possibilities, involving among others Warren Buffett and Dow Jones & Co. While media attention was almost exclusively on the *Star Tribune*, Cox made it clear in communications with employees that — for various reasons, including tax considerations — all of Cowles Media would be involved in any transaction.

In an overview story based on interviews with industry analysts and others, the *Star Tribune* listed several possible factors that caused the Voting Trustees to consider a sale in the fall of 1997, including:

1. the very high prices being paid for daily newspapers in recent years and the very strong financial position of several potential buyers;
2. record earnings at Cowles Media and a strong financial performance for several years;
3. the 1997 reduction in the capital gains tax rate from 28 to 20 percent;
4. a continued lack of success in diversification; and
5. possible capital expenditures for computer systems and additional press and production facilities at the *Star Tribune*.

While the first three were very much in the minds of the voting trustees, they were not the determining factors in their decision.

All this was occurring against the backdrop of a stock market in which the Standard & Poor's 500 Stock Index had more than doubled between the end of 1991

EPILOGUE—SUBSEQUENT EVENT

and early 1997, while the price of Cowles Media stock was about where it was in 1987.[12] Many of the news stories misstated the profitability of the *Star Tribune,* citing the 12 percent operating margin for the company as whole; publisher Joel Kramer told employees that the newspaper's margin was in excess of the industry average of around 20 percent.

On November 10 *Crain's Chicago Business* reported that the board of The Tribune Company (owner of *The Chicago Tribune* and papers in Florida) had met on November 6 and approved a bid for Cowles Media. The report said that November 10 was the deadline for bids and that the Cowles family and its advisers were expected to take at least two weeks to study proposals before choosing a buyer.[13] On November 13, the *Saint Paul Pioneer Press* reported that Times Mirror Company had withdrawn as a potential buyer "after visiting the premises and reviewing Cowles' financial data." The article went on to say that their departure "presumably leaves The Washington Post, The New York Times and the Tribune Company as possible purchasers.[14] The *Star Tribune* reported on November 13 that the Cowles Media board and members of the Cowles Family Voting Trust had met for five hours on November 12 to discuss the possible sale. Its list of possible buyers included those named by the *Pioneer Press,* plus A. H. Belo Corporation.

STAR TRIBUNE, NOVEMBER 14, 1997

THE WALL STREET JOURNAL, NOVEMBER 14, 1997

Late in the evening of November 13 the company announced that it had reached an agreement with McClatchy Newspapers, Inc. to acquire Cowles Media for approximately $1.4 billion, the equivalent of $90.50 per share. A minimum of 15 percent and a maximum of 25 percent of the Cowles shares were to be exchanged for McClatchy stock and the balance purchased for cash, a revision of the initial proposal. The Tribune Company had submitted a proposal (half cash and half stock) that was "materially lower" than the McClatchy bid. Salomon Brothers, acting as financial advisor for McClatchy, estimated the "firm value reference range" for Cowles as $1.2 to $1.5 billion — $73.06 to $96.57 per share.[15] Goldman Sachs had estimated a value between $59.75 and $98.98 per share.

McClatchy publishes *The Sacramento Bee* and nine other daily newspapers, primarily in the West. In 1995 McClatchy acquired *The News and Observer* in Raleigh, North Carolina, from the Daniels family for $337 million, thought at the time to be an aggressive price. McClatchy had revenue of $624 million in its most recent fiscal year, compared with $517 million for Cowles; its net income of $44.5 million was significantly greater than Cowles' $29.5 million. McClatchy announced that it would sell the Cowles' magazine and book publishing businesses, and that it expected to realize at least $150 million for them after taxes. The two magazine businesses were subsequently sold to Primedia for approximately $208 million.

Founded in California in 1857, McClatchy is now controlled by members of the fifth generation, only one of whom is active in management. Shares were sold to the public in 1988, but the family retains 97 percent ownership of voting shares and 75 percent of the total shares.[16]

In a press conference[17] to discuss the transaction, Gary Pruitt, president and CEO of McClatchy, described the *Star Tribune* as one of the best newspapers in the country in one of the best newspaper markets in the country, one characterized by great growth and demographics and a tradition of civic involvement. He indicated that McClatchy policy was to give considerable operating autonomy to its papers and that he anticipated no significant changes, other than to eliminate "redundant" corporate staff activities and to divest the non-*Star Tribune* businesses. McClatchy pledged to continue the company's philanthropic giving program at an annual level of $3 million for at least ten years and to rename Cowles Media Foundation "The Star Tribune Foundation."

At the same press conference, Elizabeth Ballantine, managing trustee of the Cowles Family Voting Trust, characterized the decision as "very exciting." She said that as the family had grown and dispersed throughout the country, they were less involved in the Twin Cities and less connected to its cultural and civic life. Jay Cowles reiterated her comments

ELIZABETH BALLANTINE, 1997

about the family and stressed that they had taken a long time to discuss the possibilities, noting that McClatchy had beliefs and values similar to those of the Cowles family. In response to a question he noted that a member of the Cowles family would serve on the McClatchy board of directors. Elizabeth Ballantine was later named.

Press coverage of the announcement and the reaction of the financial community reflected "surprise" that McClatchy was the successful bidder, because it had not been publicly identified as a potential bidder at all. Most agreed that it was a combination that made great strategic sense for McClatchy and one that assured the continued independence of the *Star Tribune*. Tom Goldstein, dean of the Columbia University Graduate School of Journalism, said: "Minneapolis is a journalist's paper, not afraid of trying things, and I'm a great fan of the McClatchy people, who attempt to run quality papers. They're a good, coherent family-style chain."[18]

Reaction in the Twin Cities was generally favorable. The *Saint Paul Pioneer Press* headlined: "Star Tribune's new owner appears similar to old one," and went on to say, "Like the Minneapolis newspaper, the Sacramento, Calif.-based newspaper

STAR TRIBUNE EDITORIAL, NOVEMBER 16, 1997

chain is known for its liberal editorial pages, a traditional watchdog approach to the news and an active role in the community."[19]

The fourth generation had not been not able to find a way to retain control and simultaneously achieve the desired liquidity for family stockholders. It was able, however, to meet the goals it had set for itself a year earlier. The sale of the company was accomplished in an orderly and confidential manner. The members of the Voting Trust could be confident that they were passing on a great legacy of journalism and community service by selling the company to a successful operation that had shown that its values and relationships with the communities in which it published newspapers were similar to those of the Cowles organization. Stockholders realized a high value for their holdings. The family members, many of whom felt a sense of regret about severing their direct ties to the newspaper, were united in their belief that they had exercised their stewardship responsibly.

1 In fact the trust was not simply extended. In addition, a new agreement was drawn up, in part to take into account changes in the (Delaware) laws governing such trusts.
2 The trustees were Russell Cowles II; Elizabeth Ballantine; Elizabeth Bullitt, M.D.; John (Jay) Cowles III; and Joe Scofield (son-in-law of David Kruidenier).
3 News Release, October 31, 1996.
4 A public offering would require "business segment" financial reporting, detailing the results of the Star Tribune separately from the non-newspaper operations - Cowles Enthusiast Media, Cowles Business Media and Cowles Creative Publishing. Those results had not been made public before.
5 In 1993 the New York Times Company bought the parent company of *The Boston Globe* for $1.1 billion; in 1996 A. H. Belo Company (owner of *The Dallas Morning News*) bought the Providence Journal Company (which included the newspaper and nine television stations) for $1.5 billion; and in April 1997, Knight Ridder paid $1.65 billion for *The Kansas City Star, The Fort Worth Star-Telegram* and two smaller papers. There were also reports in the press that an unsolicited offer of approximately $1 billion had been made in 1996 for The Milwaukee Sentinel Company.
6 John Cowles joined the board of General Electric Company at the same time as Sidney Weinberg, who was for many years a senior partner at Goldman Sachs.
7 "Owner of *Star Tribune* seeks buyer or partner," *Saint Paul Pioneer Press,* September 5, 1997, page 1A.
8 "Why now?" *Star Tribune,* September 4, 1997, p. 1D.
9 Ibid.
10 In fact, the Post is reported to have declined an opportunity to enter into negotiations to purchase the rest of Cowles Media because of expectations of a high price being placed on it.
11 "Knight-Ridder Decides One Twin City Is Enough," *The New York Times,* September 7, 1997.
12 See Appendix X.
13 Reported in *Star Tribune,* November 2, 1997, p. 2B "Report: *Chicago Tribune* owner makes bid for Cowles Media."
14 "Times Mirror out of Cowles bidding," *Saint Paul Pioneer Press,* November 13, 1997, p. 3E.
15 Joint Proxy Statement/Prospectus dated February 19, 1998.
16 "McClatchy Agrees to Buy Cowles Media," *The Wall Street Journal,* November 14, 1997, p. 3A.
17 Press Conference, November 14, 1997, Minneapolis.
18 "McClatchy's Surprising $1.4 Billion Purchase," *San Francisco Chronicle,* November 15, 1997, page 1D.
19 *Saint Paul Pioneer Press,* November 15, 1997, page 1A.

APPENDIX A

THE PURCHASE OF *THE MINEAPOLIS STAR*

Buying *The Minneapolis Star*
John Cowles Sr.
November 3, 1938

As several advertising men have expressed a desire to know how my brother Gardner (Mike) Cowles Jr., and I originally came to buy The Minneapolis Star, what our aims for it are, what our publishing philosophy is, etc., here is the story. If anyone is interested in more details, I shall be happy to try to answer their questions.

For several years before we bought The Minneapolis Star, we had made pretty intensive studies of various newspaper fields with a view to buying a paper somewhere that was potentially capable of being developed into a big, important, influential property. We thought The Des Moines Register and Tribune was firmly enough established and rolling ahead under its own momentum sufficiently so that we could advantageously use part of our surplus energy in building up another sizable paper in some other city.

We seriously considered seven papers, four of them in much larger cities than Minneapolis, but each time we swung back to The Minneapolis Star as offering more opportunity than any of the others.

We had, of course, been intimately acquainted with the Minneapolis newspaper situation for years. We knew that in Minneapolis, unlike most cities, the newspaper field had not crystallized into one dominant leader. In most cities some one paper was already outstanding in circulation and advertising volume and editorial merit and reader influence, such as The Milwaukee Journal, or The Kansas City Star, or The Denver Post or The Pittsburgh Press.

In Minneapolis no paper was outstanding. While the other two Minneapolis papers were better known nationally than the Star, they did not have the reader following at home to justify their prestige abroad. Actually no Minneapolis newspaper was anywhere nearly filling the field or measuring up to its opportunities. Each of the other papers had a little more than one-third of the Minneapolis pie and the Star a little less than one-third.

The Minneapolis Star had been bought in 1924 by a practical newspaper man, John Thompson, (who had been trained both on the news and business sides of The New York Times under Adolph Ochs and Carl Van Anda) and some associates.

Although Mr. Thompson was inadequately financed, he had been able, by printing the news fairly and impartially, by giving the best local news coverage, and the best sports and society news, steadily to build up The Star's home delivered Minneapolis circulation. The most vital thing that he had done to The Star was to develop in it a complete feeling of reader confidence and trust. In spite of the fact that the other Minneapolis papers then had far more elaborate telegraphic news coverage, for example, than did The Star, The Star quietly grew in home delivered city circulation year after year until it was much closer to the top than was generally realized.

Thompson's principal financial associate died in 1934, and the executors wanted to convert their Star stockholdings into cash in order to settle the estate. Although The Star had made money in eight out of the previous ten years and was currently making money, when we approached Thompson with the suggestion that we buy control of The Star, he finally agreed, because our publishing philosophies were similar and he realized that this move would provide The Star sufficient working capital so that it could go ahead and expand its facilities to take full advantage of its opportunities. Consequently, in June 1935, my brother and I paid $1,000,000 for control of The Star and joined forces with Thompson. He is publisher of The Star, in complete charge of the paper when I am not in Minneapolis, and is a substantial stockholder.

Following our purchase, we doubled The Star's wire news service, doubled the news and photographic staff, and installed a lot of new mechanical equipment. The public's response to the improved paper was immediate, and The Star's circulation has been constantly climbing upward ever since. For the six months ending September 30, 1935, The Star's circulation was 80,000. For the six months ending September 30, 1936, it was 119,000; September 1937, 135,000; and September 30, 1938, 150,000, in spite of the fact that we raised both country carrier and mail circulation prices last spring.

We have used no high pressure circulation methods or expensive promotion stunts. The same man that was circulation manager during the ten years prior to our purchase is circulation manager now. The assistant circulation manager now was the assistant prior to our purchase. No outside circulation "experts" have been imported. The Star's growth has been simply the public's voluntary response.

The Star now has more home delivered city circulation, more total city circulation and more grand total circulation, than the Minneapolis morning and evening combination paper added together, and far more than the second evening paper.

As to The Star's political leanings and editorial page philosophy, they are about as follows: If one regards The New York World-Telegram as radical, then I suppose The Minneapolis Star is radical. We believe The Star's editorial page policy would be more accurately described by calling it mildly progressive or moderately liberal.

There are two philosophies as to editing newspapers. One is that of The New York Times, which attempts to keep its news columns fair and impartial and to confine its own opinions to its editorial page. That is our publishing philosophy, both with the The Minneapolis Star and with The Des Moines Register and Tribune.

The other philosophy is exemplified by The Chicago Tribune, which believes it proper for a newspaper to editorialize in its news columns. We do not question the sincerity or good faith of publishers that follow that philosophy, but we don't agree with it. We believe that freedom of the press carries with it an obligation for a newspaper owner to keep his news columns objective and unbiased and to express his opinions only on the editorial page and not through coloring the news.

The other Minneapolis papers more or less follow the philosophy of The Chicago Tribune, while we try to live up to the same standard that The New York Times does.

The Minneapolis Star does not, for example, assume that all men who go on strike are necessarily Communists and so label them in its news columns. The fact that the general public appreciates that the *Star* tries to keep its news columns fair and impartial and confine its opinions to its editorial page has probably been more responsible for its growth in circulation and reader confidence than any other one thing.

As to the future? We expect to go right on publishing the best paper for Minneapolis readers that we know how to print. On our editorial page we expect to continue to educate the public along sound economic lines toward sound political thinking, not through invective and denunciation, but by reasonableness and persuasion.

We expect our circulation to continue to grow. We expect our advertising volume to continue to grow, not because of editorial favors that we do for advertisers, but because The Star produces the best results for the least cost.

In September 1938, The Star had the largest gain in advertising linage of any metropolitan afternoon paper in the U.S. September was also the largest month in dollar income in The Star's history, but October has topped September. The whole future looks mighty bright to The Minneapolis Star.

APPENDIX B

TIME MAGAZINE COVER STORY

When the Cowles family of Des Moines bought the Minneapolis *Star* last fortnight (TIME, June 24), they acquired the third and weakest newspaper in that community. To them that was no cause for discouragement. Their money-making Des Moines *Register & Tribune*, which today blankets Iowa like that State's own rich, black topsoil, was also third and weakest when Gardner Cowles Sr. picked it up 32 years ago.

Gardner Cowles was then 42, with six children and not much money. A small-town banker in Algona, in northern Iowa, he had taught school there, married one of the teachers, made a little money as a contractor in rural mail routes. For a while he edited a local weekly called the *Advance*. His great & good friend was the rival paper's editor, Harvey Ingham. In 1902 Editor Ingham went to Des Moines to edit the down-at-heel *Register & Leader*, persuaded his friend Cowles to buy the paper. Price: $300,000. What Mr. Cowles thought he was buying was a sheet with $160,000 debts, 33,000 circulation. When he discovered that the debts were $180,000, circulation less than 16,000, he was so disillusioned that he wanted to sell. Failing to find a buyer, he decided to go on, against the competition of the *Capital* and the Scripps-owned *News*.

FETISH. Deaf to the hoots of his advertising representatives, Publisher Cowles resolved to give out no circulation figures whatever until the *Register* had 25,000. Then & there he adopted a publishing formula which was to make him rich: He made Circulation a fetish. Hiring & firing one circulation manager after another, he finally took over the job himself. He found subscription accounts two, three, four years past due, weeded them out, put the paper on a cash-in-advance basis. On the theory that men & women are creatures of habit, he concentrated on the problem of getting the *Register* to them on time. Helped by his oldtime experience as an overland mail contractor, Publisher Cowles studied maps and railroad timetables, learned the location of every town and hamlet in Iowa, memorized the schedules of every train out of Des Moines. As the *Register* circulation machine began to work, a *Register*-habit grew steadily throughout the State. At the end of the first year the paper earned $9,000, has never failed to make money since. Circulation mounted to 25,000 in 1906, 50,000 in 1912.

In 1908 the *Register* gobbled the newly established *Tribune*. In 1924 Publisher Roy Wilson Howard (Scripps-Howard) visited Des Moines, asked Gardner Cowles ("G.C.") to call at his hotel. In an hour "G.C." had bought the Scripps-Howard *News* for $150,000. Three years later the *Capital*, owned by the late Senator

157

Lafayette Young, gave up the battle and the *Register & Tribune* remained the only newspaper in Des Moines.

Not only did the *Register & Tribune* saturate the city circulation (83,000 morning & evening in a population of 142,500), but is pushed its frontiers to the farthest of Iowa's 99 counties, became for all practical purposes Iowa's State newspaper. Its serious competitors are not the Sioux City *Journal* nor the Cedar Rapids *Gazette*, but big dailies from outside the State. On the east the invasion of the *Chicago Tribune* must be — and is — vigilantly resisted; on the west the Omaha *World-Herald* and *Bee-News* knock at the Nebraska-Iowa border. But the *Register & Tribune* has its State — most literate and fourth wealthiest per capita in the U.S. — sewed up tight. Reason: It gets and prints all Iowa news, and knows how to deliver it. Its 254 State correspondents report not only hot news, but every marriage and death in their communities. A single day's edition of the *Register & Tribune* may be replated as often as 20 times, to front-page news of special interest to this distant town or that remote county. Once printed, the news is rushed to the *Register & Tribune*'s quarter-million subscribers (including 72,000 farm families) by the most elaborate and thoroughgoing carrier system in the U.S. Old "G.C." with his head full of route numbers and train schedules, built an organization of 4,820 carriers who swarm over Iowa. Where train schedules are not adequate, a fleet of motor trucks does the job. On Sundays, when R.F.D. is off duty, carriers cover the farm regions. Fifty-six circulation managers, 90 supervisors — all crack men — keep the machine running. Chief of them all is the *Register & Tribune*'s circulation manager, William A. ("Bill") Cordingley, whose red-topped pate peers over the same roll top desk at which Gardner Cowles first placed him 30 years ago.

YOUNG BLOOD. Three daughters, three sons has Gardner Cowles. Daughter Helen, who used to edit the *Register & Tribune* book page, collaborated on four volumes including *1,000 Ways to Please a Husband*. Pleased by Daughter Helen is Husband James LeCron, secretary to Secretary of Agriculture Henry Agard Wallace. (Since the Cowleses are traditionally Republican, Son-in-law LeCron's New Dealism is a subject for family jokes.) Son Russell, living in Santa Fe, N. Mex., is a Prix de Rome muralist, an abstractionist who does portraits of himself in a bathtub (TIME, Feb. 11). Daughter Bertha's husband, Sumner Quarton, manages a Cowles radio station at Cedar Rapids. Daughter Florence's husband is in the automobile business. Remaining are two sons who now, with their 74-year-old father's counsel, rule his publishing domain. They are John and Gardner Jr. ("Mike").

JOHN. At 36, with the title of associate publisher, John Cowles is in effect the boss of the Des Moines *Register & Tribune*. That he is able, is largely due to his intelligent inquisitiveness. Home on holiday from Phillips Exeter 20 years ago small John often would go with his father to the *Register & Tribune* office, perch himself on the desk of his father's secretary, Agnes ("Mac") MacDonald, spout a stream of questions: "What does so-&-so do? Is he smart?…What is that voucher for? Why is there a 2% discount marked on it? …How much does newsprint cost?… How fast can the presses turn out 1,000 copies?…" He was still asking questions when he rushed through Harvard (cum laude) in three years while taking Professor Charles Townsend ("Copey") Copeland's famed English 12 course and working on the editorial staffs of all three campus publications — *Crimson, Advocate, Lampoon*. He asked questions when he accompanied his father to newspaper conventions, and when after graduation in 1920, he started on the *Register & Tribune* as a plain reporter. He still asks questions wherever he goes, on his frequent visits to Manhattan and Washington. No corn-fed bumpkin, no dallying rich-man's-son, inquisitive John

Cowles has stored behind his thick-lensed glasses and his moon face a wealth of essential fact. An excellence of perspective on top of a sound judgment makes him one of the most important young newspaper publishers in the land.

Individual accomplishments are difficult to classify in the *Register & Tribune* plant. But it was during John Cowles's ascendancy that circulation was upped from 114,000 to 280,000; that national features were added until the paper now offers 17, from Walter Lippmann to Walter Winchell — more headliners than any other newspaper in the U.S.; that three radio stations were established; that profits mounted to a prodigious figure with 48% of revenue coming from circulation. Definitely credited to John Cowles is the Register & Tribune Syndicate, started eleven years ago and now serving some 40 features to clients in every state in the Union.

John now occupies his father's old office on the ground floor of the 13-story building in Des Moines "Loop." He works hard, loves to play. He will bet on anything, any time, for any amount from a pack of cigarettes up. His favorite gambling companion is his young brother "Mike," and when they play golf there are bets on nearly every stroke. John has a duffer's swing but manages to score about 90.

With his vivacious, black-eyed wife, Elizabeth Morley Bates Cowles, sister of Actress Sally Bates, John lives in a big, old red brick house, owned successively by two late Secretaries of Agriculture (Wilson's Meredith, Harding's Wallace). "But," says John Cowles, "I don't want anyone to think my ambition is ever to be secretary of Agriculture." The Cowleses entertain often and well. Their bedded guests within a fortnight included such an assortment as Herbert Hoover, Thomas S. Lamont, Nicholas Roosevelt and Philip Ludwell Jackson, ebullient publisher of the (Portland) *Oregon Journal* who rarely gets to the office before noon and,

having an elderly secretary who cannot take shorthand, never dictates a letter.

When Cowles parties threaten to be dulled by stuffy guests, John, who drinks pleasantly, sometimes produces a large, flat bowl, places it on the hardwood floor. The unbending guest is persuaded to sit in the bowl, which is then spun for a record number of turns. By the time the guest has won the contest or fallen over from dizziness, the party is considerably enlivened. John Cowles plays bridge everywhere except Des Moines, where he has not the time to become involved in many local festivities.

The John Cowleses have three children, Daughter Morley, 10, Sally, 8, John, 6.

GARDNER, JR., 33, followed his brother four years later to Exeter and Harvard where he was president of the *Crimson* and where his good friend was his cousin Corliss Lamont, Red son of the Morgan partner. Slow-spoken, deliberate, "Mike" Cowles is called executive editor. From his office on the balcony of the second floor he watches over the news rooms, keeps elbow to elbow with the associate editor and managing editor on either side. He cooks up many a smart feature, directs the three radio stations, which last year netted a profit of about $20,000. Breezier, more imaginative than Brother John, Gardner Jr. is not so invariably right. However, the only office wager he is known to have lost was $1 each to five employees whom he bet that Kansas City was bigger than St. Louis.

Once an enthusiastic airplane pilot, Mike let his license lapse for want of flying time. He introduced squash racquets to Des Moines, helped build the first courts, became of the town's best players, twice city champion. Popular Mike Cowles's second wife is pretty Lois Thonburg, who was his pupil in a University of Iowa journalism class, later a crack newshawk on his staff. They have a one-year-old daughter. Just before Citizen Hoover arrived to spend the week-end, Gardner Jr. managed to have his hair cut — a necessity which both he and John regularly put off as long as possible.

CONFERENCES. No accident is the *Register & Tribune*'s dominance of Iowa. Besides his perseverance and his insistent emphasis on circulation, "G.C." had the wisdom to hire the best men available, pay them well, and above all, get them to work together. No *Register & Tribune* editor may look down his nose at a circulation hustler. No mechanical superintendent may harbor a secret contempt of a white-collar advertising manager. The Cowles method: Conferences. *Register & Tribune* conferences are a serious business. Every Monday there is a conference of all departments, at which any man can — and is expected to — speak his mind on any subject, criticize anyone from old "G.C." down.* Fridays at lunch the "planning committee" meets to plot promotion stunts and civic campaigns.

In on the Monday conference sit the owners and such key men as:

Editor Harvey Ingham, now 76, snow-thatched and paunchy, still pegs out a daily editorial column, makes speeches, is supposed to know more Iowans than any other man alive.

William Wesley Waymack, 46, associate editor, has been in charge of the editorial page since Editor Ingham's virtual retirement. Like the *Register & Tribune*'s famed Cartoonist Jay Norwood ("Ding") Darling, now on leave of absence as Chief of U.S. Biological Survey, he was hired from the *Sioux City Journal.* He is reputed the best amateur candy maker in the Midwest.

Basil L. ("Stuffy") Walters, 39, short, barrel-shaped (200-lb.) and genial, is managing editor of both the *Register* (morning) and *Tribune* (evening). Between his two staffs, entirely separate for each paper, has grown a genuine news rivalry, essential in a city where there is not other local competition.

Joyce Swan, beaming promotion manager, sees to such enterprises as giving thousands of Iowa schoolchildren free rides in the newspaper's airplane.

Vernon Pope is in charge of the rotogravure, which, instead of being the usual Sunday dump for left-over news pictures, is used as a sustained circulation getter. A prime factor in the Cowles formula is to develop long picture series which will run for a dozen weeks or more.

And always on hand is Gardner Cowles. He comes to his office, reads the papers or has them read to him, listens to reports, smokes countless cigarettes, prods his sons for circulation and more circulation. Two "G.C." maxims: "Take the subscriptions and let the street sales go."… "A mediocre paper with a good circulation department can put out of business the best newspaper in the land with a poor circulation department."

The Senior Cowles plays bridge at the Des Moines Club every day after lunch. He hates poker, likes popcorn, has his wife read to him in the evenings while he plays solitaire.

TO MINNEAPOLIS. If the Cowles boys were less ambitious they might easily have been content to remain the No. 1 publishers in Iowa for the rest of their lives. Their *Register & Tribune* has paid dividends for 30 years to its 60 stockholders, almost all of whom are active workers on the newspapers. And their riches would doubtless multiply. But the Brothers Cowles began to have other ideas three years ago when they decided to expand. Sharing their plans was Brother John's good Harvard friend Davis Merwin, who in Bloomington, Ill., was running has family's 99-year-old *Pantagraph,* and running it well enough to make it top-flight among small-town papers. For their first step, Messrs. Cowles & Merwin sought a community with a high rating of literacy and education, a high percentage of native-born U.S. citizens, preferably of northern European stock, an even distribution of purchasing power with few rich, few poor. The paper they wanted was to be an evening sheet with strong reader loyalty and strong emphasis on home circulation. The specifications led them to Minneapolis and the *Star*.

Minneapolis is one of the few cities in the Midwest where the newspaper situation has not completely jelled. The farm-booming *Tribune* and the *Journal* share leadership and prestige, but neither has anything like the circulation coverage that denotes a dominant paper. The liberal *Star* (called by its competitors the "Workingman's Paper" because its mechanical departments are completely unionized and because it is shunned in the silk-stocking areas) gained slowly while the leaders stood still. Home-delivered circulation of all Minneapolis papers totaled only 145,000 in a population of 488,000. The field looked ripe for the sort of circulation ability in which the Cowleses are well versed. They bought the *Star* for $1,000,000, installed Friend Merwin as publisher with full authority to run the paper his way. Working with General Manager John Thompson and Managing Editor George Adams, he will be free of interference from Des Moines.

Slight, handsome Dave Merwin, 35, was something of a wild man, a jolly drinker, an able cartoonist, at Harvard. After college and a round-the-world trip, with tiger-hunting in Indo-China, he quieted down, succeeded his ailing uncle as publisher of the *Pantagraph*. A licensed transport pilot, he flies about in his orange-colored airplane called Scoop, loves to whisk his small son & daughter 100 miles or so for an ice cream soda. To the Cowles team, Publisher Merwin takes financial wizardry and a profound knowledge of all newspaper mechanical operations which both brothers lack.

TO WHERE? If Cowles & Co. should fail in their Minneapolis venture, they would doubtless retire to their Iowa pasture for a long time. If they succeed, it is a practical certainty that the next year or so will see them buying into another city. They have long been surveying the field, have in their files a complete detailed index about almost every newspaper in the U.S. that might be for sale. With 30 years of active publishing ahead of them, with William Randolph Hearst settling into old age, with Scripps & Howard in their prime, the youthful Brothers Cowles of Iowa may yet step out as one of the great chain newspaper publishers of tomorrow.

*The *Register & Tribune* is Republican, but not blindly so. It did not support Warren Harding and it favors many a Democrat for State office. It defended Henry Wallace's AAA reduction program as a temporary measure, flayed NRA. It sponsored the League of Nations, World Court, low tariffs.

APPENDIX C

COWLES MEDIA COMPANY (AND PREDECESSOR CORPORATIONS)
STOCK DATA

The company was capitalized initially with 50,000 shares of common and 8,000 shares of preferred stock. Most of the common stock was held in roughly equal proportions by John and Mike Cowles, with the Des Moines Register and Tribune Company owning most of the preferred. The brothers purchased shares in 1936 at $10.30 per share and offered a portion of it to other common stockholders. Stock could be issued only with the consent of the Register and Tribune Company, as owner of the preferred stock.[1] In 1937 an additional 50,000 shares of common was authorized.

The preferred stock was converted to common stock and paid out to Register and Tribune shareholders as a stock dividend in December 1940 and March 1941. Gardner Cowles Sr. is reported to have said that the Register and Tribune stockholders took the risk and should get some return.[2]

The new Star Journal and Tribune Company had 150,000 shares of common stock, of which 100,000 was held by former Star Journal stockholders. In 1946 John Cowles wrote to Kingsley Murphy, offering to purchase his stock for $50 per share, the price at which the company had purchased approximately 7,400 shares originally owned by Gardner Cowles Sr. (Murphy declined the offer.)[3] The Register and Tribune Company acquired 5,000 shares in 1950 and an additional 12,000 shares from Mike Cowles in 1953 at $100 per share.[4]

The stock was first split in 1956, with a 3:1 ratio increasing authorized shares to 450,000, making more shares available for purchase by employees. In 1958 the number of authorized shares was increased to 750,000, of which 450,000 were voting and 300,000 non-voting. This was accomplished through a special stock dividend of two shares of non-voting for each three shares of voting stock outstanding. The value was placed at $27. (The year before it was noted that stock had been sold and purchased in the two or three preceding years at $100 per share, and that treasury shares were to be sold to employees for $37.50. That places the comparable price in 1957 at $112.50 per share. When the estate of Kingsley Murphy Sr. was settled in 1957, the Internal Revenue Service placed a value of $78.51 per share.)

In 1963 a stock dividend of two shares of non-voting for each five shares outstanding increased the authorized non-voting shares to 450,000. The new price was set at $30, compared to $40 before the dividend. In 1969 1,050,000 shares of non-voting common stock were issued, with one share to each current holder of common stock, voting and non-voting. The new price was set at $29.

In 1978 the stock was again split two-for-one. The new price was $27. In his report to stockholders, John Cowles Jr. said: "Our principal reason for this change is to maintain similarity and comparability with publicly held publishing companies, although we have no plan to take the company 'public'."

In 1981 the company discontinued its general practice of buying back common stock from stockholders. The purpose was to eliminate a large potential cash drain caused by repurchase of stock. In 1982 the company created a class of convertible preferred stock, offered to stockholders (largely employees) who had an option to sell their stock back to the company. At the same time, the company began publishing financial statements and other disclosures that would permit stockholders and broker-dealers to sell shares among themselves in compliance with federal securities laws. During 1984 two Minneapolis brokerage firms began to serve as intermediaries between buyers and sellers of Cowles Media Company stock. The preferred stock was redeemed in 1988.

An Incentive Stock Option Plan for key employees was adopted in 1984. Two years later this was followed by grants of restricted stock to selected management employees, subject to meeting specified financial performance measures.

The Employee Stock Plan in 1990 brought most regular employees into stock ownership. An initial grant of 6,500 shares began the plan, with future year contributions determined by profitability.

In 1992 the board authorized a program to purchase 90,000 shares in the open market, in part to meet the needs of the employee stock plan. The first open-market purchases were in 1993, with authorization for additional 200,000 shares made in 1996. In 1993 the stock was split six-for-one "to bring the share price more in line with other companies in the industry."[5]

1 John Cowles Sr., Letter to Gardner Cowles Jr., December 21, 1935.
2 Philip Sherburne, author interview, May 20, 1997.
3 John Cowles Sr., Letter to Kingsley Murphy, August 20, 1946.
4 William Friedricks, July 23, 1997 correspondence with the author regarding minutes of the Board of Directors of the Register and Tribune Company in 1953.
5 Cowles Media Company, *Annual Report,* Fiscal 1993.

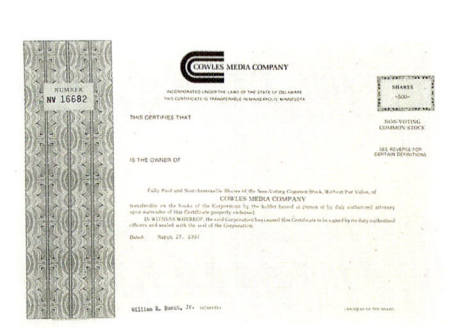

STOCK PRICES AND DIVIDENDS, 1935-1997

Year	Stock Price (adjusted for stock splits)	Total Stock Value (not adjusted for stock splits)	Dividend (adjusted for stock splits)	Year	Stock Price (adjusted for stock splits)	Total Stock Value (not adjusted for stock splits)	Dividend (adjusted for stock splits)
1935	$00.06	$ 10.00	—	1935	$00.06	$ 10.00	—
1936	$00.06	$ 10.30	—	1970	$02.42	$ 406.00	$0.13
1937	$00.06	$ 10.75	—	1971	$02.42	$ 406.00	$0.13
1938	$00.06	$ 10.75	—	1972	$02.79	$ 469.00	$0.14
1939	$00.08	$ 13.15	—	1973	$03.27	$ 549.50	$0.14
1940	$00.06	$ 10.00	—	1974	$03.27	$ 549.50	$0.15
1941	$00.09	$ 15.10	—	1975	$03.27	$ 549.50	$0.16
1942	$00.09	$ 15.00	$0.01	1976	$03.65	$ 612.50	$0.17
1943	$00.12	$ 20.00	$0.01	1977	$03.94	$ 661.50	$0.19
1944	$00.15	$ 25.00	—	1978	$05.00[5]	$ 840.00	$0.24[5]
1945	$00.15	$ 25.00	$0.01	1979	$05.00	$ 840.00	$0.24
1946	$00.30	$ 50.00	$0.01	1980	$05.00	$ 840.00	$0.24
1947	$00.30	$ 50.00	$0.01	1981	$05.00	$ 840.00	$0.24
1948	$00.30	$ 50.00	$0.04	1982	$05.00	$ 840.00	$0.24
1949	$00.30	$ 50.00	$0.04	1983	$04.25	$ 714.00	$0.24
1950	$00.30	$ 50.00	$0.05	1984	$06.50	$1,092.00	$0.25
1951	$00.45	$ 75.00	$0.06	1985	$20.37	$3,472.00	$0.26
1952	$00.45	$ 75.00	$0.05	1986	$27.08	$4,550.00	$0.28
1953	$00.45	$ 75.00	$0.04	1987	$25.00	$4,200.00	$0.33
1954	$00.60	$100.00	$0.05	1988	$20.83	$3,500.00	$0.37
1955	$00.60	$100.00	$0.05	1989	$19.50	$3,265.00	$0.41
1956	$00.60[1]	$100.00	$0.05[1]	1990	$25.50	$4,284.00	$0.45
1957	$00.67	$112.50	$0.05	1991	$20.50	$3,444.00	$0.47
1958	$00.80[2]	$135.00	$0.07[2]	1992	$19.17	$3,220.00	$0.48
1959	$01.04	$175.00	$0.07	1993	$21.50[6]	$3,612.00	$0.51[6]
1960	$01.19	$200.00	$0.07	1994	$23.00	$3,864.00	$0.55
1961	$01.19	$200.00	$0.07	1995	$24.00	$4,032.00	$0.59
1962	$01.19	$200.00	$0.07	1996	$25.00	$4,200.00	$0.63
1963	$01.25[3]	$210.00	$0.08[3]	1997	$90.50	$9,240.00	$0.67
1964	$01.46	$245.00	$0.09				
1965	$01.67	$280.00	$0.10				
1966	$01.88	$315.00	$0.11				
1967	$02.08	$350.00	$0.13				
1968	$02.08	$350.00	$0.13				
1969	$02.42[4]	$406.00	$0.13[4]				

(1) Reflects a 3 for 1 stock split
(2) Reflects a 5-for-3 stock split
(3) Reflects a 7-for-5 stock split
(4) Reflects a 2-for-1 stock split
(5) Reflects a 2-for-1 stock split
(6) Reflects a 6-for-1 stock split

Source: Sherburne & Coughlin, Ltd.

APPENDIX D

MAJOR PLANT AND EQUIPMENT INVESTMENTS

Year	Press Addition	Building Addition
1919	2 - Five unit Scott presses 3 Folders	Original 99' x 99' four-story building
1939	4 - Five unit, or 3-6 unit press Comic press	Pressroom addition
1941	12 unit and three folder Goss anti-friction presses	
1948	14 new Headliner units and two folders added to total 26 units, 11 folders	Mailroom second- and fourth-story addition Century Vault (time capsule) Facade - Medallions, art deco/stream line/modern
1960	5 - nine unit presses and 1 eight unit press. Seven color half-decks added. All Headliner units and color half-decks were converted to Dilitho in 1976.	Addition to mailroom Four-story addition along 5th Street Two-story addition to 1948 addition towards 4th Street

1978		Newsprint warehouse Large tunnel under street for link-belt conveyor system 34,000 square feet 30+ day supply 7 rolls high
1979	New 9-unit Goss Metro offset press, 5-color half-decks and a double 3/2 folder added, one old 8-unit anti-friction press removed	
1982		Occupancy of new 5-story, 75,000-square-feet Gale W. Freeman building
1987	5 ten-unit Goss presses (straight-flow processing lines) 4 Ferag inserting systems 3 72-P supplement inserting systems 19 conveyor lines linking presses and inserting systems 3 Interrelated computer systems	Heritage Center New land and building, 16 acres 425,000-square-feet Fleet repair garage New mailroom and bundle distribution facility Newsprint handling and automatic press loading 19 truck loading docks
1995	Converted vacated production space at the Star Tribune building into office environment	3-story in pressroom 39,000-square-feet

APPENDIX E

NEWSPRINT

Newsprint accounts for roughly 25 percent of a newspaper's total costs, and its price and availability are often critical factors in a newspaper's profitability. The price of newsprint tends to increase abruptly when there are labor disputes at paper mills or railroads servicing the mills; when demand for newsprint accelerates during an economic and advertising upswing in the economy; and/or when there is a lag in bringing new production capacity on line.

In 1973 a series of Canadian newsprint and railroad strikes lasted over four months. Resulting newsprint shortages cost the Minneapolis newspapers $2.6 million in lost advertising revenue. In 1972 suppliers were offering price discounts for multiyear contracts. In less than two years the quoted price went from $190 per ton to $259; the cost increase to the Minneapolis newspapers was approximately $5 million. Otto Silha explained the situation to stockholders in June 1974: "…newspapers need an assured newsprint supply. They won't have it in the latter part of this decade unless new machines are built. New newsprint machines won't be built unless newsprint companies are profitable enough to finance $100 million investments. You can see a scenario wherein the high price of newsprint forces higher and higher advertising and circulation rates which reduce circulation and advertising volume enough so that not so much newsprint is needed and the new newsprint machines are not profitable."[1] Between 1973 and 1977 the cost of newsprint increased by two-thirds.

The Minneapolis newspapers have historically used suppliers in Ontario, the site of the closest mills and hence shortest transportation links. While newsprint is a national or international commodity in theory, newspapers tend to be limited to buying paper in only a relatively small geographic segment of the newsprint industry for cost reasons. Newsprint producers are similarly limited, with the result that the industry is characterized by an intricate price-discounting system that reflects imperfections in the market mechanism and the nature of relationships between buyers and sellers.

When it became desirable to begin using large amounts of newsprint with a high recycled fiber content (from old "recycled" newspapers) in the late 1980s, there was a realignment of suppliers because it was difficult (and expensive) for western Ontario mills to use old newspapers to create recycled newsprint. There were two reasons: the mills had deliberately been built close to sources of timber and were distant from urban sources of old newspapers to recycle. A facility to process old newspapers then cost $50 million or more and construction took up to two years. (A complete new mill cost over $200 million, and its large capacity would represent a significant increase in supply, potentially depressing prices.) By 1996 the *Star Tribune* had increased its recycled newsprint content to 30 percent.

The newsprint price cycle again moved dramatically between 1988 and 1997. During the late eighties industry capacity increased as several new high yield machines came on line, reacting to good demand. The price per ton then dropped from $601 in 1988 to $440 in 1992; the recession of 1990-91 had resulted in a sharp decline in advertising expenditures. At that point suppliers began removing obsolete machines, reducing capacity. The price remained relatively stable into 1994, then moved abruptly as demand increased against a supply that had actually shrunk slightly. Demand was artificially inflated when many customers tried to build inventories as the price was rising, driving it up more rapidly.

By 1997 the price had eased again as the market came into better balance.

1 "Stockholders Told Newsprint Shortage the Financial Culprit in Fiscal '74," *Newsmakers*, June 1974, p. 1.

NEWSPRINT PRICES 1940-1997*

Year	Per Short Ton	Year	Per Short Ton
1940	$ 50.00	1969	$ 147.00
1941	$ 50.00	1970	$ 152.00
1942	$ 50.00	1971	$ 157.33
1943	$ 54.66	1972	$ 164.58
1944	$ 58.00	1973	$ 175.00
1945	$ 60.25	1974	$ 210.00
1946	$ 72.25	1975	$ 260.00
1947	$ 88.50	1976	$ 282.50
1948	$ 97.67	1977	$ 302.50
1949	$ 100.00	1978	$ 320.00
1950	$ 101.00	1979	$ 386.11
1951	$ 111.00	1980	$ 436.50
1952	$ 112.00	1981	$ 482.50
1953	$ 126.00	1982	$ 485.00
1954	$ 126.00	1983	$ 484.25
1955	$ 126.00	1984	$ 515.40
1956	$ 130.00	1985	$ 535.00
1957	$ 133.00	1986	$ 543.75
1958	$ 134.00	1987	$ 590.00
1959	$ 134.00	1988	$ 650.00
1960	$ 134.00	1989	$ 650.00
1961	$ 134.00	1990	$ 670.42
1962	$ 134.00	1991	$ 685.00
1963	$ 134.00	1992	$ 438.33
1964	$ 134.00	1993	$ 457.53
1965	$ 134.00	1994	$ 470.37
1966	$ 136.92	1995	$ 664.20
1967	$ 140.50	1996	$ 624.25
1968	$ 142.00	1997	$ 553.00

*Annual average contract price per ton delivered at New York City. Prices through 1973 are for 32-pound paper; thereafter for 30-pound. One metric ton equals 1.1023 short tons.

Source: Canadian Pulp and Paper Association

APPENDIX F

"THE RESPONSIBILITY OF A FREE PRESS IN A WORLD IN CRISIS"

An Address by John Cowles Delivered at the School of Journalism, University of Missouri, *May 4, 1951*

The Minneapolis Star and Tribune
at That Time Being Awarded a Missouri Medal for Distinguished Services to Journalism

Reprinted in *The University of Missouri Bulletin*
Volume 52-Number 33
Earl English, Ph.D., Editor
Journalism Series, No. 124

It is a great honor to be invited to speak on this occasion. For thirty years I have held the view that the country has no better school of journalism than the University of Missouri. My opinion results from personal contact with many graduates of the school over many years, and I am happy to have an opportunity to pay this tribute to Frank Mott and his predecessors who have served as dean of the school, and to Dr. Middlebush, as president of the university.

A revolution in the communication of information, ideas and opinion has been, and is, taking place in America.

Some of us newspapermen fail to realize the extent and nature of the changes that have occurred during the last generation. When reminded of it, we recall that newspapers used to put out frequent "extras" to give the results of sporting events, etc., which we no longer do, but many of us are not conscious of other more significant changes. Many of us also seem unaware of the ways in which newspapers will probably be affected by near future developments.

There is considerable reason to believe, I think, that television, when its facilities become nationwide, when telecasts are in color, and when the number of receiving sets has doubled, will become the nation's most powerful single instrument for the mass transmission of ideas and entertainment.

This does not in any sense mean, however, that newspapers generally are destined to dwindle into unimportance. Certain types of newspapers and other publications will, I think, find the economic road ahead rough, too rough for their survival. But other types of newspapers will, I believe, play an even more important role than they have in the past. Most newspapers, if they are well operated, can, I feel sure, look forward with confidence to continuing prosperity; and there may be even deeper satisfaction in editing such papers in the period ahead than there has ever been in the past.

Later on I want to talk more about the impact that color television will have on American life and what changes I think newspapers should — and will have to — make in their editorial and publishing techniques in the decade ahead. But before getting into that, I want to summarize briefly the revolution in the communication of information, ideas and opinions that quietly took place in the thirty years before anyone ever saw a telecast.

The number of different sources from which the public gets information and ideas has expanded enormously during the past generation.

There was almost no radio broadcasting in 1920. In 1950 we made a survey in Minneapolis that showed that eleven radio and TV stations were on the air with news broadcasts or news commentators for a total of 129 hours per week. This did not include speeches, round table discussions or any of the other types of programs that impart at least some information and opinion.

The Minneapolis radio and TV stations broadcast about a million words of news and news comment a week. This is almost as many words as the two Minneapolis papers print in the same period.

Unless one stretches the definition to include the old Literary Digest, there were not news magazines of importance thirty years ago. Today such news weeklies as Time, Quick, Newsweek and the U.S. News bring news to, and help shape the opinions of, large segments of the population. The youngest of the news weeklies, Quick, has gone from nothing to more than a million circulation in the past two years.

There were no picture magazines of the type of Life and LOOK until sixteen years ago. Scientific surveys indicate that some 28 million people now read each copy of Life and some 18 million read each issue of LOOK, substantially larger numbers than is the case with the older, more traditionally edited, weeklies. Since Reader's Digest does not carry advertising in its domestic editions, it publishes no circulation figures, but perhaps more Americans read it than any other publication, and Reader's Digest's circulation growth has come almost entirely in the past two decades.

Book publishing has also expanded enormously in recent years, particularly in the popular price paper bound field.

The news letters — Kiplinger, Whaley-Eaton, and a dozen others — have also come to play a sizable role in informing and influencing the public.

Nor should one underestimate the extremely important part in the distribution of information and opinion that labor unions have in the past fifteen years achieved.

During the last generation, the average American boy and girl have both attended school for a significantly greater number of years than did their fathers and mothers. The percentage of our population attending high school and college has approximately doubled since 1920. Two million more young people are going to college each year, and almost four million more to high school. As a result of better education, the public's tastes and interests in reading matter have steadily changed. Many newspapers, magazines and Sunday supplements that had wide popular appeal twenty or thirty years ago have either altered their editorial techniques or succumbed. Still others will die during the years immediately ahead if they don't change their formulas.

As the average American became better educated and also acquired access to far more numerous sources of information and opinion than before, most newspapers put increased emphasis on making their news columns objective and unbiased. Newspapers generally ceased being mouthpieces for a political party or an economic group. The public responded to this better journalism by giving to those papers that tried to present the news honestly and fully and accurately and impartially increased circulation and increased advertising patronage.

There are, of course, still a few outstanding exceptions. These fall into two classes. The first are newspapers owned by vigorous egoists who sincerely believe that their own peculiar prejudices are divinely revealed truth, and who consequently feel justified in slanting the news to conform to their convictions. The second group of exceptions are newspapers operated by cynics who believe that there is more circulation and consequently more profit, erroneously I believe, in inflaming passions and pandering to the ignorant than in issuing responsible publications. It is regrettable that most of the critics of the press cite papers in one of these two groups, and then generalize and indict the whole press for the sins of a small minority.

It is significant, however, that most of the papers in either of these two classes are currently doing less well in circulation than many of their editorially more responsible contemporaries.

Part of the credit for improving the objectivity and fairness and impartiality of the news columns of American papers in the last generation has been due to the reporters, copy readers and sub-editors who have taken increasing pride in their profession as its standards of integrity have risen. Part of the credit stems from the long-time policy of the Associated Press and the United Press, which have made full and fair news coverage their major goal.

In any event, newspaper standards of editorial objectivity and fairness and integrity are immeasurably higher than they were a generation ago.

During the last thirty years, newspaper publishing costs have steadily mounted and at an accelerated rate. The survival of marginal papers has become increasingly difficult and will become more so.

In addition to rising publishing costs, however, it has been the public itself which has dictated the reduction in the number of newspapers. As the public acquired many more sources than formerly from which it received information and news — radio, news magazines, news letters, labor union papers, etc. — the public tended to concentrate its newspaper reading on whatever was the best one afternoon paper and the best one morning paper in each community. As a result, the poorer and weaker papers simply could not survive.

In a highly thoughtful speech last March, Secretary of Commerce Sawyer said that in 1910 when the United States had a population of 92 million we had 2,600 daily newspapers. Today with a population of 150 million, we have 1,772 dailies.

In discussing the trend toward fewer newspapers, Secretary Sawyer made the following statements:

"An examination of the consolidation phenomenon indicates that it is due largely to increased costs of operation — especially the cost of labor and newsprint. In many cases the choice was combination or bankruptcy. In my opinion such combinations as have occurred have not resulted in deterioration of product. Some of our greatest newspapers exist in towns where the ownership is limited to one form. The Minneapolis Star and Tribune, The Louisville Courier-Journal, The Atlanta Constitution and Journal, The Kansas City Star and Times are examples."

Although many people wring their hands in sorrow whenever there is a newspaper suspension or merger, I want to say emphatically that I think the trend toward fewer and better daily newspapers has been clearly beneficial to the people of this country. But, whether one thinks it is beneficial or harmful is immaterial. As a practical matter, there are going to be many more consolidations and suspensions in the next few years, and the total number of daily newspapers in America is going to decline further. But that does not mean that the number and variety of the sources of information and opinion will be reduced.

Actually, I am convinced that where newspapers have combined or suspended and single ownership newspaper cities or fields have evolved, the resulting product has, in almost every instance, been much superior to the newspapers that preceded it.

I say flatly that with only a small number of exceptions the best newspapers in American are those which do not have a newspaper competing with them in their local field. By best I mean the most responsibly edited, the fairest, the most complete, the most accurate, the best written, and the most objective.

The Milwaukee Journal is alone in the afternoon field in Milwaukee. With the two possible exceptions of St. Louis and Washington, is there an afternoon paper anywhere in the country that has local competition that compares in high quality with The Milwaukee

Journal? I know of none.

Again excluding St. Louis and Washington, and also excluding New York which is an exception that I shall discuss in a moment, there aren't a handful of newspapers published anywhere else in the United States that, in my judgment, are as responsibly and well edited, as complete, as fair, as objective and which serve the public interest as well as do at least forty or fifty of the newspapers which are published in so-called monopoly or single ownership cities.

These newspaper institutions which have no local daily competition are not monopolies in the sense that they control the sole source from which the public gets its news and information and ideas. It is impossible to overemphasize this point. There are dozens of sources — radio, television, news magazines, labor papers, community papers, outside dailies, etc. — which also provide them.

The reasons why the newspapers that do not have local daily newspaper competition in their home field are superior, generally speaking, to those that do have competition are manifold.

In the first place, the publishers and editors have, I believe, a deeper feeling of responsibility because they are alone in their field.

Secondly, those newspapers that are not in hotly competitive fields are better able to resist the constant pressure to oversensationalize the news, to play up the cheap crime or sex story, to headline the story that will sell the most copies instead of another story that is actually far more important. The daily that is alone in its field can be as free as it wants to be from the urge to magnify the tawdry and salacious out of its importance in the news of the day. The newspaper that is alone in its field can present the news in better perspective and can free the news of the details which pander rather than inform.

Newspapers that don't have local newspaper competition are better able to resist the pressure of premature reporting. This pressure has become one of the worst enemies of responsible reporting. It breeds inaccuracies which can never be overtaken. It is responsible for distorted emphasis and lack of perspective. The newspaper in a single ownership city doesn't have to rush on to the streets with a bulletin rumor that Russian troops are invading Yugoslavia if it has reason to suspect that the unconfirmed report may not be true. It does not have to protect itself against a rival in case the story turns out by a long shot chance to be accurate.

Newspapers in single ownership cities can be, and usually are, less inhibited about correcting their errors adequately, fully and fairly.

Many other examples will occur to you as to why the newspapers in single ownership cities have both the opportunity and the obligation to lead the way toward a more responsible press.

And if a "monopoly newspaper" is really bad, then it won't last as a monopoly. New competition by abler and more socially moral newspapermen will eventually displace and supersede it.

A moment ago I referred to New York as being a unique exception to the condition I was describing. This is because New York has such a huge population that it can profitably support many different types of daily publications. Smaller cities can't.

The New York Times, which I regard as the world's best, is a national newspaper, deliberately edited for only the top segment of the population, that which is interested in important and serious news.

Although The New York Times is outstandingly successful, it is read by less than 15% of the families in New York City. It is only in our multi-million population cities where there is a huge amount of potential advertising revenue that a paper can prosper even though it reaches only a small percentage of the total potential audience, such as is the case with The New York Times and to an even greater degree with The Herald-Tribune. Boston wasn't large enough to support the Transcript.

Certainly in cities of less than a million population, newspapers, if they are to be economically self-sustaining, simply must be edited to interest and serve all the people, not just one class. Just as a department store carries a wide range of merchandise that will appeal to all different economic groups, or as a big cafeteria provides a variety of foods to appeal to different tastes, so must most newspapers, in order to survive, carry news and feature content that will interest people of both sexes, of all ages, of all vocations and educational levels.

In my opinion, the great mistake in the Hutchins Commission report on "A Free and Responsible Press" was its assumption that restoration of local daily competition was the only answer to the need for more responsible journalism. I think much in the Hutchins Commission report was excellent, but its basic premise was completely erroneous. As a newspaperman who has had many years' experience in both hotly competitive and in single ownership cities, I am convinced that an increase in the number of competing dailies would have precisely the opposite effect from the one the Hutchins Commission assumed. Secondly, newspaper competition as it existed in the U.S. when newspapers were virtually the only medium of information and opinion is simply not going to return. There are going to be fewer, not more, newspapers.

I agree thoroughly with the implication contained in the Hutchins Report that unless the press generally manifests more self discipline and shows more obvious concern for the genuine public interest than some papers show, the dangers of restrictions upon our free press are very real.

Although I accept the judgment of the American Society of Newspaper Editors that it would be unwise for the ASNE to create an agency to sit in judgment upon the performance of the American press, I think there is a widespread need for more self-examination on the part of American newspapers. I welcome the idea of more critical studies of the press, if made in good faith by competent, independent agencies.

We in Minneapolis have given a lot of thought to the possibility of creating an independent agency that would continuously examine how well the Minneapolis newspapers were performing their functions and fulfilling their obligations to the people of the Upper Midwest. We would be happy to regularly publish the full reports of such an agency, detailing its opinions as to our specific sins of omission or commission. The great difficulty that has so far thwarted our setting up such an agency is the finding of competent personnel in whom the general reading public would have complete confidence and who would, at the same time, know the practical problems and difficulties of metropolitan newspaper operations. If any of my hearers should have any constructive ideas in this regard I would be happy to have them.

There seems to be a widespread belief among the bench and bar throughout the United States that newspaper reporting of crime, trials and punishment sometimes contributes to the obstruction or miscarriage of justice, and that unless the situation is improved the press ought to be put under certain prohibitions in regard to such reporting. The idea of legislation limiting the right of the press freely to report the news in any field is utterly repugnant to me as a newspaper man, but I wonder whether the newspapers in single ownership cities might not jointly endeavor to explore the problem with a view toward possibly discovering ways of covering crime and trial news more responsibly. Perhaps a group of newspapers could undertake a two-year or a five-year study of crime and trial coverage, counseled by a committee on which attorneys, judges and the general public would be represented. Undoubtedly the newspaper men would never agree with the judges on precisely what ought to be done. But out of such a study and through an exchange of viewpoints there might develop a new concept of the proper function of the press in this important field of reporting, one which would better serve the public interest without infringing in the slightest upon the constitutional right of the people to a free press.

All of us there today believe in, and recognize the importance of, a free press. We agree that there can be no outside control of the press of any kind and still have it a free press. The way to reduce the likelihood that freedom of the press will be abridged is, it seems to me, for newspapers generally to demonstrate by their daily performance that they deserve their freedom. That means we must be more responsible in the way we use our franchise. We must show that we understand that the basic reason for a free press is to have and preserve a free society.

The goal of maintaining a free society is not served, it seems to me, by newspapers' whipping the public into a frenzy with cartoons, news stories and editorials that are so violent as to be almost psychopathic. I personally admire General MacArthur and regard him as one of the leading figures of this generation. I deplore the manner in which he was removed. But regardless of whether one agrees or disagrees with the administration's Asiatic policy, regardless of whether one thinks the president should or should not have relieved General MacArthur, is the preservation of our free society being enhanced by the emotional orgy that some of our newspapers are currently stimulating?

Would not qualified psychologists, regardless of their political views, say that what we have been witnessing in the United States in the last couple of weeks bears some resemblance to what took place in Germany and Italy not too long ago for some of us to remember?

Because of its powerful impact, television may tend to make the maintenance of our free society more difficult. Badly informed, emotionally adolescent TV viewers may tend to adopt hysterically extreme views on complicated political and economic issues concerning which they know, and would otherwise care, little. This will put increasing responsibilities on newspapers to try to prevent the country from being swept by mob emotion into ill considered and dangerous decisions.

Television may be the greatest potential agency for adult education we have, but there is a grave danger that it will develop in a pattern where it will not serve the public welfare as it might.

If television develops along the general line of commercial AM broadcasting it will mean that the advertiser, whose choices control programs, will push the programs down to the patterns with the lowest common denominators of interest in order to get the maximum numerical audience. The various commercial TV stations in their competition for audiences will thus all tend to vulgarize their programs. This will mean that the television station operators will be under the same type of pressures as newspapers in overly competitive fields. I discussed earlier how excessive competition for circulation in over-newspapered cities has resulted in lower quality publications, generally speaking, than where the newspapers are alone in their fields. Since there will obviously be several or many television stations in most cities, and since television stations are necessarily licensed by the government, which newspapers are fortunately not, perhaps a partial solution would be to require all television stations to allocate a very substantial number of hours, including some in the best viewing periods, for non-commercial and educational programs. Just how these programs can be of the type and quality they should be and just how their content can be kept free of government control is a problem I pass to wiser men.

The constantly growing pressure for people's time, which the coming of television intensifies, means that the less serviceable newspapers will find it more difficult to survive. The people living in metropolitan areas will increasingly concentrate on the one morning and the one afternoon paper that serves them best. In smaller cities and towns, the public will increasingly tend to read the one metropolitan daily that serves it best, plus its own local newspaper.

People will want far more interpretive news from their papers so that they can understand what is happening. People will want more background information. People will want not only the bare facts of what did happen yesterday but will want from their newspapers information on what is probably going to happen tomorrow or next week or next month.

The relative importance of editorial writers will greatly increase. It will not be tub-thumping, violent, partisan editorial assertions that the readers will want, but understandable analyses of the complicated problems that trouble them.

This means that we will need better reporters and better editors, and must give them more latitude than most papers now do.

A good newspaper reporter, whether in the field of science, government, industrial relations, education, politics, religion or crime news, ought to know as much in his field as a good college instructor knows in his. A good reporter should be able to tell the facts simply and clearly enough to interest and inform the layman without insulting the intelligence of the specialist.

A good reporter should be as objective and untiring in this pursuit of truth as a scientist doing research work at a university. In selecting and organizing his staff the editor of a large newspaper will actually, in some degree, be performing the function of a university dean.

Although complete control of a publication's editorial policy must remain in management's hands, more variety in the expression of editorial and interpretive opinion will be permitted. Men equal in intellectual caliber and character to university professors naturally will expect — and deserve — more latitude than less able men.

Frequently in The New York Times we read conflicting opinions by staff members. Charlie Merz in the editorial column may take one slant on a particular issue. Arthur Krock in his column may take another. Hanson Baldwin in his column may differ somewhat from both. Over Scotty Reston's signature we may read opinions slightly different from the other three. Is that bad? I say it is good. I have more respect for The Times because it permits this variety of opinion. It is, as a result, a more serviceable paper. In addition the readers have far more confidence in its integrity than they do in publications whose writers all follow an identical line, laid down from on high by an omnipotent and theoretically omniscient publisher.

As long as I remain a publisher I intend, of course, to reserve final authority over what does or does not go into the paper, but that is an authority that I rarely use, or feel any need of using. If a newspaper is staffed by men of high professional competence, intelligence and character, men whose basic philosophy is similar, the newspaper is better if the team is driven with loose reins.

Woodrow Wilson once said, "The highest form of efficiency is the spontaneous cooperation of a free people." I am convinced that this certainly applies to newspaper organizations!

In stressing the importance of the interpretation

of serious news I don't want to give the impression that newspapers should be solemn and dull. Quite the reverse. Unless newspapers are inviting and appealing to read, unless they have wit and humor and human interest, unless they have typographical attractiveness, unless they have many brief stories along with the long ones, they simply won't be read. We want everyone in our area to read our papers. Therefore we are trying to make them less formal. We are trying to make heavy news and editorial comment less forbidding.

We want more circulation not solely because it is a means toward more profit but because we think the more people we can persuade to read our papers the better informed they will be, and the wiser, consequently, will be their decisions. But we try never to forget that we must keep our papers responsible, for a free press won't, in our opinion, permanently survive unless it is also a responsible press. And, after all, we must never forget that the free press is a public right, not a private one.

APPENDIX G

CORPORATE AIRPLANES

After 24 Years, Airplane Operations Make
Final Landing
by Norm Mitchell, *Star Tribune* Pilot
Newsmakers, February 1976

After 24½ years of flying without an injury, *The Minneapolis Star* and *Tribune* has closed its aviation operation.

John Cowles Sr. ordered the first plane, a DC-3, from Remmert Werner in St. Louis, after he, Joyce Swan, Gideon Seymour and Otto Silha had an unbelievably hard time getting to the University of Missouri where Cowles was to receive an Outstanding Journalism Award. After going part way by train, only to have a flood stop rail and auto traffic in Iowa, two small planes were chartered to complete the trip from somewhere in Iowa to Columbia, Mo. A hair-raising experience on that charter and a comfortable, fast flight in the Pulitzer DC-3 convinced them to order a similar plane to Pulitzer's.

I was hired July 1, 1951, by Harold Perkins, then secretary of the company, and John Cowles to be the chief pilot and was sent to United Airlines in Denver for a checkout as a captain in the United DC-3. Wayne Hinderaker was hired by July 15 of that year as a co-pilot mechanic.

The DC-3 was flown without accident for 5,000 hours, eight years, 744,750 miles and over 2¾ million passenger miles. Some of the most interesting flights were to Caracas, Venezuela, Camaguey and Havana, Cuba, Bermuda, and throughout the West Indies.

1959 saw the changeover from the piston-powered DC-3 to the turbo-prop Gulfstream I, a 350 m.p.h. plane designed expressly for corporations. The Gulfstream I seated 12 passengers and had over a 2,000

TOP TO BOTTOM: DC-3, GULFSTREAM I, GULFSTREAM II

mile range, and could operate in and out of fields less than 4,000 feet long. It was pressurized so that while cruising at 25,000 feet the cabin pressure altitude was about 8,000 feet. That plane was flown for ten years and just under 5,000 hours.

The company sold the Gulfstream I in 1969 and put into operation the Gulfstream II pure jet aircraft. The GII, as it was called, incorporated many of the design features of the GI. It was approximately the same size and would operate out of relatively short fields. Pressurization was improved and its cabin altitude was 6,000 feet while the plane cruised at 43,000 feet above all scheduled airliners. It was truly a worldwide airplane with a range of well over 3,450 statue miles and cruised at speeds up to Mach .85 (about 590 m.p.h.). In it was installed one of the first inertial navigation systems used in private or commercial airplanes.

The safety record of the aircraft operation wasn't happenstance. It was due to a combination of factors. Some of these were:

1. The desire of the management to put safety foremost. That policy was responsible for the remaining factors.
2. Proper scheduling to permit crew rest for top efficiency for the flight.
3. The best aircraft available for clear vision.
4. The best and latest safety equipment.
5. The best recurrent flight training available.
6. The best maintenance available.

Twenty four and a half years of flying is summarized by listing a few impressive statistics:

Miles flown	3,383,990
Passenger miles flown	14,753,000
Total passengers	21,539
Hours flown	12,027
Flights (landings and take-offs)	5,649

Worth noting are a few of the flights and uses of the company plane. The first passenger carrying flight was September 25, 1951, from Minneapolis to Kansas City. Flight time was two hours, 42 minutes. The last flight was December 8, 1975, from Des Moines to Minneapolis in 41 minutes.

Some of the interesting uses of the plane were to take photographers and reporters to Williston, N.D., in October 1952 to observe the first oil well in the Williston basin. The plane was used to cover the opening (or more properly closing) of the Garrison dam north of Bismark in August 1953.

We flew to the political conventions of 1952, '56, '60, '64, '68 and '72, many football games including the Minnesota Rose Bowl games of 1961 and 1962, and, of course, the three Vikings Super Bowl games.

In May 1953, the DC-3 flew to Las Vegas where John Cowles Sr. was one of a few select guests to observe an atomic explosion. Every May and October for 22 years we joined most of the other leading U.S. corporations' airplanes on the top of the hill at Hot Springs, Va., for meetings of the Business Council held at the Homestead Hotel. The top business executives of the U.S. were always present at the meetings as well as senior government officials, and often the President of the United States.

Famous people were frequent guests aboard *The Star* and *Tribune* plane. Among the most notable were Dean Acheson, Archibald MacLeish, Hubert Humphrey, Richard Nixon, Paul Hoffman and Admiral Land, inventor of the Polaroid Land Camera.

On one flight our DC-3 had half of the atomic brains of the free world with us. Eminent physicists were: Harold Urey, University of California, discoverer of heavy water; Dr. Allen Waterman, director, National Science Foundation; Dr. Dael Wolfle, director, AAAS; Dr. Roger Revelle, director, Scripps Oceanography, La Jolla; Dr. Edward Teller, University of California; Dr. Laurence Gould, president, Carleton College; Dr. Athelstan Spilhaus; Dr. Paul Sears, Yale University; Dr. Frank Brown, Woods Hole, Massachusetts; Robert Garrabrant, National Science Foundation; Dr. Harlow Shapley, Harvard astronomer; and Dr. Wendell Stanley, University of California.

The circulation department filled the plane in the 50s and 60s when *Star* and *Tribune* executives and staff flew to regional circulation meetings. They also made use of the plane to deliver the city edition of the

Sunday paper with results of the state basketball finals. An example of that was delivery of the Sunday, March 24, 1968, sections flown to Fargo-Moorhead. Ninety-three bundles of 50 papers, a total of 4,650, arrived at the Minneapolis airport at 1:00 a.m. Sunday. At 1:17 the plan was airborne and by 2:20 a.m. the papers were in the trucks at Fargo where the sections were inserted with the waiting papers.

Gregg Gammack was hired in January 1969 to supplement myself and Hinderaker. Gammack had both helicopter and fixed wing experience. He was needed to assure that the new Gulfstream II jet would not be grounded for lack of a crew from illness or vacation. His helicopter background was considered an advantage in the event we added a helicopter for news use. We had already built an area on the roof of the new building suitable as a heliport. (Gammack resigned in November to join McDonald Corp.)

Many of our long flights reached record proportions for the type of aircraft involved. A DC-3 flight from Seven Islands, Quebec, to Minneapolis over the sparsely settled Canadian wilderness was an event to be remembered. The Gulfstream I stretched its legs to fly from Minneapolis to Antigua non-stop in January 1961. The longest flight in the GII was from Granada to Minneapolis and two flights set records — Antigua to Dakar, Senegal, in 5 hours, 6 minutes, and from Cairo to London in 5 hours, 44 minutes. Both flights set world and United States records for jet aircraft.

Despite its recognition as one of the most successful corporate aviation operations in the United States, *The Minneapolis Star* and *Tribune* airplane operation has always been a low profile affair. On occasions when business passengers didn't fill all seats, the remainder were often used for company personnel traveling on vacation.

The aviation department reported to a senior executive of *The Minneapolis Star* and *Tribune*. In succession they were Harold Perkins, Stanley Hawks, Joyce Swan and Otto Silha.

APPENDIX H

THE IMPORTANCE OF THE ELECTRONIC MEDIA

Confidential Memorandum
From John Cowles Sr.
September 1, 1944

Informed people who are familiar with wartime electronics discoveries and uses believe that revolutionary developments are impending in the postwar radio field: FM, television, and facsimile. Through facsimile, for example, news and pictures can be transmitted with a better quality of reproduction than most newspapers give. It is now possible, for example, automatically to turn on and turn off a facsimile receiving set by an electric impulse from the transmitting station. Enormous new fields of public service are apparently going to open up in radio, along with an attractive possibility for profit for venturesome broadcasters who actually do serve the public interest and convenience.

The type of public service that broadcasting with its enlarged facilities will be able to furnish is along exactly the same general lines as that which the Star Journal and Tribune Company renders through its newspapers.

There are many indications that in the next decade newspapers as we now know them will become relatively less important and broadcasting progressively more important as a means for the dissemination of news, information, pictures, advertising, entertainment and all other forms of public service.

One should not forget that when the "horseless carriage" first appeared on the horizon most buggy manufacturers thought the automobile was simply an interesting new toy, but nothing that would conceivably change traditional methods of transportation.

The Federal Communications Commission's so-called "duopoly policy" prevents the granting of a new broadcasting license to any corporation any of whose officers or substantial stockholders have a direct or indirect interest of any kind in another radio station in that same community. Members of the FCC indicate that this rule will be broadly interpreted and rigidly enforced.

The Minnesota Tribune Company owns 22,000 shares of the 150,000 shares of stock of the Star Journal and Tribune Company. This is 14 2/3%. The Minnesota Tribune Company also owns a 50% interest in radio station WTCN. The other 50% of WTCN is owned by the St. Paul Pioneer Press-Dispatch, and we all know that the Star Journal and Tribune Company has absolutely no voice or influence whatsoever in the management, policies or operations of WTCN. There is vigorous competition between the St. Paul and Minneapolis papers, and the St. Paul publishers have demonstrated no love for their Minneapolis competitors. Regardless of the merits of the situation, the facts seem to be that so long as the Minnesota Tribune Company remains part owner of WTCN it will apparently be impossible for the Star Journal and Tribune Company to become the licensee of a Twin Cities radio station.

Kingsley Murphy owns 19,000 shares of the 150,000 shares of stock of the Star Journal and Tribune Company. This is 12 2/3%. Kingsley Murphy is a director of the Star Journal and Tribune Company and also of the company owning WTCN. He also has some financial interest in the Minnesota Tribune Company, and is a director of it. Consequently, because Kingsley Murphy is a substantial stockholder and a director of the Star Journal and Tribune Company, and is also a director both of the company owning WTCN directly and of Minnesota Tribune Company, which owns 50% of WTCN, under the present FCC policy Kingsley

Murphy's stock holdings and connections, as well as those of the Minnesota Tribune Company, apparently constitute a barrier to the granting of a license to the Star Journal and Tribune Company to operate a broadcasting station in the Twin Cities. (Kingsley Murphy has indicated his complete willingness to resign as a director of WTCN and of the Minnesota Tribune Company if such action would be helpful. This would slightly reduce the complications but in no way solve our basic difficulties.)

The Minneapolis situation is further complicated by the twin facts that the controlling stockholders of the Star Journal and Tribune Company indirectly control a company that holds the license for radio station KRNT in Des Moines, and Kingsley Murphy is the licensee of radio station KSO, Des Moines. While actually there is complete competition at Des Moines between KSO and KRNT, and there are no understandings or agreements of any kind that reduce competition between those two licensees, the association of the parties in their ownership of stock in the Minneapolis Star Journal and Tribune Company has apparently created doubt, although it is wholly unjustified, in the minds of some people in the radio industry as to the reality of the radio competition in Des Moines.

The present situation is extremely unfortunate from every angle. No one is responsible, but we find ourselves facing a difficult and pressing problem. It seems obviously unfair for a condition to continue to exist where the outside holdings of minority SJT stockholders prevent the Star Journal and Tribune Company's achieving what clearly appears to be both in the public interest and in the best interests of the majority of its stockholders. The Cowles brothers will do anything within reason to try to help solve the dilemma.

Several possible alternative solutions suggest themselves:

1. Minnesota Tribune Company might divest itself of all of its ownership of WTCN by selling its 50% interest to the Ridders, or to some other outside party, so that there would be no connection between it and WTCN. Even if this were done, however, there would still be a serious question as to whether the FCC might not even then regard the KSO-KRNT situation at Des Moines as a sufficient barrier to prevent granting of a broadcasting license to the Star Journal and Tribune Company in Minneapolis.

2. Kingsley Murphy might acquire the Minnesota Tribune Company's 50% interest in WTCN and simultaneously divest himself of all of his stockholdings in the Star Journal and Tribune Company. The SJT Company would be willing to pay a liberal price for his SJT stock to help accomplish this, if Kingsley Murphy wished to follow this course. Then the Minnesota Tribune Company could continue permanently as an SJT stockholder if it wished, and the KSO-KRNT difficulty would be eliminated.

3. The Minnesota Tribune Company might divest itself of all of its Star Journal and Tribune Company stock and continue to hold its half interest in WTCN. If the Minnesota Tribune Company so wished, the Star Journal and Tribune Company would be willing to pay a liberal price to the Minnesota Tribune Company for its SJT stock to help clear up the situation in this way. However, the KSO-KRNT situation might still offer serious complications if Kingsley Murphy continued as a SJT stockholder.

4. Both Kingsley Murphy and the Minnesota Tribune Company might divest themselves of their Star Journal and Tribune stock so that there would be no conflict either because of the 50% ownership of WTCN or because of Kingsley Murphy's ownership of KSO. Controlling SJT stockholders would be willing to pay a liberal price for the SJT stock to help clear up the situa-

tion in this way. Conceivably a deal might be worked out to sell to Kingsley Murphy or the Minnesota Tribune Company one of the other radio stations that the Cowles brothers control, if they were anxious to acquire it in place of SJT stock, to help remove all the barriers that apparently prevent the Star Journal and Tribune Company from getting into the Twin Cities broadcasting field.

There may be other preferable alternative methods by which the barriers can be eliminated so that the Star Journal and Tribune Company can secure approval for a Twin Cities radio station.

The fact that The St. Paul Pioneer Press and Dispatch, our chief newspaper competitors in Minnesota, have a 50% ownership of a Twin Cities radio station give them not only a present but, more important, a potentially extremely great future competitive advantage as compared with the Star Journal and Tribune. This obvious inequity merits prompt remedy.

The Star Journal and Tribune Company has a large staff, special news reports and various other assets that are eminently adapted for use in serving the public interest in the broadcasting field just as through the medium of its newspapers. The SJT staff knows community interests and problems. The public will be the loser if we are not permitted directly to engage in radio. Actually, it is no exaggeration to say that the Star Journal and Tribune organization is uniquely fitted in the Twin Cities area to render public service through broadcasting.

It is the deep hope of the officers of the Star Journal and Tribune Company that some solution may be promptly found whereby the company can qualify as the licensee of a Twin Cities radio station.

In the absence of any other solution, the Cowles brothers contemplate immediately organizing a separate company in the Twin Cities, none of the stock of which would be held by any party having conflicting radio ownership connections, which new company could anticipate favorable action by the Federal Communications Commission on any request by it for the transfer or approval of a Twin Cities broadcasting license to it.

APPENDIX I

"THE NEWSPAPER BUSINESS IS A STRANGE ANIMAL"

A Speech Given to the Harvard Business
School Club of the Twin Cities
By John Cowles Sr.
September 24, 1963

The newspaper business is a strange animal because it is a mixture of a business and a profession, and at times there appear to be conflicts between what might seem expedient if the decision were to be based solely on short-run business advantages rather than on professional standards and intellectual convictions.

I don't think this apparent conflict between the professional aspects and the business-side of a newspaper is real, but, before I discuss that, I would like to summarize the nature of newspapering solely from its business aspects, so that some of you will have a better insight into the operations of two metropolitan newspapers.

Forgetting for a moment a newspaper's news and editorial functions, we are a manufacturing and sales organization, but probably more complicated than most businesses.

The Minneapolis Star and Tribune Company does about forty million dollars of business a year. Advertising provides about two-thirds of this revenue. Our readers, after deducting the share that our carriers and dealers keep for distributing our papers, provide us with about a third of our total revenue. It takes nearly 15,000 people to distribute The Star and Tribune; about 13,500 of these are boys and the rest adults. Most of the members of this distribution army are not our employees; they are independent contractors who buy from us at wholesale and sell to their customers at retail.

Unlike most manufactured products, our two finished models are each completely changed every twenty-four hours, as each day's Tribune and each day's Star are, of course, completely different from the previous day's issues. We also make many minor changes in The Star four or five times during each day and in The Tribune four or five times during each night, as successive editions carry later news which is substituted for less important or less timely news in the earlier editions.

PLANT HAS ABOUT 2,400 EMPLOYEES

If one gives it a moment's thought, one will realize how much more complicated newspaper production problems are than is the case with those manufacturers who change their models or products only once or twice a year.

We have about 2,400 employees in our plant, more than two-thirds of whom are full-time. The balance are part-time workers such as university students who may take want ad orders or circulation orders over the phone one or two afternoons or evenings during the week.

Incidentally, there are only a few newspapers in the country which carry more want ads than we do. We will print more than 1,500,000 separate want ads this year. Sometimes we carry more than 10,000 separate want ads in a single issue of a Sunday Tribune. Since all of these advertisements have to be billed and handled separately, and since most of our thousands of carriers' accounts — the number of papers each receives fluctuates from day to day due to new orders or cancellations — have to be handled separately, you can get some idea of the magnitude of our bookkeeping operations.

Our total payroll, wholly apart from the commissions that the carrier boys receive for distributing our papers, amounts to over a million dollars a month, and the cost of our newsprint and rotogravure paper is nearly a million dollars a month. These are two of the largest of the many hundreds of costs that go into the editing, production, sales and distribution of The Tribune and The Star.

We have separate contracts with 11 different labor unions, with different wage scales and working conditions in each, so you can realize how much more complicated and time-consuming union contract negotiations are in the newspaper business than is the case with most industries of comparable size which normally would have to negotiate with only one or two plant-wide unions.

We spend more than $3 million a year on our news and editorial page departments. We buy not only the full services of the Associated Press and the United Press International, but also The Tribune has leased wires that provide it with the news services of The New York Times, The New York Herald Tribune and Dow Jones News Service, while The Star has leased wires for the special news services of The Chicago Daily News and Reuters, the British news agency. In addition, The Tribune maintains a leased wire from our five-man news bureau in Washington, and also maintains two full-time foreign correspondents, Graham Hovey based in London and Bob Hewett in Hong Kong.

PUBLISHING COSTS ARE HIGH

The reason why there has been a steady decline in the number of metropolitan dailies is purely economic. The costs of publishing a metropolitan paper have become so great that few cities in the country are large enough to support more than one profitable morning paper and one profitable afternoon paper. It is generally believed by the other publishers that only two of the New York papers, for example, are profitable.

Cities as large in population as Los Angeles and Detroit and Cleveland now have only one metropolitan morning paper and one metropolitan afternoon paper. Chicago has the same number of daily newspapers as do the Twin Cities — two morning and two afternoon — and those four Chicago papers are owned by just two companies with each publishing one morning and one afternoon paper from its plant, as is the case with The Tribune and The Star in Minneapolis and The Pioneer Press and The Dispatch in St. Paul. I believe that New York and Boston are now the only two cities in America that have more daily papers than the Twin Cities.

Obviously, there are major economies if both a morning and an afternoon paper are published in the same plant as contrasted with having two separate plants where the equipment, which costs many millions of dollars for a large paper, sits idle half the time. This is another reason for the trend toward single ownership of metropolitan daily newspaper cities in the larger cities.

There are many cities like Minneapolis where the only morning paper and the only afternoon paper are owned by the same company. Milwaukee and Kansas City are two nearby examples. There are also many other cities where the city's only morning paper and the only afternoon are published in the same plant, although the ownership is separate. St. Louis and Pittsburgh and Nashville and Birmingham are examples. The degree of actual, as contrasted with theoretical, competition in cities having such joint publishing setups varies from place to place.

We here encourage the utmost competition between the news staffs of The Tribune and The Star. Each newspaper has its own managing editor and its own staff of reporters, photographers and editors. Each paper tries its best to scoop the other on news. There is actually great rivalry between the news staffs of our two papers, and we believe that through encouraging this, each paper is better than it otherwise would be. Moreover, if The Tribune and The Star were separately owned and published in separate plants, neither paper would be financially able to spend nearly as much money for news services and staff as it does now, and the quality of each paper would be much inferior to what is now is.

We at The Star and Tribune were enormously pleased when The Saturday Review magazine polled the university journalism school deans and senior professors throughout the United States and asked them to give their opinions as to what were the best newspaper in the entire country. Both The Minneapolis Tribune and The Minneapolis Star were voted among the twenty best. Only three other cities, New York, Chicago and Washington, had more than one newspaper listed in the top twenty best, so it was a real satisfaction to us that both of the Minneapolis papers should be ranked this highly.

A newspaper has several completely different functions. Its primary purpose, of course, is to present the news so that its readers will know what is happening in their local community, their state, the nation and the rest of the world. This is done through a newspaper's news columns.

THE NEWSPAPERS AND POLITICS

We make every effort to keep our news columns completely fair and objective. We pay just as much attention in our news columns to the activities of those candidates for political office whom we are opposing on our editorial pages as we do to those we are supporting.

During political campaigns partisan feeling runs high, and on some occasions we have received complaints about the same news story from both candidates, each one charging that the news story favored his opponent.

It is misleading to judge a newspaper's coverage of a political campaign on the issues. In the 1960 campaign on the days when Kennedy was stumping Minnesota, naturally more space was devoted to Kennedy than to Nixon, and similarly when Nixon was campaigning in Minnesota more news space was devoted to him than to Kennedy. For the campaign as a whole, however, both candidates and parties got approximately the same amount of news space.

Occasionally someone asks me why the Minneapolis papers don't carry as much foreign news as does The New York Times. The answer is simple. The New York Times is a national newspaper edited for a specialized group, primarily for the best educated people in the country. Excellent as The New York Times is, fewer than $1/8$ of the families in New York City and the New York suburbs read it. It simply doesn't appeal to the $7/8$ of the population who have less education and less intellectual curiosity. No Minneapolis newspaper that appealed to only 1/8 of the people here could possibly survive. We edit our papers to appeal to all segments of the population, and either The Star or The Tribune or both are read by more than 9 out of every 10 families in Hennepin County. Nearly half of all the families in the entire state of Minnesota read either the morning Tribune or the afternoon Star. And nearly 60% of the families throughout the entire state regularly read The Tribune on Sunday.

We do try to serve the highest common denominator of our readers' interest, and we are constantly trying to raise the level of that common denominator.

While our papers are aimed at all educational and economic and occupational groups in the Upper Midwest, we consistently try to widen and whet the public's interest in serious subjects. The World Affairs Program, which runs in The Star each week, and the Science Reading Program, which runs in The Tribune each week, are two examples of this.

MINNEAPOLIS PAPERS BLAZED TRAILS

Both Minneapolis papers were among the trailblazers in the country in employing specialists to cover such relatively neglected areas of news as science and education and religion.

Vic Cohn is once of the best science reporters in the country, Dick Kleeman one of the best educational reporters, and Bill Thorkelson, who is shortly returning to the Ecumenical Congress at Rome for his second trip there this year, is one of the best writers in the religious news field. We have many other specialized experts on our two staffs. I mention these three only as examples.

In addition to printing the news, we have a second important function, the editorial function. This is to attempt to lead and influence public opinion by persuading our readers to make what we regard as sound judgments on the issues confronting the community, state and nation. We never use our news columns to try to do this. We confine the expression of our own opinions to our editorial and opinion pages.

Just as we try on our editorial pages to encourage our readers to support worthwhile projects, we believe that our executives likewise have an obligation to work actively in the support of major projects that will improve Minneapolis and the Upper Midwest. I am proud that over the years many of my associates have been among the leaders in almost every important civic campaign. The list is long: the redevelopment of the lower loop, the new North Star Research Center, the Tyrone Guthrie Theater, the United Hospital Fund campaign, Metropolitan Stadium and the bringing of major league baseball here are a few examples. These activities are wholly in addition to continuing participation and occasionally leadership by Star and Tribune executives in such worthwhile annual drives as those of the United Fund, the Symphony, the Art Institute, etc. We at The Star and Tribune believe that one of the functions of a good newspaper organization is to help make the community in which the papers are published a better place to live.

Because newspapers, unless they are spineless, should express their own editorial opinions even on hot and highly controversial subjects about which people feel strongly, our editorials inevitably displease many of our readers. Some strongly dislike, for example, our editorial positions on birth control, on racial discrimination, or on the John Birch Society.

OPPOSING VIEWS ARE OFFERED

On the editorial and opinion pages, we deliberately print opposing viewpoints so that readers will have a chance to read the arguments of qualified people who differ from us. We consciously select columnists whose philosophies cover the whole political spectrum — some liberal, some middle of the road, and some conservative. We may on the same day in adjoining columns carry one writer's opinion that Barry Goldwater would make a fine President, and another's view that it would be a national calamity if he were elected.

Similarly, one of our columnists may write that the administration is pushing civil rights too rapidly, while another may write that progress isn't being made rapidly enough.

We consistently try to have both the conservative and the liberal points of view expressed on the editorial and opinion pages in each of our two papers. While it is difficult to categorize most writers' philosophies, I would say that in The Minneapolis Star, for example, Evans and Novak, Max Freedman and Eric Sevareid generally write as liberals, while Arthur Krock and Holmes Alexander usually write from the conservative side.

On The Tribune's editorial pages, I regard Walter Lippmann and Doris Fleeson as liberals. I regard Richard Wilson and James Reston and Charles Bartlett as middle-of-the-roaders, and David Lawrence as a conservative. Some of you may feel that my labels are wrong. You may regard Richard Wilson as a conservative, for example, or you may regard Bartlett as a liberal.

In addition to these columnists — and we deliberately buy more of them than we can regularly use and simply pick what we regard as the most interesting of their columns — we also run miscellaneous material and condensations of all kinds of ideas which we think will interest or inform our readers.

Also, we devote a lot of space to readers' letters to the editor, printing those that disagree with our editorial conclusions along with those that concur.

The third important function of a newspaper, in addition to reporting the news and expressing editorial judgments, is to foster commerce and industry through its advertising columns. Clear evidence that newspaper advertising does stimulate business is the fact that during our long strike in the spring and summer of 1962, not only retail sales but almost all types of business activity in the Minneapolis area declined. The Federal Reserve figures indicate that the same thing happened both in Cleveland and in New York City during their long newspaper strikes.

THERE'S ENTERTAINMENT, TOO

Then, wholly, in addition to these three major functions that I have mentioned, news coverage, editorial opinions and advertising, most newspapers also carry various entertainment features — Ann Landers or Abby Van Buren, comic strips and panels, features on bridge, menus, beauty, health, etc. While these aren't necessarily an essential part of any newspaper, their inclusion does help attract readers and makes readership more thorough so that the advertising columns produce better results. Many people probably would not subscribe to a newspaper if it weren't for some of these entertainment and service features, and in addition to reading them, many people tend also to begin to read the more serious news and editorial comment.

Earlier I referred to the fact that sometimes there is an apparent conflict between the business aspects and the professional ethics of newspapers. We at The Star and Tribune regard the professional side as paramount, and we are convinced that in the long run it is also good business to base our decisions on professional standards.

These apparent conflicts are rare, but they stem from two sources. First, from some advertising customers who occasionally may try to put pressure on a newspaper to suppress or minimize or distort some news story with a veiled threat that they may reduce or eliminate their advertising patronage if the newspaper does not comply, and, second, from organized pressure groups, whether economic or political or religious, who threaten that large numbers of subscribers will stop taking the paper or boycott its advertisers unless the paper adopts the editorial position or follows news practices that the pressure group favors, or refrains from printing editorials criticizing it.

Fortunately, both types of pressure have steadily decreased over the years.

I have been in the newspaper business since 1920. Two or three or four decades ago, there was much more pressure for news suppression or distortion than exists today. This is true not only in Minneapolis but throughout the country. This stems partially from the fact that those newspapers that have survived are numerically fewer but economically stronger than was the case twenty or thirty years ago, and so better able to withstand pressure. Also, standards of professional integrity have steadily risen over the years, and now the greater majority of newspapers pursue the same policies that we have long followed at The Star and Tribune, namely that whether or not a company or an individual is a large or small advertising customer, makes no difference in the handling of news about him or his business.

Fortunately, all of the largest merchants in Minneapolis and most of the heads of other businesses which advertise substantially in our papers are enlightened men, who clearly recognize the soundness of this policy. This has also enabled our reporters and editors, in turn, to welcome and indeed request, with no strings attached, advice or expert knowledge from business and civic leaders whose advertising in the papers — or lack of it — is immaterial.

THERE ARE PRESSURES

Some years ago, when the community became disturbed about an upsurge in drunken driving, and the *Tribune* began to run a complete list of everyone arrested in Minneapolis for drunken driving, you would have been amazed at how many people charged with drunken driving called us to claim they have either a wife or a mother with heart trouble who would probably die if their names were published, or who had a relative who was one of our advertisers who would cease advertising if we published his name. All kinds of pressure were applied to persuade us not to print their names. However, we firmly refused to omit any, and both papers consistently print the disposition of every drunken driving case in Hennepin County. The public has now apparently come to accept this as proper journalism, and we now rarely get even a phone call asking for suppression.

Similarly, if there is a serious elevator or escalator accident in Minneapolis, we don't simply say that it took place in a downtown store or hotel or building. We name the store or hotel or building, as we think the public has a right to know the facts.

Years ago, when the first medical reports began to be issued to the effect that cigarette smoking tended to produce cancer, I understand that some of the tobacco companies made veiled threats that they might reduce or withdraw their advertising from those newspapers that printed these reports in any extended way. However, most newspapers, including The Tribune and The Star, continued to print such reports as their news executives thought newsworthy, and the cigarette companies have continued their newspaper advertising.

Some of you may recall that a few years ago one of the largest automobile manufacturers cancelled all of its advertising schedules in The Wall Street Journal because the Journal had printed detailed descriptions of their new car models prior to the time that the manufacturer wanted to release the official news and pictures of these new models. The Wall Street Journal's attitude was that since the competing manufacturers had secretly photographed these new models, why shouldn't the reading public also be informed? Within a short time, the motor manufacturer realized that it had made a mistake in attempting to use its advertising patronage to coerce the editors of The Wall Street Journal, and quietly reinstated its full advertising schedules.

Twenty or thirty or forty years ago, many businessmen assumed that in return for their purchase of advertising space they were entitled to some measure of influence or control over a paper's news and editorial policies. Happily, that unfortunate assumption has almost entirely evaporated everywhere, and, with minor exceptions in a few cities, newspaper advertising space is now bought and sold solely on its merits as a sales and promotion medium.

IRRITATIONS ARE NATURAL

By the very nature of its functions, a newspaper can't avoid irritating a lot of people in the course of the year. No businessman is happy over the ensuing publicity if his company is charged with law violations. Some of the chemical manufacturers and the merchants who sell insecticides naturally weren't happy over the publication by The Star and other papers earlier this year of a condensed version of Rachel Carson's "Silent Spring."

No movie producer or exhibitor is happy if one of our movie critics suggests that his current offering isn't a superlative movie. However, a steadily increasing proportion of advertisers has come to realize that the reading public has more confidence and trust in those papers that don't suppress or distort news or their critics' honest opinions, and that consequently such papers do produce better advertising results.

Speaking of movies, when some movie exhibitors offer us suggestive ads, we have to tell them that unless they eliminate or change objectionable wording or illustrations we will decline the advertising copy on grounds of bad taste. And sometimes, because the advertising is toned down, we are blamed for that movie's box office troubles.

The Star and Tribune have some of the strictest policies in the country on medical advertising, and occasionally advertisers of products claiming certain medical benefits or cures will object when we tell them that they must make copy changes or we will decline their ads.

We also cooperate wholeheartedly with the Better Business Bureau because we believe that is simply good business to decline all misleading copy.

Occasionally, our handling of labor difficulties or strikes provokes criticism. We generally try to carry statements setting forth both the union's and the employer's positions in the same day's paper in every labor dispute, but some employers occasionally can't be located before we must go to press or decline to make any comment, so our news story may appear to be one-sided. Then, some other employers on reading that story may be inclined to say our news columns are always "pro-union."

NEWS ISN'T MONOPOLIZED

Frequently, people criticize The Star and Tribune on the grounds that we are a monopoly, apparently not realizing that, even though fewer and fewer cities can afford more than one daily newspaper publishing company, still no single publishing company can possibly monopolize or even critically restrict the flow of information and advertising available to the public. There are too many other daily newspapers, weekly newspapers, suburban newspapers, local radio and television stations, news magazines, etc., for any single publishing company to monopolize a city or area. Similarly, many people who don't like our editorials fail to give us credit for publishing various columnists whose views differ strongly from ours.

We make many, many mistakes in news and editorial judgment and in news handling, but we try to give the people of Minneapolis and the Upper Midwest the whole picture, not just the picture we see through our own spectacles which you may think are philosophically tinted by one color or another.

Some people seem to think that newspapers generally are declining in importance and influence. I disagree completely. Newspapers are changing but so is everything else.

If you have a son who is undecided as to his future vocation or profession, suggest that he consider journalism. It has all the problems and opportunities of a manufacturing or sales organization but in addition has something special that most other businesses don't have: it deals with news and ideas. And it is these aspects that give newspapering its deep appeals and satisfactions.

Some people suggest that television is gradually replacing the printed word. I don't accept that view for a moment. Television is an excellent entertainment medium, and some of its special current events programs are first-rate and highly informative. They contribute a great deal to the total education of the public, but television can never remotely take the place of well-edited daily newspapers, which are, in my opinion, essential to the successful functioning of a democratic and self-governing nation.

Today, there are only a few remaining traces of the bad conditions that existed in the early part of the twentieth century which prompted Upton Sinclair and others to muckrake the press as being the mouthpiece of special privilege and which gave rise to the expression "yellow journalism."

As one who has been in journalism for 43 years, and who has had an opportunity to be intimately acquainted with many different newspapers and their editors and publishers, it is my judgment that both the quality and the integrity of most newspapers and their services to the reading public have improved enormously in the past generation, and are continuing to rise every year.

APPENDIX J

REDEDICATION OF THE GUTHRIE THEATER

Remarks by John Cowles Jr.
June 3, 1993

Of course we never really know how things are going to turn out: baseball seasons, love affairs, appeals to the Supreme Court, theater companies…but we go ahead anyway, hoping for serendipity.

For me, the Guthrie began in the fall of 1959 on a special train to Iowa City for the Minnesota-Iowa football game — a really big event in those days before the Vikings, Twins, or freeways, and when the tallest building between Chicago and the West Coast was the Foshay Tower.

The previous night Sage and I had met Oliver Rea, a young Broadway producer, and his wife, Betty; and on that train ride I learned from Oliver that he and Tyrone Guthrie, the noted British director, were to visit Minneapolis a few weeks later at the suggestion of Frank Whiting, then head of the University of Minnesota Theater. Guthrie, Rea and Peter Zeisler, a young Broadway stage manager, had recently announced their hopes to establish a new resident repertory theater company, playing mainly the classics, somewhere in the hinterland of America, far from the distractions and sometimes dubious values of Gotham City.

I thereupon read Guthrie's just-published book about his "Life in the Theater," liked the sound of him, organized a lunch and other meetings for Guthrie and Rea's visit, and so it began.

Seeking a venue for the new theater, I finally came to the door of H. Harvard Arnason, who in those days was running both the University fine arts department and the then relatively modest Walker Art Center. Harvey was invaluable in helping persuade the T.B. Walker Foundation's trustees — many of whom lived in California or New York — to entrust not only $400,000 but also this land, this plot of ground, this place so dear to the Art Center's own image and activities, to a new theater. The Walker family crashed through, and so began many trips to and from New York, Stratford, Ontario, and elsewhere.

On Memorial Day weekend of 1960, on the steps of the old Walker, the triumvirate of Guthrie, Rea and Zeisler announced their choice of Minneapolis over Detroit and Milwaukee, the other finalists. Now the organizing, designing and money-raising shifted into high gear.

We had formed a nine-man steering committee for the project, and hired Lou Gelfand, a sports writer and railroad man, as our administrator. We used the Jade Gallery in the old Walker as Lou's office and our meeting place, with a couple of tables, chairs and a telephone.

Yet another University of Minnesota faculty member, Ralph Rapson, head of the school of architecture and a member of the Walker's board of directors, volunteered to redesign the new theater…and succeeded handsomely, even to the liking — more or less — of Guthrie, Rea, Zeisler and Tanya Moiseiwitsch, who was Guthrie's favorite designer of theatrical sets, costumes and thrust stages.

A most essential member of the steering committee was Philip Von Blon, then with International Milling, who not only helped raise money but also, as chairman of the building committee (a) helped keep the tempestuous design process on track, (b) presided over some drastic design changes and cost reductions when the original bids came in too high, and (c) selected and supervised a most supportive construction contractor, Fred Watson.

By opening night the whole project, including formation of the acting company, had cost $2.4 million dollars; and by the end of the decade most of the rehearsal and production space cut out in 1961 had been restored using a million dollars from the campaign for a new Walker Art Center designed by Ed Barnes.

The other members of that original steering committee were Pierce Butler, then a St. Paul lawyer; Martin Friedman, who succeeded Harvey Arnason when Harvey went to run the Guggenheim in New York; Roger Kennedy, then a St. Paul banker, today President Clinton's nominee, I believe, to head the National Park Service; Otto Silha, my long-time colleague at The Star and Tribune; the late Justin Smith, managing trustee of the T.B. Walker Foundation; Frank Whiting; and Louis Zelle of the Jefferson Company.

I mention names because it is easy to forget that, as my grandfather used to say, when Kiplingesque aphorisms were in vogue earlier in this century, "Things don't just happen — people make them happen." And people make things happen when they are seized by a vision. Tony Guthrie gave us such a vision.

Now, 30 years later, Garland Wright and Ed Martenson stand where Guthrie, Rea and Zeisler once stood. As one who was present at the creation, so to speak, I am proud and happy today to celebrate Garland's vision.

APPENDIX K

"HOW I BECAME INTERESTED IN RACIAL JUSTICE"

By Elizabeth Bates Cowles
Opportunity, Winter Issue, 1948

There was no one *How* or *Why* in my interest in the Negro problem.

In the upstate New York town of my childhood there was one Negro family. The father was the sexton of the Episcopalian Church. One of the children sang in the choir. That one dark face among the white faces in the sea of white robes was a point of interest as were the candles on the altar. Just a part of the usual Sunday scene.

In 1918, in my Smith College gym class, a southern white student once was rude to a Negro student. The southerner embarrassed us. No strong emotions were aroused. It was simply a question of manners.

When during early married years in the twenties in Des Moines I took part in civil and charitable causes, Negro problems did not seem distinct from white problems. There was a Negro community center and a Jewish community center but the word "segregation" had no special meaning for me then. And I had never heard the saying "the last to be hired and the first to be fired."

But on a trip to New York, in St. Paul's I had my first adult experience of worshipping in a congregation in which there were some Negroes. And I began to wonder why all churches were not for all people. And about this time there was the poetry of Countee Cullen and Vandercook's *Black Majesty* and Claude McKay's *Home in Harlem* and the books of Peterkin and DuBose Heyward.

However, I didn't begin to wake up until just before and during the war years in Minneapolis.

Housing for a Negro employee was a terrible problem. It was the sordid sections where Negroes had to live. The Red Cross refused or segregated Negro blood donors. In the public hospitals where I worked I saw two Negro nurses in all those weary months. I knew the national need for nurses. There were vast numbers of Negro girls who could be trained. Why weren't they trained? I knew the need for doctors. Why hadn't Negro doctors been trained?

I learned from the Planned Parenthood League of the terrible death rate of colored mothers and babies in the South and of the shorter life expectancy of Negroes, of the lack of hospital beds and medical care for them. Now I had long known that my own life was held cheap in two states. I knew that in Massachusetts and Connecticut I would be denied preventive medical care to save my life or preserve my health as a wife and mother of four children. I felt a bond with colored people whose lives are held cheap in varying degrees in forty-eight states.

More books came along—*Black Boy, Strange Fruit, Freedom Road*, and the life of George Washington Carver. I read a Negro newspaper, *The Minneapolis Spokesman*, and learned of injustices to Negro servicemen, of brutalities unpunished, of senseless discriminations.

So when there was fine talk of fighting Nazism for the sake of freedom and human and civil rights, I felt an angry sense of national hypocrisy. Basic freedoms and rights were denied to millions in the United States. Unless we as a national while preaching high ideals abroad, worked to make good at home those ideals to fourteen million Negroes, we were a dishonest nation. The world, overwhelmingly NOT white, would not trust us. Why should it?

It had taken me a long time, but when the Urban League asked me to join it, I was certainly more than ready.

APPENDIX L

FIRST AMENDMENT FREEDOMS AWARDS SPEECH

A speech by John Cowles Jr.
Presented to the Society of Fellows of the
Anti-Defamation League of B'nai B'rith
Minneapolis, Minnesota

October 26, 1977

Governor Andersen, Rabbi Shapiro, Father Eales, Mr. Aberman, Senator Mathias, Mr. Latz, Senator Anderson, Chief Justice Sheran, Mr. Joseph, colleagues, friends, ladies and gentlemen:

Having known and admired many of you in a personal way for years, and others of you from a distance, I am more stirred by this occasion than you might expect a presumably well-traveled and perhaps even jaded newspaper person to be.

Pride is not quite the right word, though that is certainly part of it — and one only hopes not too much of it. Self-righteousness, to which Western man is seemingly addicted, is also doubtless present, though I hope to only a minimal level.

I think maybe a simple joy in consensus, in feeling together, shared and related to things much larger, might better describe it. I remember that joy during the Bicentennial last year when the tall ships sailed into New York harbor. The Los Angeles Rams apparently had a version of it Monday night, and it surely happened in Washington yesterday when Hubert Humphrey returned to the Senate.

To be near the center of such a moment is very nice indeed, and one remembers not to inhale too many of the kind words.

My father, whose advancing years to his profound regret have kept him at home tonight, has been for many of us a steadfast model of intellectual inquiry combined with energetic practicality; and the newspapers he has led have consistently sought to publish a much wider spectrum of opinions than could be held by himself or any one person. Sometimes it isn't easy or pleasant to publish controversial material, whether your own or someone else's, much less advocate a controversial point of view; but my father was always, so far as I know, sustained by my mother, whose strong feelings for fair play were well matched by her courage and fixity of purpose. They created the modern-day Minneapolis Star and Tribune with whose accomplishments and staffs I am proud to be associated.

There is quite a variety of background and beliefs represented here tonight, which I find appropriate. It is often assumed, for example, that only liberal Democrats put high priority on things like freedom of religion, speech, press and assembly; but twenty years ago when I was serving on the board of directors of the Minnesota Civil Liberties Union, the chairman of that board, John Pemberton, was also the Republican party chairman of Olmsted county. I am not surprised that the chairman of this evening is a former Republican senator from Maryland. Of course, some of us wish there were more such Republicans.

Implicit in the first amendment, I think, are several notions. First, freedom of speech implies diversity of information, ideas and values. (Parenthetically, it is arguable that newspapers and other publications have a vested economic interest in free speech because it is more interesting, i.e., it "sells more newspapers" than would happen if newspapers and magazines and books could reflect only an establishment or government line of thought. To whatever extent this argument might be valid — and I think the economic difference probably would be only marginal — I think we are all fortunate that economic self-interest would in this instance seem to reinforce, not undermine, the desired political framework. As a society, we should nurture and invent if necessary other such economic reinforcements.)

Diversity of information and ideas, in turn, implies, I think, two other notions: confidence in people's ability to sort out "truth" (however temporary or permanent) from "error," and the notion that a debate of conflicting data and ideas will eventually advance human knowledge and therefore the human condition.

The trouble is that, in an increasingly crowded, complex and technology-dependent world, there is a tendency toward an education-based elite which does not always have Thomas Jefferson's confidence in the average man's ability to understand and sort things out.

Also, whatever the long-range benefits to human knowledge, in the short run conflicting data and diversity of values produces hesitancy and stalemate and delay. In short, political engineering perceives freedom of thought, at least in the short run, as inherently inefficient. These days, delays in responding to situations perceived as serious are increasingly seen as dangerous.

Fear is the other great enemy of diversity and dissent, and the various communications technologies now linking almost all of the four billion inhabitants of our global village greatly increase the prospects for massive propaganda as well as enlightenment.

So be it. Each generation sees the world in its own fashion, and while to some relatively recent generations the future may have looked rosy, I doubt that it's ever looked easy.

Burton Joseph, on behalf of my father and my colleagues at The Star and Tribune, I accept with pleasure and thankfulness this First Amendment Freedoms Award from the Society of Fellows of the Anti-Defamation League of B'nai B'rith. It is an honor to be associated with you in such a cause.

APPENDIX M

CIVIC RESPONSIBILITY

Civic responsibility was a concept espoused by John Cowles almost from the moment he bought *The Minneapolis Star*. He felt strongly about the responsibility of a newspaper to be a part of its community and was acutely aware of his status as an outsider in Minneapolis. He saw both an inherent duty and a competitive edge. During the first several years, officers and managers were encouraged to participate in civic activities, a tradition that has continued.

In 1945, the Minneapolis Star Journal and Tribune Fund was established, with funds coming largely in the form of listed stocks held as investments by the company. Sometime around 1947 when the tax laws changed to permit companies to make charitable contributions of up to five percent of their pretax profits, John Cowles and Bruce Dayton met to map out a common strategy. They compared notes of their earnings and agreed on the ratio at which they should support community organizations like the United Way and the Minnesota Orchestra. The two companies were the dominant forces working in the community at that time.

While there are no records to confirm the exact date at which the company began its five percent giving policy, Bower Hawthorne placed it shortly after 1947.[1] In 1977, the company's internal publication, *Newsmakers*, noted, "Almost 30 years ago, John Cowles began giving five percent of pretax earnings to philanthropy." The company was one of the 10 charter members of the Five Percent Club started in 1976. From 1960 through 1978 the company made grants of almost $11 million.

While not a charity of the company, Santa Anonymous began in 1948 when George Grim wrote a column for *The Minneapolis Tribune* asking readers to send in toys for needy children. By 1980 cash contributions reached $69,999 and almost 60,000 toys were distributed. While the company covered many direct expenses and employees spent hundreds of hours, the success of Santa Anonymous was possible only because it was embraced by individuals and organizations throughout the community. They helped with publicity, encouraging volunteers, setting up drop-off points for donated toys, and many other activities. Funds not needed for toys are used to provide summer camperships for disadvantaged children. By 1996 the program — still administered by *The Star Tribune* — had grown to provide 115,000 toys to 57,000 children, and received contributions of $403,000.

In 1959, the annual report announced that at least 53 *Minneapolis Star and Tribune* people were currently active in some 276 different roles in the community. During the late fifties Joyce Swan and Charles Johnson, executive sports editor of the papers, were leaders in the drive to bring professional sports teams to the Twin Cities. In 1960 they and their associates saw a professional football franchise awarded to the Vikings. (In recognition of his service, Swan was offered an ownership interest in the football team, but turned it down.) In 1961 an American League baseball franchise was awarded and the Metropolitan Stadium was built in suburban Bloomington. Members of the newspapers' marketing staff even prepared sales presentations that were used with the New York Giants, the Cleveland Indians, and the Washington Senators — who moved to become the Minnesota Twins. The company was one of the two largest stadium bondholders.

Minnesota Keystone Program℠

In 1966 *Saturday Review* reported that, "In the top civic leadership positions for the years 1960-64, the Cowles papers had twice the representation of the next highest company."[2] They cited John Cowles as "a first-rate example of what a publisher who has a sense of public obligation and public relations can do."

One of the most impressive civic activities undertaken by the company was the Gideon Seymour Memorial Lecture series which began in 1955. Speakers included Arnold Toynbee, T. S. Eliot, James B. Conant, Lester B. Pearson, Walter Lippmann, Archibald MacLeish and the Maharaja of Mysore.

In 1970, John Cowles Jr. confirmed the company's position in his annual report: "We recently concluded, despite some difficult provisions in the new tax law, to continue our long-standing policy of contributing up to five percent of our newspapers' pretax operating earnings to educational, social welfare, cultural, public affairs and other philanthropic institutions and programs. So far as I know, Dayton Hudson is the only other major company in this area with a similar policy."[3]

In 1972, he created a public affairs department to focus on corporate citizenship and social responsibility, appointing Bower Hawthorne as vice president for public affairs. Hawthorne had served in senior news management since 1960, and had been executive editor of each paper. In making the appointment Cowles said: "Bower's new post reflects our belief that helping improve the social, economic and physical environment wherever a company does business is a major public obligation of that company as well as a matter of long-range self-interest."[4] Harry Davis joined the office in 1976; a former Minneapolis mayoral candidate and school board chairman, he had been assistant to the publisher. "We donate money to things we think are most important," Hawthorne said. "One of the areas of our support is the redevelopment of the central city."[5] The largest contributions that year were to the United Way (at $135,752, the company was the largest contributor); Greater Minneapolis Metropolitan Housing Corporation, $20,019; the YMCA, $75,195; the Minnesota Orchestral Association, $13,500; the Minneapolis Society of Fine Arts, $12,000; the St. Paul/Ramsey Arts and Science Council, $10,000; and the Minnesota Private College Fund, $18,000. The company also gave 120 acres of land to the Hennepin County Park Reserve District that year. In 1977 contributions exceeded $1 million for the first time.

Matching of employee gifts to educational institutions began in 1973; the program was later extended to include civic organizations in which employees serve on the governing boards. In fiscal 1997 employees made 397 gifts to 203 different institutions totaling $199,445 — each matched by the Cowles Media Foundation. In 1990 an Employee Contributions Committee was given $50,000 to be granted to community organizations, with the guidelines to be determined by the committee itself, within the broad foundation guidelines.

During the late 1980s the company combined all its giving into the Cowles Media Foundation, which began to build a corpus to provide its own income and to help assure a consistent pattern of grants over time. By 1997 the corpus had grown to over $12 million and total grants were over $2.5 million. Almost half of total grants were for unrestricted general operating support of charities and public service institutions. Most of the contributions were still made in the Twin Cities, but each non-Minneapolis operating unit has responsibility for developing its own contributions program.

The largest recipients of total grants — in addition to the downtown Minneapolis stadium project in the late seventies, which received a total of $4.6 million — have been: the United Way, over $4.5 million; the Minnesota Orchestra, $2.6 million; the Walker Art Center, $2.4 million; the Guthrie Theater, $2.1 million;

the Minneapolis Institute of Art, $1.2 million; the Science Museum of Minnesota, $930,000; Planned Parenthood of Minnesota, $535,000; and the University of Minnesota, $525,000. The foundation also made grants totaling $800,000 to literacy programs since 1980, and over $500,000 to small nonprofit literary presses and related writing organizations in the Twin Cities between 1985-96. Company executives have held leadership positions in all these organizations, except for Planned Parenthood and the university. The foundation directors are all members of senior management of CMC and the Star Tribune. The company ranks 16th among corporate donors in the Twin Cities; it ranks 46th in revenue among Twin Cities public companies. In fiscal 1997 grants of $2,497,303 were made to 219 organizations.

[1] "Carrying Out Our Social Responsibilty," *Newsmakers,* January 1977, p. 3.
[2] L.L.L. Golden, "Public Relations — Cowles Knows How," *Saturday Review,* January 11, 1966.
[3] "Cowles Jr.: Must Regain Adequate Earnings Margin," *Newsmakers,* June 1970, p. 7.
[4] Minneapolis Star and Tribune Company, news release, May 2, 1972.
[5] Op. Cit., "Carrying Out Our Social Responsibility," *Newsmakers,* p. 3.

APPENDIX N

JOHN COWLES SR. REMARKS AT HIS RETIREMENT

Star Tribune Company Twenty Year Club
February 25, 1973

Members of the Twenty Year Club, or rather may I simply say friends:

We have been working together for 20 years and for many of you much longer than that toward a common objective: building The Star and Tribune toward being a stronger and better institution.

It was back in the spring of 1935 when the Cowles interest bought The Minneapolis Star, which was the smallest and weakest of the three Minneapolis newspapers. Only the old-timers will recall how rough the going was for us in those early years. The Star had come out of the bankruptcy court not very long before we acquired it, and the company continued to lose money for the three or four years after we bought it, until we finally got it into black ink. We only had a hundred and some employees in those early days, and at The Star our total revenues in a year were only about as much as a week's revenue is today. Fortunately, however, our circulation and advertising revenue began to grow steadily, and we kept plowing back our increased revenues to improve the quality of our product and develop our staff.

I started full time in the newspaper business back in 1920, after I had graduated from college, as a reporter for The Des Moines Register. I well remember hearing my father frequently quote a sentence from Rudyard Kipling: "It ain't the individual nor the army as a whole, but the everlasting teamwork of every bloomin' soul." I believe that quotation applies particularly to a newspaper organization because by its very nature a newspaper requires the complete cooperation of so many different departments — production, distribution, news, advertising, etc.

I am particularly happy that my long-time friend Joyce Swan is here today. He joined The Star back, I believe, in 1937 and became a right arm to me in building the organization. We had of course many other extremely able and valuable staff members (it would take too long to name them all), but none was more dedicated or effective than Joyce in helping build The Star and Tribune into the institution it has become.

I have been and am extremely proud of the organization that we have developed. An institution is no stronger than its personnel, and the more than 500 members of the Twenty Year Club are the backbone of the institution. I extend my gratitude to all of you.

Today marks the start of a new fiscal year for the company, and I wanted to tell the members of the Twenty Year Club, before anyone else knows it, that I have resigned as chairman of the board and as an employee of the company effective today. Probably I have already overstayed my time with 38 years as either president or chairman of this institution. They have been 38 extremely happy years for me.

The infirmities of old age have steadily galloped, not crept up on me. My cataract operations a year ago have not proved as successful as I had hoped, and my eyesight is impaired, my deafness is increasing, and my energy is slackening. Consequently, I have concluded to retire completely effective starting today, although I will continue as a director of the company.

I think the organization is stronger than it ever has been, and I have complete confidence in the judgment and abilities of the people, headed by John Cowles Jr., who will henceforth be running the company. I think both The Star and The Tribune are already great newspapers, but I believe they can be an even more constructive force for the benefit of the Upper Midwest and of the whole nation than in the past. Moreover, I think the company's outlook has never been brighter.

As I retire from all operational management responsibilities, I simply want to express my deep gratitude and thanks to all the members of the organization who have worked so cooperatively with me over so many years.

APPENDIX O

PROPOSED MERGER OF THE MINNEAPOLIS STAR & TRIBUNE AND THE DES MOINES REGISTER AND TRIBUNE COMPANIES

Minneapolis Star & Tribune Company News Release
September 9, 1981

Minneapolis, Minn.—Directors of the Minneapolis Star & Tribune Company and the Des Moines Register and Tribune Company have agreed in principle to merge the two companies. Terms of the merger have not yet been set.

Both companies are privately held corporations controlled by members of the Cowles family. Each company owns several newspapers and broadcast stations. Combined, the two companies would have annual revenues of $330 million.

The merger is subject to completion of a definitive merger agreement including terms of the merger, and to approval by shareholders and various regulatory bodies this winter.

John Cowles Jr., president of the Minneapolis company, would be chairman and chief executive of the combined company. Cowles' cousin, David Kruidenier, chairman of the Des Moines company, would be president. The combined company would be headquartered in Minneapolis.

The responsibilities of three senior Minneapolis executives would continue largely unchanged in the combined company: Otto A. Silha, chairman of the Minneapolis company, would continue as vice chairman of the combined company, overseeing the company's newspaper and cable companies in Buffalo, N.Y.; Donald R. Dwight would continue as an executive vice president of the combined company and publisher of Star and Tribune Newspapers in Minneapolis; and David C. Cox would continue as an executive vice president of the combined company responsible for finance, human resources and planning.

Michael G. Gartner, president and editor of the Des Moines company, would be a third executive vice president of the combined company with expanded responsibilities. Reporting to Gartner would be Gary G. Gerlach, now executive vice president and general counsel of the Des Moines company, who would become a fourth executive vice president of the combined company and succeed Kruidenier as publisher of the Des Moines Register and Tribune newspapers; Richard W. Gilbert, now president of the Des Moines Register Broadcast Group, who would also supervise the Minneapolis company's television stations in Wichita and Louisville; and Stephen S. Ingham, now vice president for newspaper operations of the Des Moines company, who would supervise the Rapid City (South Dakota) Journal, the Great Falls (Montana) Tribune, the Burley (Idaho) South Idaho News, the Jackson (Tennessee) Sun and the Waukesha (Wisconsin) Freeman, the Sentinel weekly newspapers in suburban Denver and all commercial printing operations of the combined companies.

Succeeding Gartner as editor of the Des Moines newspapers would be James P. Gannon, now executive editor. Gartner would become editorial chairman of the Des Moines newspapers.

Kruidenier, Gartner and Gerlach would be in Minneapolis at least weekly for management meetings, but not move their residence from Des Moines.

The only senior vice president leaving the Minneapolis company as a result of the merger would be Paul A. Tattersall, whose supervisory responsibility for the Minneapolis company's smaller newspapers and broadcasting operations would be assigned to Ingham and Gilbert.

Charles W. Arnason, senior vice president and secretary of the Minneapolis company, would continue as associate general counsel and secretary of the combined company. A new general counsel for the combined company would be recruited by Cowles.

"The merging of the companies will enable us to move into the next generation editorially and financially vigorous," Kruidenier and Cowles said in a statement. "The merger will continue and enhance strong, independent editorial voices in Des Moines and Minneapolis and the other cities where we operate."

The name of the combined company has not yet been determined. The combined company does not propose initially to offer stock to the public, although it is anticipated that a secondary public market in stock of the combined company will develop.

In the fiscal year ended December 30, 1980, the Des Moines company reported operating revenues of $86 million and net earnings of $6.8 million. The company operates the Des Moines Register and Tribune, the Jackson (Tenn.) Sun, the Waukesha (Wisc.) Freeman and weekly newspapers in Independence, Iowa. it also owns WQAD-TV in Moline, Ill.; KHON-TV in Honolulu; radio stations KYXI and KGON-FM in the Portland, Oregon, market; stations KLAK and KPPL-FM in the Denver, Colorado, market; and stations WIBA and WIBA-FM in Madison, Wisconsin. In addition, the company owns 13 percent of the stock of the Minneapolis Star & Tribune Company.

In the fiscal year ended February 28, 1981, the Minneapolis company reported revenues of $213 million and net earnings of $7 million. Operating units of the company, in addition to Star and Tribune Newspapers in Minneapolis, include: The Buffalo Courier-Express in New York; the Rapid City Journal in South Dakota; the Great Falls Tribune in Montana; the South Idaho Press in Burley; Community Publications Company — the Sentinel weekly newspapers — in the Denver metropolitan area; television station KTVH in Wichita-Hutchinson, Kansas; WDRB-TV, a UHF station in Louisville, Kentucky; a cable system, CableScope, in Buffalo, New York; and Information Publishers, Inc. — commercial printing and community directories — in Edina, Minnesota.

Cowles and Kruidenier are grandsons of Gardner Cowles, Sr., who bought the Des Moines Register and Leader in 1903 and moved from Algona, Iowa, to Des Moines. The Cowles interests purchased The Minneapolis Star in 1935 and the Minneapolis Journal in 1939, and acquired through merger the Minneapolis Tribune in 1941. John Cowles, Sr., now retired, led the Minneapolis company from 1935 to 1968.

Minneapolis Star & Tribune Company News Release
October 2, 1981

Minneapolis, Minn.—A slate for the Board of Directors to be recommended to stockholders of the new company formed out of a prospective merger of the Minneapolis Star & Tribune Company and the Des Moines Register and Tribune Company was announced today by John Cowles Jr. and David Kruidenier. Cowles is President of the Minneapolis company, and Kruidenier is Chairman of the Des Moines company.

The individuals to be recommended as directors of the new company are:

- John Cowles Jr. of Minneapolis, President of the Minneapolis Star & Tribune Company; he would become Chairman and Chief Executive of the new company.
- David Kruidenier of Des Moines, Chairman and Chief Executive of the Des Moines Register and Tribune Company, and Publisher of the Des Moines Register and Tribune newspapers; he would become President of the new company.
- Otto A. Silha of Minneapolis, Chairman of the Board of the Minneapolis Star & Tribune Company; he would be Vice Chairman of the new company.
- Morley Cowles Ballantine of Durango, Colo., Publisher and Editor of the Durango Herald.
- John Chrystal of Coon Rapids, Iowa, President, Iowa Savings Bank.
- David C. Cox of Minneapolis, Executive Vice President of the Minneapolis Star & Tribune Company; he would become an Executive Vice President of the new company responsible for finance, human resources and planning.
- Donald R. Dwight of Minneapolis, President and Publisher of the Star & Tribune Newspapers and Executive Vice President of the Minneapolis Star & Tribune Company; he would remain Publisher of Star and Tribune Newspapers and become an Executive Vice President of the new company.
- Michael Gartner of Des Moines, President and Chief Operating officer of the Des Moines Register and Tribune Company and Editor of the Des Moines Register and Tribune; he would become Editorial Chairman of the Des Moines newspapers and an Executive Vice President of the new company responsible for the Des Moines newspapers, smaller newspapers and broadcasting.
- Gary G. Gerlach of Des Moines, Executive Vice President, Secretary and General Counsel of the Des Moines Register and Tribune Company; he would become Publisher of the Des Moines Register and Tribune newspapers and an Executive Vice President of the new company.
- Lois Cowles Harrison of Lakeland, Florida, Director, League of Women Voters of the U.S.
- James L. Heskett of Cambridge, Mass., Senior Associate Dean, Harvard University Graduate School of Business Administration.
- Luther L. Hill Jr. of Des Moines, Executive Vice President and Secretary, Equitable of Iowa Companies.
- Winthrop Knowlton of New York, Chairman of the Board, Harper & Row, Publishers, Inc.
- Burke Marshall of New Haven, Conn., Professor of Law, Yale University Law School.
- Kingsley H. Murphy Jr. of Minneapolis, President, Northland Stations, Inc.

Cowles, Kruidenier, Silha, Dwight, Harrison, Hill, Knowlton and Murphy are currently members of the Board of Directors of Minneapolis Star & Tribune

Company, together with John B. Davis Jr. of St. Paul, President of Macalester College, who would not become a member of the board of the new company.

Kruidenier, Gartner, Gerlach, Ballantine, Chrystal, Cowles, Hill, Heskett and Marshall serve as directors of the Des Moines Register and Tribune Company. J. Robert Hudson, Vice President for Corporate Planning for the Des Moines Register and Tribune Company; Carolyn S. Bucksbaum, Des Moines civic leader; and Kenneth MacDonald, retired Editor of the Des Moines Register and Tribune, are members of the board of the Des Moines company who would not join the board of the new combined company.

Announcement of agreement in principle on the proposed merger was made September 9, 1981; the merger is subject to completion of a definitive merger agreement including terms of the merger, and to approval this winter by shareholders and various regulatory bodies. The combined company would be headquartered in Minneapolis.

APPENDIX P

JOHN COWLES JR. BECOMES PUBLISHER

John Cowles Jr. To Become Publisher of
The Minneapolis Star and Tribune
Cowles Media Company News Release
November 1, 1982

MINNEAPOLIS, MN — John Cowles Jr., president and chief executive officer of Cowles Media Company, announced today that he would also become publisher of The Minneapolis Star and Tribune, Cowles Media's flagship newspaper, next Monday, November 8.

Cowles said he had asked Donald R. Dwight, publisher of the newspaper since 1976, to relinquish that position as part of a reorganization of the company and newspaper's top management.

Cowles, who will continue as president and chief executive officer of Cowles Media, will move his office from the IDS building back to the newspaper's main building, at Fifth and Portland.

Otto A. Silha, chairman of the board, and Cowles Media's corporate staff headed by David C. Cox, executive vice president, will move as soon as practical from the IDS building to the newspaper's newly-built Gale W. Freeman building at Fourth and Portland.

Cox will become chief operating officer of Cowles Media, responsible for all corporate staff functions and operating units other than The Star and Tribune.

Cowles also announced today the appointment of Roger P. Parkinson as a new senior vice president and deputy publisher of The Star and Tribune. Cowles said Parkinson, Norton L. Armour, the newspaper's senior vice president for administration and general counsel, Lee Canning, senior vice president and business manager, and a new editor yet to be chosen, would report to Cowles as publisher.

Parkinson was publisher of The Buffalo (New York) Courier-Express for the three years it was owned and published by Cowles Media. The company closed down The Courier-Express September 19.

Before going to Buffalo, Parkinson held executive positions at Newsweek magazine and then The Washington Post, attaining the position of vice president for administration.

Cowles said he was assuming the publisher's role at The Minneapolis Star and Tribune "to help strengthen the sense of teamwork and common purpose" among the newspaper and headquarters staff of Cowles Media and the other operating units. "Some years ago we concluded to conduct the business of this company as if we were publicly owned," Cowles said, "even though we have no present intention to go public. This means we subject ourselves to the same financial and management disciplines as do publicly held companies, including return on investment, operating efficiency and overall profitability.

"As a company, we have concluded that in these difficult economic times we must focus our resources and management capabilities on those elements of our company which offer the greatest potential for sustained profit and growth. The sales of our interest in Harper & Row and of television station KTVH in Wichita, the combining of The Star and Tribune, and the closing of The Courier-Express in Buffalo have all been steps in a strategic process to restructure this company, and to concentrate on where we are strongest so that we can compete more effectively and prepare for developing opportunities in the information business.

"Because The Minneapolis Star and Tribune is by far our biggest operating unit — next year about three quarters of the company's revenue — it is important that I spend more time with it," Cowles said.

"The past few years have been difficult for The Star and Tribune," Cowles said, "including the 27-day strike in 1980, the voluntary early retirements of many long-term middle and senior managers last winter and the current recession.

"The Minneapolis newspaper is profitable, but is not performing at the levels needed for the long-term renewal and growth of capital investment required to maintain excellence and compete in the rapidly changing information industry. Our profit margins at The Star and Tribune are roughly half those for comparable newspapers elsewhere.

"The merger of the evening Star into the morning Tribune last April under Don Dwight's leadership was an enormously important initiative toward strengthening the long-term economic health of the newspaper. Don has properly focused the organization on issues of productivity and flexibility.

"Speaking personally, I shall miss the companionship of Don's energy, courage and humor. This community has benefited greatly from his leadership of The Star and Tribune and of community institutions including the Guthrie Theater Foundation. I wish him all possible success in whatever he next chooses to do."

Dwight joined The Star and Tribune in 1975 as associate publisher after serving as Lieutenant Governor of Massachusetts from 1971 to 1975. He had earlier served in various capacities both in Massachusetts state government and at his family's newspaper in western Massachusetts, The Holyoke Transcript-Telegram.

Cowles, 53, joined The Tribune as a reporter in 1953. After working in various departments of the newspaper he succeeded his father, John Cowles Sr. (now an honorary director of Cowles Media), as editor of The Star and Tribune in 1961 and chief executive of the company in 1968. He was a director of the Associated Press from 1966 to 1975, a director of the American Newspaper Publishers Association from 1975 to 1977, and has been a member of the Pulitzer Prize Board at Columbia University since 1970.

"I look forward to returning to an active role at the newspaper and to working with the many capable managers already there and with a new editor whom we hope to select within the next few months," Cowles said. The search for a new editor began in July in anticipation of Charles W. Bailey's plan to leave the editor's post by the end of the year.

"With a news and editorial staff for the combined Star and Tribune newspaper one-third larger than the staff of the former morning and Sunday Tribune, we have the human and financial resources to provide an outstanding paper to our readers and advertisers," Cowles said.

"Paid circulation of The Star and Tribune is strong, above last spring's pre-merger projections of 360,000 daily and 575,000 Sunday," Cowles said, "and has not been noticeably affected either by the dropping of its small afternoon street sale edition or by the recent appearance in Minnesota of USA Today, the Gannett Company's experimental national newspaper. The Wall Street Journal's circulation throughout Minnesota is approximately 36,000," Cowles said, "while The New York Times sells about 2,000 copies daily and 5,000 Sunday.

"Circulation of The St. Paul Pioneer Press and Dispatch, owned by Knight-Ridder, continues at about 106,000 morning, 113,000 evening and 246,000 on Sunday," Cowles said.

The responsibilities of Parkinson, 41, The Minneapolis Star and Tribune's new deputy publisher, will include the advertising, circulation, promotion and research departments. Those departments had been under the supervision of Christopher Burns, associate publisher, who announced last week his resignation from that position.

"In 1979," Cowles said, "we began to emphasize the development of the corporation as a whole, as distinct from the Minneapolis newspaper operation, and moved the corporate offices to the IDS building. During the past few years, we have improved our corporate competence in finance, human resources, strategic planning and other corporate services which support our operating units. We expect that moving our corporate staff adjacent to The Star and Tribune building will help the coordination of headquarters and our largest operating unit."

In addition to The Minneapolis Star and Tribune, principal operating units of the company include The Rapid City Journal in South Dakota; The Great Falls Tribune in Montana; South Idaho Press in Burley; Community Publications Company (Sentinel weekly newspapers) in the Denver metropolitan area; Information Publishers, Inc. (commercial printing and community directories) in Edina, Minnesota; WDRB-TV, an independent UHF station in Louisville, Kentucky; CableScope, the cable television system in Buffalo, New York; and KTVH, a CBS television affiliate in Wichita-Hutchinson, Kansas, pending approval by the Federal Communications Commission of the sale of the station to new ownership in Kansas.

Statement of Donald R. Dwight,
President and Publisher,
The Minneapolis Star and Tribune

November 1, 1982

"The consolidation of corporate and newspaper interests in the person of the owner, John Cowles Jr., makes sense for The Minneapolis Star and Tribune at this point in its history.

"I have loved my association with the people of The Star and Tribune and Minneapolis, and regret deeply that it comes to an end.

"I feel very good about what has started to happen with the newspaper and wish it continuing success."

APPENDIX Q

THE HERITAGE CENTER

The Heritage Center
Newsmakers, June 1987

Heritage Center is the largest and one of the most important investments made by Cowles Media since the acquisition of The Minneapolis Tribune in 1941. The building itself was begun in October 1985, following three years of extensive analysis and planning. The plant will be "officially" completed in July of 1988 when all copies of the *Star Tribune* are printed, assembled and distributed from Heritage Center. At the end of 1987 all daily newspapers will be printed there. Since March sixth of this year, printing has been split between the new facility and 425 Portland, with the balance continuously shifting to Heritage Center.

The facility has 425,000 square feet of space, housing five press lines and costing approximately $110 million. Approximately $30 million is accounted for by the land and building, with the balance being equipment and supporting systems which make it a modern newspaper plant.

Only product functions will be housed at Heritage Center. Part of photoplatemaking, all of printing, newsprint handling, mailroom, fleet and supporting services will operate from the new site. All other activities will remain at 425 Portland Avenue for the foreseeable future. News and advertising material will continue to be prepared as at present, with the final page content laser-scanned and transmitted through fiber optic lines to Heritage Center where plates are made and mounted on the presses. Most of the present production equipment — much of which is technically obsolete — will be sold or scrapped. The only major equipment to be moved are three 72-P inserting units.

Heritage Center is approximately 440 feet by 660 feet, designed so that there is a straight flow of material through the plant to achieve maximum efficiency. Newsprint enters the plant on rail cars holding 50 rolls of paper. Most paper goes directly to a laydown area adjacent to the press reel room, which has a capacity of 230 rolls; the rest goes into a storage area with a capacity of 30 day's supply. When all systems are completed, a press will be able to notify a computer that it needs a roll of paper. The computer will activate an automatic guided vehicle which will go to the rack area, pick up the paper and deliver it to the press, actually inserting the paper onto the reel which feeds the press.

The five press lines, laid out in parallel with the production flow, contain ten units each of Goss offset presses. Each line is capable of printing a 12-section, 160-page black and white newspaper with 48 spot color pages at a maximum printing rate of 35,000 papers per hour. A six-section, 80-page black and white newspaper with 24 spot color pages can be printed at a maximum rate of 70,000 papers per hour. The presses in use currently include one nine-unit offset press and five other presses which were converted to Dilitho, a direct lithography process, in the 1970s. These presses are limited to printing a 144-page newspaper of eight sections with some slower speeds. Depending on the configuration, the new presses will permit up to 16 pages of full process color plus almost unlimited spot color for advertising and news.

Newspapers are wrapped, bundled and tied in the mailroom where preprinted advertising supplements are inserted into the regular sections. There will be four Swiss-developed Ferag inserting systems in the new mailroom, each capable of inserting up to eight supplements at a single pass. They will be augmented with three 72-P inserting machines which have a capacity of 12 supplements in a single pass. In total, it will be possible to have as many as 40 supplements in a Sunday newspaper, compared with 28 today. The time and manpower required for inserting will be significantly reduced, resulting in greater productivity.

Nineteen conveyor "tie lines" handle the six press conveyors coming from the pressroom and the inserting systems in the mailroom which ultimately feed into a complementary bundle distribution system. That system permits zoned editions to be assembled and sent automatically to one of 19 truck loading docks for subsequent distribution. The dock area is completely enclosed to facilitate loading in all weather conditions and to afford greater security.

The production system is controlled by three interrelated computer systems, all housed in a secure climate-controlled room on the second floor of Heritage Center. The principal equipment is a VAX series of computers, produced by Digital Equipment Corporation. There are duplicated systems to substantially reduce the possibility of shutdown.

The building was designed to provide a superior work environment as well as a highly efficient production system. There are soundproof control rooms between each two press lines, where operators control press speed, ink supply, folding and the general quality of the process.

The walls have sound suppression characteristics akin to those used in some concert halls. There are two lunchrooms in the building and an industrial medical facility. The "ready room" for drivers adjoins the truck dock area. Employee access to the building is at a security entrance adjacent to the employee parking lot.

Training for the new systems and facility has been extensive, including trips by employees to other newspaper plants throughout the country having similar equipment, special training at the equipment vendor manufacturing plants, and formal "hands-on" training programs at Heritage Center. All major equipment is being installed and tested by specialists who are also available during the break-in periods to assist in training and in fine-tuning of the equipment.

While all equipment in Heritage Center is commercially available, a number of innovations have been designed to take advantage of the best experience in the industry:

The fiber optic transmission of copy over a distance of 18 blocks is superior to that available either by microwave or coaxial cable; it can handle 45 million bits of information per second.

The newsprint storage area adjacent to the presses utilizes a space-saving rack system which is an industry first.

The automatic guided vehicle system is widely used in other industries, but its use for handling newsprint and automatically loading newsprint into the presses has been developed by IDAB specifically for the *Star Tribune*.

The parallel alignment of press lines, in the direction of process flow, is unlike that found in most newspaper production facilities; it affords much greater flexibility in printing configurations and will permit future individual press expansion to 12 units, as well as future expansion of the total battery of presses within the limits of the site acreage.

Heritage Center stands as a symbol of the future of the *Star Tribune* and a reflection of the exacting performance which has characterized the organization over the past fifty years.

APPENDIX R

THE 1985 GOVERNANCE CHANGES

January 7, 1985

Mr. David Kruidenier
Chairman
Cowles Media Company
425 Portland Avenue
Minneapolis, Minnesota 55415

Dear David:

I have been thinking in recent weeks about the management of Cowles Media Company (CMC) and the Voting Trust and here are my suggestions.

A. I think David Cox should be named chief executive as well as president of the company no later than the company's annual meeting in July of 1985; and that David Kruidenier should continue as chairman of the board (with appropriate compensation and expense reimbursement). As for myself, I should not return to the management or board of the company.

B. I think the two Davids should recruit two business executives, on the younger side if possible, to join the board at the annual meeting in July. These two new directors should be experienced in the management of larger business organizations. I think Lois should plan to leave the board in July of 1985, and Morley in 1986.

C. I think the present Voting Trust, which terminates in May of 1990, should be promptly amended — or a new Voting Trust created — to accomplish the following:

1. Establish that each of us four children of John and Elizabeth Bates Cowles, together with our respective spouses and adult children, is entitled to decide who shall represent each of our respective families as a Trustee of the Voting Trust, approximately in proportion to our respective stakes in the assets of the Voting Trust, as follows: Morley (19.1%); Sally (21.3%) and Russell (13.2%) — one Trustee each; John (41.9%) — two Trustees.

Initially, this would be accomplished by Morley's and my continuing as Trustees, by naming Sally and Russell to replace Lois and Luther, and by regarding David Kruidenier as a representative of my family for at least three years. Vacancies resulting from resignation, disability or death would be filled by the family entitled to that seat. (Tessa would be regarded as one of my family for this purpose.)

2. Permit termination of the Trust by affirmative vote of four-fifths (4/5ths) of the Trustees instead of the present requirement for unanimity (5/5ths). Keep the present alternative procedure for termination which is an affirmative vote by holders of three-fourths (3/4ths) of the Voting Trust certificates.

3. Delete the obsolete language about approval by the FCC.

4. If a new Voting Trust is created instead of amending the present Voting Trust, specify that the new Trust will terminate in five years (January of 1990) unless the R&T has been liquidated or sold and the proceeds distributed to its shareholders by January 1987 — in which case the new Voting Trust would run the maximum limit of ten years until January of 1995.

D. Substitute Sally for David Kruidenier as a Trustee (with me and First Bank Minneapolis) of the John Cowles Family Trust, and substitute Russell for David as Trustee (with me and First Bank Minneapolis) of the four EBC Family Trusts, so that any vote by these Trusts as certificate holders in the Voting Trust will more nearly reflect the desires of their beneficiaries.

E. Later this year consider inviting the adult children of Morley, Sally and Russell — plus Tessa and Fuller — to deposit their CMC voting shares in the Voting Trust, and consider inviting present certificate holders to deposit any additional voting shares that may have come into their ownership in recent years. Of course the Voting Trust would still need the support of David's and Lois' families and our other cousins.

F. David Cox is talking with Jay about coming to work for CMC in long-range planning, which is what Jay worked on for the company in 1982. Personally, I would much enjoy having Jay and Page here in Minneapolis. However, because Jay is not yet proven in management and because I think he should feel entirely free to choose his own future, I am not counting on him as a factor in this situation. That's completely up to Jay and David Cox.

Attached is a sheet illustrating how I arrive at attributing 19.1% of the present Voting Trust to Morley, etc.

I am asking Jim Wittenburg, who is head of the Doherty, Rumble & Butler office in Minneapolis and has been Sage's and my lawyer for some years, to send you a redraft of the present Voting Trust showing the changes I have mentioned above.

Please let me have your thoughts on any of this at your earliest convenience. Considering the pending sale or liquidation of the Register and Tribune, time is of the essence.

Regards,
John

John Cowles Jr.
430 First Avenue North
Minneapolis, Minnesota 55401

APPENDIX S

COWLES MEDIA COMPANY (AND PREDECESSORS) BOARD OF DIRECTORS

Board Member	Election	Service Concluded	Board Member	Election	Service Concluded
George Adams	1935	1935	Philip VonBlon	1962	1970
John Cowles	1935	1976	Robert Witte	1971	1976
Gardner Cowles Jr.	1935	1953	David Kruidenier	1972	1993
Arthur Gormley	1935, 1938	1936, 1941	Kingsley H. Murphy Jr.	1973	1985
			Luther L. Hill Jr.	1974	1990
Davis Merwin	1935	1937	Robert W. Smith	1974	1976
John Thompson	1935	1954	John B. Davis Jr.	1976	1989
Truman Weller	1935	1937	Donald R. Dwight	1976	1982
Lloyd Bock	1936	1937	Lois Cowles Harrison	1976	1985
Nelson Poynter	1937	1938	Winthrop Knowlton	1976	1986
Basil Walters	1937	1944	Morley Cowles Ballantine	1982	1986
George Ronald	1940	1941	David C. Cox	1982	1998
Gideon Seymour	1940	1954	Roger P. Parkinson	1983	1993
Joyce Swan	1940	1977	Anthony L. Andersen	1985	1996
G. Bickelhaupt	1941	1944	William A. Hodder	1985	1998
William McNally	1941	1944	Carol R. Goldberg	1986	1990
Kingsley Murphy	1941	1953	Terry T. Saario	1987	1998
Lyle Anderson	1944	1960	Richard G. Ballantine	1988	1993
Harold Perkins	1944	1952	John Cowles III	1990	1998
Stanley Hawks	1944	1962	K. Prescott Low	1990	1998
Howard Mithun	1954	1975	James N. Rosse	1990	1998
John Moffet	1954	1970	Elizabeth Ballantine	1993	1998
Otto Silha	1954	1984	Elizabeth Bullitt	1993	1998
William Steven	1954	1960	Herbert P. Wilkins Sr.	1994	1998
John Cowles Jr.	1956	1984			

APPENDIX T

COWLES MEDIA COMPANY CHRONOLOGY

1935 Acquisition of the stock of the Minneapolis Daily Star Company for $1 million. John Cowles elected president; Gardner Cowles Jr., vice president; Davis Merwin, vice president and treasurer; John Thompson, secretary. Basil L. "Stuffy" Walters named editor. Cedric Adams begins column.

1936 Willis Brown named classified advertising manager. Walters returns to Des Moines and is replaced by Thompson as editor. Total circulation reached 119,314, the largest evening circulation in the Northwest.

1937 George Grim named promotion manager, Davis Merwin resigns as publisher, replaced by John Thompson. Walters returns as editor. *LOOK* magazine started.

1938 Circulation reaches 150,056, the largest in Minneapolis. Lyle Anderson named auditor, came from Des Moines. Sears Roebuck ran over 10.5 pages of advertising on one day, the most of any Minneapolis newspaper.

1939 Joyce A. Swan named sales promotion manager, came from Des Moines. New pressroom completed with new presses and stereotyping equipment. Acquisition of *The Minneapolis Journal*. Additional presses ordered and plant addition begun. Name changed to Star Journal Company.

1940 Gideon Seymour chief editorial writer, came from Des Moines. Sunday *Star Journal* circulation over 190,000, daily is 240,000; circulation sign erected on building. New building dedicated — finest plant between Chicago and Pacific coast. Otto A. Silha joined editorial department, William A. Cordingley Jr., the merchandising department.

1941 John Cowles returns from trip to England with Wendell Wilkie. Merger with Minneapolis Tribune Company, with Star and Journal Company holding 2/3 of stock in new company. Name changed to Minneapolis Star Journal and Tribune Company. William J. McNally named vice president; McNally, Kingsley H. Murphy and George Bickelhaupt joined John Cowles, Gardner Cowles Jr., John Thompson, Basil Walters, Joyce Swan and Gideon Seymour as directors. Bickelhaupt publisher of evening *Minneapolis Daily Times*.

1942 Dividend of $1.00 per share. New press units installed.

1943 John Cowles given eight-month leave of absence to serve with Lend-Lease Administration. 175 employees in service. First newsprint rationing.

1944 Intent to enter broadcast field. Gardner Cowles Jr. elected chairman of the board; Walters resigns, Seymour becomes executive editor, McNally resigns. Stanley Hawks elected to board; dividend of $1.00. Additional newsprint rationing to 75% of 1941 consumption, all advertising rationed. Minnesota Poll begun.

1945 Minneapolis Star Journal and Tribune Fund created for charitable, scientific and educational purposes. Northwest Broadcasting Company incorporated by Cowles brothers, to be sold to company. Airplane delivery service of *The Minneapolis Tribune* to Sioux Falls and Fargo.

1946 New building plans announced to double space to 252,000 square feet with new facade on Portland Avenue; Sunday circulation passed 500,000. John Moffett named assistant to the president, came from Des Moines.

1947 Name changed to Minneapolis Star and Tribune Company. Dividend of $2.50. New mailroom opened, largest in Upper Midwest.

1948 Purchase of shares in Minnesota and Ontario Paper Company. *The Minneapolis Daily Times* ceases publication. FCC awarded provisional construction permit to build a television station.

1949 John Thompson retires as publisher; replaced by John Cowles who remains president and editor. Dedication of new building. Morning circulation 179,878; evening 301,668; Sunday 604,728. Employee retirement plan begun.

1950 1,959 employees; newsprint costs $101 per ton; 7,654 carriers deliver papers.

1951 DC-3 airplane acquired, Norman Mitchell named chief pilot. John Cowles around-the-world trip as trustee of Ford Foundation. University of Missouri Medal for Distinguished Service to Journalism.

1952 Arthur and Morley Cowles Ballantine purchase *The Durango Herald*. WTCN and WCCO merge. Joyce Swan promoted to VP and general manager.

1953 Gardner Cowles Jr. did not stand for reelection to the board. Brief strike by drivers.

1954 Dayton's first Sunday advertising. Carl Rowan and Clark Mollenoff receive Sigma Delta Chi awards for reporting; Richard Wilson, head of Washington Bureau, receives Pulitzer for national reporting. Howard Mithun, John Moffett, Otto Silha and William Steven elected directors. Death of Gideon Seymour. Purchase of bonds for baseball stadium. Purchase of 47% interest in Midwest Radio-Television (WCCO) for $3,950,000.

1955 KTVH-TV acquired in Kansas. 11,837 carrier/farm salesmen.

1956 John Cowles received honorary LLD from Harvard, Ralph D. Casey Minnesota Award; plant expansion plans announced, including ten new press units. Stock split 3-for-1; ten-year paper contracts signed; John Cowles Jr. elected to board.

1957 Press installation brings total to 45 press units; building air conditioned; first productivity analysis published. *The Minneapolis Star* zoned for advertising.

1958 Non-voting stock created.

1959 50 acres of land purchased at Highways 100 and 12. Purchase of Grumann Gulfstream airplane authorized. Expanded mailroom and eight additional press units authorized. *The Valley Times* purchased. Retirement plan improved.

1960 Lyle Anderson retires; William Steven resigns. New press units ordered; billing expanded.

1961 New circulation highs for all three papers reached. Swan elected publisher, John Cowles Jr., editor. Philip VonBlon joins company.

1962 112-day strike. Hawks retires. VonBlon joins board.

1963 *The Valley Times* sold. 2-for-5 stock dividend. 1,000-acre farm acquired in Champlin. Gale Freeman named industrial relations director. Guthrie Theater opens.

1964 *The Rapid City Journal* acquired; Willis Brown named publisher. Investment in Harper & Row made.

1965 *The Great Falls Tribune* acquired; William Cordingley named publisher. *Harper's* magazine interest purchased. First IBM computer ordered.

1966 Plant to be expanded by 20%.

1967 Ad linage hits all-time high.

1968 Swan elected vice-chairman, John Cowles Jr. president, Otto Silha publisher. First diversity meetings. Swan becomes publisher in Rapid City. John Cowles Jr. elected chairman of Harper & Row. Handgun advertising banned. Charles Bailey heads Washington Bureau.

1969 Newsprint warehouse building authorized. Stock split 1:1. WCCO license renewal hearing ordered.

1970 Security system instituted. VonBlon resigns.

1971 Robert Witte elected director. Community Publications Company in Denver acquired. James W. Swan named publisher in Rapid City.

1972 Sohmer + Partners acquired. David Kruidenier elected to board. Bailey named new editor of *The Minneapolis Tribune*. Hawthorne named vice president for public affairs. Liquor advertising accepted. Stromberg Publications acquired in Baltimore area. Sale of land development at Highways 12 and 100.

1973 John Cowles retires as chairman, succeeded by John Cowles Jr. Silha elected president, Smith publisher of Minneapolis newspapers. Kingsley Murphy Jr. elected to board. Alcoholism program announced for employees.

1974 Luther L. Hill Jr. and Robert Smith elected to board. Mithun retires. Stadium task force formed.

1975 Donald R. Dwight hired as associate publisher. Death of Robert Smith. *Sun Newspapers* lawsuit begun.

1976 Witte retires. Airplane sold. WCCO interest sold. Dwight named publisher. Lois Cowles Harrison, John B. Davis Jr., Winthrop Knowlton and Dwight elected to board. Sale of Steve Sohmer Inc. Death of Elizabeth Bates Cowles.

1977 Acquisition of WDRB-TV in Louisville and *The South Idaho Press;* financial participation in downtown stadium authorized. *Sun Newspaper* litigation concluded. Contract awarded for new offset press. Sale of Quayle, Plesser.

1978 Authorization of new building for newspaper circulation activities. Steven Isaacs named editor of *The Minneapolis Star*. ATEX electronic news system operational. 2:1 stock split.

1979 Acquisition of the *Buffalo Courier-Express*, borrowing authorized to finance. John Cowles Jr. becomes president, Otto Silha chairman. Stromberg Publications sold. New *Star* format adopted. Cowles heads Stadium Site Task Force, downtown land donated. Corporate headquarters moved to IDS Center.

1980 Sale of *Harper's* magazine. 27-day newspaper strike. Roger Parkinson named publisher in Buffalo, Joel Kramer editor. Cowles Family Voting Trust created.

1981 Merger with The Register and Tribune Company announced. WDRB sold. David Cox hired. Sale of stock in Harper & Row. Short-term loan to Register and Tribune. Moratorium on purchase of stock by company.

1982 Merger discussions terminated. Closing of *The Star* as separate paper. VIRP early retirement plan. Name changed to Cowles Media Company. Fiscal year-end changed to March. Closedown of the *Courier-Express*. Bailey resigns as editor of *The Tribune*. Dwight resigns as publisher, succeeded by Cowles. Cox and Morley Cowles Ballantine join board. Preferred stock issued.

1983 Cowles resigns, Kruidenier elected president and CEO, Parkinson publisher. Death of John Cowles Sr. U.S. Supreme Court voids newsprint tax. Cowles Media Company headquarters moved to Freeman Building. Sale of KTVH. Kramer named executive editor. Limited stock trading begins.

1984 Facilities plan presented to board, Voting Trust. Silha retires, Kruidenier becomes chairman and CEO, Cox president and COO. Register and Tribune sale process begins. Murphy announced intent to sell his 17% stock interest in Cowles Media Company. Sale of cable system in Buffalo and WDRB-TV.

1985 Voting Trust commits to renew through 2000; John Cowles III becomes director of planning. Murphy stock sold to Washington Post Company. Register and Tribune Company and Cowles Media Company stock sold to Gannett. Cox named CEO, Kruidenier remains chairman. William Hodder and Anthony Andersen elected to board; Harrison and Murphy do not stand for reelection. James Swan retires as publisher in Rapid City and Cordingley in Great Falls. Construction begun on $110 million Minneapolis newspaper plant.

1986 Knowlton and Ballantine resign from board, Carol Goldberg joins board. Metro newspaper strategy approved. Acquisition of Historical Times, Inc., publisher of consumer special interest magazines and books, later named Cowles Enthusiast Media.

1987 Terry Saario joins board. Scottsdale paper acquired.

1988 Cowles Media Company stock owned by Gannett acquired for $128 million. Preferred stock redeemed. Richard Ballantine joins board. Hanson Publishing Company acquired, publisher of business magazines; acquisition of *Bowhunter* magazine and Empire Press, publisher of several history magazines. Issued $50 million in senior notes. Cowles Media Charter adopted.

1989 Tender offer for 10% of Cowles Media Company stock. Davis retires from board. Acquisition of *Practical Horseman* magazines.

1990 *The Great Falls Tribune* and *The Rapid City Journal* sold. Employee stock plan approved. Goldberg and Hill leave board, John Cowles III, K. Prescott Low and James Rosse join board. Voting Trust announces John Cowles III and Elizabeth Ballantine elected trustees, Kruidenier, Morley Ballantine and John Cowles Jr. resign.

1991 John Cowles III named vice chairman; Elizabeth Bullitt and Gardner Cowles III elected trustees. Community Publications sold. Acquisition of *Vegetarian Times* and *Horse & Rider* magazines. Glendalough farm given to The Nature Conservancy.

1992 Kramer named publisher. Acquisition of *Doll Reader* and *Teddy Bear and Friends* specialty magazines and of Simba and several other business information service providers.

1993 Kruidenier retires from board, John Cowles III becomes chairman, Elizabeth Bullitt, Elizabeth Ballantine and Herbert P. Wilkins Sr. join board, Richard Ballantine and Roger Parkinson resign. Scottsdale paper sold. Stock split 6:1. Acquisition of *Mobile Office* and *Cable World* magazines.

1994 Acquired Cy DeCosse, publisher of special interest books. Acquired *Walking* magazine.

1995 Acquisition of *Southwest Art*.

1996 Voting Trust extended to 2010. Acquisition of The Virtual Flyshop. Acquisition of *Dressage & CT*. Acquisition of *Kitplanes*. Sale of *Mobile Office*. Acquisition of *PROMO* magazine.

1997 Cowles Media Company Board of Directors vote to explore "strategic alternatives." Acquisition of *Nautical Collector*. Sale of *Walking* magazine. Acquisition of *Climbing*. Acquisition of *Military History Quarterly*. Agreement in principle reached for Cowles Media Company to be acquired by McClatchy Newspapers Inc. for $1.4 billion. Acquisition of *Circulation Management* magazine. Acquisition of *American Demographics* magazine.

1998 McClatchy Newspapers Inc. acquires Cowles Media Company.

APPENDIX U

THE FAMILY OF GARDNER COWLES

(INCLUDING SECOND AND THIRD GENERATION MEMBERS ACTIVE IN COWLES MEDIA COMPANY AND THE REGISTER AND TRIBUNE COMPANY)

- **GARDNER COWLES** (1861 - 1946)
- **FLORENCE CALL COWLES** (1861 - 1950)

BERTHA COWLES QUARTON (1882 - 1980)

HELEN COWLES LECRON (1886 - 1963)

RUSSELL COWLES (1887 - 1979)

FLORENCE COWLES KRUIDENIER (1895 - 1985)

- **DAVID KRUIDENIER JR. (1921 -)**

  Register and Tribune Company Director 1952-1985

  Register and Tribune Company Chairman 1978-1983

  Register and Tribune Company CEO 1971-1985

  Cowles Media Company 1948-1952

  Cowles Media Company Director 1972-1993

  Cowles Media Company CEO 1983-1984

  Cowles Media Company Chairman 1984-1993

JOHN COWLES SR. (1898 - 1983)

Cowles Media Company Director 1935-1976

Cowles Media Company CEO 1935-1968

Register and Tribune Company Chairman 1945-1970

Register and Tribune Company 1920-1970

Cowles Communications, Inc. 1941-1954

- **MORLEY COWLES BALLANTINE (1925 -)**

  Register and Tribune Company Director 1977-1985

  Cowles Media Company Director 1982-1986

- **JOHN COWLES JR. (1929 -)**

  Cowles Media Company 1951-1984

  Cowles Media Company Director 1956-1984

  Cowles Media Company CEO 1968-1983

  Register and Tribune Company Director 1960-1984

  Cowles Communications, Inc. Director 1960

GARDNER COWLES JR. (1903 - 1985)

Register and Tribune Company Director

Register and Tribune Company CEO

Cowles Media Company Chairman 1935-1953

Cowles Communications, Inc. Chairman 1936-1973

- **LOIS COWLES HARRISON (1934 -)**

  Cowles Media Company Director 1976-1985

229

APPENDIX V

THE FAMILY OF JOHN COWLES
(INCLUDING THIRD GENERATION MEMBERS ACTIVE IN COWLES MEDIA COMPANY)

- **JOHN COWLES (1898 - 1983)**

  Register and Tribune Company
  1920-1970

  Register and Tribune Company
  Chairman 1945-1970

  Cowles Media Company
  Director 1935-1976

  Cowles Media Company
  CEO 1935-1968

  Cowles Communications, Inc.
  1941-1954

- **ELIZABETH BATES COWLES (1900-1976)**

  - **MORLEY COWLES BALLANTINE (1925 -)**

    Cowles Media Company Director 1982-1986

    Register and Tribune Company Director 1977-1985

    - **RICHARD BALLANTINE (1945 -)**

      Cowles Media Company Director 1988-1993

    - **ELIZABETH BALLANTINE (1948 -)**

      Cowles Media Company Director 1993-1998

  - **SARAH COWLES DOERING (1926 -)**

    - **ELIZABETH BULLITT (1949 -)**

      Cowles Media Company Director 1993-1998

  - **JOHN COWLES JR. (1929 -)**

    Cowles Media Company 1951-1984

    Cowles Media Company Director 1956-1984

    Cowles Media Company CEO 1968-1983

    Register and Tribune Company Director 1960-1984

    Cowles Communications, Inc. Director 1960

    - **JOHN COWLES III (1953 -)**

      Cowles Media Company 1985-1998

      Cowles Media Company Director 1990-1998

      Cowles Media Company Chairman 1993-1998

  - **RUSSELL COWLES II (1936 -)**

231

APPENDIX W

STAR TRIBUNE (AND PREDECESSOR NEWSPAPERS) CIRCULATION 1935-1997

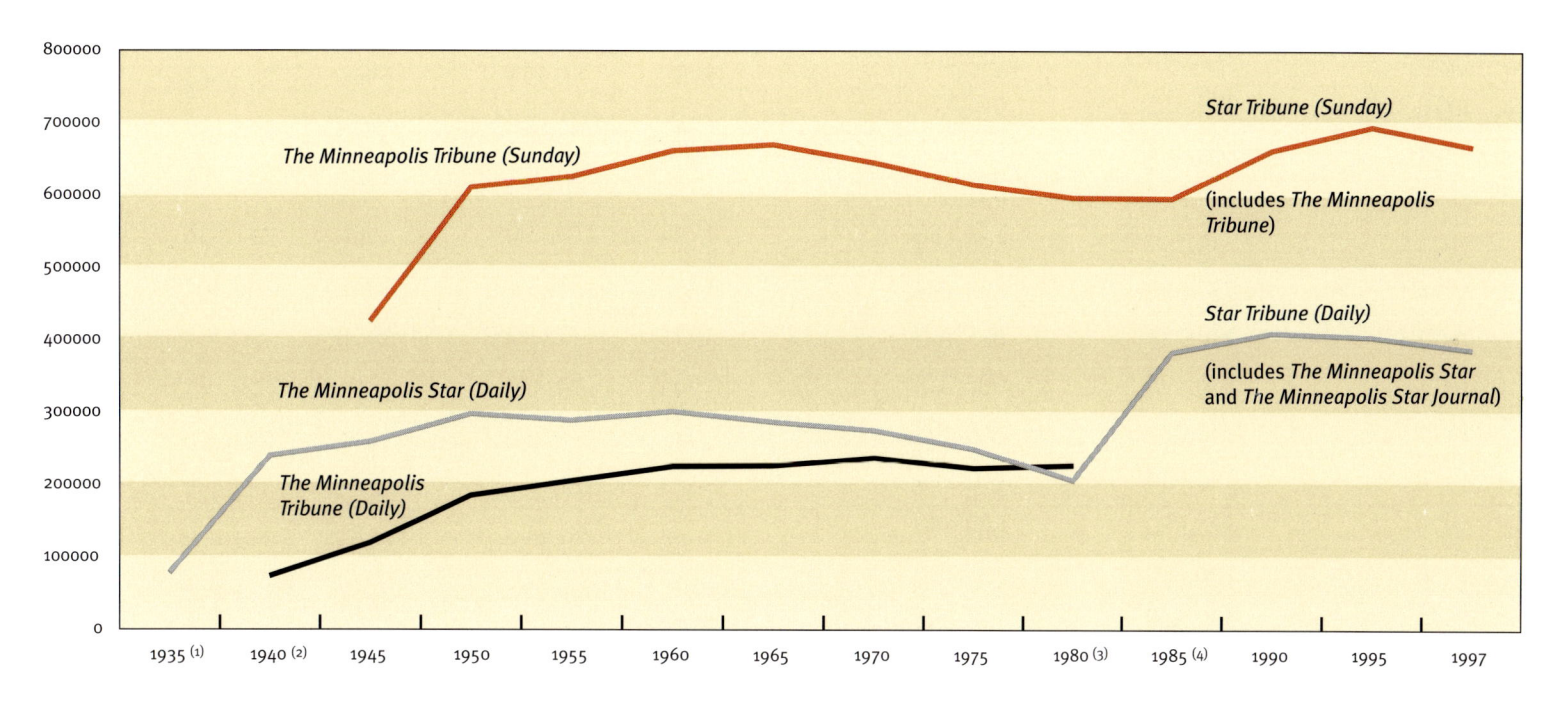

(1) 1939–Cowles purchases *The Minneapolis Journal* to form *The Minneapolis Star Journal*.
(2) 1941–*The Minneapolis Tribune* is combined with the Cowles organization.
(3) 1982–*The Minneapolis Star* is combined with *The Minneapolis Tribune* to form an all-day morning newspaper, *The Minneapolis Star and Tribune*.
(4) 1987–*The Minneapolis Star and Tribune* changes its name to the *Star Tribune* in recognition of its circulation and reach through the Twin Cities Metro Area.

Year	Daily *Star Tribune*	Sunday *Star Tribune*	Year	Daily *Star Tribune*	Sunday *Star Tribune*
1935	79,000		1954	285,797	621,627
1936	119,314		1955	289,629	626,214
1938	150,056		1957	290,542	627,498
1939[1]	241,200		1958	290,960	630,035
1941[2]	240,172	350,164	1959	291,795	640,554
1946	270,000	465,000	1960	301,719	662,074
1947	281,358	535,622	1961	302,738	666,395
1948	283,924	565,979	1962	301,133	672,162
1949	301,668	604,728	1963	279,010	654,623
1950	298,320	611,183	1964	286,881	658,764
1951	295,471	615,888	1965	287,193	670,436
1953	289,695	616,060	1966	287,211	673,391

Year	Daily Star Tribune	Sunday Star Tribune
1967	286,864	664,951
1968	284,691	674,407
1969	285,048	677,808
1970	275,671	645,575
1971	265,454	634,332
1972	257,838	631,093
1973	258,169	646,158
1974	257,680	634,195
1975	250,238	615,169
1976	240,594	604,763
1977	246,233	610,408
1978	236,634	607,194
1979	226,680	608,550
1980	206,700	597,180
1981	192,508	587,255
1982[3]	169,184	576,994
1983	362,015	579,847
1984	372,179	586,876
1985	383,657	596,181
1986	382,499	612,604
1987[4]	382,832	625,504
1988	406,246	648,062
1989	403,300	650,317
1990	410,226	663,063
1991	413,237	673,773
1992	412,871	685,975
1993	413,603	695,710
1994	412,438	696,084
1995	404,757	695,548
1996	388,120	682,318
1997 (September)	387,412	668,466

THE MINNEAPOLIS TRIBUNE

Year	Daily	Year	Daily
1936	74,397	1964	221,981
1938	80,151	1965	226,663
1941[2]	63,610	1966	233,189
1945	120,048	1967	235,921
1946	130,000	1968	241,836
1947	141,377	1969	240,467
1948	151,192	1970	237,747
1949	179,870	1971	229,143
1950	185,460	1972	232,270
1951	190,276	1973	233,025
1953	195,830	1974	228,291
1954	196,473	1975	223,455
1955	205,710	1976	224,412
1956	207,271	1977	225,415
1957	207,538	1978	226,899
1958	208,236	1979	229,754
1959	215,175	1980	227,392
1960	225,436	1981	234,730
1961	229,421	1982[3]	362,505
1962	229,481		
1963	211,471		

SOURCE: ABC STATEMENTS

APPENDIX X

COWLES MEDIA COMPANY (AND PREDECESSOR CORPORATIONS)
FINANCIAL PERFORMANCE 1935–1997*

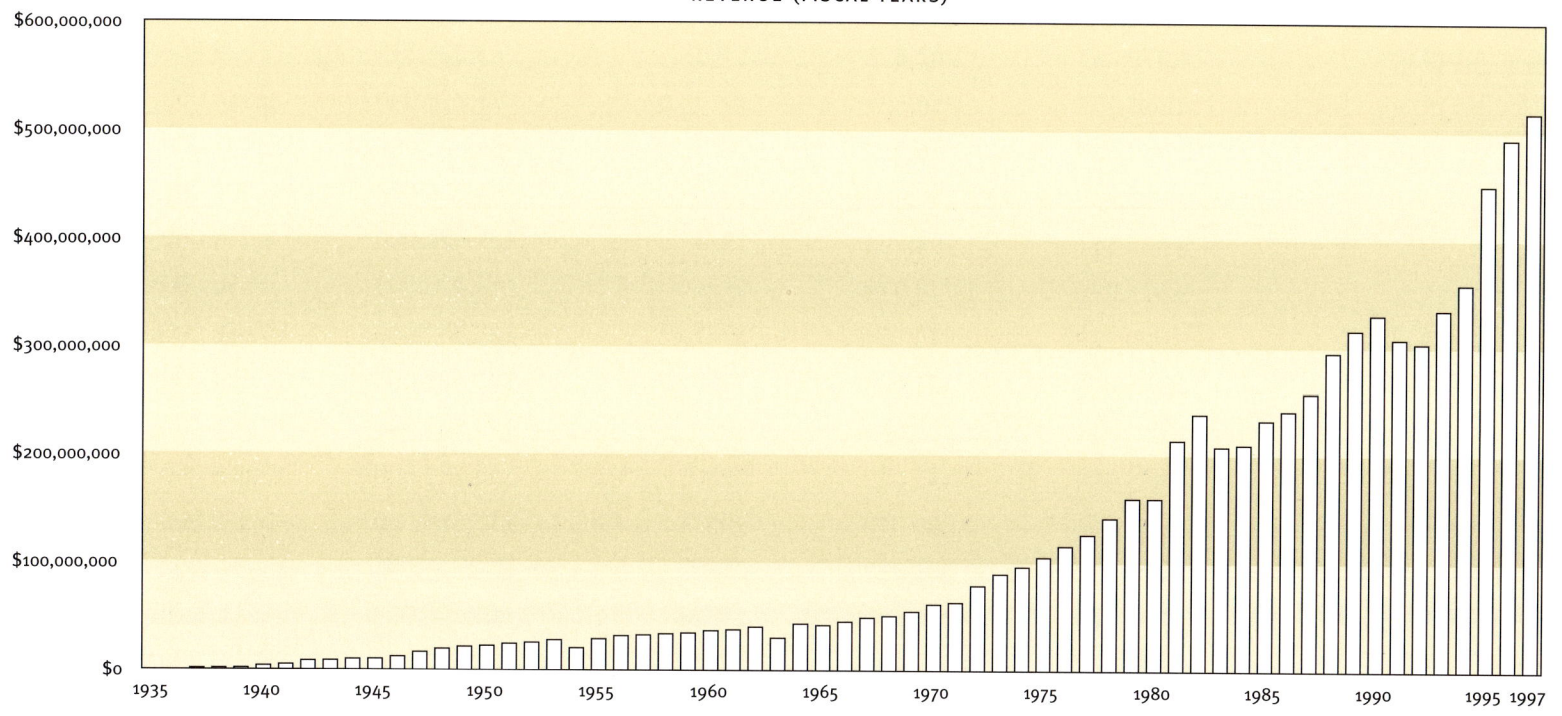

REVENUE (FISCAL YEARS)

NET EARNINGS (FISCAL YEARS)

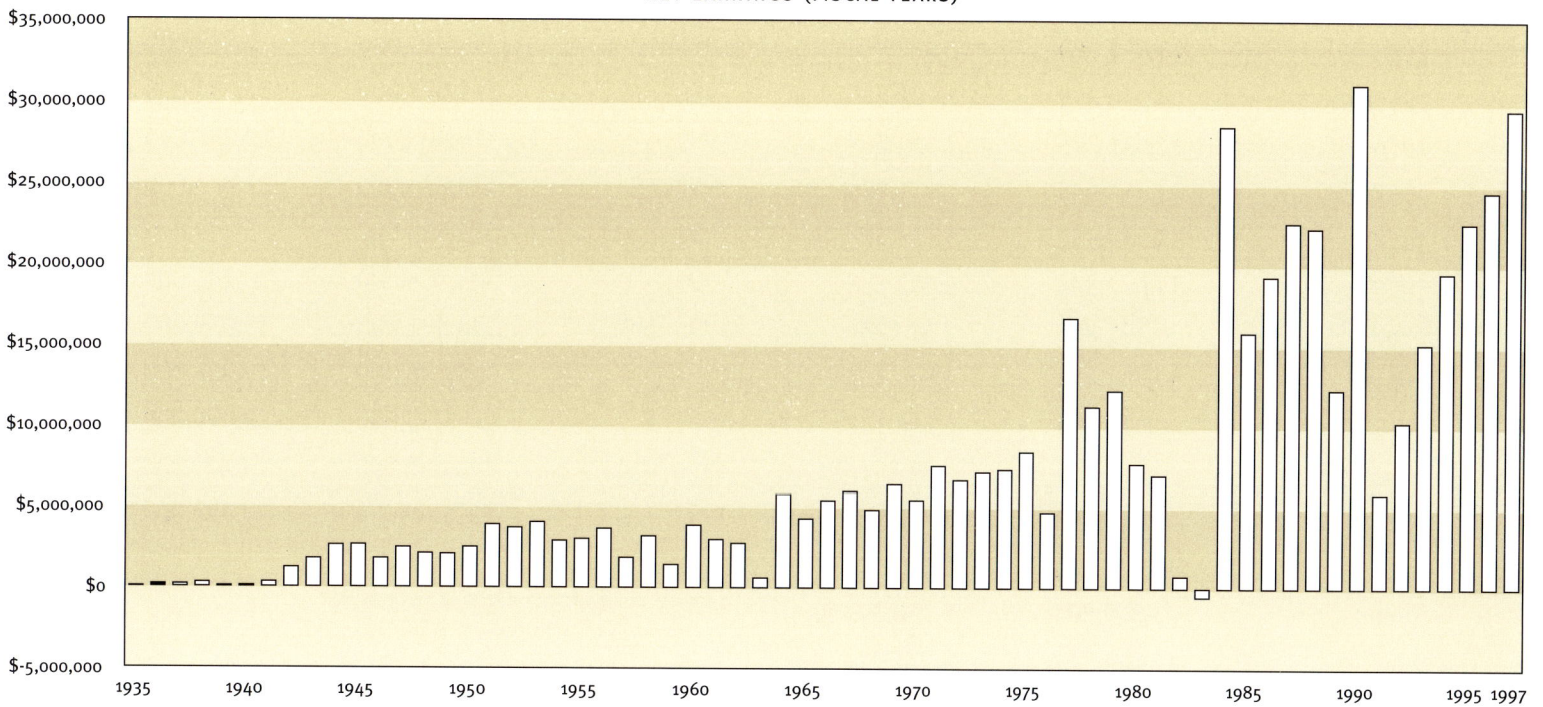

*Amounts prior to 1972 are from the company's unconsolidated federal tax returns; after 1972, amounts are from the company's annual reports to shareholders.

Fiscal Year	Revenue	Net Earnings	Fiscal Year	Revenue	Net Earnings
1935		$ 23,875 [1]	1968	50,754,574	4,783,007
1936		157,487	1969	54,932,199	6,392,524
1937	$ 1,301,855	152,791	1970	61,558,532	5,385,897
1938	1,379,465	262,421	1971	63,226,219	7,522,856
1939	1,647,795	56,629 [2]	1972	78,795,000	6,656,000 [5]
1940	3,752,829	76,257	1973	89,640,000	7,142,000
1941	4,901,450	296,949 [3]	1974	96,236,000	7,301,000
1942	8,334,111	1,194,706	1975	105,024,000	8,399,000
1943	8,626,240	1,744,938	1976	115,430,000	4,650,000 [5]
1944	9,900,158	2,582,724	1977	125,982,000	16,658,000
1945	10,161,492	2,608,966	1978	141,639,000	11,194,000
1946	12,297,511	1,766,055	1979	159,752,000	12,176,000
1947	16,485,184	2,445,052	1980	159,752,000	7,658,000 [6]
1948	19,616,193	2,080,370	1981	213,589,000	6,959,000
1949	21,602,520	2,045,452	1982	237,744,000	747,000 [7]
1950	22,469,469	2,470,640	1983	207,740,000	(531,000)
1951	24,476,864	3,861,894	1984	209,491,000	28,477,000 [8]
1952	25,604,556	3,668,034	1985	232,077,000	15,743,000
1953	27,951,996	4,008,662	1986	240,614,000	19,207,000
1954	20,632,689	2,867,559	1987	256,813,000	22,515,000
1955	29,070,889	2,982,246	1988	295,095,000	22,195,000
1956	32,031,396	3,619,267	1989	315,800,000	12,238,000
1957	32,814,045	1,831,976	1990	329,834,000	31,065,000 [9]
1958	33,923,552	3,158,778	1991	307,558,000	5,794,000
1959	34,672,346	1,402,888	1992	303,574,000	10,231,000
1960	36,895,853	3,827,286	1993	334,591,000	15,039,000
1961	37,793,414	2,944,367	1994	358,196,000	19,428,000
1962	40,419,264	2,716,147	1995	449,738,000	22,499,000
1963	30,284,793	595,416 [4]	1996	492,635,000	24,427,000
1964	43,330,742	5,732,937	1997	517,069,000	29,492,000
1965	42,109,046	4,239,381			
1966	45,377,804	5,350,392			
1967	49,124,327	5,957,917			

SOURCE: COMPANY TAX RETURNS 1935-1971;
COMPANY ANNUAL REPORTS 1971-1997

1 Cowles purchases *The Minneapolis Daily Star.*
2 Cowles purchases *The Minneapolis Journal* to form *The Minneapolis Star Journal.*
3 *The Minneapolis Tribune* merges with the Cowles organization to form the Minneapolis Star Journal and Tribune Company, which publishes the morning *Minneapolis Tribune* and the evening *Minneapolis Star Journal.*
4 Includes the impact of the 1962 strike against the company.
5 Includes the sale of Midwest Radio-Television and WCCO-Television.
6 Includes the impact of the 1980 strike against the company.
7 Includes the closure of the *Buffalo Courier-Express.*
8 Includes the sale of CableScope.
9 Includes the sale of *The Great Falls Tribune* and *The Rapid City Journal.*

APPENDIX Y

GLENDALOUGH

Glendalough game farm was acquired by the company as part of *The Minneapolis Tribune* transaction in 1941. Started in 1903 as an 80-acre summer lakeside retreat, it was bought by F. E. Murphy in 1927 and named Glendalough, after a monastery in County Wicklow in Ireland. In 1932, he established a hatchery where he raised turkeys, pheasants and other game birds as "a supplement to *The Minneapolis Tribune* program for a well-balanced Northwest agriculture."[1] During the Depression, he added adjacent farms, a practice that was continued under Cowles ownership until it was almost 2,000 acres with roughly 30,000 feet of shoreline on five lakes.

It was used by the Cowles family for summer vacations, and by the newspaper advertising department in the fall for hunting weekends. One of those weekends was designated the "Eastern Weekend" — the opening of pheasant season. Bankers, media executives and political leaders from "the East" were invited, most of them friends and associates of John Cowles Sr. Mike Cowles was a regular participant.

Shortly after he came to work for the company, John Cowles Jr. was given responsibility for organizing Glendalough hunting weekends. While he was still in college, his father arranged for him to be in a duck blind with Bruce Dayton with instructions to get acquainted, in spite of the fact that John didn't hunt and felt a cold coming on.[2] Guests came at other times as well; over the years they included Dwight Eisenhower (who visited after being nominated for President), Richard Nixon, and Walter Mondale.

Located about 200 miles west of the Twin Cities, it was a place for the family to get away and relax, although John Cowles Sr. conducted business by telephone with people across the country and often dictated letters and memos to his secretary in Minneapolis. Mike Cowles and his family came from Des Moines when they lived there, often bringing friends. After Arthur and Morley Ballantine bought *The Durango Herald* in Colorado in 1952, they continued to come back for summer visits with their children. There was a main house of relatively modest size and several cottages for guests, located near the northwest shore of Annie Battle Lake. There were also tennis courts, a croquet court, a bowling alley, and later a paddle tennis court. (Croquet was actually a British Army variation of the usual lawn game, requiring oversize square-headed mallets with different rules and etiquette than its conventional cousin.) Bridge in the main house was often the featured social activity, but it was the dining room that was the heart of the place.

Jay Cowles remembers that children were not permitted at the table until age 12, when their table manners would be good enough for adult company. His grandfather treated Jay and his cousins just as he did other guests — with discussions about politics and world affairs in which they were expected to participate. (This was apparently a continuation of a tradition in the Gardner Cowles household in Des Moines, which is well remembered by most members of that third generation.) Richard Ballantine recalls that six or eight copies of *The Minneapolis Tribune* arrived every morning, and that "everyone jumped in," reading aloud and discussing parts of stories they found particularly interesting. They enjoyed their grandfather and his stories of current events, and were encouraged to think about the life of the community and the world. From these experiences came their understanding of the civic role of the newspaper, as an institution of information and ideas. The values learned at Glendalough continue to influence the family today.

The game fowl operations were considerable; the farm raised ducks, partridge, pheasants, turkeys and even cattle for a while. Millet, oats and other grain was grown, part of which was used for feed and part for migrating birds. For many years a Glendalough turkey was a prized gift at Thanksgiving or Christmas.

Glendalough was also used for management retreats for a week in the summer. By the late eighties, however, the hunting weekends were no longer the valuable marketing opportunities they once were, and family members visited less frequently. The cost of maintaining the farm and camp could no longer be justified, and the company gave the property to The Nature Conservancy, so that it could be made available to the State of Minnesota for a park. The property, valued then at $2.6 million was given to the Conservancy on Earth Day, 1990. In the audience that day was Joseph E. Murphy Jr., a nephew of F. E. Murphy and a member of the board of the the Minnesota Chapter of The Nature Conservancy. Because it had remained in private ownership for so long, Glendalough was valued not only for its beauty but because it was one of the last large tracts of undeveloped lake shore and land in the state. There had been no logging operations and very little fishing on the lakes.

Les Estes, then the farm manager, remained as the new manager of the state park. He and his wife, Helen, came to Glendalough in 1965, succeeding Mr. and Mrs. Alex Johnson.

1 Bradley L. Morison, *Sunlight on Your Doorstep* (Minneapolis: Ross & Haines, Inc., 1966), p. 31.
2 Bruce Dayton, author interview, June 6, 1996.

APPENDIX Z

SELECTED BIOGRAPHIES

JOHN COWLES (1898–1983)

John Cowles was president of the Minneapolis Star and Tribune Company (and predecessor companies) from 1935–1968. He served as both editor and publisher during much of that time, relinquishing both posts in 1961. He was chairman of the board from 1953 to 1973 and a director from 1935 until 1976 when he became an honorary director.

He began working for the Des Moines Register and Tribune Company in 1920, and in 1923 became vice president, general manager and associate publisher. He was chairman from 1945 to 1970.

He graduated from Phillips Exeter Academy in 1917, served in the U. S. Army and graduated from Harvard University in 1920. He married Elizabeth Morley Bates in 1923. They had four children: Elizabeth Morley, Sarah Richardson, John Jr., and Russell II.

He was a trustee of The Ford Foundation (1950–68), Drake University (1929–45), Carleton College (1945–61), Phillips Exeter Academy (1936–54), The Minneapolis Foundation, the Minneapolis Society of Fine Arts, the American Assembly, the Carnegie Endowment for International Peace, and the Gardner and Florence Call Cowles Foundation.

He was a member of the Board of Directors of the Associated Press (1934–43) and of the Audit Bureau of Circulations (1929–33). He was a director of The First National Bank of Minneapolis (1944–68), General Electric (1945–49), General Mills (1944–58) and the Equitable Life Insurance Company of Iowa (1955–64).

He was a member of the Board of Overseers of Harvard University (1944–50 and 1960–66), the Business Council, the General Advisory Committee to the U.S. Arms Control and Disarmament Agency (1966–1969), the Hoover Commission Committee on the National Defense Establishment (1948), the National Citizens Commission for the Public Schools (1950–56), the Committee for The White House Conference on Education (1954–55), consultant to the National Security Council (1953) and president of the Harvard Alumni Association (1953–54).

He received the Presidential Certificate of Merit of Service as Special Assistant to the Lend-Lease Administrator in 1943, was an honorary national president of Sigma Delta Chi in 1954, received the Centennial Award from Northwestern University in 1951 and the Minnesota Award for Distinguished Service in Journalism from the University of Minnesota in 1956.

He held honorary degrees from Boston University (1941), Jamestown College (1946), Grinnell College (1955), Coe College (1956), Harvard University (1956), Simpson College (1957), Drake University (1958), Macalester College (1958), Rochester University (1959), Carleton College (1961) and Allegheny College (1963).

JOHN COWLES JR. (1929–)

John Cowles Jr. was chief executive officer of Cowles Media Company (formerly Minneapolis Star and Tribune Company) (1968–83), a director (1956–84) and chairman of the board (1973–79). He was editor of *The Minneapolis Star and Tribune* 1961–69. From 1953–61 he worked in a number of business and editorial positions. He was a director of the Des Moines Register and Tribune Company (1960–84) and Cowles Communications, Inc. (1960).

He graduated from Phillips Exeter Academy in 1947, received an A. B. from Harvard College in 1951, and served in the U.S. Army (1951–53). He married Jane Sage Fuller in 1952. They have four children: Tessa Sage Flores, John III (Jay), Jane Sage and Charles Fuller.

He served on the Pulitzer Prize Board, Columbia University (1970–83), and was a director of the Associated Press (1966–75), and the American Newspaper Publishers Association (1975–77). He was a director (1965–81) and chairman of Harper & Row Publishers, Inc. (1968–79) and director of Farmers & Mechanics Savings Bank (1960–65), Equitable Life Insurance Company of Iowa (1964–66), First Bank System, Inc. (1964–68), and Midwest Radio-Television, Inc. (1967–76).

He was a director or trustee of the John and Elizabeth Bates Cowles Foundation (1954–87), Minnesota Civil Liberties Union (1956–61), Minnesota Orchestral Association (1958–61), Walker Art Center (1960–69 and 1987–92), Phillips Exeter Academy (1960–65), Guthrie Theater Foundation (1960–71), president (1960–63) and chairman (1964–65), Urban Coalition of Minneapolis (1968–70), Gardner and Florence Call Cowles Foundation (1968–84), The Minneapolis Foundation (1970–75), The German Marshall Fund of the United States (1975–78), the Stadium Site Task Force (Chairman) of the Greater Minneapolis Chamber of Commerce (1977–82), President (1978–81) and chairman (1982–84) of Industry Square Development Company, and Greater Minneapolis Chamber of Commerce (1978–81).

He was named one of ten outstanding young men of 1964 by the U. S. Junior Chamber of Commerce, one of 200 Rising Leaders in America by *Time* magazine in 1974, and received the First Amendment Freedoms Award from Anti-Defamation League of B'nai B'rith (1977) and the John Phillips award of Phillips Exeter Academy (1977).

JOHN (JAY) COWLES III (1953–)

Jay Cowles was chairman of the board of directors of Cowles Media Company (1993–1998), vice chairman (1991–1993), and director. He was an intern in 1982, director of planning (1985–88), and vice president and director of operations of Sentinel Publishing Company (1988–91).

He attended Prescott College and graduated from Harvard University in 1981 and from the Harvard Business School in 1983. He is married to Page Knudsen, and they have three children: Lucia, Colin and Maxwell.

He was director of internal operations and of financial analysis for United Satellite Communications, Inc. (1983–85) and a consultant to the Mayor's Office of Cable Television in Boston (1980–81). He is chairman of Women's Professional Fastpitch, LLC (1993–) and was vice president of Book Ventures, Inc. (1991–93).

He has been a director of the Guthrie Theater (1994–), the St. Paul Riverfront Corporation (1994–), Unity Avenue Foundation (1985–), and Minnesota Center for Book Arts (1987–98, chairman 1995–97). He has been a trustee of The Minneapolis Foundation (1987–88), board member at Prescott College, Headwaters Fund (1986–88), the St. Paul Chamber of Commerce (1993–96), and an advisory board member of the Environmental Defense Fund/Rocky Mountains (1988).

DAVID KRUIDENIER (1921–)

David Kruidenier was chief executive officer of Cowles Media Company (1983–84). President in 1983, he was chairman of the board (1984–1993). He became a director in 1972. He began his newspaper career there as a trainee in 1948.

He was chief executive officer of the Des Moines Register and Tribune Company (1971–1985), president and publisher (1971–1978), and chairman and publisher (1978–1983). He joined that company in 1952 and became vice president and general manager in 1960.

He graduated from Phillips Exeter Academy in 1940, from Yale University in 1946 and the Harvard Business School in 1948. He served in the U. S. Air Force (1942–45), receiving the Distinguished Flying Cross and the Air Medal with three clusters.

He was a director of the Audit Bureau of Circulations (1974–78), where he served as treasurer (1978–84), and of the Newspaper Advertising Bureau (1983–90). He was a director of Norwest Bank/ Des Moines N.A. (1955–1987).

He has been a trustee of Grinnell College (1953 and 1986–98) and served as vice-chair (1988–94), of Drake University (1960–98) and was chairman (1970–74), Des Moines Art Center (1953–78) and (1986–97), The Menninger Foundation (1957–97), Midwest Research Institute (1971–86), Walker Art Center (1983–89), and Civic Center of Greater Des Moines (1975–88) where he was a founder and first chairman, and the Gardner and Florence Call Cowles Foundation, where he has been president (1960–98).

He received honorary degrees from Buena Vista College (1960), Simpson College (1963), Luther College (1990), and Drake University (1990). He received the 1992 Honor Award from the American Library Trustee Association, the 1992 Outstanding Leadership Award from the Des Moines Human Rights Commission, the Des Moines Mid-City Vision Committee Annual Award, the 1993 Iowa Business Hall of Fame Award, and the Ralph D. Casey Minnesota Award (1994).

JOYCE A. SWAN (1906–)

Joyce Swan was executive vice-president and publisher of the Minneapolis Star and Tribune Company (1961–68) and a director (1940–77), serving as vice-chairman (1968–73). He joined the company in 1939 and was successively business manager, publisher of *The Minneapolis Daily Times,* and general manager. He was president of the Rapid City Journal Company, the Great Falls Tribune Company and Wichita-Hutchinson Company. He worked at the Des Moines Register and Tribune Company (1928–39).

He graduated from the University of Missouri School of Journalism in 1928. He married Pauline Snider and they have two children: Sonya and James W. ("Rusty").

He was treasurer of the American Newspaper Publishers Association (1964–66) and a board member (1958–66), chairman of the Newspaper Advertising Bureau (1954–56) and a board member (1950–74). He was president of the Des Moines Advertising Club, Minnesota Advertising Club, Minneapolis Aquatennial Association, Upper Midwest Research and Development Council, United Fund, Minneapolis Chamber of Commerce, Downtown Council and the Rapid City Regional Hospital. He was chairman of the Federal Reserve Bank of Minneapolis, a director of the First National Bank of the Black Hills (1969–74) and trustee of the University of Missouri Development Fund.

He received the University of Missouri School of Journalism Honor Award in 1948, the Minneapolis Silver Medal from the American Federation of Advertising-Printers' *Ink Magazine,* the National Newspaper Promotion Association's Silver Shovel Award in 1961 and the James McGovern Memorial Award from the Association of Newspaper Classified Managers in 1971.

OTTO A. SILHA (1919–)

Otto Silha was chairman of the board of Cowles Media Company (and predecessor company) (1979–1984), and president (1973–79). He was publisher of the Minneapolis newspapers (1968–73). He joined the company in 1940 and was promotion director, business manager and general manager. He was a director of Harper & Row, Publishers, Inc. (1972–1981) and Midwest Radio-Television, Inc. (1974–76).

He was a 1940 magna cum laude graduate of the University. He served in the Air Force (1942–46). He is married to Helen Fitch; they had four children: Stephen, David, Alice, and Mark.

He was president of the International Newspaper Promotion Association (1953–54), director of the Newspaper Advertising Bureau (1970–84) and chairman (1976–78), director of the Associated Press (1978–84), director of the American Newspaper Publishers Association Research Institute (1960–70) and president (1967–69), Co-chairman of the Newspaper Readership Council (1977–83) and chairman of the Newspaper Industry Joint Postal Task Force (1982–84).

He was vice chairman of City Venture Corporation (1978–86), a director of Norwest Bank Minneapolis (1975–84) and Norwest Corporation (1980–84).

He was a member of the University of Minnesota Board of Regents (1961–69), chairman of the Minnesota Experimental City Project, City Innovation, and the National Retiree Volunteer Coalition (1991–), president of the Minneapolis Aquatennial Association (1955–56), and Upper Midwest Council (1975–77); a director of the Greater Minneapolis Chamber of Commerce, the United Way of Minneapolis Area, Greater Minneapolis Metropolitan Housing Corporation, Advertising Club of Minneapolis, Minneapolis Society for the Blind, Citizens League, Minneapolis Area Development Corporation, the Guthrie Theater Foundation, North Star Research Institute; and trustee of Midwest Research Institute, the Minneapolis Society of Fine Arts, and the University of Minnesota Foundation.

He received the 1972 Silver Medal Award from the American Advertising Federation, Outstanding Achievement Award from the University of Minnesota in 1974, Minnesota Award for Distinguished Service in Journalism in 1978, and the First Amendment Defense Award from St. Cloud State University in 1986.

DAVID C. COX (1937–)

David Cox was president and chief executive officer of Cowles Media Company (1985–98). He was chief operating officer (1983–85) and a director (1983–98).

He was an officer of The Toro Company (1979–81), of Litton Microwave Cooking Products (1975–79), and Lawry's Foods, Inc. (1972–75).

He graduated from Stanford University Magna Cum Laude in 1959 with Honors in Economics and from the Harvard Business School in 1961. He married Vicki Bever; they have two sons, Brian and Carson.

He was chairman of the Newspaper Association of America (1997–98) and served on the Board of Directors (1991–98). He was a director of The Guthrie Theater (1977–86), (1988–92) and (1994–98); he was also chairman and president. He was chairman of the United Way of Greater Minneapolis (1996–97) and a director (1991–1998). He was a member of the Page Education Foundation Board of Advisors (1992–98) and of the board of the Humphrey Institute at the University of Minnesota (1992–1998).

He is a director of National Computer Systems (1983–98), ReliaStar Financial Corporation (1988–98) and the Tennant Company (1991–1998).

APPENDIX AA

JOINT PROXY STATEMENT

Excerpt from the Joint Proxy Statement for Special Meetings of the Stockholders of McClatchy Newspapers, Inc. and Cowles Media Company to be Held March 19, 1998

THE REORGANIZATION

This section of the Joint Proxy Statement/Prospectus describes certain aspects of the Mergers. This description does not purport to be complete and is qualified by reference to the Reorganization Agreement, which is attached as Annex A hereto and is incorporated by reference herein.

BACKGROUND OF THE COWLES MERGER

The proposed Cowles Merger is the result of a review by the Cowles Board of strategic alternatives available to Cowles. This review included consideration of factors affecting the newspaper business and other parts of the media industry, plus an exploration of opportunities for continued growth available to Cowles and opportunities for liquidity and enhanced value available to Cowles stockholders. As discussed below, the Cowles Board has concluded that the proposed Cowles Merger is in the best interest of Cowles and its stockholders.

In July 1997, representatives of the Cowles Family Voting Trust (which holds approximately 56 percent of all outstanding shares of Cowles Voting Common Stock) requested that the Cowles Board explore strategic alternatives available to Cowles and indicated support for a possible combination with, or acquisition by, a third party having experience in managing large daily newspaper operations. The Cowles Family Voting Trust expressed interest in considering a possible transaction that would include a tax-deferred equity component and liquidity for some of the proceeds.

Following receipt of the Cowles Family Voting Trust's request for an exploration of strategic alternatives, Goldman Sachs, a full-service investment banking and securities firm that has served as Cowles' principal financial advisor for many years, made a presentation to the Cowles Board and senior management of Cowles on July 29, 1997, that included a discussion of possible processes for identifying and evaluating strategic alternatives and analyses of historic and recent performance of the newspaper industry, emerging technological changes in media markets and related opportunities and challenges for newspapers, and competitive effects arising from development of large, sophisticated news-gathering and distribution networks. Goldman Sachs also discussed valuation considerations for newspaper companies in private and public markets, and provided an overview of various other newspaper companies. On August 12, 1997, Cowles formally engaged Goldman Sachs to act as its financial advisor. The scope of Goldman Sachs' engagement included reviewing alternatives, evaluating possible strategic transactions and rendering an opinion as to the fairness from a financial point of view of the consideration to be received in a possible transaction.

After meeting with representatives of the Cowles Family Voting Trust who expressed their general goals and objectives with respect to a possible strategic transaction, Cowles developed a list, with the assistance of Goldman Sachs, of potential candidates considered qualified for preliminary contacts regarding a possible strategic transaction. During August 1997, Goldman Sachs contacted the potential candidates and obtained confidentiality agreements from several of them. Following receipt of the confidentiality agreements,

Goldman Sachs provided to the candidates a confidential memorandum that included detailed information about Cowles and each of its business units.

During the week of September 1, 1997, Cowles and Goldman Sachs became aware of speculation within parts of the newspaper industry that Cowles was considering various strategic alternatives. While it is Cowles' long-standing general policy not to comment on rumors or speculation, Cowles management preferred to have any public discussion about the process occur on an orderly basis so as to avoid a situation where employees and stockholders of Cowles would face uncertainty and other distractions because of potentially inaccurate rumors and speculation. Accordingly, on September 4, 1997, Cowles announced publicly that it had commenced an exploration of strategic alternatives at the request of the Cowles Family Voting Trust.

Following the September 4, 1997 public announcement, McClatchy and certain other companies also expressed interest in a possible strategic transaction with Cowles. Thereafter, McClatchy and other interested companies entered into confidentiality agreements with Cowles, obtained the confidential memorandum and began conducting due diligence.

Of the candidates who signed confidentiality agreements, several, including McClatchy, submitted non-binding proposals in late September and early October for a possible transaction with Cowles within various price ranges. Most of the candidates who submitted such proposals then reviewed additional information about Cowles and its businesses, visited Cowles facilities and met with Cowles management during October 1997.

On October 20, 1997, Goldman Sachs reviewed with the Cowles Board the terms of the non-binding proposals received to date. The Cowles Board instructed Goldman Sachs to engage in further discussions with the candidates that submitted proposals in order to refine such proposals and make them more definitive. Thereafter, Cowles provided additional due diligence information to the candidates, and Goldman Sachs requested final proposals from the candidates, including any comments on a proposed form of merger agreement previously distributed by counsel to Cowles. During the week of November 3, 1997, the candidates, including McClatchy, made separate presentations to senior management of Cowles and representatives of the Cowles Board. In connection with such presentations, Cowles and its legal and financial advisors conducted due diligence with respect to the candidates. On November 10, 1997, the candidates, including McClatchy, submitted definitive proposals.

McClatchy submitted two alternative proposals having the same per-share offer price: one proposal contemplated an all-cash transaction and the other contemplated 75 percent of the merger consideration being paid in cash and 25 percent being paid in New McClatchy Class A Common Stock. In evaluating McClatchy's proposals, Cowles expressed a concern that 25 percent of the consideration in New McClatchy Class A Common Stock may require some Cowles stockholders to take more stock than they might otherwise elect. Therefore, Cowles requested that McClatchy modify its combination cash/stock proposals so as to include an election to receive up to 25 percent of the merger consideration in stock. On November 11, 1997, McClatchy agreed, among other things, to modify the stock component of the merger consideration so as to include an election to receive a minimum stock consideration component of 15 percent (with a maximum stock consideration component of 25 percent) and to make certain other nonfinancial changes to its proposal. The Tribune Company also submitted a proposal contemplating both cash and stock, each providing approximately 50 percent of the total proposed consideration.

The Tribune Company proposal represented a per share price that was materially lower than the per share price proposed by McClatchy.

A meeting of the Cowles Board was held in two sessions on November 12, 1997. At the first session, Cowles management and Goldman Sachs made a presentation that included an updated review of the exploration process, a comparison of final proposals, an analysis of the business operations, financial capabilities and other attributes of the candidates submitting proposals and the results of financial due diligence performed with respect to the candidates. Cowles' legal counsel presented the results of legal due diligence with respect to the candidates and described the terms of the proposed merger agreements submitted by the candidates. Such session also included a discussion of the proposals in the absence of those directors who are also trustees of the Cowles Family Voting Trust. Between the two sessions, senior executives of Cowles and representatives of Goldman Sachs attended part of a meeting of certificateholders and trustees of the Cowles Family Voting Trust and described the final proposals. At the second session of the meeting of the Cowles Board, representatives of the Cowles Family Voting Trust reported that the trustees were prepared to vote the shares of Cowles Voting Common Stock held by them in favor of the McClatchy proposal that included a stock component of 15 percent to 25 percent of the total merger consideration. Following additional discussions with Goldman Sachs and legal counsel to Cowles (including discussions in the absence of those directors who are also trustees of the Cowles Family Voting Trust), the Cowles Board concluded, for reasons stated below under "—Recommendations of the Cowles Board and Reasons for the Cowles Merger," that the McClatchy proposal was the superior alternative for Cowles and its stockholders. The Cowles Board concluded to accept and recommend the version of the McClatchy proposal that included issuance of McClatchy Class A Common Stock, given the expressed intent (but not a commitment) of certificateholders of the Cowles Family Voting Trust to elect to receive at least two-thirds of the minimum stock consideration component of 15 percent. At the conclusion of the meeting, the Cowles Board voted to authorize the execution and delivery of the Reorganization Agreement and to recommend the proposed Cowles Merger to the holders of Cowles Voting Common Stock. On November 13, 1997, Cowles and McClatchy executed the Reorganization Agreement.

RECOMMENDATION OF THE COWLES BOARD AND REASONS FOR THE COWLES MERGER

The Cowles Board has approved the Reorganization Agreement and recommends the proposed Cowles Merger to stockholders of Cowles. The Cowles Board believes that the proposed Cowles Merger is fair to and in the best interests of Cowles and is stockholders, and recommends that the holders of Cowles Voting Common Stock vote FOR the Cowles Proposal. The Cowles Board's actions regarding the Reorganization Agreement were taken in a meeting attended by eight of the nine directors of Cowles. All directors present voted in favor of the Reorganization Agreement.

Prior to taking action on the proposed Cowles Merger, the Cowles Board reviewed and carefully considered reports and other materials relevant to the proposed Cowles Merger and received reports and presentations from Goldman Sachs, senior officers of Cowles and legal counsel to Cowles, including a detailed review of terms and conditions of the Reorganization Agreement and the transactions contemplated thereby. The decision of the Cowles Board to approve the Reorganization Agreement and recommend the proposed Cowles Merger was the result of the exploration process described above. (See "—Background of the Cowles Merger.")

In its evaluation of the Cowles Merger, the Cowles

Board did not quantify or otherwise attempt to assign relative weights to the specific factors considered in reaching its determination. In determining whether to approve and recommend the Reorganization Agreement and the Cowles Merger, the Cowles Board considered the following factors:

ENHANCED STOCKHOLDER VALUE. The Cowles Board reviewed possible strategic alternatives to enhance stockholder value and concluded that the proposed Cowles Merger presents the most favorable opportunity to do so.

PUBLIC ANNOUNCEMENT AND PROCESS. Cowles publicly announced that it would consider a strategic transaction. Execution of the Reorganization Agreement occurred well after such announcement and after an exploration of various strategic alternatives by Goldman Sachs. Because information regarding the exploration of strategic alternatives was publicly available for over two months before execution of the Reorganization Agreement, the Cowles Board believes that any qualified candidate interested in making a proposal had sufficient opportunity to do so.

FINANCIAL CAPABILITY OF MCCLATCHY. The Cowles Board considered McClatchy's financial ability to complete the proposed Cowles Merger, including its financing commitments and the fact that the Reorganization Agreement does not include any financing-related conditions to McClatchy's obligation to complete the Cowles Merger.

OPINION OF FINANCIAL ADVISOR. Goldman Sachs has provided its opinion to the Cowles Board that, as of November 13, 1997, the Cash Consideration and the Stock Consideration to be received by the holders of Cowles Common Stock under the Reorganization Agreement, taken as a unitary transaction, is fair from a financial point of view to such holders.

INCREASED POTENTIAL FOR CONTINUED SUCCESS. The Cowles Board believes that prospects for continued performance at the levels achieved by the *Star Tribune* in recent years will be enhanced by greater size and scale. In the Reorganization, the *Star Tribune* will become part of a substantially larger enterprise, and the Cowles Board believes that the *Star Tribune*'s enhanced access to capital and other resources as a result of the proposed merger would substantially increase its ability to compete successfully in the increasingly consolidating newspaper industry.

CONTINUED ACCESS TO OUTSTANDING MANAGEMENT. The Cowles Board believes that opportunities and challenges in the newspaper industry will become more complex in the future, especially as technological advances and other industry developments continue to emerge. The Cowles Board also believes that the *Star Tribune*'s performance in recent years has been substantially enhanced by its ability to attract and retain outstanding management and that continued success will require continued access to outstanding executive talent. Cowles' planning for development and succession among senior executives has demonstrated that larger enterprises have an increasing advantage in attracting and retaining outstanding executives, including the ability to provide long-term equity based compensation, stronger opportunities for career development within a single organization, and capital resources and support functions necessary for development and execution of aggressive strategic and operating plans.

LIQUIDITY OF STOCK FOR COWLES. Although Cowles stock has traded on a local over-the-counter basis since 1981 and bid-and-asked prices for Cowles stock have been publicly quoted since 1993, opportunities to buy and sell Cowles stock have remained limited and relatively unpredictable. The Cowles Board believes that stockholder interest in greater liquidity and diversification has increased, and stockholders have continued to make inquiries to Cowles about opportunities for additional liquidity. Certain stockholders (including, among others, members of the Cowles family and current and former employees of Cowles) have substantial percentages of their personal assets invested in Cowles stock. Such stockholders currently do not have reliable opportunities to liquidate such stock to fund personal needs for retirement, education and other purposes at values that are representative of those available in public markets for stock of other media or publishing companies.

SUPPORT OF MAJORITY HOLDER. Trustees of the Cowles Family Voting Trust, which holds a majority of all outstanding shares of Cowles Voting Common Stock, have indicated their support for the proposed Cowles Merger and their commitment to vote such shares in favor of the Cowles Proposal pursuant to the Cowles Stockholders Voting Agreement.

OTHER FACTORS. In addition to the foregoing, the Cowles Board also considered certain disadvantages of the Reorganization, such as the fact that the minimum stock consideration of 15 percent may cause some Cowles stockholders to receive more New McClatchy Class A Common Stock than they might otherwise elect; the fact that McClatchy is a family-controlled company and some elements of liquidity (including, among others, average trading volume) for New McClatchy Class A Common Stock will be more limited than those of other possible candidates; and the fact that, immediately following the Reorganization, New McClatchy will be substantially more leveraged than before the Reorganization.

INDEX

American Broadcasting Company   68
Acquisitions   71-74
Adams, Cedric   12, 21, 50
Adams, George   11-12
Airplanes   58-9, Appendix G
Albuquerque NM newspapers   74
Alcohol   52, 63
Algona (Iowa)   1, 12
Anaconda Copper Company   72
Andersen, Anthony L.   131
Andersen, Elmer L.   95
Anderson, Lyle   53, 65, 71, 81-2
Anti-trust   51, 93
Austin (Texas) *American-Statesman*   71
Bailey, Charles   97, 113
Ballantine, Arthur   51
Ballantine, Elizabeth   130, 141-2, 146, 150
Ballantine, Morley Cowles   5, 15, 20, 51, 59, 105-8, 123, 141
Ballantine, Richard   141-2
Baseball   73, 104, 128
Bates, Elizabeth   5 (See also Elizabeth Bates Cowles)
Bell, James Ford   30, 41, 64, 94
Bickelhaupt, George   24, 38, 41
Blandin, Charles   30-1
Building   35-6, 46-7, 63, 94, 126-7, Appendices D, Q
Bogart, Leo   54
Boise Cascade   57
Brown, Willis   13, 74
Buffalo *Courier-Express*   115-119
Buffalo *Evening News*   115-119
Buffett, Warren   115-117, 148
Bullitt, Elizabeth   142
Canfield, Cass   88
CableScope   117-19
Carriers   48
Columbia Broadcasting System   68-70, 95
Central Newspapers, Inc.   66
Charter   138
Community Publications Company   94, 137
Cooney, Richard   53, 109
Copeland, Lamont Jr.   73
Cordingley, William A.   12
Cordingley, William A. Jr.   53, 74, 137
Corporate responsibility   97-8, Appendix M
Cowles, Elizabeth Bates   5, 61, 92, Appendix K

Cowles, Gardner Sr.   1, 2, 5, 9, 23
Cowles, Gardner Jr. (Mike)   5, 6, 9, 18, 36, 40, 59-62, 65-7
Cowles, Gardner III (Pat)   142
Cowles, John Sr.   5, 6, 9, 19, 39, 42, 45, 48, 50 52, 55, 58-62, 64, 72, 83-4, 90, 122-139
   Des Moines Register and Tribune Company   5, 6
   Purchase of Star   9
   Purchase of *Minneapolis Journal*   23, 25-7
   Purchase of *Minneapolis Tribune*   23-4, 32-3
   Advertising   15, 20, 24-5
   Acquisitions   40, 65-6, 72-75
   Management style   51-2
   Broadcasting interest   65-67
   Wendell Willkie   32, 36-7
   LOOK magazine   36
   Kingsley Murphy   42-3
   Strike   76-8
   Retirement   82-3, 98
   Appendices A, B, F, H, I, N, V
Cowles, John Jr.   5, 15, 53-4, 74, 79, 81-5, 96, 103-4, 130, 141
   Early career   81-2
   Editor   82, 87-91, 93
   Guthrie Theater   85
   Publishing philosophy   87, 103
   Harper & Row and *Harper's*   88-90
   Executive positions   90, 98, 104, 107, 121
   Management style   53-7, 93, 103, 115
   Buffalo   117-81
   Resignation   122
   Appendices J, L, P
Cowles, John III (Jay)   81, 131, 141-2, 146, 147, 150
Cowles, Morley   5, 15, 20 (See also Morley Cowles Ballantine)
Cowles, Russell II   5, 15, 141-2
Cowles, Sarah (Doering)   5, 15, 141
Cowles Broadcasting Company   68
Cowles Business Media   136, 140
Cowles Enthusiast Media   136, 140
Cowles formula   2, 12, 17, 38, 51
Cowles Media Company   123, 147, 148, 150, Appendices C, M, S, T, W, AA
Cowles Media Foundation   150, Appendix M
Cowles Magazines, Inc.   61
Cox, David C.   104, 107, 110, 121, 123-4, 131-2, 147
Crawford, Carroll E.   94
Davis, John B. Jr.   99

251

Davis, W. Harry 92
Dayton, Bruce 97, 122
Dayton, Donald 49, 64
Dayton, Kenneth 103
Dayton, Nelson 19, 25, 41, 62
Dayton, George 30
Daytons's 20, 24, 25, 49, 128
Des Moines Register and Tribune Company 1, 3, 6, 10, 33, 43, 49, 62, 106-8, 147
   Sale of 129-32
Digital services 139
Dillon, Thomas 38
Diversification 65, 71-4, 93-6
Dividends 38, 45, 75, 132, 142
Donaldson's 20, 49
Dow Jones 129, 132, 148
Durango *Herald* 51
Dwight, Donald R. 98-101, 103, 107, 109, 111, 121
Earnings 13, 35, 57-8, 75-6, 96-7, 117, 124, 132, 142-3
Edwards, Charles 148
Eisenhower, Dwight D. 40, 59, 73
Electronic publishing 140
Empire Press 135
Employee benefits 41, 52-2, 57, 76, 79, 96
Employee stock plan 137-8
Energy crisis 96, 99
Enid, Oklahoma newspapers 136
Everett (Washington) *Herald* 106
Federal Communications Commission 43, 67, 93, 95
Femco Farms 30-1
Fenton, Fleur 61
Financial reporting 96-7
First Boston Corporation 130
First National Bank 40
Fischer, John 88
Flair 61
Ford Foundation 58
Fuller, Sage 81
Fourth generation 130, 141, 147
Freeman, Gale 77, 93, 87-8, 100, 109
Frizell, A. B. 3, 7
Gallup, George 18
Gannett 41, 129-30, 132, 136-7, 147, 148
Gartner, Michael 105-7, 129
General Electric 41, 64
General Mills 40, 64, 95
Gensmer, Bruce 127
Glendalough 33, 142, Appendix Y
Goldman, Sachs & Co. 147, 149, Appendix AA
Graham, Katherine 107

Graham, Philip 72
Grand Forks (ND) *Plaindealer* 29
Great Falls *Tribune* 74, 93, 137
Grim, George 17, 21
Guthrie Theater 84-5, 104
Hanson Publishing Company 136
Harmon, Reuell 30
Harper & Row 74, 88-90, 99, 123
Harper's magazine 74, 88-90, 93-4
Harper's Magazine Press 89
Harrison, Lois Cowles 99, 106, 132, 148
Harvard Business School Club 80, Appendix I
Harvard University 5, 51, 58
Hatch, Francis W. 51, 80
Hawks, Stanley 16, 67, 69
Hawthorne, Bower 82, 90, 90-1, 97
Heritage Center 125-27, 135, Appendix Q
Hill, Luther L. Jr. 98, 105-6, 141
Historical Times, Inc. 135
Hodder, William 132
Hoffa, Jimmy 78
Howard, Roy 40, 65
Hubbard, Stanley 69
Indianapolis *Times* 40, 65
Initial Public Offering 146
Ingham, Harvey 1, 2, 5, 42
IDS Center 103
Inskip, Leonard 123
Iowa Broadcasting Company 66
Isaacs, Stephen D. 111-2
International Typographical Union 100
Jacksonville, Florida *Times Union* 71
Jaffray, C. T. 24
Jones, Carl 10, 13, 23-6
Jones, Herschel V. 24
Jones, Moses 24, 28
Jones, Waring 26
Kansas City Star 105
Knight-Ridder 42, 95, 146, 148
Knowlton, Winthrop 89, 99
Kramer, Joel 116, 124, 139, 147, 149
Kruidenier, David 98, 107-7, 122-5, 128-32, 141-2, 148
KSO 43, 67
KSTP 69
KTVH 70, 93, 123
Labor disputes 7, 62-3, 76-9, 100-1, 127
Labor unions 63, 76-9, 100-2, 127
Lapham, Lewis H. 90
Larsen, Dale 71
Larsen, Roy 36

INDEX

Lee Enterprises   72, 137
Lend-Lease Administration   37, 40-1
Liberalism   11-12
Liquidity   137, 145, 146, 147, 151
Liquor advertising   20
LOOK magazine   13, 36, 61
Louisville television   94, 124
Low, K. Prescott   141
Lowry, Thomas   29
Luce, Henry   36
Mall of America   138
Management Style   51-54
Manistique Paper Company   30, 57
McCambridge, Jack   53
McClatchy Newspapers, Inc.   96, 145, 147, 149, 150, Appendix AA
McNally, W. J.   31-2, 37, 42, 69
The Menninger Foundation   54
Merger discussions   103-4, 129, Appendix O
Merwin, Davis   9, 12, 13
Metro Strategy   127-8, 135, 139
Midwest Radio-Television   69, 95-6
Minneapolis   7, 15
Minneapolis Daily Times   38
Minneapolis Daily Star   20
Minneapolis Herald   78
The Minneapolis Journal   10, 23-38, 46
The Minneapolis Star   99, 109-12
    Circulation 10, 13, 17, 21-2, 24, 29, 39, 45-6, 63, 79-80, 113-4
    Advertising 13, 20-1, 29, 46, 48-50, 57, 62-3, 75, 79-80
    Promotion 17, 20, 47-8, 50
Minneapolis Star Journal   26-8, 35
Minneapolis Star Journal and Tribune Company   33, 37, 43, 45
Minneapolis Star and Tribune Company   46, 61
Minneapolis Star and Tribune   41, 111, 113
Minneapolis Times   38, 41
Minneapolis Times-Tribune   22, 37
The Minneapolis Tribune   10, 23, 29-32, 38
Minnesota Broadcasting Company   67, 69, 95
Minnesota Daily Star   2
Minnesota Loan and Trust Company   30
Minnesota and Ontario Paper Company   49, 57
Minnesota Tribune Company   30, 32-3, 42-3, 67-9, 95-6
Minnesota Twins   128
Minority employment   91-2
Mithun, Howard   53, 77-8, 98
Morris, Willie   98
Murphy, F. E.   10, 23, 29-32
Murphy, Kingsley H.   31, 33, 37, 43, 67-8
Murphy, Kingsley H. Jr.   98, 122, 129, 131-2

Murphy, W. J.   10, 29-30
Mutual Holding Company   30-1
Neuharth, Al   129-30
New York Times Company   145, 148, 149
Newman, Cecil E.   92
Newspaper of the Twin Cities   128
Newspaper Guild   8, 38, 100-1, 118
Newsprint   39, 48, 57, 96, Appendix E
Newsprint use tax   123
Non-Partisan Political League   3
Northwest Broadcasting Company   67-8
Northwestern National Bank   31
Oakland Tribune   96, 105
Objectives   115, 135
Oklahoma Publishing Company   93
Orlando, Florida newspaper   71
Owens, Leo   30-1
Ownership   9-11, 33, 43, 61, 98, 105
Parkinson, Roger P.   116-7, 124, 126-7
Pension plans   3, 14, 78
Phoenix, Arizona newspapers   65
Plan for the 80's   110
Plant and equipment investment   22, 35-6, 46-7, 75, 94, 111, 115, 125-7, Appendix D
Plant pattern   100-2
Portland, Oregon newspapers   74
Productivity   63, 76-7, 81, 96, 99, 126
Profitability   97, 105, 119, 138, 142
Quick   61
Racial Justice   91-2
Radio   65-69
Rapid City Journal   74, 90, 137
Real estate investments   88
Register and Tribune Syndicate   6
Republicanism   12, 38, 59, 73
Revenue   47, 57-8, 97, 142-3
Ridder family   31, 42, 67, 69, 127
Rockford, Illinois, newspapers   74
Ronald, George   23, 25, 28
Rosse, James N.   128, 141
Rowan, Carl   62
Saario, Terry T.   141
Saint Paul   7, 95, 127
St. Paul newspapers   31, 95
San Bernardino, California newspapers   71
San Fernando Valley Times   72-3
Scofield, Joe   142
Scottsdale Progress   136-7
Seymour, Gideon   42-3, 53, 58, 64, 82
Shaffer, James B.   116

Sheboygan, Wisconsin, *Press*   136
Silha, Otto A.   53-4, 74, 77, 81, 91, 98, 104, 107, 109, 129-30
Silverman, David   83
Smith, Robert W.   90-1, 98-100
Socialism   3, 17
Southern Production Program   100
Stadium Site Task Force   103-4
William Steven   82
Star Tribune   130, 140-3, 145-151
Strategy   131, 135, 138-9
Strikes   7, 62-3, 76-8, 100-1
Stromberg Publications   94, 116
Swan, James W.   98, 137
Swan, Joyce A.   20, 22, 27, 41, 50, 58, 64, 66, 71-4, 76-7, 82, 90, 98
Sun Newspapers   94-5
Taft, Robert   37, 59
Tacoma *News Tribune*   96
Teamsters   63, 76-7, 100-1
Television   65-9
Tele-Communications, Inc.   119
Tender offer   137
Thompson, John   3, 9, 16
Times Mirror Company   145, 148, 149
Tribune Company   148, 149
Tucson Daily Star   74
Upper Midwest   48, 72, 74, 82
University of Minnesota   30
University of Missouri   13, 22, 58
U.S. Junior Chamber of Commerce   85
VIRP (Voluntary Incentive Retirement Plan)   109
VonBlon, Philip   84, 93, 98
Voting trusts   105-6, 128-9, 131, 141-2, 145, 146, 147, 148, 149, 150
Walters, Basil (Stuffy)   9, 13, 17-8, 42, 53
Watts lawsuit   105, 129
The Washington Post   100-1
The Washington Post Company   106-7, 132, 145, 147, 148, 149
Waymack, W. W.   5, 43
WCCO   21, 69, 93, 95-6
Weed, Robert   53, 72
Wichita, Kansas, newspapers   66, 74
Willkie, Wendell   32, 36-7
Witte, Robert   53, 93
Woodhill   15
World War II   39, 45, 55
WTCN   31, 33, 43, 6-8

PHOTO CREDITS

CHAPTER 1

p. 1 *The Des Moines Register,* May 21, 1927, reprinted with permission by the Des Moines Register

p. 2 Harvey Ingham and Gardner Cowles, 1937, Courtesy of the John Cowles Sr. Archives, Drake University, Des Moines, Iowa

p. 2 Iowa Railroad Map, 1884, Map prepared for the Iowa Railroad Commissioners By Rand McNally & Co., Chicago; Courtesy of the State Historical Society of Iowa

p. 3 Des Moines Skyline, Early 20th Century, The Haines Photo Company, Connecticut, Ohio; Courtesy of the State Historical Society of Iowa

p. 3 *The Des Moines Register and Tribune* Building, 1940, Courtesy of the State Historical Society of Iowa

CHAPTER 2

p. 5 *Minneapolis Daily Star,* May 26, 1927, Courtesy of the Minnesota Historical Society

p. 6 Oskar Kokoschka
Portrait of Mr. and Mrs. John Cowles, 1949
oil on canvas
44¾ x 60 inches
Gift of John and Elizabeth Bates Cowles; Des Moines Art Center Permanent Collections, 1963

p. 6 John, Russell, Gardner Sr. and Gardner (Mike) Cowles, Jr., 1910, Courtesy of the John Cowles Sr. Archives, Drake University, Des Moines, Iowa)

p. 7 Minneapolis Skyline, 1928, Courtesy of the *Star Tribune* Library

CHAPTER 3

p. 9 *Time,* July 1, 1935, Courtesy of Time, Inc.

p. 10 *The Minneapolis Star,* June 14, 1935, Courtesy of the Minnesota Historical Society

p. 10 Minneapolis' "Newspaper Row" at the turn of the century, Courtesy of the *Star Tribune* Library

p. 11 Minneapolis Skyline, 1935, Courtesy of the *Star Tribune* Library

p. 12 *The Minneapolis Star* Building, 1928, Courtesy of the *Star Tribune* Library

p. 12 The Great Depression, 1933, Courtesy of the *Star Tribune* Library

p. 13 Minneapolis Star Company first certificate of sale of stock to John Cowles Sr., 1935, Courtesy of Cowles Media Company

CHAPTER 4

p. 15 *Minneapolis Star Journal,* November 24, 1939 Classified Ads, Courtesy of the Minnesota Historical Society

p. 16 Home of John Cowles Sr., Minneapolis, Courtesy of the *Star Tribune* Library

p. 16 John Thompson, 1947, Courtesy of the *Star Tribune* Library

p. 19 *The Minneapolis Star,* July 15, 1935, Courtesy of the Minnesota Historical Society

p. 20 A Christmas ad for the Dayton Company, *Minneapolis Star Journal,* December 21, 1939, Courtesy of the Minnesota Historical Society

p. 21 Foshay Tower Telesign, 1939, Courtesy of the *Star Tribune* Library

p. 21 Cedric Adams, 1941, Courtesy the *Star Tribune* Library

CHAPTER 5

p. 23 *The Minneapolis Sunday Tribune,* March 8, 1936, Courtesy of the Minnesota Historical Society

p. 24 *The Minneapolis Journal,* July 22, 1934, Courtesy of the Minnesota Historical Society

p. 25 A Dayton Company ad, *The Minneapolis Journal,* December 18, 1939, Courtesy of the Minnesota Historical Society

p. 26 *Minneapolis Star Journal* merger notice, August 1, 1939, Courtesy of the Minnesota Historical Society

p. 27 The Star Journal Frolic, 1939, Courtesy of the Star Tribune

p. 28 *The Minneapolis Tribune,* August 10, 1939, Courtesy of the Minnesota Historical Society

CHAPTER 6

p. 29 *Minneapolis Tribune,* November 12, 1940, Courtesy of the Minnesota Historical Society

p. 30 Early offices of *The Minneapolis Tribune* were in the Minneapolis City Hall, circa 1870, Courtesy of the *Star Tribune* Library

p. 30 W. J. Murphy, about 1910, Courtesy of the Murphy Family

p. 31 Radio photo, circa 1938, Courtesy of the *Star Tribune* Library

p. 32 The Minneapolis Star Journal Company Stock Certificate, 1940, Courtesy of Cowles Media Company

CHAPTER 7

p. 35 *Minneapolis Star Journal,* April 30, 1941, Courtesy of the Minnesota Historical Society

p. 36 *The Minneapolis Star* Building, 1920, Courtesy of the *Star Tribune* Library

p. 36 *The Minneapolis Star* Building, 1960, Courtesy of the *Star Tribune* Library

p. 36 Gardner Cowles Jr. (Mike) and John Cowles Sr. at *LOOK* magazine, about 1941, Courtesy of the John Cowles Sr. Archives, Drake University, Des Moines, Iowa

p. 37 John Cowles Sr., Wendell Willkie, and Gardner Cowles Jr. (Mike), about 1941, Courtesy of the *Star Tribune* Library

p. 38 *The Minneapolis Times-Tribune,* August 14, 1939, Courtesy of the Minnesota Historical Society

CHAPTER 8

p. 39 *Minneapolis Morning Tribune,* December 8, 1941, Courtesy of the Minnesota Historical Society

p. 40 The War Memorial in the lobby of *The Minneapolis Star and Tribune* Building, Courtesy of the *Star Tribune* Library

p. 41 Correspondence from and to John Cowles Sr. in 1942 and 1943 regarding his service with the Lend-Lease Administration, Courtesy of the John Cowles Sr. Archives, Drake University, Des Moines, Iowa

p. 42 Gideon Seymour, circa 1945, Courtesy of the *Star Tribune* Library

p. 42 *The S.J.T. Makers,* February 1942, Courtesy of the *Star Tribune*

p. 43 *Minneapolis Morning Tribune,* May 8, 1945, Courtesy of the Minnesota Historical Society

CHAPTER 9

p. 45 *Minneapolis Morning Tribune,* August 15, 1945, Courtesy of the Minnesota Historical Society

p. 46 *The Minneapolis Star and Tribune* Building, about 1949, Courtesy of the *Star Tribune* Library

p. 47 *The Minneapolis Star and Tribune* Goss Presses, 1949, Courtesy of the *Star Tribune* Library

p. 48 Carrier Boy, circa 1941, Courtesy of the *Star Tribune* Library

p. 49 *The Minneapolis Star,* Parade of Champions Coverage, May 24, 1949, Courtesy of the Minnesota Historical Society

p. 49 The Dayton Company Ad, *Minneapolis Star,* December 7, 1948, Courtesy of the Minnesota Historical Society

p. 50 John Cowles and Globe, 1959, Courtesy of the *Star Tribune* Library

p. 50 Cedric Adams Column, *The New Yorker,* 1949, Courtesy of *The New Yorker*

p. 51 Spelling Bee, 1965, Courtesy of the *Star Tribune* Library

p. 51 *Minneapolis Star* Truck, about 1936, Courtesy of the *Star Tribune* Library

p. 52 John Cowles Sr., "How Are We Doing?" column, Courtesy of the *Star Tribune*

p. 53 *Corporate Report,* August 1979, Courtesy of *Corporate Report*

CHAPTER 10

p. 57 *Minneapolis Morning Tribune,* November 5, 1952, Courtesy of the Minnesota Historical Society

p. 58 John Cowles Sr.'s LL.D. degree from Harvard University, Courtesy of the John Cowles Sr. Archives, Drake University, Des Moines, Iowa

p. 59 Newsprint supplies, Courtesy of the *Star Tribune* Library

p. 59 The Star Tribune Company's DC-3 airplane, Courtesy of the *Star Tribune* Library

p. 60 John Cowles Sr. and President Dwight D. Eisenhower at the company's Glendalough Retreat in West-Central Minnesota, in 1952, Courtesy of the *Star Tribune* Library

p. 61 *Look, Quick,* and *Flair,* Courtesy of Cowles Communications, Inc.

p. 62 *Minneapolis Morning Tribune,* May 15, 1948, Courtesy of the Minnesota Historical Society

p. 63 Press Row Bar and Cafe, circa 1948, Courtesy of the *Star Tribune* Library

p. 64 *Star Tribune* Building, 1997, Photo by Lars Hanson

CHAPTER 11

p. 65 *Minneapolis Star and Tribune,* advertising supplement, 1955, Courtesy of the *Star Tribune*

p. 68 WTCN-TV, Courtesy of the *Star Tribune* Library

p. 69 The Kansas CBS affiliate, Courtesy of *The Star Tribune*

CHAPTER 12

p. 71 *Minnneapolis Morning Tribune,* October 29, 1962, Courtesy of the Minnesota Historical Society

p. 72 The San Fernando Valley, about 1960, served by *The Valley Times,* Courtesy of Cowles Media Company

p. 73 *The Great Falls Tribune* and *The Rapid City Journal,* Courtesy of *The Great Falls Tribune* and *The Rapid City Journal*

CHAPTER 13

p. 75 *The Minneapolis Star,* November 22, 1963, Courtesy of the Minnesota Historical Society

p. 76 *Newsmakers,* 1956, Job Dividends Reminder, Courtesy of the *Star Tribune*

p. 77 *The Minneapolis Star* (Strike Edition), April 13, 1962, Courtesy of the Minnesota Historical Society

p. 78 *The Minneapolis Star,* August 7, 1962, Courtesy of the Minnesota Historical Society

p. 80 *The Minneapolis Star,* June 14, 1965, Courtesy of the Minnesota Historical Society

CHAPTER 14

p. 81 *Minneapolis Morning Tribune,* May 18, 1954, Courtesy of the Minnesota Historical Society

p. 83 Joyce A. Swan, 1963, Courtesy of the *Star Tribune* Library

p. 84 Guthrie Theater, 1974, Courtesy of the *Star Tribune* Library

CHAPTER 15

p. 87 *Minneapolis Tribune,* November 4, 1964, Courtesy of the Minnesota Historical Society

p. 88 John Cowles Jr., 1978, Courtesy of the *Star Tribune* Library

p. 89 *Harper's* magazine, November 1968 and August 1969, Courtesy of Cowles Communications, Inc.

p. 90 Bower Hawthorne, 1967, Courtesy of the *Star Tribune* Library

p. 90 Robert W. Smith, 1969, Courtesy of the *Star Tribune* Library

p. 91 Otto Silha, 1968, Courtesy of the *Star Tribune* Library

p. 92 *Minneapolis Tribune,* July 3, 1964, Courtesy of the Minnesota Historical Society

p. 92 Elizabeth Cowles article, *Opportunity Magazine,* Winter, 1948, Courtesy of the National Urban League

CHAPTER 16

- p. 93 *The Minneapolis Tribune,* July 21, 1969, Courtesy of the Minnesota Historical Society
- p. 94 Computer Composition, 1968, Courtesy of the *Star Tribune* Library
- p. 94 *The Star and Tribune* Newsprint Warehouse, 1982, Courtesy of the *Star Tribune* Library
- p. 95 Sun Newspapers Inc., 1978, Courtesy of the Minnesota Historical Society and the Minnesota Sun-Post Publications
- p. 97 *Minneapolis Tribune,* April 30, 1975, Courtesy of the Minnesota Historical Society
- p. 98 Donald Dwight, 1980, Courtesy of the *Star Tribune* Library
- p. 99 *The Minneapolis Tribune,* August 9, 1974, Courtesy of the Minnesota Historical Society

CHAPTER 17

- p. 103 *Minneapolis Tribune,* January 14, 1978, Courtesy of the Minnesota Historical Society
- p. 104 Minneapolis Skyline, showing the Hubert H. Humphrey Metrodome, 1993, Courtesy of the *Star Tribune* Library
- p. 104 The IDS Tower, Minneapolis, 1978, Courtesy of the *Star Tribune* Library
- p. 105 David C. Cox, 1985, Courtesy of the *Star Tribune* Library
- p. 106 *The Des Moines Register,* September 10, 1981, Courtesy of UMI and reprinted with permission by *The Des Moines Register*
- p. 107 *Business Week* article, December 7, 1981, Courtesy of *Business Week*

CHAPTER 18

- p. 109 *Minneapolis Tribune,* January 21, 1981, Courtesy of the Minnesota Historical Society
- p. 110 *Newsmakers,* November 1981, Courtesy of the *Star Tribune*
- p. 111 Atex System 1978, Courtesy of the *Star Tribune* Library
- p. 112 *The Minneapolis Star* Final Edition, April 2, 1982, Courtesy of the *Star Tribune* Library
- p. 112 *The Minneapolis Star,* March 25, 1982, Courtesy of the Minnesota Historical Society

CHAPTER 19

- p. 115 Buffalo Skyline, 1982, Courtesy of the Buffalo and Erie County Historical Society and *The Buffalo News*
- p. 118 *Buffalo Courier-Express* Final Edition, September 19, 1982, Courtesy of the Buffalo and Erie County Historical Society
- p. 119 *The Buffalo News,* December 26, 1983, Courtesy of the Buffalo and Erie County Historical Society and *The Buffalo News*

CHAPTER 20

- p. 121 *Minneapolis Star and Tribune,* November 7, 1984, Courtesy of the Minnesota Historical Society
- p. 122 Roger Parkinson, 1983, Courtesy of the *Star Tribune* Library
- p. 122 David C. Cox, 1985, Courtesy of the *Star Tribune* Library
- p. 122 *The New York Times,* February 26, 1983, Courtesy of UMI and The New York Times, Inc.
- p. 123 *Minneapolis Star and Tribune,* February 26, 1983, Courtesy of the Minnesota Historical Society
- p. 123 Cowles Media Company Logo, 1997, Courtesy of Cowles Media Company
- p. 124 David Krudenier, 1983, Courtesy of the *Star Tribune* Library
- p. 124 *Editor & Publisher,* March 24, 1984, Courtesy of Editor & Publisher Company, Inc.

CHAPTER 21

- p. 125 *Minneapolis Star and Tribune,* January 29, 1986, Courtesy of the Minnesota Historical Society
- p. 126 Heritage Plant, 1997, Photo by Lars Hanson
- p. 126 Heritage Plant, 1988, Courtesy of the *Star Tribune*
- p. 127 *Star Tribune,* July 1, 1987, Courtesy of the Minnesota Historical Society
- p. 128 *Star Tribune,* October 28, 1991, Courtesy of the Minnesota Historical Society
- p. 129 Homer Hanky, Photo by Lars Hanson
- p. 129 *The Des Moines Register,* December 11, 1984, Courtesy of UMI and reprinted with permission by *The Des Moines Register*
- p. 132 Cowles Media Company Board of Directors, 1991, Courtesy of Cowles Media Company

CHAPTER 22

- p. 135 *Star Tribune,* October 20, 1987, Courtesy of the Minnesota Historical Society
- p. 137 *Scottsdale Progress,* October 14, 1990, Courtesy of *The Scottsdale Progress*
- p. 138 Pulitzer Prize, 1990, Courtesy of the *Star Tribune* Library
- p. 139 Joel Kramer, 1995, Courtesy of the *Star Tribune* Library
- p. 139 The Star Tribune Online, The Virtual Vegetarian, The Virtual Flyshop and Media Central, Photos by Brady Willette
- p. 140 The titles produced in 1997 by Star Tribune, Cowles Enthusiast Media, Cowles Business Media and Cowles Creative Publishing, Photos by Gary Thoen

CHAPTER 23

- p. 141 *Star Tribune,* January 17, 1991, Courtesy of the Minnesota Historical Society
- p. 142 John Cowles III (Jay), 1991, Courtesy of the *Star Tribune* Library

CHAPTER 24

- p. 145 *Star Tribune,* April 20, 1997, Courtesy of the *Star Tribune*
- p. 146 *Star Tribune,* September 4, 1997, Courtesy of the *Star Tribune*
- p. 147 *Star Tribune,* September 5, 1997, Courtesy of the *Star Tribune*
- p. 149 *Star Tribune,* November 14, 1997, Courtesy of the *Star Tribune*
- p. 149 *The Wall Street Journal,* November 14, 1997, Courtesy of UMI and Dow Jones & Co., Inc.
- p. 150 Elizabeth Ballantine, 1997, Courtesy of Cowles Media Company

p. 150 *Star Tribune*, November 16, 1997, Courtesy of the *Star Tribune*

APPENDIX B

p. 157 *Time,* July 1, 1935, Courtesy of Time, Inc.

APPENDIX C

p. 164 Stock Certificates of Cowles Media Company and predecessors, Courtesy of Cowles Media Company

APPENDIX D

p. 167 All photos courtesy of *Star Tribune* Library, except the Gale W. Freeman Building and the Heritage Center, which are by Lars Hanson

APPENDIX G

p. 179 All photos courtesy of the *Star Tribune* Library

APPENDIX K

p. 197 All photos courtesy of the National Urban League

APPENDIX M

p. 201 Keystone 5% Program logo, Courtesy of the Greater Minneapolis Chamber of Commerce

APPENDIX Q

p. 215 Photos by Lars Hanson or Courtesy of the *Star Tribune* Library

APPENDIX Y

p. 239 All photos courtesy of *The Fergus Falls Daily Journal*